USSR
FOREIGN POLICIES
AFTER DETENTE

Books by Richard F. Staar

Arms Control: Myth Versus Reality (editor)

Aspects of Modern Communism (editor)

Communist Regimes in Eastern Europe

Long-Range Environmental Study of the Northern Tier of Eastern Europe in 1990–2000

Poland 1944–1962: Sovietization of a Captive People

Public Diplomacy: USA Versus USSR (editor)

Soviet Military Policies Since World War Two (co-author)

USSR Foreign Policies After Detente

Yearbook on International Communist Affairs (editor)

★

USSR FOREIGN POLICIES AFTER DETENTE

★★★

Revised Edition

Richard F. Staar

Hoover Institution Press   Stanford University

Stanford, California

Hoover Press Publication 359

Revised edition, first printing, 1987
First edition, 1985

Manufactured in the United States of America
91 90 89 88 87   9 8 7 6 5 4 3 2 1

Library of Congress Cataloging in Publication Data
Staar, Richard Felix, 1923–
    U.S.S.R. foreign policies after detente.

    Bibliography: p.
    Includes index.
    1. Soviet Union—Foreign relations—1975–   .
2. Soviet Union.   Ministerstvo inostrannykh del.
3. TSK KPSS.   Politbiūro.   4. Propaganda,
Russian.   5. Espionage, Russian.   6. Soviet
Union—Military policy.   7. Soviet Union—
Foreign economic relations.   I. Title.
DK274.S7   1987   327.47   86-27655
ISBN 0-8179-8592-1 (pbk.)

Design by Lorena Laforest Bass

TO

USMC COMMAND AND STAFF COLLEGE
STUDENTS AND FACULTY (1971–1981)
WHO PROVIDED THE INSPIRATION
FOR THIS BOOK

CONTENTS

PART I

FOUNDATIONS

1 ★ SOVIET WORLD OUTLOOK   3

PART II

INSTRUMENTALITIES

===== PART III =====

REGIONAL POLICIES

TABLES

FIGURES

PREFACE

This monograph is organized into twelve chapters. It begins with the USSR world outlook and attempts to show how Soviet perceptions differ from those of the West. Next, the Politburo's decision-making process and the problem of succession are discussed; historically the latter has almost always involved a protracted struggle for power. The third chapter deals with implementation of policies by the USSR Ministry of Foreign Affairs.

The second part of the book (Chapters 4 through 7) treats the instruments of Soviet foreign policy: propaganda, espionage and active measures, military strategy, trade. All play significant roles in the orchestration of USSR moves throughout the world.

Finally, Part Three takes a geographic approach and covers the Soviet colonial empire in Eastern Europe, relations between East and West in Europe, the Third World, the USSR in East Asia, and finally Soviet relations with the United States.

The author expresses his deep appreciation to his assistant, Joyce Cerwin, for her invaluable help throughout the laborious process of preparing the revised edition for publication. This book could not have been written without access to the world-famous library collections at the Hoover Institution on War, Revolution and Peace. The staff has been outstanding in its dedication to the pursuit of esoteric and elusive data.

INTRODUCTION

The current Soviet collective leadership appears to have a compara-
tively realistic view of what is possible to accomplish in the world arena,
and yet it has re-emphasized the doctrinal component of foreign policy
by making Egor K. Ligachev, deputy to the ruling party's general-secretary, directly responsible for ideology. That is to say, the foreign
policy of the USSR is still guided by a dogma that remains messianic in
its very nature. According to this doctrine, the world revolutionary
process has no timetable and may indeed experience temporary setbacks. In the long run, however, those who sit in the Kremlin believe
that their political and socio-economic system will prevail over that of
the West in general and of the United States in particular.

Soviet ideology continues to envision the communist movement as
essentially international in character. The core of fifteen party-states,
two of which are antagonistic and three others neutral toward the USSR,
is supported by communist organizations in about eighty other countries
or administrative units throughout the world. The so-called "national
liberation" movements, restricted for the most part to Africa and the
Middle East, are considered to be allies of the Soviet Union in the
struggle against the "imperialist" camp headed by the United States. In
addition, communism is seen as eventually spreading throughout Latin
America from its two beachheads in Cuba and Nicaragua.

Nonetheless, regarding immediate prospects for expansion, the politburocrats in Moscow seemed incapable of making any decisions of major significance until the succession problem had been resolved. The deaths of Leonid I. Brezhnev, Iurii V. Andropov, and Konstantin U. Chernenko within a 28-month period brought Mikhail S. Gorbachev to the top leadership position. At age 54, he was of the next generation from his three immediate predecessors and therefore may be more likely to attempt important changes.

In view of the fact that decisions will be arrived at collectively until Gorbachev or another man emerges and has been able to promote a majority of his own supporters into the Politburo, the current period of weakness in the Kremlin may last for several more years. During that time, implementation of basic foreign policy decisions will continue to be conducted by the men in the Ministry of Foreign Affairs bureaucracy. These officials, however, also view world developments in terms of Marxism-Leninism. Such a doctrinal framework inevitably tends to slant information dispatched from abroad on the basis of which foreign policy decisions must be made. Indeed, at times it would appear that the ruling politburocrats are the victims of a distorted view of the world, that is, the one projected by their own propaganda.

One of the oldest instruments of political warfare, applied by the Soviet regime from its very inception, has been propaganda directed at foreign audiences. Specific campaigns are supervised by the Propaganda Department in the central party apparatus, which decides how to present different aspects of USSR external policy to various publics. Slogans appearing twice each year, in April and October, provide the general themes that will be used. International communist front organizations, like the World Peace Council, are tools for dissemination of such propaganda and promote Soviet foreign policy. Their activities are supplemented by use of the printed word and by radio broadcasts via official as well as clandestine transmitters.

Press agencies and newspapers also provide cover for USSR intelligence officers, whose assignments involve espionage and implementation of so-called "active measures." The latter include the use of fronts, manipulation of foreign media, the spreading of disinformation, the planting of forgeries, and the recruitment of so-called "agents of influence" to promote the Kremlin's objectives and undermine those of any opponent. Between one-fourth and one-third of all Soviet officials abroad work for the KGB (civilian) or GRU (military) intelligence services. The United Nations is heavily penetrated by such individuals.

The KGB and its predecessor organizations have all been involved in attempted coups and terrorism. Since the end of World War II such operations have been conducted, for the most part successfully, in such diverse regions as Eastern Europe, Africa, the Middle East, Asia, and Latin America. An international terrorist network is being clandestinely financed by the Soviet Union and other bloc countries. Schools for terrorists are located not only in the USSR, but also in Bulgaria, Czechoslovakia, East Germany, and Hungary.

During the 1980s, Soviet bloc clandestine services have been propagating a flurry of forged documents in an attempt to split the NATO alliance. Racist letters threatening athletes from more than twenty developing countries were sent by the KGB (allegedly from the Ku Klux Klan) in an attempt to win support for the East's boycott of the 1984 Summer Olympics in Los Angeles. Such fake messages are designed to demonstrate that American policies are incompatible with those of the Third World, to discredit Western intelligence organizations, and in general to undermine the non-communist world's resolve to defend itself against Soviet encroachments.

Assassination as an instrument of government policy is not new for the USSR, as mentioned above. Two anti-communist Ukrainian leaders, for example, were murdered by the same Soviet intelligence officer during the late 1950s, at Munich. The assassin, who later defected to the West, had been personally decorated in Moscow for his action by the head of the KGB. According to a June 1984 report of the Italian state prosecutor, the attempt on the life of Pope John Paul II had been paid for by the Bulgarian secret services. High-level defectors have revealed that the USSR assigns these "wet" projects to other bloc intelligence organizations, and this tends to support the hypothesis that Andropov himself (at the time, head of the KGB) probably issued the orders to kill the pope.

This last endeavor, if successful, would have been important for the prosecution of a future war against NATO, especially if it were to become a protracted one. With the Polish pope gone, perhaps resistance in Poland could be crushed for good. Soviet military doctrine is directed toward seizing the initiative, which makes it imperative to strike first across a pacified Eastern Europe. Surprise and pre-emption represent the two most important elements in USSR treatises on the subject of warfare. This also applies to contingency plans for a conventional war in Central Europe.

A war-fighting and war-survival posture has characterized Soviet nuclear military doctrine from its origins. Under these precepts, a series of pre-emptive strikes would be directed at military installations and important economic sites in the continental United States, maritime lines of communication, and reconnaissance satellites. Destruction of these targets would confront the Western alliance with the probability that further escalation might only work to the East's advantage. Indeed, deployment of superior strategic offensive forces has already given Moscow the capability of destroying more than 90 percent of all United States land-based intercontinental ballistic missiles in their pre-launch configuration.

Foreign trade is also used for political purposes by the Soviet Union. Commercial sanctions have been applied in the past to such diverse countries as Cuba, Iceland, Yugoslavia, Australia, China, and Romania. (Yugoslavia and Romania are both considered to be maverick states, albeit communist-ruled ones.) In general, the USSR has been forced to support most of its client regimes in Eastern Europe.

Trade with the West, meanwhile, has included large purchases of grain, which worldwide totaled a record 55 million metric tons during the 1984–85 crop year. Over the decade of the 1970s, the Soviet Union also had acquired more than $50 billion worth of high technology from the industrialized West. Together with its dependencies in Eastern Europe, the USSR currently remains in debt to capitalist countries for more than twice that amount.

It is in the Third World that the political use of trade can be seen most clearly. Such countries as Afghanistan, Angola, Cuba, Ethiopia, South Yemen, and Vietnam lack the means to pay for imports from the USSR. Moscow permits this adverse balance of trade to continue because of the important geographic location of these states from a military point of view. Also, in certain instances, the Soviet Union obtains critical raw materials (of which it may have a surplus) in order to deny them to the West and at the same time build up its own strategic reserve.

The Kremlin pursues many different foreign policies, depending on the extent of its influence over another country and the latter's power. Even with respect to its dependencies in Eastern Europe, approaches vary. Romania belongs to the Warsaw Treaty Organization and the Council for Mutual Economic Assistance (CMEA), yet twice in the past few years (1980 and 1984) the USSR foreign minister traveled to Bucharest and in effect bribed the government of that country to change a public posture that had differed from bloc policy.

Soviet troops stationed on the "sovereign" territories of East Germany, Czechoslovakia, Hungary, and Poland represent a symbol of Kremlin authority. In the past, they have intervened to support puppet regimes and to replace recalcitrant ones. Moscow understands that if war should come, indigenous troops in bloc countries may not willingly support the Warsaw Pact against NATO, especially if Western forces were to cross the borders into Eastern Europe. Apart from the military aspects, the Soviet Union also dominates its client states economically by supplying them with indispensable raw materials and energy resources. At the November 1986 CMEA meeting in Moscow, all bloc governments agreed to concentrate on development of nuclear power and high technology, through the year 2000.

Soviet relations with Western Europe have as their main objective the decoupling of Europe from the United States, which means, of course, the withdrawal of American troops. Nonetheless, recent USSR threats that Scandinavian members of NATO will "burn in the fires of nuclear war," that all of southern Italy will be converted into "a Pompeii," and that the Federal Republic of Germany could be "ascending a nuclear gallows" did not prevent acceptance of U.S. ground-launched cruise and Pershing II ballistic missiles by Western Europe to counterbalance earlier massive Soviet deployments of triple warhead SS-20 nuclear missile launchers. Still, with the construction of the trans-Siberian pipeline, imports of natural gas could make several of these NATO countries dependent to a large extent on the USSR for this source of fuel.

That plans made in Moscow vis-à-vis Western Europe are long-term and consistent becomes apparent when one compares the 1975 Final Act at Helsinki with the objectives listed in the 1967 Karlovy Vary communiqué issued by Soviet and East European leaders after a summit meeting in Czechoslovakia. Almost all of these goals were attained. Concessions agreed upon at Helsinki in the human rights area, on the other hand, have been ignored by all communist regimes. Review conferences in Belgrade (1977–1978) and Madrid (1980–1983) both ended without specific condemnation of this behavior. The next review, which opened in November 1986 at Vienna, may have the same results.

If progress has been slow in subverting Western Europe, the opposite is true of the Third World, where the USSR has made considerable inroads. "Revolutionary democracies" and other governments that have chosen the "non-capitalist" path of development exist in twenty-four countries, with Nicaragua well on its way to becoming a second Cuba in the Western Hemisphere. Setbacks have occurred, although the trend remains one of expansion and net advantage to the Soviet Union.

Throughout East Asia, nonetheless, the USSR has met with opposition from the Chinese communists, who consider that part of the world as their sphere of influence. The Sino-Soviet conflict has continued since the official break starting in July 1960, with no end in sight. Beijing seems to have lost out to Moscow in Vietnam, Laos, Kampuchea, and perhaps also in North Korea. The Chinese have made three demands upon the USSR, as a first step toward improving relations:

1. reduction of Soviet troops along their common border;
2. an end to support by the USSR for the Vietnamese occupation of Kampuchea; and
3. Soviet military withdrawal from Afghanistan.

Moscow has made it clear, however, that no agreements will be made with China at the expense of third countries.

Finally, relations with the United States until recently seem to have been centered on arms control. Vitriolic speeches by the USSR party leader, the foreign minister, the defense chief, and others suggest that the Kremlin may have decided against any agreements, perhaps regardless of who sits in the Oval Office. Although the Soviets came back to restructured nuclear arms control talks at Geneva in March 1985, no breakthrough had been achieved as of this writing. The summit meeting in Iceland on 11–12 October 1986 adjourned without even a joint communiqué.

The record suggests that Soviet leaders are not serious about reaching equitable agreements. To Moscow negotiations have served as little more than camouflage for what has proven to be the most massive military buildup in history. When the United States offered back in 1946 to give up its atomic bomb stockpile and transfer all fissionable material to a veto-free United Nations body, the highest-ranking USSR official at the U.N. privately responded to the American presidential representative as follows: "The Soviet Union doesn't want equality. The Soviet Union wants complete freedom to pursue its own aims as it sees fit." At that time, the Kremlin had no atomic weapons.

Despite outward shifts in rhetoric from the USSR, this attitude has essentially remained unchanged. Indeed, in certain respects, it has hardened. The current U.S. secretary of state described Soviet international misconduct as based upon

1. a continuing quest for military superiority;
2. an "unconstructive involvement" in the Third World;
3. an unrelenting effort to impose an alien "model" on clients and allies; and
4. the practice of stretching treaties to the brink of violation and beyond.

The last charge has been documented to date in five successive reports to the U.S. Congress on Soviet non-compliance with arms control agreements. A more detailed study, prepared by the nonpartisan

General Advisory Committee on Arms Control and Disarmament, covers the last quarter-century. Submitted to Congress by the White House, it cites seventeen major violations by the USSR (in addition to the five revealed previously by the president) since the 1958 nuclear test moratorium. Even now, as if to flaunt their disregard for treaty obligations, the Soviets continue to encrypt signals from their own ICBM test launches to prevent U.S. monitoring of compliance with nuclear arms control agreements between the two countries.

Despite the foregoing, dialogue between the United States and the USSR continues. Talks on preventing accidental war and nuclear weapons proliferation, establishing the precise boundary between Alaska and Siberia, as well as implementation of exchange agreements are all currently in progress. President Reagan authorized a ten-year extension of the economic cooperation accord that had expired in July 1984. He also agreed to anti-satellite (ASAT) negotiations proposed by the USSR to open at Vienna. The Kremlin refused to send a delegation, explaining its decision with an Orwellian "inversion of truth" and claiming that the United States had made it impossible to hold the talks. However, two summit meetings did take place, in November 1985 at Geneva and October 1986 at Reykjavik.

Multilateral negotiations with United States and Soviet participation continued on Mutual and Balanced Force Reductions (MBFR) in Central Europe between the two military alliances; at the United Nations–sponsored 40-member Committee on Disarmament (CD); and at the Conference on Confidence- and Security-Building Measures and Disarmament in Europe (CDE), with 35 governments represented (which ended in September 1986). None of these multilateral talks, however, is likely to result in anything of importance for reasons that the following twelve chapters attempt to explore. The same may apply to the consolidated U.S.-Soviet arms control negotiations in Geneva.

★ PART I ★

FOUNDATIONS

1

SOVIET
WORLD OUTLOOK

It has been suggested that Soviet behavior in the world arena can be explained as the product of simple opportunism or *Realpolitik*. If this were true, the USSR would in the end be no different from any other aggressive power that would like to expand its influence. Yet such an assessment could even be true at the operational level and still not explain precisely what motivates the decision makers in the Kremlin. Why do these men seek confrontation, and what drives them?

One key place to find answers for such questions is in the system of beliefs on the basis of which all Soviet leaders have operated since the small group of communists seized power in 1917. Working within the framework of this ideology, the current successors to the original Bolsheviks have a world outlook that differs radically from that held by Western statesmen. According to one of Moscow's leading ideologists, the "historic mission" of the USSR involves the following three aspects:[1]

1. building socialism and communism in the Soviet Union;
2. providing assistance to those countries where this process is under way; and
3. supporting the struggle for "social progress" in *all* other countries. [Italics added.]

The importance of ideology had recently been re-emphasized in the Soviet Union by the decision that the heir apparent, Gorbachev, retain ultimate responsibility for questions in this field. In fact, even as general secretary he chaired the commission preparing a new world outlook for the Communist Party of the Soviet Union (CPSU) program just before the 1986 party congress.[2] Since that time, the deputy general-secretary has been responsible for the ideological area within the Politburo and Secretariat.[3]

The ideological framework within which the foreign policies of the USSR operate actually has as its point of departure the belief that the industrialized countries of the West are currently in the third stage of a general crisis. By positing this periodization of modern history, the Soviets project what is for them an optimistic image of the world, in which the areas under capitalist control are becoming constantly smaller and weaker. Correspondingly, in Moscow's perception, areas under "progressive" rule in the communist and lesser developed states are expanding and being strengthened (see Table 1.1).

Boris N. Ponomarev, at the time a candidate Politburo member of the CPSU and International Department head in its Central Committee apparatus, illustrated this belief when he summarized territorial advances made during the decade of the 1970s. He spoke of "the unification of Vietnam, the consolidation of people's power in Laos, the liquidation of the Pol Pot regime in Kampuchea [Cambodia]." He then added that "Ethiopia, Angola and Mozambique" had "secured liberation . . ." All of the countries listed above, he said, had carried out "major social transformations" and represented "advance posts of socialist orientation"—language generally restricted to so-called "revolutionary democracies" or governments well advanced on their way to communism. Ponomarev next stated that "South Yemen is playing an important role" in this field. He also mentioned Nicaragua, Afghanistan, Iran, and Zimbabwe [formerly Rhodesia] as examples of "blows against imperialism" in the world revolutionary process.[4]

PERIODIZATION OF HISTORY

According to Soviet ideology, stage one of the alleged crisis in world capitalism, guided by the "objective laws of social development," began with the First World War and the 1917 revolution in Russia. The next phase started during World War II and included the socialist revolutions in a number of countries of Europe and Asia. The third and contemporary stage commenced during the 1970s. An obvious differ-

TABLE 1.1
CHANGING SOCIO-POLITICAL WORLD MAP, 1950 AND 1985

CATEGORY	POPULATION (PERCENTAGE)		TERRITORY (PERCENTAGE)		INDUSTRIAL PRODUCTION (PERCENTAGE)	
	1950	*1985*	*1950*	*1985*	*1950*	*1985**
Developed capitalist countries	22.4	12.1	24.9	8.1	73.0	ca. 50.0
Communist-ruled states	35.0	32.1	25.8	26.2	ca. 20.0	over 40.0
Lesser-developed countries	42.6	51.2	49.3	61.6	7.0	ca. 7.0
Total:	100.0	95.4	100.0	95.9	100.0	97.0

*None of the figures in this column have changed since 1978, and the total probably reflects the downturn in the economies of communist-ruled states.
SOURCES: M. M. Avsenev, chief ed., *Krizis kapitalizma* (Moscow: Mysl', 1980), p. 62; USSR, *Narodnoe khoziaistvo SSSRv 1985* g. (Moscow: Finansy i Statistika, 1986), pp. 578–79. *Pravda*, 17 March 1986, p.4.

ence between the current period and both preceding ones has been the absence of a general war involving the major powers. There is "a rough military-strategic parity between socialism and imperialism."[5]

Competition and conflict between the two worldwide socio-economic systems is accompanied, in the Soviet view, by increasingly aggravated problems within all capitalist countries and the United States in particular: monetary crises, rampant inflation, decline in production, price increases, and unemployment.[6] Such domestic problems supposedly represent only one of four basic contradictions affecting the capitalist world. The others involve the conflict between the newly emergent nations and former colonial powers, the competition among the so-called imperialist countries themselves (especially the United States, Japan, and West European members of NATO) and, most important of all, the struggle between what the Soviets call "socialism" [that is, communism] and "capitalism."

This last struggle, it is claimed, will be won by means of a policy based on the principle of "peaceful coexistence," which has been enunciated from time to time ever since the days of Lenin. For example, the Bolshevik government's Foreign Affairs Commissariat [Ministry] reported to the All-Russian Central Executive Committee [Council of Ministers] on 17

June 1920 that "our slogan was and remains one and the same, peaceful coexistence with other governments of whatever kind they may be." During the 1980s, it is called "a specific form of class warfare in the international arena between capitalism and socialism."[7]

PEACEFUL COEXISTENCE AND
THE BREZHNEV DOCTRINE

The reason given by politicians in the USSR for resurrecting this more than half-century-old principle of peaceful coexistence as one basis for Soviet foreign policy can be found in what they identify as the alternative, namely, a nuclear war. Thus, the concept of peaceful coexistence provides a relatively safe framework within which to support "wars of national liberation" in the underdeveloped areas of the world, on the one hand, and so-called "active measures" within the capitalist states, on the other. In terms of propaganda, peaceful coexistence is also useful as a slogan for mobilizing domestic public opinion within non-communist-ruled countries in support of Soviet foreign policy.

In this respect peaceful coexistence, according to Mikhail A. Suslov,[8] the most prominent Soviet ideologist and a full member of the ruling party's Politburo at the time of his death in 1982, "has nothing in common with class peace between exploiter and exploited, colonialist and victims of colonial oppression, or between oppressors and oppressed." What this means, in effect, is that the USSR by definition will be on the side of any movement that has the objective of weakening and destroying governments not under Soviet control or influence. When he served as foreign minister, Andrei A. Gromyko made this clear in the following words:[9] "International detente does not in any way suggest artificial restraints on the objective processes of the historical development and struggle by oppressed people for their liberation."

Previously, communist ideology had affirmed the "inevitability of a world conflict" between capitalism and Soviet-style "socialism." This formula prevailed as dogma until February 1956, when it was revised at the Twentieth CPSU Congress. There a new position emerged—that war is not inevitable[10]—and the latter formula has been repeated at the three postwar world conferences of communist parties (1957, 1960, 1969), as well as the last four CPSU congresses (1971, 1976, 1981, 1986). Members of the international communist movement, some friendly and some not so friendly toward Moscow, send delegates to such meetings. The gatherings are used as a podium for making policy statements.

As for the so-called Brezhnev Doctrine, when originally pro-

pounded a month after the USSR military occupation of Czechoslovakia, it limited the sovereignty only of those communist-ruled states
within the USSR's reach. Every party inside the East European bloc was
said to be "responsible, not only to its own people, but to all the socialist
[that is, communist-ruled] countries and the entire communist movement."[11] Moscow thus retroactively had fulfilled its "international
duty" by invading Czechoslovakia in August 1968 and allegedly preventing a "counterrevolution" from taking place. Approximately
80,000 Soviet troops—five divisions—have remained in that country
since they entered it on a "temporary" basis.

Brezhnev personally told a group of the highest-ranking party/gov-
ernment officials, arrested in Prague and flown to Moscow as prisoners
during the invasion, that

> We in the Kremlin came to the conclusion that we could not depend
> on you any longer. You do what you feel like in domestic politics, even
> things that displease us, and you are not open to positive suggestions.
> But your country lies on territory where the Soviet soldier trod in the
> Second World War. We bought that territory at the cost of enormous
> sacrifices, and we shall never leave it. The borders of that area are our
> borders as well. Because you do not listen to us, we feel threatened. In
> the name of the dead in World War Two who laid down their lives for
> your freedom as well, we are therefore fully justified in sending our
> soldiers into your country, so that we may feel truly secure within our
> common borders. It is immaterial whether anyone is actually threaten-
> ing us or not: it is a matter of principle, independent of external
> circumstances. And that is how it will be, from the Second World War
> until "eternity."[12]

In effect, the Czechs and Slovaks present were made to understand
that the USSR's borders extended to the Elbe River and that the Soviets
considered all lands conquered during World War Two as their own.

Not quite ten years later, a coup in Afghanistan brought a *de facto*
communist regime to power. In the wake of the resulting twenty
months of anarchy, the USSR occupied Kabul at the end of December
1979 and installed its own puppet as ruler. His predecessor, Hafizullah
Amin, and most members of the deposed cabinet were murdered in
the process.[13] This could also be considered an application of the
Brezhnev Doctrine, in view of the fact that the Soviet Union and Afghanistan are territorially contiguous neighbors. The subsequent annexation of the Wakhan land corridor has given the USSR a border
with Pakistan, obviously a development of geostrategic importance.

What all of this means in Soviet eyes, apart from the claimed irreversibility of communist rule, is the following: (1) the "socialist [communist] commonwealth of nations" considers itself powerful enough to determine the course of world events; (2) the world balance of forces already favors a "socialist" encirclement of capitalism; (3) economic development has been subordinated to ideology, coercion, and the threat of force; and (4) no single country or geographic region remains immune to communism.[14] Soviet writers do not hesitate to propound these conclusions openly in Russian-language publications, although naturally they leave the third point above unmentioned.

CORRELATION OF FORCES

One explanation why war is no longer considered inevitable can be found in a concept that has been enunciated by the CPSU Central Committee in a formal resolution, adopted at a plenary session, as follows:

> Detente is the natural result of the correlation of forces in the world arena that has formed in recent decades. The military-strategic balance between the world of socialism and the world of capitalism is an achievement of principled historic significance. It is a factor which contains imperialism's aggressive aspirations and which meets the vital interests of all peoples. The hopes to shake this balance are futile.[15]

This, of course, means that Kremlin leaders believe the West was forced to accept detente or peaceful coexistence because of a "correlation of forces" that has been changing to the advantage of the USSR. One pair of Soviet writers has explained this idea in terms of the relationship between (1) military-strategic capabilities of the two "antagonistic" social systems and (2) their socio-political potentials.[16] The former issue is dealt with in subsequent chapters of this book. Only the latter will be considered here.

According to these authors, the USSR always has been opposed to the status quo for any country whose policy is not based upon the "objective requirements of world social development." This corresponds to the concept of internationalism as originally formulated by Lenin. Although the Soviet Union, "as is well known," does not export revolution, it always will give assistance to the "struggle for social progress." Only in this light can one evaluate the "revolution as well as events concerning Afghanistan, problems of the Iranian revolution, the [USSR] attitude toward the revolution in Nicaragua, and elimination [by Vietnam] of the Pol Pot regime in Kampuchea." The Soviet Union "has never made any secret of its interest in changing the correlation of forces within the world arena, so that it favors socialism [that is, communism] . . . to the disadvantage of imperialism . . ."[17]

A perceived superiority in political, economic, social, and, above all, military factors allows the USSR to apply a double standard. From the Kremlin's point of view, a Western ideological offensive that threatened the "socialist" system, United States support for "anti-progressive" movements anywhere in the world, and NATO attempts to revise East European borders would all violate detente.[18] However, the Soviets themselves accept no similar constraints, especially in areas which they consider off limits to the West, as can be seen in the definition of proletarian internationalism as "the fundamental principle of USSR foreign policy [which] means that this policy consistently upholds the basic interests of world socialism, of the forces of the international communist and workers' movements, as well as the national liberation movement."[19] These are the major components of the "world revolutionary process," as described by Soviet writers and spokesmen. A more detailed explanation follows in the next section.

WORLD REVOLUTIONARY PROCESS

Moscow, nevertheless, cannot control all fraternal communist movements. At the most recent Twenty-seventh CPSU Congress, among the ruling parties, Albania and China did not send representatives, which limited the number in attendance from that category to thirteen. On the other hand, a total of approximately 84 delegations that could be identified came from communist parties in capitalist countries (two each from Australia, Iran, Ireland, India) or administrative units like West Berlin.[20] The national liberation movement was represented by 33 "revolutionary democratic" parties and clandestine groups. Finally, there were about 23 left-socialist and social democratic delegations as well as members of the Congress and Center parties, from India and Finland, respectively.

The list above illustrates the diverse elements making up the "world revolutionary process." They are linked together because of a mutual enemy: imperialism.[21] To reiterate, components of the process include (1) the world communist movement, (2) the national liberation movement and, implicitly, (3) the left wing of the socialist movement, in the Western sense of that term, and certain other organizations.

World Communist Movement

Communist and workers' parties, recognized by the CPSU, operate in 95 countries throughout the world, and their total claimed membership has surpassed 80 million.[22] This total includes the Chinese, who claim approximately half the global figure. Only fifteen states are ruled by communist parties, and those comprise the "world socialist system." A so-called revolutionary democracy, Kampuchea, is not officially in this category. Two member states (Albania and China) are antagonistic toward the Soviet Union as well as toward each other, and three ruling parties are more or less neutral in the Sino-Soviet dispute (those in Romania, North Korea, and Yugoslavia).[23]

The "socialist commonwealth" includes the ten full members of the Council for Mutual Economic Assistance (CMEA) plus Laos, with observer status only. Thus, except for Romania, the so-called commonwealth remains limited to the pro-Soviet core of communist-ruled countries. Albania has not been a member of the USSR bloc *de facto* since 1961 and *de jure* since 1968, when it withdrew from both CMEA and the Warsaw Pact after the Soviet invasion of Czechoslovakia. Yugoslavia maintains associate status within CMEA, although it is not considered a member of the "socialist commonwealth" (see Table 1.2).

One may assume Soviet leaders expect that both Albania and Yugoslavia, in the not too distant future, can be influenced to rejoin the bloc. The Kremlin certainly hopes also that a future Chinese leadership may revise current anti-Soviet policies and draw closer to Moscow. Relations with North Korea remain ambiguous, although in 1984 Kim Il-sung did visit the USSR and Eastern Europe. The following year, about twenty Soviet delegations went to Pyongyang.

Alongside the world socialist system within the world communist movement stands, according to Soviet writers, "the revolutionary movement of the working class in capitalist countries." It consists of approximately 89 communist parties, generally one for each country or political entity (for example, Puerto Rico). Not all are pro-Moscow. Some remain neutral in the Sino-Soviet dispute, and others adopt a pro-Chinese stance.[24] CPSU leaders probably consider these latter two attitudes of a transitory nature that can be modified over time. However, no serious attempts have been made to organize an international meeting of communist parties. In 1985, Gorbachev himself spoke out against the endeavor.[25]

National Liberation Movement

When discussing organizations comprising the national liberation movement, Soviet ideologists have limited their comments largely to Africa and Asia, that is, to former colonies or semi-colonies. The situation in Latin America is different also because of a relatively developed

TABLE 1.2
WORLD COMMUNIST SYSTEM, 1986

Socialist Commonwealth of Nations	
Country	*Year Joined CMEA*
1. Bulgaria	1949
2. Cuba	1972
3. Czechoslovakia	1949
4. East Germany	1950
5. Hungary	1949
6. Laos	(observer status)
7. Mongolia	1962
8. Poland	1949
9. Romania	1949
10. Soviet Union	1949
11. Vietnam	1978
Other Communist-ruled States	
1. Albania	
2. China	
3. North Korea	
4. Yugoslavia (associate CMEA member)	

SOURCES: Speeches at the 27th CPSU Congress by party leaders from the above countries, excluding Albania and China, appeared in *Pravda,* 27 or 28 February or 1 March 1986. *World Marxist Review Information Bulletin,* September 1984, p. 4, lists only the first eleven above as represented at a meeting of Central Committee secretaries from "fraternal parties" in Moscow.

capitalism, a strong and experienced working class, a long history of revolutionary struggle, and the existence of communist parties in most of the countries throughout this region. Therefore, in USSR terms, "laws of natural evolution" could be allowed to determine the outcome here. Even in Latin America, however, implementation of these so-called laws is being hastened by Moscow. If a country's policies are anti-imperialist, Soviet leaders consider it "progressive" and therefore to be helped along the path to socialism.[26]

A good example of how Marxist-led insurgents are clandestinely assisted not only by the USSR but also by other fraternal regimes can be documented from El Salvador. During June and July of 1980, the communist party leader in that country, Shafik Jorge Handal, traveled in his capacity as a representative of the Farabundo Martí National Liberation Front to Cuba, Vietnam, Ethiopia, the USSR (twice), Bulgaria, Czechoslovakia, Hungary and East Germany. All eight countries promised to supply uniforms, weapons, and ammunition. According to captured documents, evaluated as genuine by United States intelligence agencies,[27] Handal met with the deputy head of the CPSU International Department, K. N. Brutents, and that body's Latin American sector chief, M. F. Kudachkin. Moscow also promised to provide military training for young communists from El Salvador who were studying in the USSR at that time.

More recent documentation, discovered by United States troops on Grenada and released in December 1983, indicates similar involvement on that Caribbean island. For the period 1983–1984, North Korea had obligated itself to send without charge weapons and ammunition as well as 6,000 military uniforms. These items were listed on a two-page annex to a secret agreement. Cuba specified the exact numbers of its own military personnel to be stationed in Grenada through the end of 1984. Secret agreements with the USSR included three-, seven-, and fourteen-page annexes itemizing weapons and ammunition to be delivered to the regime on the island.[28]

According to the Soviet world outlook, however, the most important grouping within the overall national liberation movement category includes those countries with a "socialist orientation," most of which are controlled by a single so-called revolutionary democratic party. USSR sources have listed some 24 of them, as indicated in Table 1.3. Although theoretically developing toward communism, these states generally

1. allow some private capital investment (foreign as well as domestic) to remain;
2. emphasize nationalism and religion in their ideologies as well as Marxism-Leninism to varying degrees; and
3. consider a multi-class (as opposed to simply a proletarian) party to be the leading revolutionary force.[29]

The "revolutionary democratic" movements that appear more highly developed with regard to ideology and pro-Soviet orientation are called "vanguard parties" by the USSR. Nine of these have been noted so far in Afghanistan, Angola, Bahrain (non-ruling and illegal), Benin, the Congo, Ethiopia, Kampuchea, Mozambique, and South Yemen.

The second grouping that Soviet ideologists identify within the "national liberation movement" consists of those still fighting to achieve power. Two examples of such organizations are the African National Congress (ANC), directed against the Republic of South Africa, and the South-West African People's Organization (SWAPO). The latter is attempting to detach and assume control of an area being administered by the Republic of South Africa. Another "liberation movement," the Polisario, remains active in the Western Sahara. Those operating in the Middle East include the People's Front for the Liberation of Oman and the Palestine Liberation Organization (PLO). The Association of Revolutionary Organizations of Guatemala and the Farabundo Martí National Liberation Movement in El Salvador belong to this same category, as does the recently identified National Liberation Movement of the Caribbean Basin.[30] These organizations are aligned with the Soviets to varying degrees. At one extreme, the ANC is almost openly dominated by the Moscow-line Communist Party of South Africa,[31] whereas the PLO relationship with the USSR might best be described as a marriage of convenience.

Left Wing of the Socialist Movement

In third place, within the broad context of the "world revolutionary process," after the world communist and national liberation movements, are the left-wing socialists from parties of various political coloration.[32] Moscow attempts to co-opt their trade unions and youth groups as well as individuals to become members of international front organizations that, in turn, can enlist them to serve Soviet foreign policy interests. In addition, over the past several years, communists have cooperated organizationally and/or individually even with such moderate socialist parties as those in France and Portugal or with the semi-socialist ones in India, Sri Lanka, and Bangladesh. At least fifteen socialist groupings of various stripes have members on the World Peace Council,[33] the best known among all Soviet-controlled international communist front organizations.

Perhaps the most important vehicle through which the Kremlin hopes to influence West European moderate socialists, especially those in the Federal Republic of Germany, Britain, and Scandinavia, has been the Socialist International (SI), which worldwide includes 75 parties and a total of about 20 million members. Only a few days after the Soviet invasion of Afghanistan, the current SI president (West German socialist Willy Brandt) stated that "the world still suffers from too little and not too much detente."[34] The following month, Brandt and his colleague, the late Olof Palme of Sweden, convinced the SI meeting in Vienna not to mention Afghanistan but rather to concentrate on promoting arms control. This conference led to the idea of an SI disarmament commission, headed by Palme.

Based on the latter's visits to Moscow and Washington, D.C., it would seem that SI may have unwittingly become an indirect instrument of USSR foreign policy. One USSR objective had been to discourage West European governments from implementing the NATO Council decision

TABLE 1.3

THIRD WORLD COUNTRIES WITH A "SOCIALIST" ORIENTATION, 1986

Country	Name of Movement
1. Afghanistan (1978)	*People's Democratic Party of Afghanistan
2. Algeria	National Liberation Front (FLN)
3. Angola (1976)	*Movement for People's Liberation of Angola—Labor Party
4. Benin (1981?)	*People's Revolutionary Party of Benin
5. Burkina-Faso	National Council of the Revolution (CNR)
6. Burundi	Union for National Progress (UPRONA)
7. Cape Verde	African Party for Independence of Cape Verde (PAICV)
8. Congo/Brazzaville (1981)	*Congolese Workers Party (PCT)
9. Ethiopia (1978)	*Workers' Party of Ethiopia
10. Ghana	Provisional National Defense Council
11. Guinea	†Democratic Party of Guinea (PDG)
12. Guinea/Bissau	African Party for Independence of Guinea (PAIGC)
13. Kampuchea	*People's Revolutionary Party of Kampuchea
14. Madagascar	Congress Party for Independence of Madagascar (AKFM), part of ruling coalition
15. Mali	Democratic Union of the Mali People (UDPM)
16. Mozambique (1977)	*Mozambique Liberation Front (FRELIMO)
17. Nicaragua (1980?)	Sandinista National Liberation Front (FSLN)
18. Sao Tome & Principe	Movement for the Liberation of Sao Tome & Principe
19. Seychelles	Seychelles Peoples' Progressive Front
20. Syria (1980)	Arab Socialist Resurrectionist (Ba'th) Party
21. Tanzania	Revolutionary Party of Tanzania (CCM)
22. Yemen/South (1979)	*Yemen Socialist Party
23. Zambia	United National Independence Party
24. Zimbabwe	Zimbabwe African National Union-Patriotic Front

*Called "vanguard parties" by Soviet writers.

†The PDG was dissolved after the April 1984 military coup.

NOTES: The Soviet Union signed twenty-year friendship treaties with certain countries during the year indicated in parentheses. A ruling party delegation from Benin spent May and June 1981 in Moscow, and a secret agreement could have been signed at this time (A. M. Prokhorov, chief ed., *Ezhegodnik bol'shoi sovetskoi entsiklopedii, 1981* [Moscow: Sovetskaia entsiklopediia, 1981], p. 212).

to commence deployment in December 1983 of Pershing II and ground-launched cruise missiles. Interviews with moderate socialist leaders throughout northern Europe indicated a definite move toward Moscow's position on this arms issue. Several of these individuals, no longer in power, called for abandonment of the original emplacement schedule even if the United States–Soviet arms control negotiations in Geneva should fail. The USSR broke off the intermediate-range and the strategic weapons reduction talks before NATO deployments commenced.

How the communists attempt to manipulate the SI can be seen, in another example, from minutes taken at a secret meeting during 6–7 January 1983 at Managua. The Sandinistas hosted representatives of El Salvador guerrillas, the Radical Party from Chile, the People's National Party of Jamaica, the New Jewel Movement on Grenada, and the Communist Party of Cuba.[35] Participants in the meeting agreed that "progressives" already controlled the SI Committee on Latin America and the Caribbean. The most important enemies were identified as socialists in Italy and Portugal as well as the Social Democrats U.S.A.; Scandinavian and Dutch socialists were counted among the best friends. Not mentioned were the ruling Greek socialists (PASOK) whose first congress in May 1984 was attended by representatives from the Sandinistas, the PLO, the Fatherland Front in Bulgaria, and the Communist Party of the Soviet Union.[36] An SI conference on disarmament took place in October 1985 at Vienna, with guests from such national liberation movements as SWAPO and the ANC.

In the case of Nicaragua, an understanding about relations between the CPSU and FSLN was signed on 19 March 1980 in Moscow. *Archiv der Gegenwart, 1980* 50, no. 23/24 (4–18 May 1980): 23533.

Grenada and Nicaragua had been described, along with Cuba, as having "taken the road of building a new society in Latin America" (see Raul Valdez Vivo, "The Latin American Proletariat and Its Allies in the Anti-Imperialist Struggle," *World Marxist Review* 23, no. 8 [August 1980]: 33). This description ceased to apply in the case of Grenada, after U.S. and Caribbean troops occupied the island during the seven weeks before 15 December 1983.

Mozambique has announced that its ruling FRELIMO has been transformed into a Marxist-Leninist party, according to *Tempo* (Maputo), 8 May 1983, p. 93.

SOURCES: Y. N. Gavrilov, "Problems in the Formation of a Vanguard Party in Countries of a Socialist Orientation," *Narody Azii i Afriki,* no. 6 (1980): 11; "The Twenty-sixth CPSU Congress and the National Liberation Movement," ibid., no. 3 (1981): 5; N. D. Kosukhin, "Development Trends in the Countries of a Socialist Orientation," *Rabochii klass i sovremennyi mir,* no. 4 (July–August 1981): 104; E. Primakov, "Countries with a Socialist Orientation," *Mirovaia ekonomika i mezhdunarodnye otnosheniia,* no. 7 (July 1981): 3; Wallace Spaulding, "The Communist Movement and Its Allies," in Ralph M. Goldman, ed., *Transnational Parties* (Lanham, Md.: University Press of America, 1983), pp. 25–60; *Pravda,* 14 February 1984; *New York Times,* 11 September 1984, for establishment of Workers' Party in Ethiopia; speeches or attendance at 27th CPSU Congress in *Pravda,* 24 February–7 March 1986; CIA, *The World Factbook, 1986,* series CR WF 86–001, June 1986, passim.

It is possible that only left-wing socialists (that category also includes certain members of moderate parties) are consciously in tune with the "world revolutionary process." The most characteristic manifestation of this involvement remains their active participation in international communist front organizations. Less reliable, but even more useful to the USSR on occasion, are people like Brandt and even the late Olof Palme and the late Mrs. Indira Gandhi because of their international influence. Such individuals do not appear to be Soviet-controlled and most probably have reached their positions—at times relatively pro-Soviet—independently. Even if certain Socialist International decisions were made as a result of action taken by "agents of influence,"[37] it would be debatable whether that body as a whole could be included in the "world revolutionary process."

FUTURE PROSPECTS

The fundamental Soviet world outlook had been re-emphasized in a series of articles by Ponomarev.[38] Short-term victories for the world revolutionary movement were envisaged throughout Latin America, which is portrayed as a "continent in upheaval." Medium-range expectations refer to what the author calls the "zone of developed capitalism." An acute socio-political crisis in the United States allegedly will become aggravated. Unfortunately, according to the writer, local communist parties in this zone (which includes Western Europe) remain unprepared for revolutionary contingencies and face problems of coordination with the USSR as well as with their socialist counterparts. It is undoubtedly true that Ponomarev's articles do not represent anything new in terms of ideology, although they are reformulated in the most recent 1986 CPSU program.[39]

It was the late Nikita S. Khrushchev, however, who had coined the term "revolutionary democracy" to justify Moscow's support for Third World leaders from within the armed forces or intelligentsia yet essentially of middle-class origin. Moscow thus endorsed a Gamal Nasser in Egypt and a Houari Boumedienne in Algeria, even though their "socialisms" did not correspond to the Soviet model. In actual fact the USSR considers middle-class or "petit-bourgeois" elements to represent budding revolutionary forces in the lesser developed countries, and it appears to be correct in this assessment.

The problem of dealing with the Third World is complicated by Sino-Soviet rivalry.[40] Among the 27 independent Asian states, only five (China, Laos, Mongolia, North Korea, Vietnam) are ruled by *recognized* communist parties. To date there are none in this category throughout

Africa, where political movements completely subservient to Moscow remain weak. However, the USSR has been working on a long-range program of academic training for youth from the lesser developed countries in general at its People's Friendship University named after the late Patrice Lumumba from the Congo. It is giving priority to providing students from "revolutionary democracies" with political training in the Soviet Union as well as in its East European client states.

Almost 35,000 young people were enrolled during 1985 in such colleges and universities.[41] China temporarily lost by default in this competition when, during the Great Cultural Revolution, all foreign students (other than those being trained in guerrilla warfare or sabotage) were forced to leave the country on two weeks' notice. Concurrently, their professors were sent to work on collective farms.

Yet, if Soviet relations with the People's Republic of China may be described as competitive regarding influence throughout the world communist movement, those vis-à-vis the West are fundamentally hostile. Peaceful coexistence or detente remained a one-way street that did not even halt Moscow's attempts to mobilize world public opinion against the United States. Diplomacy and propaganda continued to be viewed by the Soviets as two sides of the same coin. Throughout the period of so-called detente the USSR persisted in a build-up of its armed forces, with the aim of intimidating Western Europe and decoupling it from the United States. The men who make the basic decisions for the Soviet Union, and the process itself, are dealt with in the next chapter.

NOTES

1. V. V. Zagladin, *Istoricheskaia missiia sotsialisticheskogo obshchestva,* 2nd rev. ed. (Moscow: Politizdat, 1984), pp. 230–36. The essence of these points also appears in Article 28, Constitution of the USSR, in A. P. Blaustein and G. H. Flanz, eds., *Constitutions of the Countries of the World* (Dobbs Ferry, N.Y.: Oceana, December 1985), p. 25.

     Another source predicts that by the year 2017, the Soviet system will have been installed throughout the "vast majority of countries in the world" (G. Kh. Shakhnazarov, *Sotsializm i budushchee* [Moscow: Nauka, 1983], p. 723).

2. *Pravda,* 15 October 1985, p. 1; Moscow radio, domestic service in Russian, 17 February 1986, in *Foreign Broadcast Information Service,* III (18 February 1986), p. R2. Henceforth cited as *FBIS.*

3. *Pravda,* 7 March 1986, p. 1.

4. Address delivered in the Kremlin Palace of Congresses on the anniversary of Lenin's birth and entitled "The Great Living Force of Leninism," *Pravda,* 22 April 1980, p. 2.

5. I. D. Ovsianyi, chief ed., *Vneshniaia politika SSSR,* 2nd rev. ed. (Moscow: Politizdat, 1978), pp. 17–18; repeated by Vadim Zagladin, "On the Theory of World Politics," *Political Affairs* 64, no. 10 (October 1985): 38–39.

6. M. S. Gorbachev, "Political Report of the Central Committee to the 27th CPSU Congress," *Pravda,* 26 February 1986, p. 8.

7. Cited by A. E. Bovin, "Peaceful Coexistence," in A. M. Prokhorov, chief ed., *Bolshaia sovetskaia entsiklopediia,* vol. 16, 3rd ed. (Moscow, 1974), pp. 314–16, at p. 314; N. V. Ogarkov, chief ed., *Voennyi entsiklopedicheskiy slovar'* (Moscow: Voenizdat, 1983), p. 449.

8. M. A. Suslov, "The Communist Movement in the Vanguard of the Struggle for Peace and Social and National Liberation," *Kommunist,* no. 11 (July 1975): 7; see also his article in ibid., no. 4 (March 1980): 11–29.

9. A. A. Gromyko, ed., *Istoriia diplomatii* (Moscow: Politizdat, 1979), 5: 725. The same author wrote for *Kommunist,* no. 1 (January 1981): 13–27, in a similar vein.

10. Kommunisticheskaia Partiia Sovetskogo Soiuza, *XX s"ezd, 14–15 fevralia 1956 goda: Stenograficheskii otchet* (Moscow: Politizdat, 1956), 1: 37–38.

11. Sergei Kovalev, "Sovereignty and International Responsibility of Socialist Countries," *Pravda,* 26 September 1968, p. 4.

12. Zdenek Mlynar, *Nightfrost in Prague: The End of Humane Socialism* (New York: Karz Publishers, 1980), p. 240. The author claims personally to have heard Brezhnev make this statement.

13. Anthony Arnold, *Afghanistan's Two-Party Communism* (Stanford: Hoover Institution Press, 1983), pp. 97–98.

14. R. Judson Mitchell, "A New Brezhnev Doctrine," *World Politics* 30, no. 3 (April 1978): 389–90.

15. "On the International Situation and Foreign Policy of the Soviet Union," *Pravda,* 24 June 1980, p. 2. See also Onikov and Shishlin, *Kratkii slovar',* pp. 321–23; Ogarkov, "Correlation of Forces and Means," *Voennyi slovar',* p. 691.

16. Yuri Zhilin and Andrei Yermonskii, "Once Again on the Correlation of World Forces," *Novoe vremia,* no. 46 (14 November 1980): 18.

17. Ibid., p. 20. The latest USSR constitution explains the objectives of Soviet foreign policy as follows: "... consolidating the positions of world socialism, supporting the struggle of peoples for national liberation and social progress...." Article 28 in Chapter 4 of "Konstitutsiia SSSR," enclosure to *Mezhdunarodnaia zhizn',* no. 11 (1977): 26.

18. R. Judson Mitchell, *Ideology of a Superpower: Contemporary Soviet Doctrine on International Relations* (Stanford: Hoover Institution Press, 1982), especially pp. 54–70. See also Joseph G. Whelan, "Soviet-American Relations," *Issues and Studies* 20, no. 1 (Taipei, January 1984): 76–97.

19. A. A. Gromyko, "Leninist Foreign Policy in the Contemporary World," *Kommunist,* no. 1 (January 1981): 14. See also F. Konstantinov, "From the

Ideological Front," *Pravda,* 18 November 1983, on the worldwide struggle against capitalism; E. Pletnev, ibid., 1 December 1986, pp. 4, 6.

20. Some of the communist party delegations remained unidentified, probably because they operate on an illegal basis. *Pravda,* 24 February–7 March 1986, listed the delegation heads. Other numbers are from Heinz Timmermann, *Der XXVII KPdSU Kongress* (Cologne: Biost, 1986), report no. 16, p. 5.

21. V. V. Zagladin, ed., *Mirovoe kommunisticheskoe dvizhenie* (Moscow: Politizdat, 1984), pp. 12–16. See also Onikov and Shishlin, *Kratkii slovar',* pp. 230–31.

22. V. V. Zagladin, "On the Contemporary Communist Movement," *Tribuna* (Prague), no. 5 (30 January 1985): 3.

23. Richard F. Staar, ed., "Introduction," *1986 Yearbook on International Communist Affairs* (Stanford: Hoover Institution Press, 1986), pp. xxix–xxxvii.

24. Australia, Costa Rica, Great Britain, India, New Zealand, Spain, and Sweden each have two Soviet-recognized communist parties (Richard F. Staar, "Checklist of Communist Parties," *Problems of Communism* 33, no. 2 [March–April 1986]: 58–71.

25. *Rude pravo* (Prague), 6 May 1983, stated that a majority of parties favored a conference. *Trybuna ludu* (Warsaw), 24 February 1984, claimed the total in favor to be 60 but gave no source. Gorbachev admitted that holding such a conference would be "inappropriate" (*L'Unità* [Milan], 22 May 1985).

26. B. N. Ponomarev, "Inevitability of the Liberation Movement," *Kommunist,* no. 1 (January 1980): 12. See also his "Teachings of Marx: A Guide to Action," *Pravda,* 31 March 1983, pp. 2–3.

27. U.S. Department of State, *Communist Interference in El Salvador,* Special Report no. 80, 23 February 1981; documents are reproduced in an appendix. See also John Norton Moore, "The Secret War in Central America and the Future of World Order," *American Journal of International Law* 80, no. 1 (January 1986): esp. 80–103.

28. United States Information Agency, *Documents Pertaining to Relations Between Grenada, the USSR, and Cuba,* December 1983, in three packets. The agreements with the USSR are dated 27 October 1980, 9 February 1981, and 27 July 1982, in Russian and English. See also U.S. Department of State, *Lessons of Grenada* (Washington, D.C.: GPO, February 1986), publ. no. 9457.

29. G.N. Volkov, chief ed., *The Basics of Marxist-Leninist Theory* (Moscow: Progress, 1982), pp. 304–13; V. V. Zagladin, chief ed., *Revoliutsionnyi protsess* (Moscow: Mysl', 1985), pp. 167–81.

30. Represented at the Eighth Congress of the Guadeloupe Communist Party, as reported by TASS in *Pravda,* 1 May 1984, p. 4. See also Wallace Spaulding, "Checklist of the 'National Liberation Movement,' " *Problems of Communism* 31, no. 2 (March–April 1982): 77–82.

31. Moses Mabhida, recently deceased SACP general secretary, is identified as having "long been a leading figure" in the ANC (*Political Affairs* 62, nos. 4–5 [April–May 1983]: 42, published by the Communist Party USA in New York).

32. V. V. Zagladin et al., *Mezhdunarodnoe rabochee dvizhenie* (Moscow: Politizdat, 1984), pp. 72–106, on the Socialist International.

33. World Peace Council, *List of Members, 1980–1983* (Helsinki: WPC, 1981), pp. 5, 20, 28, 44, 76, 92, 102; *New Perspectives* 12, no. 1 (1982): 2. The latter also is published in Helsinki. See the essay by Wallace Spaulding, "Communist Fronts in 1985," *Problems of Communism* 35, no. 2 (March–April 1986): 72–78.

34. Quoted by William R. Kintner, "The End of Socialist Anti-Communism?" *National Review,* 12 December 1980, p. 1505. Forty parties belonging to the SI Bureau, by contrast, condemned the United States for mining Nicaraguan ports (see *Aktuelt* [Copenhagen], 27 April 1984, p. 4).

35. *New York Times,* 29 and 30 November 1983; *Wall Street Journal,* 2 December 1983, p. 22; *Il Giornale Nuovo* (Milan), 11 December 1983. Only the groups from Chile, Jamaica, and Grenada belonged to the Socialist International.

36. Athens radio, 11 May 1984; *U.S. Foreign Broadcast Information Service,* 14 May 1984, p. S-1 (henceforth abbreviated as *FBIS*). Socialist Prime Minister Andreas Papandreou of Greece has stated publicly that "the world is now convinced the [Korean] jumbo jet was on a spy mission for the CIA and that it really did violate Soviet airspace for intelligence gathering purposes," without citing any evidence (*International Herald Tribune* [Hong Kong], 6–7 October 1984).

37. See the SI publication, *Common Security: A Programme for Disarmament* (London: Pan Books, 1982). The Seventeenth Socialist International Congress held in Lima, Peru, called for settlement of problems in Central America, Namibia, and the Middle East but did not mention Afghanistan or Kampuchea (Moscow radio, 24 June 1986; *FBIS,* 25 June 1986, p. CC-1). See also *Pravda,* 18 August 1986, p. 6; "Kremlin Gambits in SI," *Disinformation,* no. 4 (Fall 1986): 4–5.

38. B. N. Ponomarev, "Socialism's Role in the Present Day World," *World Marxist Review* 18, no. 1 (January 1975): 4–19; "Real Socialism and Its National Meaning," *Kommunist,* no. 2 (January 1979): 17–36; "Invincibility of the Liberation Movement," ibid., no. 1 (January 1980): 11–27; "Teachings of Marx: A Guide to Action," *Pravda,* 31 March 1983, pp. 1–2.

39. The text of the latest program appeared in *Pravda,* 7 March 1986, pp. 3–8.

40. Dieter Heinzig, "Die Ursprünge der sowjetisch-chinesischen Entspannung," *Berichte des Biost* (Cologne), no. 2, 1986.

41. Central Intelligence Agency, *Handbook of Economic Statistics, 1986* (Washington, D.C.: Directorate of Intelligence, September 1986), CPAS-86-10003, table 91, p. 126. For the ideological content of what these students are taught, see P. N. Fedoseev et al., *Nauchnyi kommunizm: Uchebnik,* 6th ed. (Moscow: Politizdat, 1984). Over half of all foreign students in the USSR come from Asia, Africa, and Latin America. Forty percent are from "fraternal socialist countries" (speech by M. S. Gorbachev at the Kremlin, as published in *Izvestiia,* 23 June 1984, p. 2).

2

THE DECISION-MAKING PROCESS

It is accepted by most scholars that the locus of power in the Soviet foreign policy decision-making process is the Communist Party of the Soviet Union (CPSU), and specifically its Political Bureau, or Politburo, rather than the government. A U.S. Senate study that appeared one year prior to Khrushchev's ouster concluded that this former leader had applied the "balance of interests" principle whenever the Politburo convened to discuss policy alternatives.[1] This has probably also been the general pattern of Soviet decision making in external affairs. That is, fundamental decisions concerning the five-year economic plan and the annual budget, both of which involve basic resource allocations and thus represent important foreign policy constraints, have in all likelihood been dealt with by a plenary session of full members and "candidates" for membership in the Political Bureau.

On the other hand, candidate, as opposed to full, members of the Politburo for the most part are occupied with domestic affairs and, hence, would seldom be involved in a discussion of foreign policy issues (see Table 2.1). The two exceptions among the seven alternates are S. L. Sokolov and N. V. Talyzin, both of whom have specialized duties relating to foreign policy concerns outside USSR borders. It is probable that all candidates participate in meetings but without the right to vote on decisions. The CPSU statute makes no distinction between candi-

TABLE 2.1
CPSU POWER ELITE, EARLY 1987

Name	Born	Age	Nationality	Responsibility (appointed)
Politburo members (11)				
*Gorbachev, M. S.	1931	55	Russian	General-secretary (March 1985)
Aliev, G. A.	1923	63	Azerbaijani	1st Dpty. chmn., Council of Ministers (Nov. 1982)
Chebrikov, V. M.	1923	63	Ukrainian	Chmn., USSR Committee for State Security, or KGB (Dec. 1982)
Gromyko, A. A.	1909	77	Russian	Chmn., Presidium, Supreme Soviet (July 1985)
*Ligachev, E. K.	1920	66	Russian	Deputy to General-secretary (April 1985)
Ryzhkov, N. I.	1929	57	Russian	Chmn., Council of Ministers (April 1985)
Shcherbitskii, V. V.	1918	68	Ukrainian	1st Secr., Ukraine (April 1971)
Shevardnadze, E. A.	1928	58	Georgian	Foreign minister (July 1985)
Solomentsev, M. S.	1913	73	Russian	Chmn., CPSU Control Committee (Dec. 1983)
Vorotnikov, V. I.	1927	59	Russian	Chmn., RSFSR Council of Ministers (Dec. 1983)
*Zaikov, L. N.	1923	63	Russian	Secretary for industrial policy & defense (July 1985)

Politburo candidates (8)

Demichev, P. N.	1918	68	Russian	1st Dpty. chmn., Presidium, Supreme Soviet (June 1986)
*Dolgikh, V. I.	1924	62	Russian	Secr., heavy ind. (May 1982)
El'tsin, B. N.	1931	55	Russian	1st Secr., Moscow City (Feb. 1986)
*Iakovlev, A. N.	1923	63	Russian	Propaganda (January 1987)
*Sliun'kov, N. N.	1929	57	Belorussian	
Sokolov, S. L.	1911	75	Russian	Defense minister (April 1985)
Solov'ev, Iu. F.	1925	61	Russian	1st Secr. Leningrad province (July 1985)
Talyzin, N. V.	1929	57	Russian	Chmn., Gosplan (October 1985)

Other Secretaries (six above with asterisks plus six below = twelve)

Biriukova, A. P.	1929	57	Russian	Light industry (March 1986)
Dobrynin, A. F.	1919	67	Russian	International (March 1986)
Luk'ianov, A. I.	1930	56	Russian	General Dept. (1985)
Medvedev, V. A.	1929	57	Russian	Bloc parties (March 1986)
Nikonov, V. P.	1929	57	Russian	Agriculture (April 1985)
Razumovskii, G. P.	1936	50	Russian	Org. Party Work (March 1986)
Kapitonov, I. V.	1915	71	Russian	Chmn. CPSU Audit Commission (1986)

SOURCES: *Pravda*, 7 March 1986, as elected at the Twenty-seventh CPSU Congress; CIA, Directorate of Intelligence, *Directory of Soviet Officials: National Organizations*, series CR 86–11691, June 1986, pp. 3–4; *CPSU Politburo and Secretariat: Positions and Responsibilities*, July 1986, LDA 86–10436. For biographic sketches, see Alexander G. Rahr, comp., *A Biographic Directory of 100 Leading Soviet Officials*, 3rd ed. (Munich: Radio Liberty Research, March 1986). *Pravda*, 29 January 1987, for latest changes.

dates and full members and only specifies that the Political Bureau is elected "for [the purpose of] directing the work of the party between plenary sessions of the Central Committee."[2]

THE POLITICAL BUREAU

In view of its size (eleven full members plus eight candidates in early 1987) and the foregoing limitations, the Politburo probably is broken down into several policy-making teams that must deal with various issues concerning such broad global subjects as diplomacy/foreign trade, military/intelligence, and world communism/propaganda.[3] (See Table 2.2.) Gorbachev, as general secretary of the party, is apparently the only individual who participates in all key foreign policy decisions, even though he has had limited prior experience. The other full members, Politburo candidates, and national secretaries have been placed on various teams in accordance with their particular responsibilities. The same criterion has been used in Table 2.2 for advisors, whose positions indicate their expertise. Special commissions are probably also established to work on important foreign policy problems. A recent example in the domestic arena included M. S. Gorbachev (chairman), G. A. Aliev, V. I. Vorotnikov, V. V. Kuznetsov, E. K. Ligachev, and N. I. Ryzhkov.[4]

Little information exists on the functioning of the Politburo and exactly how foreign policy decisions are made. Obviously, each successive leader or "collective leadership" group has had a specific *modus operandi*. According to a speech, given by Leonid Brezhnev at the Twenty-sixth CPSU Congress,

> All its [that is, the Politburo's] work has been concentrated on key points connected with the practical fulfillment of the decisions of the 25th CPSU congress and Central Committee plenums and with new happenings in domestic and foreign policy. Questions submitted for the examination of the Politburo have been carefully studied in advance. The range of such questions is extraordinarily wide and varied. The degree of complexity of many of them is increasing all the time. In certain instances the *Politburo sets up special commissions* to study thoroughly and to make general conclusions about the things that must have happened as well as to take, as the situation demands, appropriate practical measures.
>
> In the preparation for sessions and during discussions, different opinions were expressed—something that is quite natural—and numerous criticisms and proposals were submitted. However, *all decisions were adopted in a spirit of complete unanimity.* [Italics added.][5]

TABLE 2.2
PROBABLE FOREIGN POLICY-MAKING TEAMS, LATE 1986

Diplomacy & Trade	*Military & Intelligence*	*World Communism & Propaganda*
Gorbachev, M. S.	Gorbachev, M. S.	Gorbachev, M. S.
Shevardnadze, E. A.	Chebrikov, V. M.	Dobrynin, A. F.
Advisors:		
Gromyko, A. A.	Zaikov, L. N.	Medvedev, V. A.
Talyzin, N. V.	Sokolov, S. L.	Iakovlev, A. N.

Identifications:

1.	Gorbachev	CPSU General secretary: chairman, Defense Council
2.	Shevardnadze	Foreign minister
3.	Gromyko	Chairman, Presidium, Supreme Soviet
4.	Talyzin	Chairman, Gosplan
5.	Chebrikov	Chairman, KGB
6.	Zaikov	Secretary for industrial policy and defense
7.	Sokolov	Defense minister
8.	Dobrynin	Secretary for international affairs
9.	Medvedev	Secretary for Bloc parties
10.	Iakovlev	Secretary for propaganda

NOTE: The unofficial deputy to the general secretary, E. K. Ligachev, probably chairs meetings in the absence of Gorbachev.
SOURCES: *Pravda*, 7 March 1986, p. 1; CIA, Directorate of Intelligence, *Directory of Soviet Officials: National Organizations*, series CR 86/-11691, June 1986; and current press identifications.

The Central Committee, at its plenary sessions twice each year, approves all Politburo decisions without discussion or dissent.

During a meeting in Moscow with American correspondents, Brezhnev stated that 99.9 percent of the time "an agreed point of view is arrived at after long discussion." If a consensus could not be reached, he said, a small group was selected to resolve the matter.[6] Regular meetings were held at 3:00 P.M. every Thursday and lasted from three to six hours. Foreign policy issues had priority over domestic problems, according to Brezhnev. During a recent five-year period (1976–1981), a total of 237 Politburo sessions were held, an average of almost one per week.[7]

Chernenko, the man whom Brezhnev had selected to become his successor but who was passed over at first, gave the following description of work by the two most important CPSU organs:

The Politburo and the Secretariat are working efficiently, concertedly, in an atmosphere of high-principledness and full and genuine unity. Every condition has been created at their meetings for free discussion and evaluation of questions of foreign and domestic policy and for a comradely exchange of opinion.[8]

The foregoing, of course, ignored the friction between two major Politburo factions: those members who had supported Chernenko and those favoring Andropov for the CPSU general secretaryship.

In any event, decisions must depend to a large extent on the quality of information that reaches the highest level. Reports are prepared by political, economic, and military agencies of government with representatives stationed abroad as well as by corresponding departments within the central apparatus of the CPSU Secretariat. In addition, a classified and unedited digest of the foreign press, called "white TASS" after the color of its cover, is reportedly distributed among Politburo members. Other information may be submitted periodically on specialized problems.

The requirement for data from independent sources is understandable, since only on this basis can decisions be made with reference to the real world. One may compare the current situation to conditions under Stalin, when the reporting system generally yielded information conforming to that leader's distorted image of areas outside USSR borders. Apparently some improvement has occurred. However, distortions of information cannot be avoided completely because those reporting from foreign countries are forced always to evaluate developments in terms of a theoretical class struggle, a world outlook they have absorbed since kindergarten.

In the past there have been at least three different channels through which a matter might find its way on to the agenda of the Politburo.[9] First, each Politburo member or candidate has his own personal secretariat through which a subordinate might gain a hearing. Second, the national CPSU Secretariat also maintains an executive staff, and this has represented another channel for approaching those secretaries who are either full or candidate members of the Politburo. Finally, certain among the governmental agencies, such as those charged with responsibility for foreign trade or economic planning, might be called upon to brief the decision makers on issues involving their areas of expertise.

It is likely that proposals coming from lower echelons within the CPSU apparatus and/or the government must be coordinated laterally prior to submission through one of the three channels mentioned above. In most cases, the next stage would involve clearance by the executive staff of the national CPSU Secretariat. The central party apparatus, supervised by the latter, might consider a particular question independently. A process of review and approval, including staff work and in certain instances modification of a proposal, certainly would occur before submission to the Politburo.[10] Minor issues can be decided by any one of the four national secretaries in their capacity as Politburo members or candidates for membership.

THE CENTRAL APPARATUS

The executive staff of the national Secretariat thus represents in actuality the main locus of power for both formulation of policy alternatives (though not decision making *per se*) and subsequent implementation. A central apparatus department employs between 100 and 150 persons, subdivided into branches and sections. Each department's responsibilities are carefully defined. (See Figure 2.1 for department designations and incumbents.)

Administration of Affairs supervises operations of the entire central apparatus. Defense Industry performs the same function for eight ministries: defense, aviation, shipbuilding, electronics, radio, general machine building, "medium" machine building (a cover name for nuclear weapons' production), and machine building, all of which work on requirements for the armed forces. The Main Political Directorate of the Armed Forces exercises political control over the military. The General Department is responsible for all staff work and the Politburo's agenda. Administrative Organs approves important appointments in the armed forces and the KGB through the *Nomenklatura*[11] system, which includes approximately 300,000 positions in the CPSU and government. Cadres Abroad decides on travel by key personnel to foreign countries.

CPSU relations with other political parties and movements are handled by two departments: (1) International, for non-ruling communist parties and also non-communist movements; (2) Liaison, with the bloc, for those communist parties in power.[12] Either may have representatives in a Soviet embassy, depending upon the status of indigenous communists.

It has been asserted that the International Department exercises decisive influence on Soviet foreign policy.[13] Headed by A. F. Dobrynin since 1986, this organization controls the monthly journal *World Marxist Review*. Several deputy chiefs have responsibilities allocated to them by

FIGURE 2.1

THE 1987 CENTRAL PARTY MACHINE

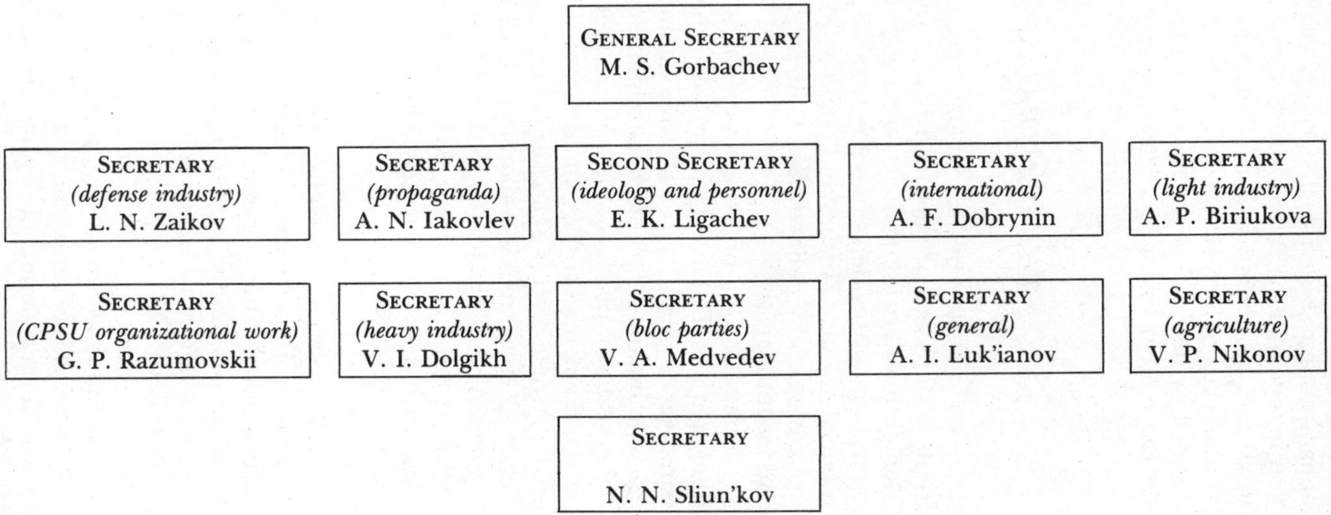

GENERAL SECRETARY
M. S. Gorbachev

SECOND SECRETARY
(ideology and personnel)
E. K. Ligachev

SECRETARY
(propaganda)
A. N. Iakovlev

SECRETARY
(defense industry)
L. N. Zaikov

SECRETARY
(CPSU organizational work)
G. P. Razumovskii

SECRETARY
(heavy industry)
V. I. Dolgikh

SECRETARY
(bloc parties)
V. A. Medvedev

SECRETARY
(international)
A. F. Dobrynin

SECRETARY
(light industry)
A. P. Biriukova

SECRETARY
N. N. Sliun'kov

SECRETARY
(general)
A. I. Luk'ianov

SECRETARY
(agriculture)
V. P. Nikonov

DEPARTMENTS (22)

Administration of Affairs
N. E. Kruchina (1983)

Administrative Organs
N. I. Savinkin (1986)

Agriculture & Food Industry
V. A. Karlov (1983)

Cadres Abroad
S. V. Chervonenko (1983)

Chemical Industry
V. G. Afonin (1980)

Construction
A. G. Mel'nikov (1986)

Culture
Iu. P. Voronov (1986)

Defense Industry
O. S. Beliakov (1986)

Economic
V. P. Mozhin (1986)
First Deputy

General
*A. I. Luk'ianov (1985)

Heavy Industry & Power
I. P. Iastrebov (1984)

International
*A. F. Dobrynin (1986)

Letters
B. P. Iakovlev (1979)

Liaison with Bloc Parties
*V. A. Medvedev (1986)

Light Industry & Consumer Goods
L. F. Bobykin (1986)

Machine Building
A. I. Vol'ski (1986)

Main Political Directorate of the Armed Forces
A. D. Lizichev (1985)

Organizational Party Work
*G. P. Razumovskii (1985)

Propaganda
Iu. A. Skliarov

Science & Educational Institutions
V. A. Grigoriev (1986)
1st Deputy

Trade & Domestic Services
N. A. Stashenkov (1986)

Transport & Communications
V. S. Pasternak (1986)

NOTES: *Secretary of the Central Committee.
Year appointed in parentheses.

SOURCES: Central Intelligence Agency, *Directory of Soviet Officials: National Organizations*, CR 86-11691 (Washington, D.C., June 1986), pp. 3–18; and *CPSU Central Committee: Executive and Administrative Apparatus* (July 1986), LDA 86-10433; *Pravda*, 29 January 1987.

geographic area or function (for example, arms control or international communist front organizations). More than 50 others have been identified in the press since 1979 as section heads, their deputies, and other high-ranking officials.

The central apparatus as a whole reportedly performs the following duties:[14]

1. disseminates Politburo decisions to lower CPSU levels, explaining and interpreting them;
2. implements CPSU policy;
3. controls and ensures implementation of policy by government agencies;
4. mobilizes the economy and society to implement CPSU policies;
5. allocates personnel and CPSU funds;
6. gathers and edits information, prepares reports and analyses for the Secretariat and Politburo;
7. alerts the Secretariat and Politburo to problems, performs preparatory work, and recommends solutions.

Little information is available on how the Secretariat operates. Each one of the national secretaries involved with foreign affairs, however, must exercise considerable power in his own right, since he may be in a position to deny access to the Politburo. The full Secretariat reportedly held 250 meetings—that is, more than the Politburo—during the same 1976–1981 five-year period mentioned above.[15]

RESEARCH INSTITUTES

In addition to handling the staff work on reports and drawing up the Politburo's actual agenda (the responsibility of its General Department), the Secretariat most probably reviews position papers submitted by various government agencies and specialized research institutes before they are transmitted to the Political Bureau. Among the best known in this second category are the Institute on the World Economy and International Relations (IMEMO), the Institute of the USA and Canada (ISShAiK), and the corresponding regional centers for Africa, Latin America, and the Far East.[16]

IMEMO, founded in 1956, had been headed from the beginning by Central Committee member N. N. Inozemtsev, who died in 1983.

The current director is E. M. Primakov. This institute, with some 800 employees, may still be regarded as the leading research center for international affairs but overlaps with the regional ones mentioned above. The latter is apparent in the duplication of effort that takes place with regard to the so-called national liberation movements throughout Africa, Latin America, and Asia. Apart from the Russian-language journal, *World Economics and International Relations,* IMEMO publications have included a volume on the "International Revolutionary Movement" edited by Ponomarev.

Since its establishment in 1968, the USA and Canada Institute, with more than 300 specialists, has been directed by G. A. Arbatov, also a full Central Committee member.[17] A former U.S. secretary of state gives the following assessment of that man in his memoirs:

> Arbatov was a faithful expounder of the Kremlin line, whom I had met at various international conferences on arms control when I was still a professor. He knew much about America and was skillful in adjusting his arguments to the prevailing fashions. He was especially subtle in playing to the inexhaustible masochism of American intellectuals who took it as an article of faith that every difficulty in U.S.-Soviet relations had to be caused by American stupidity or intransigence. He was endlessly ingenious in demonstrating how American rebuffs were frustrating the peaceful, sensitive leaders in the Kremlin, who were being driven reluctantly by our inflexibility into conflicts that offended their inherently gentle natures.[18]

Galina Orionova, who had worked during a ten-year period at this research center and subsequently defected at Heathrow Airport in London, flatly states that the USA and Canada Institute has no impact on Soviet foreign policy. She claims it is being used to influence the United States by means of disinformation. A KGB general (R. G. Bogdanov) serves as ideology department head and one of the three deputy directors for the institute, according to Orionova.[19] Domestic developments and foreign relations of the United States are covered by the institute's monthly magazine in the Russian language, *U.S.A.: Economics, Politics, Ideology.*

The Africa Institute, organized in 1959, had been headed by a former IMEMO director, V. G. Solodovnikov. This individual was succeeded in December 1976 by A. A. Gromyko (son of the Politburo member), who had served as a section chief at the USA and Canada Institute. Apart from Soviet relations with Africa, the so-called non-capitalist path of development, various economic and socio-political problems, the phenomenon of "neo-colonialism," and the effects of Chinese influence are studied by almost 500 members of this research center.

The Far East Institute publishes *Problems of the Far East*. The institute has a staff of about 300 and, since establishment in 1961, had been directed by M. I. Sladkovskii, who was succeeded in late 1985 by M. L. Titarenko. Most research efforts are concentrated on the People's Republic of China. It works closely with IMEMO, particularly regarding Japan. Information about Far Eastern studies is difficult to obtain, perhaps because of the sensitivity regarding Sino-Soviet relations in general.[20] The Africa and Far East institutes jointly publish two magazines, entitled *Peoples of Asia and Africa* and *Asia and Africa Today,* in three languages: Russian, English, and French.

The Latin America Institute, founded in 1961, is led by V. V. Volskii and publishes in Russian a bimonthly journal called *Latin America.* Research sections deal with economics, socio-political problems, foreign policy and international relations, culture, and Cuba as a model for the Western Hemisphere. The institute has expanded its staff to more than 350, in line with growing trade between that part of the world and the USSR.

SHORT- AND LONG-RANGE PLANS

Although it participates in submitting proposals to the Politburo, there is no specific evidence that the Secretariat functions as a long-range planning staff in foreign affairs. It may only work on an *ad hoc* basis. If a project involves several areas of responsibility, a small group of secretaries probably would form a subcommittee. This group might then study the reports and policy papers, arriving at a consensus as a basis for recommendations. The expertise and personality of each subcommittee participant certainly would influence the proposed course of action.

Individual departments in the central party apparatus receive, process, and analyze data on which foreign policy staff studies are based. They maintain contact with Soviet diplomatic and military installations abroad, so that communications are sent either directly to them or through an intermediary like the Main Intelligence Directorate (GRU) in the Defense Ministry.[21] Some of this information will come via East European military attachés and bloc intelligence officers stationed abroad, or even from members of non-ruling foreign communist parties loyal to Moscow.

It would seem that Soviet foreign policy remains both consistent and coordinated, which suggests that the Politburo must approve two types of plans: (1) a strategic one, setting forth the basic objectives for different geographic areas of the world to be implemented only within a relatively long-range time frame; and (2) an operational one for individual countries, which delineates specific goals to be achieved in order to fulfill overall objectives.[22]

These plans, especially the short-range operational type, are reviewed by departments in the central party apparatus and also by the Foreign Affairs Ministry. It is this latter governmental agency that implements foreign policy decisions. Along with the career diplomats stationed at Soviet missions abroad are representatives of other governmental agencies. It is commonly known that the various USSR intelligence services operate independently of one another, probably even on a competitive basis.[23] Organizations whose operatives report directly to their own headquarters in Moscow, bypassing the ambassador, include the secret police (KGB) as well as military intelligence (GRU) and the State Committee on Foreign Economic Relations.

This last agency represents the vehicle through which foreign aid and military assistance are channeled to recipient countries and to so-called national liberation movements abroad. In addition, the Foreign Trade Ministry has its commercial personnel, as part of or at times even physically separated from the Soviet embassy. Yet another organization involved in this field would be the Council for Mutual Economic Assistance,[24] particularly in lesser developed countries, where the East European regimes provide foreign aid in coordination with the Soviet Union (see Chapter 8).

THE SUCCESSION PROBLEM

The CPSU ended its Twenty-sixth Congress on 3 March 1981 with unanimous re-election of all Politburo members and candidates as well as all Central Committee secretaries. In the unlikely event that these same individuals had remained in their positions until the next congress met in 1986, their average age would have been 75 or almost double that of the 1919 leadership (see Figure 2.2). Many changes already have occurred since L. I. Brezhnev's death in November 1982 and his replacement by Andropov, who died only fifteen months later in February 1984. His successor, K. U. Chernenko, lasted until March 1985. The current leader is M. S. Gorbachev, formally confirmed as general-secretary at the Twenty-seventh CPSU Congress.

The previous Politburo core group had been composed almost entirely of individuals who reached the supreme decision-making level

FIGURE 2.2
AGE OF POLITBURO MEMBERS
1919–1986

YEAR

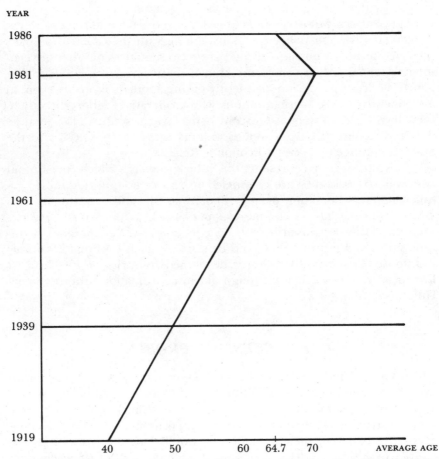

SOURCES: John Lowenhardt, *The Soviet Politburo,* trans. Dymphna Clark (New York: St. Martin's Press, 1982); Herwig Kraus, comp., "The Composition of Leading Organs of the CPSU, 1952–1982," *Radio Liberty Research Bulletin* (Munich, 1982); Alexander G. Rahr, comp., *A Biographic Directory of 100 Leading Soviet Officials* (Munich: Radio Liberty Research, March 1986), 234 p.

because Stalin's terror machine had cleared the way for their advancement. They themselves participated vigorously in denouncing their superiors from the relatively safe third- and fourth-echelon positions during the Great Purge[25] in the mid-1930s. Most of them never received a secondary education, having been selected for their technical or political training with only an elementary school background. Many thus were semi-educated in the conventional sense of the word. Their outlook had been constrained by ideological blinders, and their advancement depended on ruthless cunning.

Certain analysts in the West expressed hope that a new generation of Soviet leaders, perhaps after the 1986 CPSU Congress, might be different. Such reasoning ignored the fact that those who were in a position to succeed the previous gerontocracy had been recruited into the party machine as local Komsomol (Communist Youth League) secretaries and are totally devoted to the system. They could not have reached positions close to the top without constantly displaying absolute dedication to their superiors. The "new generation" thus remains narrow-minded and cynical in its opposition to governments, even communist-ruled ones, that are not under USSR influence. This mentality can be summed up by Lenin's slogan, *kto kogo?* or "who [will eliminate] whom?"[26]

One of the great weaknesses of the Soviet system is that no means exist for any constitutional transfer of power or for removal of overaged leaders except by conspiracy. In the past, heirs apparent have been victims of intrigue by rivals or have become impatient for the mantle. The most recent example was Brezhnev himself, who organized a successful plot in October 1964 against his benefactor, Khrushchev.

Prior to Brezhnev's death, it seemed that the favorite to succeed him as party leader would be Chernenko, promoted to secretary of the Central Committee, candidate, and then full Politburo member within a brief period of two years. Such a rapid rise is unusual. A protégé of the general secretary, he had been the youngest politburocrat to possess all five prerequisites for the top position: ethnic Russian background, experience in the party apparatus, some knowledge of both foreign and economic affairs, plus membership in the Brezhnev faction.[27] These qualifications did not ensure immediate success, however.

THE ANDROPOV INTERLUDE

Although much of what follows is based on informed speculation, the final struggle for power probably commenced in January 1982 after chief ideologist Mikhail Suslov had died. The KGB arrested a certain

Boris Buriatia for possession of stolen diamonds. He also happened to
be a friend of Mrs. Galina Churbanova, daughter of Brezhnev. Such a
development, that is, the arrest of an individual so close to the general
secretary's immediate family, indicated that the party/state head may no
longer have been in full control. Brezhnev reportedly suffered heart
spasms during both February and March. The following month, Andropov delivered the address commemorating Lenin's birthday; by May he
had succeeded Suslov as secretary in charge of ideology, the position
that heir apparent Chernenko should have received.[28]

Next came the disinformation campaign directed at Western journalists, portraying Andropov as an educated and cultured individual
who spoke English and had an affinity for jazz. Supposedly he had
voted in the Politburo against both the invasion of Afghanistan and the
declaration of martial law in Poland. Scientists and intellectuals should
have access to scholarly publications from the West, he was alleged to
have believed. The "liberal" Andropov, if he assumed power, would
promote Jews to high positions in the Soviet Union. None of these
"leaks" could be corroborated, and none of them corresponded to the
man's actual background.[29]

In fact, Andropov had begun his career by assisting in deportation
of thousands of inhabitants from the Karelo-Finnish Republic—that is,
the part of Finland that had been recently occupied by the Red Army—
who were sent to forced labor camps in the Gulag Archipelago during
the years 1940–1941. As ambassador to Budapest in 1956, he promised
safe-conduct to Prime Minister Imre Nagy and other Hungarian cabinet members. They were arrested and executed after two years in
prison. Under the fifteen-year chairmanship of Andropov, the KGB
introduced a scientific innovation: psychiatric hospitals to suppress
dissidents.[30] This career pattern should have led observers to conclude
that the new Soviet leader would be a ruthless individual, much more
dangerous to deal with than even his predecessor.

Andropov became chairman of the Supreme Soviet presidium, that
is, president or chief-of-state, on 16 June 1983, which gave him the third
key post in the USSR. He had been identified previously as Defense
Council chairman. Thus, within a little more than half a year, Andropov
attained what it had taken Brezhnev thirteen years to accomplish. In late
1983 it was anticipated that Andropov would appear either at the Central
Committee plenum or the meeting of the Supreme Soviet during the last
week of December, even though he had not been seen since 18 August.
He attended neither, obviously suffering from a protracted illness. Nonetheless, other Central Committee plenary sessions had promoted several
Andropov supporters.

Still, despite the several statements and even speeches read in Andropov's name, the decision-making process seemed to have become moribund. Nobody appeared certain either that the leader definitely would or that he would not return to his office in the Kremlin; hence, the situation came to resemble a stalemate. Moreover, even on the expanded thirteen-member Politburo, the line-up did not overwhelmingly favor Andropov.

Because of this delicate balance of power, Andropov had to move cautiously and slowly in consolidating his power position on the Politburo. On the other hand, a large number of lower-ranking leaders (75 years or older) were retired from Central Committee membership, Secretariat departments, government ministries, lower-ranking CPSU organizations (20 percent of the regional first secretaries), and even embassies in attempts to break apparatus fossilization. This process reflected the tension between the Andropov and Chernenko factions, with the latter supporting the *status quo*.

ASCENDANCY OF CHERNENKO

Andropov, already ten years older[31] than either Brezhnev or Khrushchev when they acceded to power, died on 9 February 1984. Elected four days later as the new CPSU general secretary, Chernenko was of the same generation as his predecessor. In choosing him, the Politburo probably considered seniority and experience in the central party apparatus[32] and also avoided the difficulties that might have resulted if a choice had been made from among the younger politburocrats. Any one of the latter, once firmly in power, might have been tempted to retire the septuagenarians.

Appointment of Chernenko as funeral commission chairman indicated that he would be Andropov's successor, and there seems to have been no other serious contender. The "old guard" dominated the scene, with Chernenko (then age 72), Gromyko (74), and Ustinov (75) as main speakers at the funeral. Tikhonov (78) proposed only one candidate for general secretary, and the motion received unanimous endorsement by the Politburo. Exactly two months later the Supreme Soviet, also without a single dissenting vote, elected Chernenko chairman of its presidium or titular USSR president.[33] This time, it was Gorbachev (53) who made the nomination speech.

Gorbachev apparently ranked third in the official hierarchy, after Chernenko and Tikhonov, that status having been confirmed by his place (third from last) among speakers during the February–March

1984 election campaign for the Supreme Soviet. These and other events seemed to indicate Gorbachev's emergence as the unofficial second secretary or deputy to Chernenko.[34] Whether he would remain the heir apparent, and for how long, could not be predicted with any degree of certainty. In the past, individuals in such a position for the most part had been eliminated from the race.

Among the eleven full Politburo members, only three others, in addition to Gorbachev, were under 65 years of age: Aliev (61), Romanov (61), and Vorotnikov (57). The first is an Azerbaijani, which should have disqualified him from becoming the next general secretary. He served formerly as KGB chief in his native republic. Vorotnikov would seem to have had a better chance, with foreign affairs experience (1979–1982) as ambassador to Cuba.

Each leader in the past has been a Central Committee secretary in addition to holding Politburo membership. Only two contenders were in this category: Gorbachev and Romanov.[35] The latter apparently had made a good record as CPSU first secretary for Leningrad province before moving to Moscow. His family name, however—coincidentally the same as that of the last tsarist dynasty—conjures up images of the *ancien regime*, unwelcome to the communists.

Neither should one discount candidate Politburo members who, at the same time, are national secretaries. Only two held such dual positions: Ponomarev (79) and Dolgikh (60). The former would seem to be eliminated because of age. The latter had been in charge of the heavy industry department (1976–1984) in the central party apparatus and still supervises that important part of the economy. In addition, he gave the anniversary address[36] commemorating Lenin's birthday in 1984, which may indicate future promotion to full Politburo status. It should be noted that Chernenko delivered this speech in 1981, as Brezhnev's protégé and heir apparent at the time.

GORBACHEV AT THE TOP

In actual fact, this time the heir apparent did emerge as general secretary. Mikhail S. Gorbachev had been born of peasant stock on a collective farm in the Stavropol region. Because of his work at a local machine-tractor station and activities in the Communist Union of Youth (Komsomol), he was selected to study law at Moscow State University. As secretary of the Komsomol organization in law school, Gorbachev reportedly assisted the KGB in developing cases against other students.[37]

The new CPSU leader never practiced law, but became instead a full-time apparatus worker. It was the late KGB chief Andropov who promoted Gorbachev and saw to his protégé's advancement. Although Chernenko received the mantle, he lived only thirteen months. Gromyko nominated Gorbachev ("this man has a nice smile but iron teeth"), who was elected unopposed and unanimously as general secretary on 11 March 1985. On 1 July he removed his only serious rival, Grigori Romanov, and began coopting supporters into the Politburo. The 27th CPSU Congress confirmed Gorbachev in his position almost exactly one year after his initial election. The current CPSU general secretary has the opportunity to direct foreign policy and see that it is being executed. Implementation is the subject of the next chapter.

NOTES

1. U.S. Congress, Senate, Committee on Government Operations, Subcommittee on National Security Staffing and Operations, *Study on Staffing Procedures and Problems in the Soviet Union,* 88th Cong., 1st sess., 1963, p. 24. More recent discussions of this policy-making organ can be found in John Lowenhardt, *The Soviet Politburo,* trans. Dymphna Clark (New York: St. Martin's Press, 1982), and Roy D. Laird, *The Politburo* (Boulder, Colo.: Westview Press, 1986).

2. Chapter 4, Article 38, on Higher Party Organs, in "Ustav KPSS" *Pravda,* 7 March 1986, p. 9.

3. For texts of recent decisions, see Donald V. Schwartz, ed., *Resolutions and Decisions of the Communist Party of the Soviet Union: The Brezhnev Years, 1964– 1981* (Toronto: University of Toronto Press, 1982), 5:301.

4. The Politburo commission membership appeared in *Pravda,* 2 August 1984, p. 2.

5. *Pravda,* 24 February 1981, p. 8; "Proceedings of the 26th CPSU Congress," *FBIS,* 24 February 1981, p. 47. This supposedly was not the case in August 1968, when the decision to invade Czechoslovakia allegedly resulted from a six-to-five split vote, with "Brezhnev having hesitated a long time" before casting the decisive one (Vasilii M. Kulish, deputy director of the Institute on the World Economy and International Relations [IMEMO], in a private conversation with the author. A former colonel in Soviet military intelligence, this individual obviously had received disinformation training).

6. *New York Times,* 15 January 1973.

7. L. I. Brezhnev report to the Twenty-sixth CPSU Congress, in *FBIS,* 24 February 1981. See also the report based on an eyewitness account by M. H. Heikal, *The Road to Ramadan* (New York: Quadrangle Books, 1975), especially p. 04, according to which it took five Politburo members to approve a telegram to Major General Muhammad Siad Barre in Somalia.

8. Chernenko speech in *Pravda,* 15 June 1983, pp. 1–3. An innovation is

regular reporting in the press about Politburo discussions, which suggests that the body meets on Wednesdays or Thursdays. Moscow radio on 6, 13, 20, 26 June 1986, reported meetings for those days; *Pravda*, 13, 17, 21, 25 July 1986; the third a "special session" concerning the Chernobyl accident.

9. U.S. Congress, Senate, Committee on Government Operations, *Report on National Policy Machinery in the Soviet Union*, 86th Cong., 2nd sess., 1960, p. 19.

10. Ibid., p. 20. See also Thane Gustafson and Dawn Mann, "Gorbachev's First Year: Building Power and Authority," *Problems of Communism* 35, no. 3 (May–June 1986): 1–19.

11. On this key personnel appointment system, see Michael Voslensky, *Nomenklatura: The Soviet Ruling Class* (Garden City, N.Y.: Doubleday, 1984), esp. pp. 356–85.

12. Institute for the Study of Conflict, *The Strategic Intentions of the Soviet Union* (London, 1978), pp. 13–15.

13. Robert W. Kitrinos, "International Department of the CPSU," *Problems of Communism* 33, no. 5 (September–October 1984): 47–75; Wallace Spaulding, "Shifts in CPSU ID," ibid. 35, no. 4 (July–August 1986): 80–86.

14. Michael Voslensky, *Nomenklatura*, pp. 271–78.

15. These dealt with "selection of cadres, organization and checking of execution, and virtually all current questions of party life," according to Brezhnev's report to the Twenty-sixth CPSU Congress (*Pravda*, 24 February 1981).

16. Richard S. Soll, Arthur Zuehlke, Jr., and Richard B. Foster, *The Role of Social Science Research Institutes in Formulation and Execution of Soviet Foreign Policy* (Arlington, Va.: SRI Strategic Center, n.d.), pp. 18–31. This same source lists on pp. 58–59 about a dozen relatives of high-ranking CPSU officials who work at these institutes, which suggests widespread nepotism. See also Igor S. Glagolev, *Post-Andropov Kremlin Strategy* (Washington, D.C.: Association for Cooperation with Democratic Countries, 1984), pp. 21–26, on his work at IMEMO.

17. V. A. Fedorovich, "USA Institute of the USSR Academy of Sciences," *SShA: Ekonomika, politika, ideologiia* 5, no. 5 (May 1974): 12–16; Central Intelligence Agency, *Biographic Report: USSR Institute of the United States of America and Canada*, series CR 76–10864, April 1976, pp. 3–4.

18. Henry Kissinger, *White House Years* (Boston: Little, Brown & Co., 1979), p. 112. For KGB connections with Arbatov's institute, see Glagolev, *Post-Andropov*, pp. 79–80.

19. Barbara L. Dash, *A Defector Reports: The Institute of the USA and Canada* (Falls Church, Va.: Delphic Associates, May 1982) (volume includes an appendix of biographic sketches totaling another 198 pages); and Stanislav A. Levchenko, "Unmasking Moscow's 'Institute of the U.S.A.,' " *Heritage Foundation Backgrounder* (Washington, D.C., 17 December 1982), for an exposé by a defector from the KGB.

20. Soll et al., *Role of Social Science Research Institutes,* pp. 27–30. Numbers of institute staffs are from Daniel C. Matuszewski, "Soviet International Relations Research," *Foreign Area Research in the National Interest: American and Soviet Perspectives* (New York, International Research and Exchanges Board), *IREX Occasional Papers* 1, no. 8 (1982): 33–44. Matuszewski states that 7,400 specialists work at twelve key Moscow institutes.

21. Oleg Penkovskiy, *The Penkovskiy Papers* (Garden City, N.Y.: Doubleday, 1965), pp. 65–93. Colonel Penkovskiy had served as a GRU officer until arrested and subsequently executed in Moscow.

22. Senate, Committee on Government Operations, *National Policy Machinery,* pp. 40–41.

23. Ladislav Bittman, *The KGB and Soviet Disinformation* (Washington, D.C.: Pergamon-Brassey's, 1985), pp. 18–19.

24. Richard F. Staar, *Communist Regimes in Eastern Europe,* 4th rev. ed. (Stanford: Hoover Institution Press, 1982), pp. 301–24.

25. Robert Conquest, *The Great Terror: Stalin's Purge of the Thirties,* rev. ed. (New York: Collier Books, 1973), especially pp. 638–96.

26. Richard F. Staar, "Soviet Union," in Peter Duignan and Alvin Rabushka, eds., *The United States in the 1980s* (Stanford: Hoover Institution Press, 1980), pp. 735–55. See also Boris Meissner, "Brezhnev's Legacy in Soviet Politics," *Aussenpolitik* 34, no. 2 (1983): 107–21.

27. R. Judson Mitchell, "The Soviet Succession," *Orbis* 23, no. 1 (Spring 1979): 25. See also Joseph G. Whelan, "Soviet Successions from Lenin to Brezhnev: The Troubled Search for Legitimacy," *Congressional Research Service,* Report No. 82–152S, 20 September 1982, mimeographed.

28. Andrew Nagorski, "The Making of Andropov," *Harper's,* February 1983, pp. 23–26. See also Amy W. Knight, "Andropov: Myths and Realities," *Survey* 28, no. 1 (Spring 1984): 22–44.

29. Official biography in *Sovetskaia voennaia entsiklopediia* (Moscow: Voenizdat, 1976), p. 193. The best available political study is by Arnold Beichman and Mikhail S. Bernstam, *Andropov: New Challenge to the West* (New York: Stein & Day, 1983).

30. Charles Krauthammer, "The Andropov Factor," *New Republic,* 13 June 1983, pp. 19–21.

31. Ages at accession to power of the last three leaders had increased over the years as follows: Lenin (47), Stalin (44), Khrushchev (58), Brezhnev (57), Andropov (68), and Chernenko (72). See also Myron Rush, "Succeeding Brezhnev," *Problems of Communism* 32, no. 1 (January–February 1983): 2–17.

32. On the unimpressive background of Chernenko, see *Strategic Survey, 1983–1984* (London: International Institute for Strategic Studies, 1984), pp. 50–51. He completed only primary school at age twelve and much later served three years with the border guards, after which he attended the Higher School for Party Organizers.

33. *Pravda,* 12 April 1984, p. 1.

34. V. G. Afanas'ev, editor of *Pravda,* during an interview with *Dagens Nyheter,* 15 March 1984, in Stockholm, made a flat statement to this effect.

35. Marc D. Zlotnik, "Chernenko Succeeds," *Problems of Communism* 33, no. 2 (March–April 1984): 17–31.

36. *Pravda,* 21 April 1984, pp. 1–2.

37. Andrew A. Michta, *An Emigré Reports: Fridrikh Neznansky on Mikhail Gorbachev: 1950–1958* (Falls Church, Va.: Delphic Associates, October 1985), p. 55. See also R. Judson Mitchell and Teresa Gee, "The Soviet Succession Crisis," *Orbis* 29, no. 2 (Summer 1985): 293–317, and Elizabeth Teague, "Turnover in the Soviet Elite Under Gorbachev: Implications for Soviet Politics," *Radio Liberty Research* 8 July 1986, RL Supplement 1/86.

3

IMPLEMENTATION OF FOREIGN POLICY

As discussed in the preceding chapter, policy decisions in matters of great importance are made by the Political Bureau as a whole, although individual politburocrats decide matters of a routine nature on a day-to-day basis. Implementation of external policies is effected primarily through the Ministry of Foreign Affairs, while administration of military aid and civilian-type foreign assistance in general would fall within the purview of the Defense Ministry and/or Committee for Foreign Economic Relations. The daily functions of the Foreign Affairs Ministry, according to a standard textbook used at the USSR Diplomatic Academy, include:

> The study of international conditions, external and domestic policies of foreign governments, international organizations and movements; [provision of] timely information to the Central Committee and Soviet leadership on international events deserving their attention; submission of suitable recommendations on necessary action in the interest of strengthening peace, cooperation between governments, and in the struggle against the aggressive activities of imperialistic forces.[1]

Many governments throughout the world systematically publish archival materials on foreign policy. However, the first annual compendium of documents on Soviet foreign policy released by the USSR did not appear until December 1983. It covered the year 1966 and was entitled *For Peace and the Security of Nations.* Annotated documentary compilations on the 1943 Moscow conference of foreign ministers as well as the first volume on Soviet-American relations during World War II were published the following year. Another book on diplomacy in general deals with the same time span.[2]

ORGANIZATION

The Ministry of Foreign Affairs, like other Soviet government agencies, includes an inner policy group known as the collegium. This comprises the minister (E. A. Shevardnadze), two first deputy ministers (Iu. M. Vorontsov and A. G. Kovalev), nine deputies, a secretary general, and thirteen other members for a total of 25 persons.[3] The duumvirate of two first deputy ministers had the effect of establishing a new administrative structure at the apex of the Foreign Ministry, which for more than twenty years had only one individual with this rank. The existence of two positions could be explained by a failure to decide upon a single person who would be groomed to succeed as head of the ministry. Vorontsov (born 1929) is an expert on global policy and disarmament, having spent seven years during the 1970s at the Soviet embassy in Washington, D.C. Kovalev, an older (born 1923) and more experienced party member, is responsible for Western Europe and CSCE. Both have held their current rank since May 1986.

Each of the nine regular deputy ministers is responsible for a specific region of the world or certain functional aspects of foreign affairs (see Table 3.1). The remaining collegium members also may hold posts as department chiefs in the ministry. Some of these units are organized by subject matter (archives or personnel); seventeen of the units pertain to geographic regions; and there are also two divisions covering international organizations. As the standard Soviet textbook on foreign affairs puts it:

> An important branch of the central apparatus, from the point of view of day-to-day operational diplomatic guidance, is the executive diplomatic divisions. The nature of activities engaged in by these divisions is determined by their territorial and functional characteristics. Territorial departments handle questions of foreign relations with specific groups of states. These groups of countries are divided by region. For example, Europe, the USA and Latin America, Near and Middle East, Southeast and South Asia, Africa, Far East, and others.

Functional divisions in the central apparatus are divided into such sections as consular, protocol, treaty-legal, press, international organizations and international economic organizations, cultural, planning of foreign policy tasks, general international problems.[4]

A separate administration exists for servicing the foreign diplomatic corps in the USSR. The Institute of International Relations and a Diplomatic Academy also are operated by the ministry. The latter began publishing an annual *Diplomatic Bulletin* in 1983, which includes foreign policy documents and a chronicle of activities. Official, annotated materials on the Teheran and Yalta summits (1943 and 1945) did not appear until the following year, when they were released in a new series on such World War II conferences.

A report from Moscow indicates that several new functional departments have been established: arms limitation and disarmament under V. P. Karpov; international economic relations, headed by I. D. Ivanov; humanitarian and cultural relations, with Iu. B. Kashlev as chief; and a consolidation of press and information units into an administration for information, directed by G. I. Gerasimov. The same source indicates that a realignment of geographic areas has resulted in new departments for Arab countries, socialist countries of Europe, and socialist countries of Asia.[5]

The term *collegium* implies collective administration, and advice for the minister indeed may emanate from this body. However, it is more probable that the collegium operates in a coordinating capacity for decisions regarding allocation of specific tasks on the basis of overall policy guidelines. This group would almost certainly be expected to check on the implementation of directives and undertake periodic reviews to evaluate the success of Soviet foreign policy endeavors.

Foreign minister over a 28-year period, Andrei A. Gromyko's career stood in contrast to that of other such bureaucrats. His immediate predecessors, V. M. Molotov[6] and D. I. Shepilov, had involved themselves with intra-party politics. Gromyko refrained from doing so, and this may be the principal reason for his long tenure. Graduated from the Institute of Economics, he entered the foreign service in 1939 when opportunities for rapid advancement existed after the purges. From the USA department, Gromyko came to Washington as embassy counselor[7] and received promotion to ambassador at age 34. His subsequent positions included permanent U.N. representative, ambassador to Britain, and in 1957 foreign minister. In July 1985, the 76-year-old Gromyko became titular chief of state, to make way for a man without any diplomatic experience.

TABLE 3.1
USSR MINISTRY OF FOREIGN AFFAIRS, 1986

Collegium	Appointment Date	Responsibilities
Minister		
Shevardnadze, E. A.	July 1985	Direction of foreign policy
First deputy ministers (2)		
Vorontsov, Iu. M.	April 1986	Representative, USSR-US talks (Geneva)
Kovalev, A. G..	April 1986	Western Europe and CSCE
Deputy ministers (9)		
Adamishin, A. L.	May 1986	Africa
Bessmertnykh, A. A.	May 1986	United States, U.N.
Chaplin, B. N.	May 1986	Cultural, administrative, juridical affairs
Il'ichev, L. F.	Mar. 1965	China
Kapitsa, M. S.	Dec. 1982	Asia
Komplektov, V. G.	Dec. 1982	UNESCO
Loginov, V. P.	Dec. 1985	Eastern Europe
Nikiforov, V. M.	Dec. 1985	Cadres
Petrovsky, V. F.	May 1986	International Organizations
Rogachev, I. A.	Aug. 1986	Far East (chief negotiator with PRC)

		Secretary general
Secretary general		
Fokin, Iu. E.	July 1980	
Other collegium members (12)		
Bondarenko, A. P.	Oct. 1971	Chief, Third European Department
Grinevskii, O. A.	Jan. 1983	Representative, Conference on Disarmament in Europe (Stockholm)—ended September 1986
Grishchenko, A. I.	id. 1982	not identified
Israelian, V. L.	Sept. 1977	Representative at U.N. Conference on Disarmament (Geneva)
Khlestov, O. N.	Oct. 1973	Representative to International Organizations (Vienna)
Poliakov, V. P.	Sept. 1984	Chief, Near East Department
Sevostianov, P. P.	id. 1985	Chief, Historical-Diplomatic Administration
Suslov, V. P.	Nov. 1973	Chief, Second European Department
Tikhvinskii, S. L.	July 1978	Director, Diplomatic Academy
Tsybukov, V. V.	id. 1984	Not identified
Vasev, V. M.	Jan. 1983	Chief, Third African Department

SOURCES: CIA, Directorate of Intelligence, *Directory of USSR Ministry of Foreign Affairs Officials*, series CR 85-14535, September 1985, pp. 3–4; CIA, Directorate of Intelligence, *Directory of Soviet Officials: National Organizations*, series CR 86-11691, June 1986, pp. 69–70; Alexander Rahr, "Winds of Change Hit Foreign Ministry," *Radio Liberty Research* (16 July 1986), RL 274/86, pp. 7–10; Philip Taubman, "Soviet Diplomacy Given a New Look," *New York Times*, 10 August 1986. *Arizona Republic*, 11 January 1987, p. A9, for Vorontsov appointment as chief negotiator at the arms control talks in Geneva.

Fifty-seven-year-old Edward A. Shevardnadze joined the CPSU at age 20 in Georgia. He became a professional apparatus worker and served from 1965–1972 as minister of internal affairs and three-star police general in his native republic. During the next thirteen years, he headed the CPSU of Georgia and cleaned up some of the corruption. This unexpected transfer of Shevardnadze obviously meant that party leader Gorbachev wanted to be his own foreign minister. The titular head, Shevardnadze, gave the ceremonial address commemorating Lenin's birth.[8]

TRAINING AND ACTIVITIES

As already mentioned, the Foreign Affairs Ministry operates the Moscow State Institute of International Relations (IIR)[9] and a Diplomatic Academy for those who already have made the foreign service their profession. The former lasts six years and includes a rigorous curriculum: foreign languages, history, culture, economics in the geographic area of specialization, a heavy emphasis on Marxism-Leninism, and also CPSU history as subject matter, apart from six to eight hours per week of military training. This last activity is given major emphasis that equals, if not exceeds, the time allocated to the study of economics or CPSU history. And, according to a former Soviet diplomat, the regional orientation of the program tends to encourage a rigid approach rather than develop the analytical abilities of students.[10]

Approximately 20 percent of the IIR graduates are assigned to the Foreign Ministry and later go abroad; about one-third of each graduating class is sent to other government agencies to work as interpreters or consultants; the remainder receive assignments in the mass media, Committee on State Security (KGB), and the IIR for research and teaching. The Diplomatic Academy[11] apparently constitutes an in-service training center for personnel at advanced career levels.

Once attached to a geographic desk in Moscow, the young foreign service officer assists in "filtering, consolidating and synthesizing reports from field missions."[12] In general, embassies abroad are responsible for monitoring all Soviet citizens in the specific country to which they are accredited. They also prepare a comprehensive annual report or country study that analyzes political, economic, and cultural developments. Policy recommendations are added by the ambassador. Although each chief of mission is legally appointed via the Presidium of the Supreme Soviet as representative of the USSR government, he must be cleared first by a unit[13] within the central apparatus of the CPSU Secretariat.

It appears that most ambassadors to other communist-ruled states are either former high-ranking party or government officials. This is understandable, since they deal with their counterparts and with matters where such a background would represent a definite advantage. The chiefs of mission accredited to "fraternal," or other communist-ruled, states seem to have little chance in general for long-term tenure in their respective embassies. Among the ambassadors in East Central Europe (excluding Albania, which has had no Soviet representatives since December 1961), all have been changed at least twice in the past nine years.[14] Chiefs of mission in Bulgaria, Czechoslovakia, Poland, and Yugoslavia average tours of duty from two to four years.

Some of these individuals at times rotate back into governmental or CPSU positions, as did Andropov, who served as ambassador to Hungary during the 1956 revolution. The reverse occurred when N. N. Rodionov became a deputy foreign minister after serving as first CPSU secretary for the Cheliabinsk region. He next became ambassador to Yugoslavia.[15] There are also instances where a subordinate may rank higher in the party hierarchy than the mission chief himself. Conversely, an ambassador, formally at least, might hold a more important position in the party than even the foreign minister. This seemed to have been the case with Y. I. Pervukhin, a former deputy prime minister and still at that time candidate member of the CPSU Politburo, who was demoted to chief of mission in East Berlin after the June 1957 Central Committee plenum, which had resulted in defeat of the opposition to Khrushchev. Gromyko, the foreign minister at the time, did not receive Politburo status until 1973.

In 1987, the USSR maintained regular diplomatic relations with approximately 130 foreign countries. The Democratic People's Republic of Vietnam has had an ambassador to Moscow since 1969, although a Soviet envoy has been in Hanoi only since 1974. The USSR quickly founded an embassy in the newly established People's Republic of Kampuchea in May 1979. Relations exist, but no exchange of diplomats has taken place with either Guatemala or Saudi Arabia. Diplomatic ties were broken off with Israel (1967), the Ivory Coast (1969), Chile (1973), the Central African Republic (1980), Grenada (1983), and Liberia (1985). Since the Twenty-seventh CPSU Congress ended in early March 1986, more than 40 younger ambassadors have replaced older chiefs of USSR missions throughout the world.[16]

As of late 1986 only twenty-two Soviet ambassadors were members or candidates for membership on the Central Committee. Seventeen of them are stationed in other communist-ruled states or so-called "revolutionary democracies." Among those assigned to non-bloc capitals, the ambassadors to France, India, Italy, the United Kingdom, and West Germany are Central Committee members. India seems to hold special importance in USSR foreign policy, since it remains the one non-aligned lesser developed country given such distinction (see Table 3.2).

The previous Soviet ambassador to the United States served in Washington, D.C., from 1961 to 1986, or almost a quarter-century. Anatolii F. Dobrynin reportedly is still on a first-name basis with a previous American secretary of state and could reach a former U.S. president "just about whenever" he wanted. He accompanied Henry Kissinger to Moscow in April 1972 to prepare for the following month's summit meeting. In the past, the Department of State had always waived restrictions on Dobrynin's travel if he expressed a desire to visit areas off limits, allegedly because of the value to be gained from his "very accurate reporting and assessing of U.S. positions."[17]

In the wake of Dobrynin's transfer to Moscow, where he became one of the CPSU national secretaries, an unusual successor was named on 20 May 1986. He is Yuri V. Dubinin, only two months at the United Nations, with a previous background in West European assignments. A career foreign service officer, he is neither a member nor candidate on the CPSU Central Committee, having been elected in March 1986 to the Central Audit Commission, which handles party finances. Dubinin speaks no English and must rely on an interpreter,[18] which is also the case with the U.S. ambassador to Moscow, Arthur A. Hartman, who spoke no Russian upon arrival in the USSR.

In addition to regular foreign service officers and staff personnel, a Soviet embassy also includes representatives from the defense establishment, the State Committee on Foreign Economic Relations, the Foreign Trade Ministry, the Committee on State Security, and the International Department of the CPSU central apparatus.[19] All of them have their own channels of communication back to Moscow. The size of the foreign mission often reflects a combination of the above interests that bears on the specific foreign country rather than on the requirements of purely diplomatic functions. For example, the Soviet embassy in Mexico City is staffed with approximately 100 personnel plus about as many wives. Each of the latter fills a position: secretary, bookkeeper, telex operator, cook, charwoman. No foreign nationals are employed in any USSR diplomatic mission. The particular installation in Mexico is probably one of the key Soviet espionage and political agitation facilities in the non-communist world. Indeed, an East European source[20] has stated plainly that in the Soviet mind, "a diplomat who doesn't work for the intelligence service is considered only half a diplomat."

It should be noted here that consulates-general function as mini-

TABLE 3.2
SOVIET AMBASSADORS WITH CENTRAL COMMITTEE MEMBERSHIP, 1986

Country	Name	Born	Date of Appointment	CC Membership
Afghanistan	Mozhaev, P. P.	1930	14 Aug. 1986	cand. 1961
Algeria	Taratuta, V. N.	1930	9 Apr. 1983	full 1976
Bulgaria	Grekov, L. I.	1928	9 July 1983	full 1971
China (PRC)	Troianovskii, O. A.	1919	4 Apr. 1986	cand. 1986
Cuba	Kapto, A. S.	1933	15 Jan. 1986	full 1986
Czechoslovakia	Lomakin, V. P.	1926	15 Apr. 1984	full 1971
Ethiopia	Dmitriev. V. I.	1927	23 July 1986	cand. 1981
France	Riabov, Ia. P.	1928	23 Dec. 1986	full 1971
Germany (East)	Kochemasov, V. I.	1918	12 June 1983	full 1983
Germany (West)	Kvitsinskii, Iu. A.	1936	18 Apr. 1986	cand. 1986
Hungary	Stukalin, B. I.	1923	21 July 1985	full 1976
India	Rykov, V. N.	1918	11 Jan. 1983	full 1971
Italy	Lun'kov, N. M.	1919	5 Nov. 1980	cand. 1981
Korea (North)	Shubnikov, N. M.	1924	8 Dec. 1982	cand. 1986
Mongolia	Fomichenko, K. E.	1927	4 Apr. 1985	cand. 1981
Mozambique	Dybenko, N. K.	1928	4 Nov. 1986	cand. 1981
Poland	Brovikov, V. I.	1931	30 Dec. 1985	full 1981
Romania	Tiazhel'nikov, E. M.	1928	27 Dec. 1982	full 1971
United Kingdom	Zamiatin, L. M.	1922	25 Apr. 1986	full 1976
Vietnam	Kachin, D. I.	1929	3 Aug. 1986	full 1981
Yemen (South)	Rachkov, A. I.	1927	7 Apr. 1982	cand. 1981
Yugoslavia	Mal'tsev, V. F.	1917	24 Apr. 1986	full 1976

SOURCES: RFE/RL, "CPSU Central Committee Members Elected by the Twenty-seventh Party Congress in March 1986," *Radio Liberty Research* (Munich: April 1986); CIA, Directorate of Intelligence, *Directory of USSR Ministry of Foreign Affairs*, series CR 85–14535, September 1985, pp. 22–37; CIA, Directorate of Intelligence, *Directory of Soviet Officials: National Organizations*, series CR 86–11691, June 1986, pp. 73–79; John L. Scherer, ed., *USSR Facts & Figures Annual* (Gulf Breeze, Fla.: Academic International Press, 1986), 10: 25–27; *Foreign Report* (London: 20 November 1986), p. 7.

embassies in the USSR's foreign service. Thus the consul general in San Francisco, Valentin M. Kamenev, is ranked second only to Ambassador Dubinin in Washington, D.C. He reports first to the Department for the USA under a deputy foreign minister (A. A. Bessmertnykh) and only secondarily to the consular administration under V. Ia. Plechko in Moscow. The consulate-general, in addition to Kamenev, has twenty individuals listed as consul or vice-consul in San Francisco.[21] Most of them, of course, have wives who also work at the office.

In contrast with the policy of hiring only Soviet citizens to staff its missions abroad, the USSR has established a special department in Moscow for the purpose of servicing foreign diplomats residing in the USSR. The Administration for the Operation of the Diplomatic Corps (UpDK) functions as liaison between all non-communist representatives living in the Soviet Union and the various governmental and official business establishments that cater to their domestic and personal needs. This service is portrayed by the USSR government as relieving foreign diplomats from the mundane and often frustrating problems of dealing with the local population. It remains, however, another useful means of information gathering and provides a setting for controlled observation of foreign diplomats on a day-to-day basis.

OTHER AGENCIES

The Ministry of Defense maintains armed forces' attachés at all major posts abroad and junior military representatives even in the smaller ones. They are trained at the Military Diplomatic Academy. Information obtained through espionage is reported directly to the Main Intelligence Directorate (GRU). Apart from this, at times large numbers of military technicians and instructors are stationed abroad. In 1972, for example, after relations with the USSR had cooled, Egypt expelled as many as 20,000 Soviet advisers. An estimated 7,800 persons from the Soviet Union and Eastern Europe in these categories still remain in Syria, which has contracted for about $19 billion in military equipment through the year 1989 from the USSR alone.[22] Delivery of weapons to foreign countries involves the Defense Ministry, which recommends types and quantities that are considered in surplus.

In the area of trade, the chairman of the State Committee for Foreign Economic Relations enjoys cabinet rank. His agency supervises grants, the construction of enterprises, training of specialists in foreign countries, and technical cooperation abroad. A policy to expand commercial relations with another state, for example, would be implemented through this committee. In the case of an agreement, the Foreign Trade Ministry assumes responsibility. However, for other economic or technical assistance matters, the state committee is the pertinent agency involved. Originally restricted to dealings with communist-ruled states, it now covers "all countries to which the Soviet Union . . . renders economic aid."[23]

The Ministry of Foreign Trade maintains a bureaucracy that negotiates agreements with other countries and also prepares a commodity export/import plan. The actual exchange, of course, is conducted by

TABLE 3.3
SOME REPORTING UNITS ON FOREIGN AFFAIRS, 1986

Council of Ministers	CPSU Secretariat
Ministry of Foreign Affairs E. A. Shevardnadze[a]	International Department (A. F. Dobrynin)[c]
Committee on State Security (V. M. Chebrikov)[a]	General Department (A. I. Luk'ianov)[c]
Ministry of Defense (S. L. Sokolov)[b]	Main Political Directorate of the Soviet Army and Navy (A. D. Lizichev)[c]
State Committee on Foreign Economic Relations (K. F. Katushev)[c]	Department for Cadres Abroad (S. V. Chervonenko)[c]

NOTES: [a]Member, Political Bureau.
[b]Candidate member, Political Bureau.
[c]Member, Central Committee.
SOURCES: CIA, Directorate of Intelligence, *Directory of Soviet Officials: National Organizations*, series CR 86–11691, June 1986, pp. 3–17.

legal monopolies (called associations) that deal in specific commodities. They have such descriptive names as *Eksportkhleb* (grain exports), *Eksportles* (forestry products), *Promeksport* (industrial commodities), *Stankoimport* (heavy machine tool imports), and others.[24] Illustrations of how the USSR has used commercial agreements as instruments of foreign policy include the large-scale purchases of rice from Burma, cocoa from Ghana, cotton from Egypt, sugar from Cuba, and even wine from Algeria. In each instance, the magnitude of imports has been far greater than actual Soviet requirements, if there were any at all.

The Committee for State Security (KGB) is known to have intelligence officers, who serve under diplomatic cover, at all embassy and consular installations overseas. A former KGB captain estimated that half of the personnel attached to Soviet foreign missions in the West has espionage assignments.[25] Although clandestine in nature, details of such operations have become public knowledge from high-ranking defectors. The KGB station chief may and usually does occupy an ostensibly low foreign service rank, for example, that of an embassy second secretary. He reports directly to his headquarters in Moscow, bypassing the ambassador. The latter most probably is not even kept informed of undercover operations and thus is in a good position to issue a denial when these are discovered.

ACTIVITIES WITHIN THE UNITED NATIONS

USSR influence at the United Nations has increased as that of the United States has declined. Soviet policies at the U.N. have benefited from a multiplier effect, given the automatic support of the East European client states as well as of many so-called "non-aligned" Third World governments. This pattern can be documented from the voting records in both the General Assembly and Security Council during 1983 through 1985 as well as U.N. media products.[26]

In general, the USSR has utilized the United Nations as a forum in which to repeat over and over again what George Orwell called "inversions of truth." It was in this spirit that the chief Soviet delegate charged the United States with responsibility for the crime his own government had committed in shooting down an unarmed South Korean commercial airliner on 1 September 1983 off the coast of Siberia, killing all 269 civilians on board. To what degree such "double-think" actually impresses Third World diplomats remains unknown.

It is apparent, however, that the USSR has been skillfully courting the 101 non-aligned countries (out of a total of 158 U.N. members) at the United Nations. A recent study found that during all of 1985, Third World representatives voted most of the time in the General Assembly with the Soviet Union and only 22.5 percent with the United States.[27] The importance that Moscow attributes to this forum can be seen from the fact that the USSR maintains 111 diplomats at the U.N. in New York, by far the largest number of any member delegation.

The political neutrality of the Soviet citizens employed by the United Nations itself also has been questioned. Fully 474 of them work as international civil servants for the U.N. Secretariat. Supposedly impartial and loyal to the United Nations, they all live in a housing compound at Riverdale owned by the USSR government, which provides buses to transport its citizens to and from work. Most, if not all, are members of the CPSU and attend party meetings at the Soviet mission to the United Nations on East Sixty-seventh Street. Article 100 of the U.N. Charter specifically states that no staff member "shall seek or receive instruction from any government," and yet it is apparent that so-called international civil servants from the USSR at the United Nations also are deeply involved with their own country's diplomatic work. Although it contributes just over 10 percent to the U.N. budget, the Soviet Union holds 15 percent of the senior international secretariat posts.[28]

NEGOTIATIONS

Traditionally diplomacy involves negotiation. Here, fortunately, there exist considerable data on USSR attitudes and practices. Edward L. Rowny, the Joint Chiefs of Staff representative to the SALT delegation and ambassador to the START talks, has argued that U.S. foreign service officers have failed to recognize the fundamental differences between American and Soviet approaches to bargaining. In negotiating with USSR diplomats, American representatives have assumed that Moscow shares the same goals as Washington does and that the two are basically similar. The United States, according to Ambassador Rowny, tend to conduct negotiations as a problem-solving exercise; the Soviet Union, in contrast, looks upon negotiations as competition and views them as just another aspect of the ongoing struggle against "the imperialists."[29]

Others have reached similar conclusions. An expert from the London School of Economics and Political Science—one of a number of scholars who contributed to a special series of papers on negotiating with the Soviet Union commissioned by a subcommittee under the late Senator Henry M. Jackson—has suggested that the USSR follows a policy of multiple options and considers NATO as the main obstacle to "the traditional and natural area of its expansion."[30] In his opinion, many of the negotiations aim at ascertaining United States' intentions and not at solving any conflict of interest.

Adam Ulam of Harvard University concluded that Soviet foreign policy rests on an unrealistic premise, namely that "the United States is basically an enemy and a threat." He went on to write that the USSR approach to international disputes is frequently more elaborate and indirect than that of the West. Examples cited include Soviet threats to Berlin during the years 1948–1949 and 1958–1962, the latter resolved only in the aftermath of the Cuban missile crisis. Moscow, according to Ulam, respects the components of power: heavy industry, military strength, social stability, intelligence, and leadership acumen. Both decision makers and those who implement Soviet decisions look at the world arena from the perspective of power politics. The world as it exists, thus, represents for the Kremlin a stage in the "struggle for primacy" between the United States and the USSR.[31]

In the same context, Robert Conquest analyzed the talks preliminary to SALT I. He suggested that Moscow's drive for military superiority should not be thought of as being motivated by a desire to launch a nuclear war. Instead, the Soviets "would regard it as both justifiable and natural to use their advantage greatly to increase *political pressure* on the United States and its allies throughout the world [emphasis added]."[32] Conquest stressed that the judgment of Kremlin decision makers is not the best and anticipated situations fraught with danger. The next decade, he suggested, might well become the most dangerous the world has ever known. He raised this matter in connection with sudden crises that may be unanticipated by either side.

However, decisions can and are made rapidly by the Soviet leadership when the need exists. A draft four-power agreement on the status of West Berlin came soon after President Nixon's announcement of his forthcoming visit to Mainland China. Other negotiations may continue for years without any success, like the Mutual and Balanced Force Reduction talks, which started in October 1973 at Vienna between twelve NATO and seven Warsaw Pact countries. Harvard University historian Richard Pipes has observed that the Soviets have no use for compromise and are "predisposed toward exclusive possession." In his view, the USSR adopts a negotiating position that "always represents the actual expectations of the Soviet government, weighted down with additional unrealistic demands to be given up in exchange for the other side's concessions."[33] Indeed, examples of this tactic have recurred again and again in the four decades of arms control talks that have been conducted off and on since the end of World War II. American negotiators have learned and relearned that the USSR always prefers to win rather than to compromise.

OBJECTIVES

Pipes has noted that Soviet foreign policy tends to concentrate on the implementation of one major objective at any given time. During the period from 1946 to 1953, the primary goal appeared to be elimination of United States influence from Western Europe. At the invitation of Britain and France, then Foreign Minister V. M. Molotov arrived in Paris with a staff of almost 100 aides to discuss a U.S.-sponsored postwar recovery program. He left six days later on 2 July 1947, after having denounced the Marshall Plan as an instrument of American "imperialism." The USSR prevented Albania, Bulgaria, Czechoslovakia, Finland, Hungary, Poland, Romania, and Yugoslavia from participating in what turned out to be the first step toward the European Economic Community, or Common Market.

Unable to sabotage Western Europe's recovery, the Soviet Union next concentrated on the Third World. The new thrust began during the mid-1950s and might have succeeded more rapidly but for opposition from communist-ruled China. This global flanking movement involved so-called peaceful coexistence together with "nuclear saber rattling," in an attempt to intimidate the United States. Beginning with the early 1960s, a new and complete redirection of the USSR's focus extended over the most recent two decades: detente in Western Europe and confrontation with China, the latter strategy stressing containment as well as isolation.[34] In the view of Pipes, the above three primary thrusts during the recent past should be distinguished from diversionary activities that may receive considerable publicity but remain nonessential.

In really important matters, the operational code of Soviet negotiators is rather clear. As one high-ranking government official put it, USSR foreign policy and diplomacy have always been regarded as among the most important forms of class struggle. According to this former deputy minister, V. S. Semenov, even Lenin himself combined "firmness with flexibility in international politics, resolute defense of vital interests and diplomatic maneuvering, including compromise when the new is not yet strong enough to overthrow the old." This need, in times of weakness, for compromise may lead to "certain agreements with the imperialist countries in the interests of socialism."[35]

THE ROLE OF THE PARTY

The relation between ideology and expertise remains an active issue. Semenov has commented on the connection in modern times between party supervision and the day-to-day conduct of foreign affairs. Though resolutions at CPSU congresses and Central Committee plenary meetings approve general parameters laid down by the Politburo, these directives, he has argued, cannot solve specific problems. He suggests that the latter have become so complex as to require experts. Only such individuals can understand these issues down to minute details. Examples given included the general field of disarmament, the German question, Middle East problems, and policy vis-à-vis the United States. Knowledge can be acquired only after many years of work and practical experience.

Indeed, according to the director of the Moscow State Institute of International Relations, all successful diplomatic activity is based upon a Marxist-Leninist evaluation of the world situation, understanding the laws of social development in combination with concrete knowledge of particular countries as well as an understanding of their historical and national characteristics.[36] Another senior Soviet official has asserted that the Central Committee provides day-to-day direction for measures to be implemented by the Ministry of Foreign Affairs. The latter reportedly is staffed with "politically mature" individuals whose work is claimed to be efficient, accurate, and precise. A model Soviet diplomat must have the following qualities: a high level of political awareness, Marxist-Leninist training, a sense of duty, communist party maturity, and diplomatic expertise. However, on more important questions, it is not permissible for a foreign service worker to say anything that has even the least real meaning.[37] This has been corroborated by a former high-ranking Soviet official in the arms control field, who has written about the Directorate for Planning Foreign Policy Measures (UPVM) at the Ministry of Foreign Affairs. This group prepared only analyses, documents, and predictions for 1971–1975 and 1971–1980. The Directorate never actually planned the foreign policy of the USSR.[38] Although not permitted to speak on substantive matters in public, the Soviet "diplomat" frequently does assist in foreign propaganda operations, which is the subject of the next chapter.

NOTES

1. V. A. Zorin, *Osnovy diplomaticheskoi sluzhby*, 2nd rev. ed. (Moscow: Mezhdunarodnye otnosheniia, 1977), pp. 106–7. For a more recent text, see A. N. Kovalev, *Azbuka diplomatii*, 4th rev. ed. (Moscow: Mezhdunarodnye otnosheniia, 1984).

2. A. A. Gromyko, chief ed., *Za mir i bezopasnost' narodov*, 2 vols. (Moscow: Politizdat, 1983); A. A. Gromyko, ed., *Moskovskaia konferentsiia, 19–30.X.1943* (Moscow: Politizdat, 1984); Gromyko, ed., *Sovetsko-amerikanskie otnosheniia, 1941–1945*, vol. 1, *1941–1943* (Moscow: Politizdat, 1984); V. L. Israelian, *Diplomatiia v gody voiny: 1941–1945* (Moscow: Mezhdunarodnye otnosheniia, 1985).

3. Central Intelligence Agency, Directorate of Intelligence, *Directory of USSR Ministry of Foreign Affairs Officials*, series CR 85–14535, September 1985, pp. 3–4; henceforth cited as *MFA Directory*. See also Alexander Rahr, "Winds of Change Hit Foreign Ministry," *Radio Liberty Research* 16 July 1986, RL 274/86, pp. 7–10.

4. Zorin, *Osnovy sluzhby*, pp. 107–8.

5. Philip Taubman article in the *New York Times*, 10 August 1986, p. A–1.

6. Expelled from the CPSU in 1961 by Khrushchev, the 94-year-old pensioner Molotov was restored to party membership and reportedly had a "cordial" meeting with Chernenko (*L'Unità* [Rome], 5 July 1984). Molotov was interviewed two years later by *Moskovskiie novosti* (Moscow radio, 2 July 1986; *FBIS*, 3 July 1986, p. R9). He died in November 1986.

7. His son, Anatolii Andreevich, held this same post in the mid-1970s, having been previously section chief at the USA and Canada Institute in Moscow. Biographies of both father and son appear in *The International Who's Who, 1985–1986* (London: Europa Publications, 1985), p. 562.

8. "Report by Comrade E. A. Shevardnadze at the Ceremonial Session Devoted to the 116th Anniversary of V. I. Lenin's Birth," *Pravda*, 23 April 1986, pp. 1–2. See also David Shipler in the *New York Times*, 21 September 1986.

9. The director since 1974 had been N. I. Lebedev, who held the academic rank of professor (position listed as vacant in *Directory of Soviet Officials*, June 1986, p. 73).

10. U.S. Senate, Committee on Government Operations, *Staffing Procedures and Problems*, p. 60; Vladimir Sakharov and Umberto Tosi, *High Treason* (New York: G. P. Putnam's Sons, 1980), pp. 81–144, provides first-hand experience with the IRR curriculum.

11. S. L. Tikhvinskii, chief editor of the annual *Diplomatic Bulletin*, has been director since January 1982. *Directory of Soviet Officials*, June 1986, p. 73.

12. U.S. Senate, Committee on Government Operations, *National Policy Machinery*, p. 42.

13. Identified as "Department for Cadres Abroad." The current chief, appointed in January 1983, is S. V. Chervonenko. *Directory of Soviet Officials*, June 1986, p. 14.

14. Compare the *MFA Directory* from 1976 through 1985. An exception is P. A. Abrasimov, twice ambassador to East Germany (1962–1971 and 1975–1983) and last relieved at age 71, who became chairman of the State Committee for Foreign Tourism (Ronald D. Asmus, "Abrasimov Removed as Soviet Ambassador to GDR," *RAD Background Report* [Munich: RFE-RL, 14 June 1983], p. 4).

15. Moscow radio, 28 July 1970. Belgrade radio, 10 July 1986; FBIS, 14 July 1986, p. I 8, announced his successor.

16. *Directory*, June 1986, pp. 73–79. Diplomatic relations with Liberia were resumed as per *Pravda*, 22 August 1986, p. 4. On the new chiefs of mission, see David Anable in the *Christian Science Monitor*, 5 September 1986.

17. Articles in the *New York Times*, 4 June 1979; ibid., 14 January 1984; and the *New York Times Magazine* (13 May 1984), pp. 25–92 *passim*.

18. A. A. Gromyko, ed., *Diplomaticheskii slovar'* (Moscow: Nauka, 1984), I. p. 343; Elaine Sciolino in the *New York Times*, 21 May 1986.

19. Richard H. Shultz and Roy Godson, *Dezinformatsia: Active Measures in Soviet Strategy* (McLean, Va.: Pergamon-Brassey's International Defense Publishers, 1984), pp. 22–23.

20. Vladimir Kostov, a defector and former member of the Bulgarian Communist Party, as quoted by Daniel Southerland, "The World of Espionage," *Christian Science Monitor*, 22 September 1980.

21. San Francisco Consular Corps, *Roster* (San Francisco, 1986), no pagination.

22. Central Intelligence Agency, *Handbook of Economic Statistics, 1986* (Washington, D.C.: September 1986), table 90, p. 125.

23. Zorin, *Osnovy sluzhby*, p. 125.

24. Ibid.

25. Interview with Aleksei Miagkov in *Aktuelt* (Copenhagen), 2 April 1980. Five years later, the highest ranking Soviet diplomat at the U.N. estimated that more than half of all USSR citizens in New York worked for the KGB or GRU: Arkady N. Shevchenko, *Breaking with Moscow* (New York: Knopf, 1985), pp. 240–41.

26. U.S. Department of State, *Report to Congress on Voting Practices in the United Nations* (Washington, D.C.: GPO, 1984). See also U.S. General Accounting Office, *United Nations: Analysis of Selected Media Products* (Washington, D.C.: April 1986).

27. Richard L. Jackson, *The Non-Aligned, the U.N., and the Superpowers* (New York: Praeger, 1983), pp. 285–97, gives earlier data; *New York Times*, 4 July 1986 for percentage.

28. Richard Bernstein, "Soviet Defector Charges U.N. Charter Violations," *New York Times*, 17 July 1984.

29. Edward L. Rowny, "Negotiating with the Soviets," *Washington Quarterly* 3, no. 1 (Winter 1980): 60. See also his "The Soviets Are Still Russians," *Survey* 25, no. 2 (Spring 1980): 1–9.

30. Leonard Schapiro in U.S. Congress, Senate, Committee on Government Operations, Subcommittee on National Security and International Operations, *Hearing on International Negotiation*, Part 2 (16 April 1970), 91st Cong., 2nd sess., 1970, p. 33.

31. Adam B. Ulam, "Communist Doctrine and Soviet Diplomacy: Some Observations," in U.S. Congress, Senate, Committee on Government Operations, Subcommittee on National Security and International Operations, *Memorandum on International Negotiation*, 91st Cong., 2nd sess., 1970.

32. Robert Conquest in U.S. Congress, Senate, Committee on Government Operations, Subcommittee on National Security and International Operations, *International Negotiation*, Part 6 (30 April 1971), 92nd Cong., 1st sess., 1971, p. 163. See also U.S. Congress, House, Committee on Foreign Affairs, *Special Study on Soviet Diplomacy and Negotiating Behavior: Emerging New Context for U.S. Diplomacy*, prepared by Senior Specialists Division, Congressional Research Service, 96th Cong., 1st sess., 1980, vol. 1, H. Doc. 96–238.

33. Richard Pipes, *U.S.-Soviet Relations in the Era of Detente* (Boulder, Colo.: Westview Press, 1981), p. 370.

34. Ibid., pp. 41–42.

35. V. S. Semenov, "The Leninist Principles of Soviet Diplomacy," *Mezhdunarodnaia zhizn'* 16, no. 4 (1969); translation in *International Affairs*, no. 4 (April 1969): 5–6; both published in Moscow.

36. N. I. Lebedev, chief ed., *Nauchnye osnovy sovetskoi vneshnei politiki* (Moscow: Mezhdunarodnye otnosheniia, 1982), pp. 10–27.

37. Zorin, *Osnovy sluzhby*, pp. 122–24.

38. Glagolev, *Post-Andropov Strategy*, pp. 72–75.

★ *PART II* ★

INSTRUMENTALITIES

4

FOREIGN PROPAGANDA

The magnitude of Moscow's effort to influence target audiences abroad can be seen from the size of Soviet expenditures for propaganda and related covert action, which the CIA estimates conservatively to be more than $3 billion per year (see Table 4.1).[1] If one were to include also the propaganda efforts routinely directed at resident foreigners and visitors inside the Soviet Union and Eastern Europe, the total spent would increase substantially. Indeed, Western intelligence officials generally agree that the USSR probably devotes many times what the non-communist world spends, in both human and financial resources, to propaganda and related measures. Not only the dissemination of views favorable to the USSR, but also use of accusation and derogatory terminology, harassment, comprehensive censorship, radio jamming, forgery, and general "disinformation" have all become institutionalized tools of the Soviet party-state.[2]

CENTRAL COMMITTEE DEPARTMENTS

It is the Politburo that supervises agitprop (agitation and propaganda) operations through several departments of the Central Committee. A distinction should be made between "propaganda" and "agitation."[3]

TABLE 4.1
SOVIET EXPENDITURES FOR PROPAGANDA
(IN MILLIONS OF DOLLARS)

Budget Item	Cost
CPSU International Department	$ 100
CPSU International Information Department	50
TASS	550
Novosti (APN)	500
Pravda	250
Izvestiia	200
New Times and other periodicals	200
Moscow radio foreign service	700
Press sections in Soviet embassies	50
Clandestine radio stations	100
Communist international front organizations	63
Subsidies to foreign communist parties	50
KGB's Service "A"	50
Covert action operations by KGB foreign residencies	100
Support to national liberation fronts	200
Special campaigns	
anti-NATO modernization	200
Lobbying activities in the United States	5
Total:	$3,368

NOTE: The estimate of over $3 billion per year in Soviet expenditures for propaganda and covert action can be broken down as above, if one counts only proportional costs for foreign as distinct from domestic propaganda, and if other activities of the KGB are not considered. The indirect cost, borne by foreign communist organizations, is not included.

SOURCE: U.S. Congress, House, Permanent Select Committee on Intelligence, Subcommittee on Oversight, *Hearings on Soviet Covert Action: The Forgery Offensive,* 96th Cong., 2nd sess., 1980, p. 60; see Kathryn Johnson, "How Foreign Powers Play for Status in Washington," *U.S. News & World Report,* 17 June 1985, p. 39, on the $5,469,000 officially reported by lobbyists for the USSR during 1984.

The former presents many ideas, primarily through the printed word; the latter uses a single, widely known "fact" and disseminates it via the spoken word in face-to-face contact, which today includes television. [Two departments in the Central Committee apparatus deal with foreign communist parties, as mentioned in Chapter 2: one involves relations with ruling movements, the other with non-ruling parties.]

The International Department, headed by CPSU secretary A. F. Dobrynin, maintains liaison also with the many foreign organizations that are utilized to disseminate Soviet propaganda. This man, who became department chief in March 1986, had served as USSR ambassador to the United States for almost 25 years. He probably is the key advisor to the CPSU general secretary on American affairs, apart from his responsibility for the International Department.[4]

The International Information Department, (IID) of the CPSU Central Committee, formerly played a decisive role in deciding both what aspects of Soviet policy to discuss openly and how to present them to various international publics.[5] Its principal task had been to counter the potential ill effects for USSR policy from the free flow of information generated by Western media. Soviet officials appear regularly on domestic television programs and write for their own press. They frequently travel also to the West, offer propaganda lectures as well as interviews, and address meetings of international communist front organizations. Topics frequently expounded upon include such concerns as NATO deployment of medium-range missiles in Europe, proposals by Gorbachev for arms control, and the "evils" of "imperialism." The chief of the former International Information Department, Leonid M. Zamiatin, had been relieved even before his appointment in April 1986 as ambassador to the Court of St. James. His previous responsibilities reportedly[6] were taken over by the International and Propaganda departments.

Another unit in the CPSU Central Committee, the Cadres Department, functions as a coordinating center to inform diplomatic missions from other communist-ruled states and friendly countries about propaganda lines. Twice a year, before May Day and prior to the anniversary of the Bolshevik Revolution in November, a list of slogans appears in print.[7] These represent, in effect, action directives for a coordinated propaganda effort. A careful reading of them yields clues to the general line. They are prepared by the Propaganda Department, since 1986 under Iurii A. Skliarov.

The main purpose of external propaganda is to present Soviet foreign policy as dedicated to peace and to characterize the USSR as having established the only just society on earth. Essentially three methods are used to achieve this goal:

1. white or non-camouflaged psychological warfare, conducted openly by government and other official organs (Moscow radio, TASS, *Pravda*);

2. grey, emanating from putatively "independent" organizations and groups (Radio Peace and Progress, international communist front organizations, Soviet friendship societies); and

3. black, which is "a particularly insidious form of ideological diversion, closely combined with terrorist and covert activities," allegedly originating from within target countries (clandestine radio stations broadcasting from the USSR or Eastern Europe, forgeries, disinformation).[8]

FRONT ORGANIZATIONS

International communist front organizations play a key role in projecting a positive image of the USSR and an unflattering one of the West. These efforts are especially useful, because they are less likely to fall under suspicion of operating as tools of Moscow than local communist parties in each country. Officially, fronts pretend not even to adhere to the tenets of Marxism-Leninism, but in practice they are controlled by the Soviet Union. According to an authoritative study, the most important groups include the following:[9]

1. World Peace Council (WPC)
2. World Federation of Trade Unions (WFTU)
3. World Federation of Democratic Youth (WFDY)
4. International Union of Students (IUS)
5. Women's International Democratic Federation (WIDF)
6. International Organization of Journalists (IOJ)
7. International Association of Democratic Lawyers (IADL)
8. World Federation of Scientific Workers (WFSW)
9. International Federation of Resistance Fighters (IFRF)
10. International Radio and Television Organization (IRTO)
11. International Institute for Peace (IIP)
12. Christian Peace Conference (CPC), and
13. Afro-Asian Peoples' Solidarity Organization (AAPSO)

These front organizations form a vital link in the worldwide Soviet propaganda network, and the USSR provides them with an estimated subsidy of more than $63 million per year (see Table 4.2). Fronts gather support based on broad range of political appeals. Not infrequently they have enlisted the sympathies of non-communist Western scholars and scientists who, in their pacifist zeal, have become unwitting instruments of Soviet propagandists. There also exist many "friendship societies" that perform tasks similar to those of fronts on a bilateral country-to-country basis, linking groups in Western countries to various entities in the Eastern bloc.

In general, the purpose of front organizations, as one witness put it in congressional hearings on USSR covert activity, is "to spread Soviet propaganda themes and create a false impression of public support for the foreign policies of the Soviet Union."[10] Sometimes Moscow employs the fronts directly to promote its ideology abroad. Members of such organizations, called "useful idiots" by Lenin, are introduced to the alleged virtues of the USSR way of life. The most important function of the fronts, however, is to drum up support in various non-communist states for policies whose effects would be favorable to Soviet foreign objectives. Moscow formulates programs and campaigns that coincide subtly or not so subtly with its goals. Characteristically, fronts adopt a line (for example, the campaign for disarmament, the various "peace offensives," the condemnation of the West for its alleged economic subjugation of the Third World) that effectively parallels USSR initiatives abroad. Usually front leaders will insist on collaborating actively with various non-front groups that share ostensibly similar goals. At times the pro-Soviet groups will work actively as members of a much larger coalition of organizations, most of which are clearly non-communist, steering the coalition where possible in directions most agreeable to Moscow (see Table 4.3).

FRONT CONFERENCES

The most active front organizations are the World Peace Council (WPC), the World Federation of Trade Unions (WFTU), the World Federation of Democratic Youth (WFDY), and the International Union of Students (IUS). An important WPC-staged event, the World Parliament of Peoples for Peace, reportedly attracted to Bulgaria some 2,260 persons from 134 countries, representing 330 political parties and 137 international organizations. A World Assembly for Peace and Life Against Nuclear War supposedly did even better during that same year in Czechoslovakia with 2,645 delegates from 140 countries, according to the organizers.[11] Both meetings issued standard USSR appeals for peace. WPC held a world peace congress during 15–19 October 1986 at Copenhagen.

The other front organizations tend to take their lead from the WPC. Sometimes there is a show of independence by front organs or members. Interestingly enough, the WFTU secretariat condemned the

TABLE 4.2
INTERNATIONAL COMMUNIST FRONT ORGANIZATIONS, 1986

	Year Founded	Claimed Membership	Headquarters	Number of Affiliates	Number of Countries	Soviet Support
Afro-Asian Peoples' Solidarity Organization	1957	no data	Cairo	87	—	$1,260,000
Christian Peace Conference	1958	no data	Prague	—	ca. 80	210,000
International Association of Democratic Lawyers	1946	25,000	Brussels	90	ca. 80	100,000
International Federation of Resistance Fighters	1951	5,000,000	Vienna	22	—	125,000
International Institute for Peace	1958	no data	Prague	9	—	260,000
International Organization of Journalists	1946	200,000	Prague	—	ca. 100	515,000

International Union of Students	1946	10,000,000	Prague	117	109	905,000
Women's International Democratic Federation	1945	200,000,000	East Berlin	136	118	390,000
World Federation of Democratic Youth	1945	150,000,000	Budapest	270	123	1,575,000
World Federation of Scientific Workers	1946	450,000	London	33	70 plus	100,000
World Federation of Trade Unions	1945	296,000,000	Prague	ca. 90	81	8,575,000
World Peace Council	1950	no data	Helsinki	—	142 plus	49,380,000
Total:						$63,445,000

SOURCES: U.S. Congress, House, Permanent Select Committee on Intelligence, Subcommittee on Oversight, *Hearings on Soviet Covert Action: The Forgery Offensive*, 96th Cong., 2nd sess., 1980, pp. 79–80, which also gives a breakdown of Soviet financial support (staff, salaries, administration, travel, publications, conferences, and in-house meetings); Richard F. Staar, ed., *1986 Yearbook on International Communist Affairs* (Stanford: Hoover Institution Press, 1986), p. xxviii; membership for WFTU is from East Berlin radio, 21 September 1986, in *FBIS*, 24 September 1986, p. E 13; the IOJ figures appeared in *Pravda*, 23 October 1986, p. 5; IADL affiliates from *Pravda*, 10 December 1986, p. 4.

TABLE 4.3
ORGANIZATIONS CLOSELY CONNECTED WITH FRONTS

Name of Organization	Fronts
African Workers' University, Conakry	WFTU
Afro-Asian/Latin American Peoples' Solidarity Organization	AAPSO
Asian Buddhists' Conference for Peace	CPC
Berlin Conference of Catholic Christians	CPC
Center for Professional Education of Journalists	IOJ
Conference of Non-Governmental Organizations in Consultative Status with ECOSOC	WPC
Continuing Liaison Council of the World Congress of Peace Forces	WPC
Fritz Heckert Trade Union College, Bernau	WFTU
Generals for Peace and Disarmament	WPC
Georgi Dimitrov Trade Union School, Sofia	WFTU
International Association for Social Tourism and Leisure of Workers	WFTU
International Bureau of Tourism and Exchanges of Youth	WFDY
International Campaign Committee for a Just Peace in the Middle East	WPC
International Club of Agricultural Journalists	IOJ
International Club of Science and Technology	IOJ
International Commission of Children's and Adolescents' Movements	WFDY
International Commission of Enquiry into the Crimes of the Military Junta in Chile	WPC
International Commission of Enquiry into the Crimes of the Racist Regimes in Southern Africa	AAPSO
International Commission of Enquiry into Israeli Treatment of Arab People in Occupied Territories	WPC
International Commission for the Investigation of American War Crimes in Vietnam	IADL
International Committee Against Apartheid, Racism, and Colonialism in Southern Africa	WPC, AAPSO
International Committee for European Security and Cooperation	WPC
International Committee for Solidarity with Cyprus	WPC

International Committee of Lawyers for Democracy and Human Rights in South Korea	IADL
International Committee for Solidarity with the Palestinian People	WPC
International Committee of Solidarity with the Arab People and their Central Cause—Palestine	WPC
International Committee for the UN Debate on Women	WIDF
International Committee for the Cooperation of Journalists	IOJ
International Liaison Forum of Peace Forces	WPC
International School of Journalism and Agency Techniques, Prague	IOJ
International School of Solidarity for Journalists, Havana	IOJ
International Student Research Center	IUS
International Trade Union College, Moscow	WFTU
International Trade Union Committee for Peace and Disarmament ("Dublin Committee")	WFTU, WPC
International Trade Union Committee for Solidarity with the People and Workers of Africa	WFTU
International Trade Union Committee for Solidarity with the People and Workers of Chile	WFTU
International Trade Union Committee for Solidarity with the People and Workers of Korea	WFTU
International Trade Union Committee for Solidarity with the People and Workers of Palestine	WFTU
International Voluntary Service for Friendship and Solidarity of Youth	WFDY
Interpress Graphic Club	IOJ
Interpress Motoring Club	IOJ
Journalists' School of Solidarity, Bucharest	IOJ
Journalists' School of Solidarity, Sofia	IOJ
Latin American Federation of Journalists	IOJ
Latin American Information Center, Lima	IOJ
School of Solidarity of the GDR Journalists' Union, East Berlin	IOJ
Vienna Dialogue on Disarmament and Detente	WPC
World Federation of Teachers' Unions (FISE)	WFTU

SOURCE: Richard F. Staar, ed., *Yearbook on International Communist Affairs* (Stanford: Hoover Institution Press), published annually in June.

Soviet occupation of Czechoslovakia, when it met by coincidence in Prague at the height of the invasion in that country.[12] The organization held its ninth world congress ten years later in the same city. Almost 1,000 persons from 126 countries were said to have attended, representing 300 organizations, most of them from the Soviet bloc and the Third World. At this conference, the communist-controlled General Confederation of Labor (CGIL) in Italy had announced it would leave the WFTU before the congress. A spokesman for the corresponding organization (CGT) in France also made public a decision that no individual from his country would be a candidate for the post of WFTU secretary general and hinted that the CGT might emulate the CGIL.[13] The tenth world congress was held in Havana during February 1982, when the WFTU called for a new international economic order, trade union rights and democratic freedoms (only in the West, of course), security and disarmament in Europe, solidarity with Arabs and peoples of southern Africa, and support for "progressive" movements in Latin America. A similar appeal emanated from the eleventh congress in September 1986 at East Berlin.[14]

The WFDY and IUS, meanwhile, cooperate in holding a world youth festival, the largest single event sponsored by any front organization. The most successful had been the eleventh, held at Havana in Cuba. Reportedly attendance totaled about 18,500 delegates from 145 countries. WFDY and IUS meetings echo the same kind of declarations as the WPC, that is, calls for "peace, disarmament, and detente" as well as an end to "imperialist oppression." However the twelfth World Youth Festival, 27 July–3 August 1985 at Moscow, claimed 22,000 delegates. As many as sixty speakers criticized the Soviet Union for its military occupation of Afghanistan.[15]

The main assignment of all fronts is to convince well-intentioned but politically naive persons to support Soviet objectives; the fronts also serve as a non-governmental channel for free or low-cost trips to Eastern Europe or the USSR and as a means of recruiting potential communist party members. Since these functions have become widely known in the non-communist world, supplementary techniques have had to be devised for influencing public opinion in the West.

OTHER MOVEMENTS

Numerous high-level conferences and international meetings also draw together the "elite" among scientists, artists, medical doctors, academicians, and former government officials, ostensibly for open discussion of relevant topics, but in reality to serve as sounding boards for anti-American and pro-Soviet propaganda. Membership remains much smaller than that in the front organizations.

One such example is the Pugwash movement. Established by the late Canadian industrialist Cyrus Eaton, on the initiative of Albert Einstein and Bertrand Russell, its first meeting in 1957 drew only 22 participants. Since then it has attracted hundreds of prominent individuals from a total of 75 countries. The common denominator is the participant's concern for the future and acceptance of the Pugwash manifesto's call that "science must only be used for the good of mankind and never for its destruction."[16] In recent years meetings have been held in Munich, Mexico City, Warsaw, Plovdiv, Venice, Bucharest, and Geneva (nine workshops). The thirty-fourth one was held at Bjerkliden in northern Sweden to oppose the NATO decision on deployment of Pershing II and cruise missiles and to promote efforts for "stepping up the struggle against the threat of nuclear war." Preventing a future arms race in outer space was the theme at the thirty-fifth meeting in Campinas near Sao Paulo, Brazil. The same subject was discussed at the thirty-sixth session in Budapest.[17]

A different series of conferences begun in 1960, restricted to Soviet and American public figures or influential personalities, are the so-called Dartmouth meetings. The eleventh meeting was held at Jurmala, Latvia. Bilateral economic relations, the environment and conservation, urgent international problems like disarmament, prospects for peace in the Middle East, and European problems were discussed. The Soviet delegation informed American participants about the content of the six-point "peace program,"[18] first advanced at the Twenty-fourth Congress and refined by the next three CPSU congresses.

Georgii Arbatov, director of the USA and Canada Institute, attended a more recent Dartmouth conference held on the campus of Grinnell College in Iowa. A U.S. Department of State directive insisted that the visit not be used for propaganda purposes, yet Arbatov nonetheless gave interviews to the *Des Moines Register* and appeared on public television. He also took the opportunity of the supposedly private symposium to lecture in public before approximately 1,000 people as well as to speak at a series of breakfast and luncheon meetings.[19] By contrast, Lieutenant General Brent Scowcroft, USAF (ret.), was not allowed to deliver a personal letter from President Reagan to Soviet leader Chernenko on the occasion of a Dartmouth conference held the following year at Moscow.

Another kind of special gathering involved the third congress of International Physicians for the Prevention of Nuclear War (IPPNW), held in Amsterdam. The organization, formed in December 1980, claims a membership of 75,000 medical doctors (some 30,000 are USSR citizens) from 43 countries. The ostensible purpose of the first conference, held in Virginia, was to increase public awareness of the consequences of a nuclear war. The Soviet delegation at the Amsterdam meeting included Dr. Evgenii I. Chazov, personal cardiologist for Soviet leaders and the man who signed a letter to *Izvestiia* denouncing Andrei Sakharov; a nuclear physicist and director of laser research, E. P. Velikhov; and the ubiquitous Arbatov.[20] The presence of this last man, a key shaper of the USSR propaganda message, made clear that the Soviets use this forum, as they have other international peace and disarmament conferences, for propaganda purposes: to promote their image as peacemakers and supporters of disarmament. The fourth congress, held at Helsinki, repeated previous calls from Moscow for a *freeze* on testing, production, and deployment as well as for *no first use* of nuclear weapons,[21] both of which would give the USSR obvious advantages (see Chapter 12). IPPNW won the Nobel peace prize in October 1985.

RADIO BROADCASTS

Apart from the front organizations and various specialized conferences at the elite level, the bulk of Soviet propaganda floods the world via the printed word and radio broadcasts. The major theme, whether the issue at hand be the Arab-Israeli dispute or southern Africa, is the "anti-imperialist struggle." Not only military alliances such as NATO but also cooperative regional organizations like the European Economic Community (EEC) or the Association of Southeast Asian Nations (ASEAN) remain under constant attack by USSR propagandists as threats to peace.

Moscow devotes more than 2,000 hours per week to foreign radio broadcasts in 81 languages to about 100 countries. Dissemination of propaganda is supplemented by radio services from other communist-ruled states (see Table 4.4). The East European members of the Warsaw Pact broadcast 1,601 hours per week: East Germany (413) is second to the USSR and Poland (336), third. Kabul radio in Afghanistan transmits almost 40 hours per week in Urdu, English, Russian, Arabic, Pushtu, Dari, and German. Broadcasts from Cuba total 420 hours per week, with more than half directed at North, Central, and South America, the remainder at countries around the Mediterranean in the Middle East and Western Europe. Moscow also transmits in English

TABLE 4.4
COMMUNIST FOREIGN RADIO BROADCASTS, 1950–1986
(HOURS PER WEEK)

Year	USSR	Eastern Europe	China
1950	533	412	66
1960	1,015	1,072	687
1970	1,897	1,264	1,591
1980	2,097	2,210	1,374
1981	2,126	2,362	1,318
1982	2,162	1,644[b]	1,423
1986	2,547[a]	2,064[b]	n.a.

NOTES: [a]USSR includes foreign radio broadcasts from Alma Ata, Baku, Dushambe, Kiev, Magellanus (to Chile), Minsk, Peace and Progress (to Third World), Tashkent, Vilnius, and Yerevan, in addition to Moscow.
[b]Warsaw Pact members only.

SOURCES: U.S. Information Agency, "Communist International Radio Broadcasting," *Research Memorandum* (Washington, D.C., 7 December 1985), pp. 1–2; ibid. 17 December 1985 and 14 January 1985; "The War of Words," *U.S. News & World Report*, 7 October 1985, p. 37; Board for International Broadcasting, *1986 Annual Report* (Washington, D.C.: GPO, 1986), p. 2; BBC Monitoring Services, *Schedules* (London: 1986).

from Havana and can be received on any automobile radio throughout the southern United States. Southeast Asia is the main target of Radio Hanoi, which is on the air for 192 hours per week.[22]

"Radio Peace and Progress" (RPP), although it has used Moscow radio transmitters since its establishment in 1964, claims to be independent of the USSR government. This allows it to assume a more strident tone than the official broadcasts. Complaints from foreign governments about the RPP have been rebuffed by the Soviets on grounds of the station's independence, even though it remains under full government control and direction. The RPP broadcasts 161 hours per week in fifteen languages and dialects. Its programs for the Western Hemisphere are highly anti-American. For example, it quoted a guerrilla as stating that Cuba might intervene militarily in El Salvador.[23] To date Moscow radio has not suggested this possibility.

In addition, clandestine stations are operated by communist party leaders exiled to the Soviet Union from abroad. They use transmitters located in the USSR and Eastern Europe. Stations of this type broadcast for a total of some 337 hours. Two are known to be situated on Soviet territory. Radio Ba Yi ("Eight One," for the 1 August 1927 establishment of the Chinese Red Army) first came on the air in early 1979, its broadcasts directed at the armed forces of Mainland China.

The clandestine station "National Voice of Iran" has transmitted since 1959 in Farsi, Kurdish, and Azerbaijani from Baku. It made inflammatory statements prior to seizure of the U.S. embassy at Teheran. On 7 November 1979, as the world first learned about the American prisoners, this station continued inciting Iranian mobs to further violence. In July 1984, "Radio Iran Toilers" began broadcasting in Farsi from Afghanistan. Another new station, "Voice of the Communist Party of Iran," was first heard the following month, also in Farsi. Commentaries of both are hostile to Khomeini.[24]

Clandestine transmissions to Turkey have been on the air over Bizim Radyo (Our Radio) since 1958 and the Voice of the Turkish Communist Party since 1968 from Magdeburg in East Germany.[25] The Iberian peninsula in the past had been the target of so-called Radio Free Portugal (1962–1974) and Radio Independent Spain (1941–1975), the latter originating from Romania after the Second World War. Stations called Deutscher Freiheitssender 904 and Deutscher Soldatensender were at one time directed at the Federal Republic of Germany from the German Democratic Republic. Other discontinued stations include Voice of Truth to Greece (1958–1975) and Voice of Italian Emigré Workers (1971–1978). Certain of these clandestine transmitters closed down after underground communist parties received legal status.

On 20 August 1980, the USSR resumed jamming Voice of America, British Broadcasting Corporation, and Deutsche Welle (Federal Republic of Germany) transmissions, which had been free from such interference during the preceding several years in accordance with the Final Act signed on 1 August 1975 at Helsinki.[26] This move undoubtedly represented an effort by the Soviet government to keep news of the Solidarity movement in Poland from its own citizens. Jamming of Radio Free Europe and Radio Liberty commenced in 1953 and has continued ever since. Broadcasts to Czechoslovakia and Bulgaria are severely blocked, to Poland less so, to Romania and Hungary not at all since 1963 and 1964, respectively. The USSR reportedly employs about 5,000 people and uses an estimated 2,000 to 2,500 transmitters at a cost of between $100 and $300 million annually to continue these jamming efforts, which openly violate the Helsinki agreement.[27]

THE PRINTED WORD

Official USSR government news organizations also play an important role in disseminating foreign propaganda through print and radio. TASS (Telegraphic Agency of the Soviet Union) has about 200 correspondents stationed in 125 foreign countries. It transmits daily more than 1,000 air hours of material to all of its foreign subscribers. The general directorship of TASS since May 1979 has been held by Sergei A. Losev, member of the CPSU Central Audit Commission. He frequently travels abroad to appear on television talk shows. His articles are also printed in Western newspapers and magazines.[28]

Another agency called *Novosti* (News), ostensibly unofficial but in fact controlled by the CPSU, produces translations and feature articles on a worldwide basis. The Soviets refer to it as a "social organization." Chairman of the board is Valentin M. Falin. A first deputy chief of the former International Information Department, he became candidate member of the CPSU Central Committee in March 1986 soon after his appointment as head of *Novosti*.[29] The agency claims to have connections with 120 foreign publishing houses as well as 140 international and national news agencies. It reportedly has entered into agreements with more than 6,000 foreign periodicals and 70 television companies. Bureaus or correspondents operate in 115 foreign countries, and excerpts from the Soviet press are translated into 56 languages. The previous head of *Novosti,* Ivan I. Udaltsov, has been identified as a KGB officer who helped plan the 1968 invasion of Czechoslovakia. According to John Barron's study, "An entire division of *Novosti,* known as the Tenth Section, is staffed with KGB men." In fact, both news agencies are virtual centers for subversion and espionage. "A sizable portion of the Soviet nationals posted abroad as staff members of TASS, Aeroflot, *Novosti,*" Barron writes, "are KGB and GRU officers."[30]

Novosti material provides the basis for publication abroad of about 50 journals, ten newspapers, and more than 100 press bulletins. The agency claims that 4,500 titles (for the most part pamphlets) and 30 million copies of its publications are distributed each year. Titles are published also in non-communist-ruled countries under contract with the Soviet international distribution agency, *Mezhdunarodnaia kniga* (International Book). Others are sold through normal channels at reduced prices. A recent gift of 1,000 books in the French language, dealing with Marxism-Leninism for the national party school, arrived in Bamako, Mali.[31]

In the lesser developed countries, newspapers and journals are easier to circulate than books. Thus more than twenty-four Soviet periodicals and six newspapers are printed in forty-five foreign languages, including *Asia and Africa Today* (in two languages), *Culture and Life* (five), *New Times* (ten), *Soviet Literature* (ten), *Soviet Union* (twenty), and *Soviet Woman* (fourteen).

The theoretical and informational journal of communist and workers' parties is the monthly *World Marxist Review*,[32] with headquarters in Prague. In appears in 40 languages and 75 national editions, for distribution throughout 145 countries. Each print run reportedly exceeds a half-million copies. Iurii A. Skliarov, the editor-in-chief, is a candidate for membership on the CPSU Central Committee. A bimonthly *Information Bulletin* appears in six languages. It provides an additional, and more frequent, outlet for dissemination of speeches and articles by prominent figures in the world communist movement.

The weekly *Moskovskie novosti* (Moscow News) has been in existence since 1930. English, French, Spanish, and Arabic translations circulate in 140 countries; it has a press run of 800,000 copies per edition.[33] This newspaper promotes the Soviet way of life and includes articles on USSR economic "successes," communist peace initiatives, and international relations.

A rather specialized operation is conducted by the Progress Publishing House in Moscow. About 180 translators prepare the works of Lenin, socio-political literature, and documents from CPSU congresses in 40 foreign languages for sale in roughly twice as many countries.[34] The All-Union Copyright Agency (VAAP) claims to have negotiated more than 1,750 contracts with publishing enterprises in non-communist-ruled states, covering a total of 3,345 titles. In 1980, a ten-year agreement was signed between VAAP and Pergamon Press of London. The latter already had brought out Brezhnev's *Selected Speeches and Writings on Foreign Affairs*. In one article, the late CPSU leader explained that his purpose in this English-language edition was to "familiarize [the readers] with our understanding of human rights and their realization in the Soviet Union." Pergamon Press also published a volume of Andropov's articles and speeches in English translation and did the same for Chernenko.[35]

At times, a country may become the target for saturation with propaganda. This is the case in India, where 50 separate Soviet journals or bulletins appear, compared with a total of 111 for the remaining 92 foreign countries that have diplomatic representation at Delhi. Most USSR publications are distributed in the capital as well as Bombay, Calcutta, and Madras. The journal *Soviet Land* (circulation 550,000 copies in all of India) holds annual essay competitions for the "Nehru Award," with fifteen prizes that include free trips to the USSR. Five other USSR periodicals are printed locally in English and sixteen additional languages. Of approximately 150 inexpensive Soviet technical books, some 40 to 50 have been adopted by various Indian colleges and universities as texts.

AID TO LESSER DEVELOPED COUNTRIES

In addition, certain types of technical assistance are provided to the Third World as a means of establishing influence over the mass media. Provisions for radio transmitters and printing presses, training of journalists (at special schools in Moscow, Bucharest, East Berlin, Prague, and Sofia), and visits by USSR specialists are written into cultural treaties. These agreements also cover film and radio material, exchanged as a normal part of the aid program. Such cultural cooperation agreements have been signed by the USSR with 27 African states. Similar treaties have been entered into with Jordan, Lebanon, and Iraq. An agreement with the People's Democratic Republic of [South] Yemen provided for construction of a 200-kilowatt shortwave radio transmitter at Aden to reach the entire Arab world. Algeria, Egypt, and Syria also have entered into telecommunications' cooperation with the Soviet Union. Before the combined U.S.-Caribbean invasion, the USSR signed a contract with Grenada[36] to provide the latter with a ground communications station as part of the Intersputnik satellite system.

The best-publicized example of Soviet initiative in extending its influence throughout the Third World is Friendship University, founded at Moscow in 1960 and named after Patrice Lumumba, one of the Congolese leaders who had been supported by the USSR. A decade later it reportedly had 700 Africans, 650 Middle Easterners, 460 Southeast Asians, and 800 Latin Americans among its approximately 3,500 enrolled students. In one recent year, diplomas were handed out to 80 Asians, some 140 Latin Americans, more than 140 Africans, and about 100 Soviet citizens. By 1985, total enrollment reportedly had reached 5,000 from 105 foreign countries.[37]

Those selected receive one or two years of preparatory instruction to fill gaps in their previous schooling and to teach them the Russian language. Six departments open for study include economics and law, history and philosophy, agriculture, medicine, science, and engineering. Students are given free dormitory space plus 80 to 90 rubles per month for food. Many graduates support USSR foreign policy through international communist front organizations. The most important is probably the Afro-Asian People's Solidarity Organization, which maintains a strong pro-Soviet and anti-Western stance. Revolutionaries apprehended in Mexico[38] and insurgents among the radical leftists of Sri Lanka reportedly had received part of their training at Lumumba University.

However, there have been several confrontations between USSR authorities and those attending Lumumba University. One early example of such a conflict became known when a newspaper in Zambia reported how foreign students had demonstrated in Red Square to protest and demand an investigation concerning the death of a colleague from Ghana. African students were arrested subsequently for distributing pamphlets received at the Chinese embassy. Fifteen others from Kenya were expelled, allegedly for political reasons, but probably because they had resisted communist indoctrination. The 25,000 Afghan youths sent to the USSR over the past 30 years have had no choice.[39]

FUTURE ACTIVITIES

During the late 1980s the USSR will continue to direct its propaganda especially toward the lesser developed countries of Africa, Asia, and Latin America. In the view of Kremlin decision makers, the fate of these recently independent states will decide whether or not communism establishes itself as *the* socio-political and economic form of organization over most of the globe. It is for this reason that the Soviet Union attempts to identify itself with all types of national liberation or separatist movements. Elites within the Third World are the target because they decide, in effect, the direction that local developments will take. In this connection, techniques and propaganda themes vary considerably.

Throughout Latin America the USSR sometimes makes a verbal show of condemning violent revolution and terrorist movements, but in practice the Soviets are disposed to support any activity undertaken by groups that profess anti-American and anti-capitalist beliefs. Moscow has made no secret of its friendly and mutually beneficial ties with Cuba[40] and Nicaragua, attempting to promote their two communist regimes as models for the region. Meanwhile, USSR propaganda concentrates on the issue of the allegedly "oppressive" and "exploitative" policies pursued by U.S.-based multinational companies. Cuban communists are given predominant responsibility for dissemination of propaganda in the Western Hemisphere. A nationality adapted edition of the *World Marxist Review* (Cuban title, *Revista Internacional*) and a Spanish edition of the Soviet journal *Latinskaia Amerika* are published by the Soviet Union for wide distribution throughout the area. Havana also has a large network of periodicals that it distributes. The weekly edition of the communist party newspaper *Granma* is the most prominent, appearing in Spanish, English, and French.

The USSR approach to Africa shows greater variation, because the

Arab states throughout the Maghreb region of northern Africa seem more stable than the non-Arab ones south of the Sahara. The latter were long the targets of Soviet propaganda, which had previously been directed both against Portuguese control over its territories in Angola and Mozambique and against the white-dominated government of the former Rhodesia (now Zimbabwe). Currently, the target is the Republic of South Africa. Approximately 30,500 academic students from sub-Saharan Africa were being educated during 1984 in Soviet and East European colleges.[41]

The Middle East also remains a fertile area for Soviet propaganda, because the USSR has been successful in projecting the image of itself as an ally in the struggle against Israel, which is portrayed as an American "puppet." Most of the students from this region who have been schooled in the Soviet Union and Eastern Europe have come from the two Yemens, Lebanon, Iraq, Syria, and (formerly) Egypt. Currently, they number 31,395 in academic programs[42] The war between Iran and Iraq since 1980 has posed a slight complication for the USSR. Moscow remained officially neutral in reporting those military developments. Nonetheless, the Soviets continue to heap discredit upon the United States, criticize the Camp David accords, support the PLO as the sole representative of the Palestinian people, and attack Israel's "expansionism" and "oppression" in Arab lands.

In East Asia and the Pacific, propaganda activities of Moscow exploit cultural relations. A maximum of only about 200 students per year have been recruited from this region, mostly from Burma, Indonesia, and Laos, for education in the USSR or Eastern Europe[43]. Even this number is declining. In the Pacific Basin, USSR propaganda opportunities tend to be limited to such things as a trade fair in Malaysia or visits by journalists from Moscow to the Philippines.

The need for technology to develop Siberia has spurred tourist travel and frequent exchange of official delegations between Japan and the USSR. Thousands of students have been graduated from the Russian-language program at the Japanese-Soviet Academy in Tokyo. Moscow's propaganda goals also have been served effectively by communist-supported campaigns against the security treaty with the United States. A new theme,[44] prompted by U.S. efforts to persuade the Japanese to expand their defenses, alleges that Washington wants Tokyo not only to increase its military potential for the fulfillment of certain tasks currently facing the U.S. armed forces in the Far East but also to provide economic support for pro-American countries throughout the region.

The USSR is attempting to undermine the Association of Southeast Asian Nations (ASEAN). It regularly conveys messages to the governments of Indonesia, Malaysia, Singapore, Thailand, the Philippines, and other states in the area, urging them to adopt Soviet proposals for peace. However, the united stand by ASEAN members against Vietnam and resistance to the Hanoi-installed puppet regime of Heng Samrin in Kampuchea (Cambodia) represent attitudes that Moscow finds difficult to combat.

Meanwhile, with regard to the Soviet attempt to conquer Afghanistan, USSR propaganda alleges that Mainland China and the United States are aiding "counterrevolutionaries" against the "legitimate" (that is, Moscow-installed) regime of Mohammed Najibullah and that Pakistan is being used by "the imperialists" as a "base for hostile operations."[45]

A special place in Soviet foreign propaganda activities is reserved for the People's Republic of China. Although both countries again exchanged ambassadors in 1970 after a four-year hiatus, this has not prevented them from attacking each other in the media as well as at the United Nations. In this last forum, the Chinese support Pakistan, while the USSR lines up with India. Beijing is accused by Moscow of discriminating against minorities in Tibet, Sinkiang, and Inner Mongolia. Publication of a Chinese atlas in 1979, which laid claim to 600,000 square miles of territory within the Soviet Union, evoked an attack in the official government daily newspaper, *Izvestiia*.[46] Over the past seven years, these disputes have become muted as relations improved.

Throughout Western Europe, USSR propaganda themes have concentrated on peace and detente. Attacks against the Federal Republic of Germany, once a mainstay of the Soviet propaganda message, have fluctuated. As in the case of Tokyo, Moscow anticipates substantial future gains in capital investment (loans) and technology transfer from Bonn. Consequently, closer economic and political integration of Western Europe is presented as an obstacle to bilateral trade with individual Eastern bloc countries. However, the most sustained USSR propaganda campaign in postwar history was that directed during the early and mid-1980s against American deployment of Pershing II and ground-launched cruise missiles in Europe, a move requested by NATO to counter the Soviets' earlier emplacement of SS-20 intermediate-range launchers in the western parts of the USSR.[47]

Freedom of the press in the West provides the East with a multitude of printed and spoken criticism of public figures, organizations, society, and government policy that Soviet propagandists then cite in their own articles and speeches. Of more value to the Soviets is the opportunity to place full-page "advertisements" in major American newspapers,[48] paid for by the Information Department of the USSR embassy in Washington, D.C. Finally, a certain Vladimir V. Posner, commentator for Moscow radio, has made "dozens of appearances on ABC's *Nightline* and other American programs" including seven minutes to criticize the president of the United States after his speech on defense spending.[49]

As suggested in the foregoing, propaganda activities overlap with espionage and "active measures," which are discussed in the next chapter. Intelligence gathering involves professionals, who frequently use TASS or *Novosti* as covers. This should not be confused with Western-style "investigative reporting." The reports of these Soviet "journalists" go directly to KGB or GRU headquarters in Moscow.

NOTES

1. U.S. Congress, House, Permanent Select Committee on Intelligence, Subcommittee on Oversight, *Hearings on Soviet Covert Action: The Forgery Offensive*, 96th Cong., 2nd sess., 1980, p. 7. Paul A. Smith, Jr., "Propaganda: A Modernized Soviet Weapons System," *USIA World* 2, no. 10 (November 1983): 9, gives $3.5 billion as the annual budget.

2. Earlier studies of this subject include Frederick C. Barghoorn, *Soviet Foreign Propaganda* (Princeton, N.J.: Princeton University Press, 1964); Lyman B. Kirkpatrick, Jr., and Howland H. Sargeant, *Soviet Political Warfare Techniques* (New York: National Strategy Information Center, Inc., 1972), pp. 41–82; and Paul Roth, *Sow-Inform: Nachrichtenwesen und Informationspolitik der Sowjetunion* (Dusseldorf: Droste Verlag, 1980), pp. 205–47, for the Brezhnev period. The U.S. Information Agency began publishing in October 1981 *Soviet Propaganda Alert*, which appears every two months and identifies themes being used during that period by Moscow. See no. 32, 29 July 1986, pp. 1–2.

3. "Agitator's Vocation," *Pravda*, 11 January 1978. See also Baruch Hazan, *Soviet Impregnational Propaganda* (Ann Arbor, Mich.: Ardis, 1982). Both aspects would be supervised domestically by the Central Committee's propaganda department.

4. Elizabeth Teague, "International Department Now Has Two First Deputy Heads," *Radio Liberty Research* (Munich: 3 February 1986): p. 3; *Pravda*, 7 March 1986, p. 1, for Dobrynin's appointment; ibid., 15 June 1986, p. 4, on his activities in this capacity.

5. Elizabeth Teague, "The Foreign Departments of the Central Committee of the CPSU," *Radio Liberty Research Bulletin* (Munich: 27 October 1980), pp. 25–26.

6. Agence France Press over Paris radio, 20 June 1985; *FBIS*, 21 June 1985, p. R4. The IID is not listed by Alexander Rahr, "The Apparatus of the Central Committee of the CPSU," *Radio Liberty Research* (Munich: 3 June 1986), RL 215/86. See also *Foreign Report*, (London: 11 December 1986).

7. Slogans for the May Day anniversary appeared in *Pravda,* 13 April 1986, p. 1, and numbered 40. Only the last 15 dealt with foreign policy. A larger number appeared (9 out of 50) for Revolution Day in ibid., 19 October 1986, p. 1. A. N. Iakovlev's book, *Ot Trumena do Reigana* (Moscow: Molodaia gvardiia, 1984) reflects the distorted views of the man who now heads the Soviet foreign propaganda apparatus.

8. Academician P. Fedoseev, "Imperialist Aggression and Psychological Warfare," *Pravda,* 10 September 1984, p. 6. This Soviet author was writing about alleged Western propaganda, directed against the USSR, but mirror-imaged what the Soviets themselves do.

9. U.S. House, Permanent Select Committee on Intelligence, *Soviet Covert Action,* p. 80. All except (9), (10), and (11) are discussed annually in Richard F. Staar, ed., *Yearbook on International Communist Affairs* (Stanford: Hoover Institution Press). See also Wallace Spaulding, "Communist Fronts in 1985," *Problems of Communism* 35, no. 2 (March–April 1986): 72–78, who regularly contributes to the *Yearbook.*

10. U.S. House, Permanent Select Committee on Intelligence, *Soviet Covert Action,* p. 80.

11. U.S. Department of State, "Soviet Active Measures: The World Peace Council," *Foreign Affairs Note* (Washington, D.C.: April 1986). Gorbachev sent a personal message to the WPC session, according to Moscow radio, 24 June 1986; *FBIS,* pp. CC1–CC2, of the same date.

12. Richard F. Staar, ed., *1969 Yearbook on International Communist Affairs* (Stanford: Hoover Institution Press, 1969), p. 953.

13. *L'Unità* (Rome), 15 March 1978, and *L'Humanité* (Paris), 13 April 1978.

14. *Flashes from the Trade Unions* (Prague), 20 February 1982; U.S. Department of State, "World Federation of Trade Unions: Soviet Foreign Policy Tool," *Foreign Affairs Note* (Washington, D.C.: August 1983); Roy Godson, *Labor in Soviet Global Strategy* (New York: Crane, Russak, for the National Strategy Information Center, 1984). See address by WFTU chairman in *Nepszawa* (Budapest), 18 September 1986, pp. 1–3.

15. *Juventud Rebelde* (Havana), 28 July–4 August 1978; Spaulding, *op. cit.,* p. 77, on the Moscow festival.

16. The manifesto appears in *The Pugwash Conferences on Science and World Affairs* (Geneva: Pugwash Council, 1984), pp. 10–12. For KGB control of the Soviet side, see Glagolev, *Post-Andropov Strategy,* pp. 53–57.

17. Martin M. Kaplan, ed., *Proceedings of the Thirty-second Pugwash Conference on Science and World Affairs* (Geneva: Pugwash Council, 1984); *Pugwash Newsletter* 22, no. 2 (October 1984): 29–39, for the Bjerkliden meeting. Moscow radio, 9 July 1986 and 17 June 1986 in *FBIS,* 10 July 1985, p. AA–4 (Campinas) and 17 June 1986, p. AA–15 (Geneva), respectively.

18. *Literaturnaia gazeta,* 20 July 1977; A. M. Aleksandrov, ed., *Radi mira na*

zemle: Sovetskaia programma mira dlia 80-kh godov v deistvii (Moscow: Politizdat, 1983), discusses the "peace plan."

19. *Washington Post,* 1 May 1983. A few weeks later some 30 Soviet delegates appeared in Minneapolis at a conference on "creating the conditions for peace," sponsored by the Institute for Policy Studies (IPS) in Washington, D.C. A list of U.S. participants appeared in the *Minneapolis Daily American,* 17 May 1983. The same IPS sponsored Arbatov at the World Affairs Council of Northern California. See the *San Francisco Chronicle,* 5 September 1985, p. 24, and *Izvestiia,* 11 September 1985, p. 5.

20. *Los Angeles Times,* 23 June 1983; *Christian Science Monitor,* 28 February 1984; *Wall Street Journal,* 3 June 1986, p. 30, editorial on Chazov. See also IPPNW *Report* 4, no. 1 (February 1986).

21. "A Factor of Hope," *Pravda,* 6 June 1984; *New York Times,* 10 June 1984. The organization won the UNESCO Peace Education Prize for "promoting actions aimed at constructing defenses of peace in the minds of men" (*New York Times,* 1 November 1984). The sixth conference at Cologne demanded the "right to life," as reported in *Pravda,* 30 May 1986, p. 5.

22. U.S. Information Agency, "Communist International Radio Broadcasting Between 1983 and 1985," *Research Memorandum* (Washington, D.C.: 29 August 1986), tables 3 and 4; *New York Times,* 24 March 1986, op.ed. page.

23. U.S. Department of State, "Moscow's Radio Peace and Progress," *Foreign Affairs Note* (Washington, D.C.: August 1982), p. 1.

24. U.S. House, Permanent Select Committee on Intelligence, *Soviet Covert Action,* p. 79; U.S. Information Agency, "Communist International Radio Broadcasting," *Research Memorandum* (Washington, D.C.: 17 December 1985), pp. 1–2.

25. U.S. Department of State, "Communist Clandestine Broadcasting," *Foreign Affairs Note* (Washington, D.C.: December 1982), p. 3.

26. U.S. Board for International Broadcasting, *1986 Annual Report* (Washington: GPO, 1986), pp. 24–30.

27. Jamming transmitters in the USSR and Eastern Europe cost an estimated one-quarter of a billion dollars to construct (David Brand, "Soviets Continue Jamming," *Wall Street Journal,* 14 July 1983; U.S.I.A., *Jamming of Western Radio Broadcasts to the Soviet Union and Eastern Europe,* Research Report, April 1983, p. 5). See also "The War of Words," *U.S. News & World Report,* 7 October 1985, p. 37; Radio Liberty Research (7 November 1986).

28. Sh. P. Sanakoev, ed., *Voprosy sovetskoi vneshnepoliticheskoi propagandy* (Moscow: Mezhdunarodnye otnosheniia, 1980), pp. 203–4; *U.S. News & World Report,* 30 March 1981, p. 37; John J. Karch, "News and Its Uses in the Communist World," in L. J. Martin and A. G. Chaudhary, eds., *Comparative Mass Media Systems* (New York: Longman, Inc., 1983), pp. 111–31; S. A. Losev, "Two Approaches to Information Policy," *Mezhdunarodnaia zhizn'* 32, no. 12 (December 1985): 28–36.

29. Sanakoev, *Voprosy propagandy*, p. 207; *The International Who's Who, 1985–1986* (London: Europa 1985), p. 440, carries a biography of Falin.

30. John Barron, *KGB: The Secret Work of Soviet Secret Agents* (New York: Bantam Books, 1974), pp. 15 and 27.

31. One example is Leonid I. Brezhnev, *Istoricheskii rubezh na puti k kommunizmu* (Moscow: Politizdat, 1977). More than 1.5 million copies of this pamphlet were published in English, Arabic, Spanish, German, and French translations. The number of publications distributed during 1982 totaled 74 million copies, according to Colin Walters, "World's Bookshelves out of Kilter," *Insight*, 17 March 1986, p. 72. *Pravda*, 26 January 1985, reported the gift.

32. It is known also as *Problems of Peace and Socialism*. See Wallace Spaulding, "World Marxist Review," in Richard F. Staar, ed., *1984 Yearbook on International Communist Affairs* (Stanford: Hoover Institution Press, 1984), pp. 426–27. *WMR* editor Skliarov moved to Agitprop in late 1986.

33. Sanakoev, *Voprosy propagandy*, p. 191. See also S. I. Beglov. *Vneshnepoliticheskaia propaganda* 2nd rev. ed. (Moscow: Vysshaia shkola, 1984), pp. 283–89.

34. A. M. Prokhorov, chief ed., *Bol'shaia sovetskaia entsiklopediia*, 3rd ed. (Moscow: Sovetskaia entsiklopediia, 1975), 21:29–30.

35. L. I. Brezhnev, "Socialism, Democracy and the Rights of Man," *Kommunist*, no. 2 (January 1981): 14; Iu. V. Andropov, *Speeches and Writings* (1983); K. U. Chernenko, *Selected Speeches and Writings* (1984). However, another U.S. company (Richardson and Steirman) published two similar volumes by Gorbachev, *A Time of Peace* and *The Coming Century of Peace*, according to *Pravda*, 5 April 1986, p. 1.

36. Timothy Ashby, "Grenada: Soviet Stepping Stone," *Proceedings of the U.S. Naval Institute* 109, no. 12 (December 1983): 34. See also V. Listov, "Lessons from Grenada," *Pravda*, 25 October 1985, p. 5.

37. Alvin Z. Rubinstein, "Lumumba University: An Assessment," *Problems of Communism* 20, no. 6 (November–December 1971): 65–67; more than 13,000 graduates are working in 110 Third World countries, according to Moscow radio, 7 February 1985, in *FBIS*, 11 February 1985, p. R-16; Edward B. Fiske, "Education Watch," *New York Times*, 16 June 1985, for latest enrollment.

38. Barron, *KGB*, pp. 317–25, provides a discussion of activities in Mexico by former students from Lumumba University.

39. U.S. Department of State, "Soviet Influence on Afghan Youth," *Special Report*, no. 139 (February 1986), p. 2.

40. About 70,000 Cubans were assisting the USSR in Africa and another 8,000 in Nicaragua, according to U.S. officials (*New York Times*, 2 May 1984).

41. U.S. Department of State, Bureau of Intelligence and Research, *Warsaw Pact Economic Aid to Non-Communist LDCs, 1984*, Publication 9345, May 1986, table 7, p. 6.

42. Ibid.

43. Ibid.

44. U.S. Information Agency, *Soviet Propaganda Alert,* no. 18 (31 January 1984): 11; U.S. Arms Control and Disarmament Agency, *Soviet Campaign Against SDI* (Washington, D.C.: August 1986), p. 15.

45. Tass dispatch from the United Nations in *Pravda,* 9 February 1986, p. 5.

46. Cited by Richard F. Staar, "Bear and Dragon in the Third World," *Policy Review* 2, no. 7 (Winter 1979): 97. See, however, Gorbachev's speech at Vladivostok, which called for better relations with the PRC (Moscow television, 28 July 1986; *FBIS,* 29 July 1986, pp. R14–15).

47. Alexander R. Alexiev, *The Soviet Campaign Against INF* (Santa Monica, Calif.: Rand, February 1985), N-2280-AF.

48. See, e.g., Gorbachev's report to the 27th CPSU Congress in *Pravda,* 26 February 1986, pp. 2–10.

49. Quotation from Philip Taubman article in the *New York Times,* 30 December 1985; editorial from the *Wall Street Journal,* 5 March 1986.

5

ESPIONAGE AND ACTIVE MEASURES

Since the 1917 revolution, the Soviet civilian intelligence organization has had fifteen different chiefs. Four were executed, and only two of the last seven incumbents can be classified as career secret police officials. The majority had been transferred from work in the CPSU apparatus. This would indicate an attempt to maintain tight party supervision over activities that include a substantial domestic component. The chapter that follows will discuss the foreign operations of the USSR intelligence services.

After the execution in 1953 of secret police chief and CPSU functionary Lavrentyi P. Beria, who had attempted to seize power upon Stalin's death, a professional intelligence officer, General Ivan A. Serov, took over the organization. Serov had directed the mass deportation of Lithuanians, Latvians, and Estonians at the beginning of World War II and later also of Chechens, Kalmyks, and Crimean Tatars, among other nationalities. Party control over the secret police could not be firmly re-established until 1958, when Khrushchev appointed former Komsomol leader Aleksandr N. Shelepin to head what was now called the State Security Committee, or KGB. It had been placed under the Council of Ministers four years earlier.

The KGB soon accelerated its operations abroad, slightly curtailing domestic work. A meeting with its military counterpart, the GRU (by then under the direction of Serov), and foreign intelligence organizations from fourteen other communist-ruled countries resulted in an agreement to cooperate on the basis of "equality." The Chinese and Albanians broke this compact in 1960, and the KGB began to direct operations against Mainland China.[1]

Vladimir Y. Semichastniy, also a former Komsomol leader, took over the secret police in October 1961. One of his missions included penetration of the International Confederation of Free Trade Unions in Brussels. A year and a half later, the trial of a senior GRU colonel, Oleg Penkovskiy, revealed that this man had delivered approximately 10,000 negatives from photographs of classified documents to British and American intelligence services over an eighteen-month period.[2] Apparently, one motive for his activity had been Penkovskiy's hatred of the KGB and its personnel.

In 1965 it was revealed that General Serov had been expelled from the communist party for "violations of socialist legality" while serving as deputy to Beria. This reflected on both the KGB and GRU, because Serov also served as head of the latter from 1958 to 1962. His dismissal from this last position occurred as a result of the Penkovskiy case. Semichastniy was succeeded in May 1967 by Iurii V. Andropov, a career party apparatus worker without any previous experience in intelligence activities. This appointment indicated an upgrading of the KGB, due to Andropov's status as candidate Politburo member at the time.[3]

After fifteen years as head of the secret police, Andropov moved into the position of a CPSU national secretary. His replacement, V. V. Fedorchuk, was transferred in May 1982 from the Ukraine, where he had directed KGB activities for that republic. As the new CPSU general secretary, Andropov shifted Fedorchuk to the Internal Affairs Ministry and promoted him to general of the army. The first deputy KGB chief, Viktor Mikhailovich Chebrikov, succeeded to the chairmanship on 17 December 1982, the seventh secret police head in three decades.

Unlike his predecessor, Chebrikov had not made a career in such work. He served in the army during the Second World War, completed engineering studies at Dniepropetrovsk, and worked briefly in a factory. Between 1951 and 1967, Chebrikov occupied full-time CPSU positions. Brezhnev called him to Moscow and placed him in charge of KGB personnel, and in April 1982 he became first deputy chairman for the whole organization. In other words, Chebrikov and Andropov had worked for the KGB during the same fifteen-year period. At the end of 1983, Chebrikov became a candidate member of the Politburo and the following spring received a marshal's star, which is appropriate for his rank as general of the army. He was promoted to full Politburo membership on 6 March 1986, at the 27th CPSU Congress.[4]

ORGANIZATION

The center of the Soviet Union's worldwide espionage operation and active measures is located in the State Security Committee (*Komitet Gosudarstvennoi Bezopastnosti*), with headquarters at No. 22 Lubianka Street, off Dzerzhinskii Square[5] in Moscow. The KGB employs up to 1.4 million persons, half of them part-time informants, both inside and outside the Soviet Union. Theoretically a government organization, the KGB in fact is controlled by the Politburo and Secretariat of the Central Committee. Although the agency exercises day-to-day responsibility for its own operations, work plans and especially intricate operations are first approved at the top levels of the party. The KGB is subdivided into directorates, services, and departments (see Figure 5.1).

The First Chief Directorate, sharing responsibility with military intelligence (GRU) for all Soviet clandestine activities abroad, is staffed by about 10,000 officers. It maintains three sub-directorates, three special services, two special departments, eleven geographic departments, and several functional ones.[6] From 1959 through 1967 the "disinformation" department, comprising 40 to 50 employees, was headed by a Major General Ivan I. Agaiants. In 1968, however, this unit underwent reorganization and expansion. Now referred to as Service "A," it exists to coordinate and plan dissemination of "false and provocative information," designed to deceive foreign governments or the public in countries outside the Soviet bloc under the name "active measures."[7]

One of several subdirectorates (Directorate "S") has responsibility for foreign intelligence, or "illegals," that is, agents who reside abroad under deep cover and have no apparent connection with the USSR. The scientific and technical sub-directorate (Directorate "T") coordinates the theft of Western technology and military secrets. It has a staff of several hundred officers in Moscow, in addition to specialists at each major diplomatic mission. This sub-directorate determines the composition of Soviet delegations to international scientific conferences as well as individuals sent abroad on exchange programs. Soviet citizens who travel to foreign countries are all considered important for intelligence-gathering purposes. Each must sign a form prior to departure (see Figure 5.2) and, upon return, undergo a debriefing. "Executive Action" (Department Eight of Directorate "S") involves terrorism, kidnapping, and assassination under the euphemism *mokrye dela* or "wet" (bloody) business. Formerly designated as "the thirteenth," and then Department "V," it underwent reorganization in 1969 with an additional emphasis on capabilities to sabotage foreign communications, transport, and public utilities.

The Second Chief Directorate is responsible for internal security and surveillance over foreigners inside the USSR. About half of the personnel is assigned to subvert foreign diplomats and prevent them from contact with ordinary Soviet citizens. The other half concentrates on tourists, artists, scientists, businessmen, students, and journalists from foreign countries. The Fifth Chief Directorate concerns itself with internal dissidents and reinforcement of controls over the general populace. The Chief Directorate for Border Guards[8] controls the frontiers and is occupied more with keeping Soviet citizens within the USSR than with preventing others from entering the country. Its personnel is estimated to number 250,000 uniformed and armed men.

PROMINENT ESPIONAGE CASES

Among Soviet intelligence successes, some of which have been publicized inside the USSR, is that of former German communist Richard Sorge.[9] This man was able to obtain advance information from the Nazi embassy in Tokyo, where he worked ostensibly as a journalist, on the exact date the Wehrmacht would invade the Soviet Union, and he transmitted this to Moscow. Stalin did not believe the message. Arrested by Japanese counterintelligence, Sorge was executed before the end of the Second World War. Another important agent, Rudolf I. Abel, operated from 1948 to 1957 in the United States.[10] Lieutenant Colonel Evgenii V. Runge worked successfully against the Federal Republic of Germany and NATO for twelve years until 1967, when he defected to the West. The vast majority of Soviet intelligence officers, however, operates under diplomatic cover.

A request for political asylum in 1971 by Captain Oleg Lialin, an operative in what was then Department "V," precipitated the expulsion of 105 individuals or one-fifth of all personnel from the Soviet embassy, its trade mission, Aeroflot office, and Narodnyi Bank in London. This defection also had repercussions for the worldwide USSR espionage network. A number of Soviet intelligence officers throughout the Western Hemisphere, Asia, Europe, and Africa received orders to return home, since their cover might have been compromised by the defector.[11] In 1983 the French government declared 45 Soviet diplo-

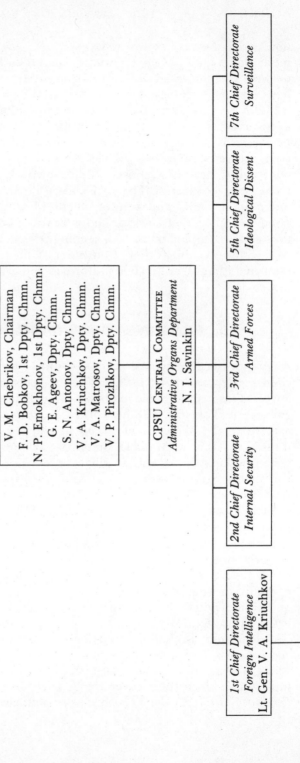

FIGURE 5.1

COMMITTEE FOR STATE SECURITY OF THE USSR, 1986

V. M. Chebrikov, Chairman
F. D. Bobkov, 1st Dpty. Chmn.
N. P. Emokhonov, 1st Dpty. Chmn.
G. E. Ageev, Dpty. Chmn.
S. N. Antonov, Dpty. Chmn.
V. A. Kriuchkov, Dpty. Chmn.
V. A. Matrosov, Dpty. Chmn.
V. P. Pirozhkov, Dpty. Chmn.

CPSU CENTRAL COMMITTEE
Administrative Organs Department
N. I. Savinkin

1st Chief Directorate
Foreign Intelligence
Lt. Gen. V. A. Kriuchkov

2nd Chief Directorate
Internal Security

3rd Chief Directorate
Armed Forces

5th Chief Directorate
Ideological Dissent

7th Chief Directorate
Surveillance

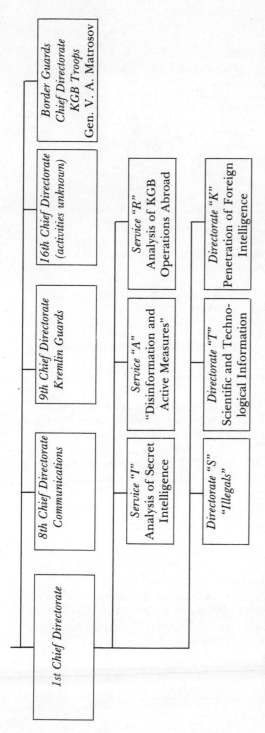

Sources: John Barron, *KGB Today* (New York: Reader's Digest Press, 1983), pp. 444–53; Alexander Rahr, "KGB Chief Gets New First Deputy," *Radio Liberty Research Bulletin* (Munich), RL 221/84, (4 June 1984), p. 2; "KGB: Das Schwert trifft auch Unschuldige," *Der Spiegel* 38, no. 27 (2 July 1984): 128 (fig.); John J. Dziak, "Soviet 'Active Measures,'" *Problems of Communism* 33, no. 6 (November–December 1984), p. 67; CIA, *Directorate of Intelligence, Directory of Soviet Officials: National Organizations*, series CR 86-11691, June 1986, pp. 185–86; and *Moskovskaia pravda*, 2 July 1986, p. 2, for Matrosov.

FIGURE 5.2
INSTRUCTIONS FOR [SOVIET] SCIENTISTS TRAVELING ABROAD
(TRANSLATION)

"APPROVED"

Academician-Secretary of the Department of Biochemistry, Biophysics and the Chemistry of Physiologically Active Combinations of the Academy of Sciences of the USSR,

    Academician

_____ A. A. Baev

_____ 1978

Scientific-Technical Assignment

to the scientific employee of laboratory .... of the
institute ..... of the Academy of Sciences of the USSR, [grade-rank] [position] [Name: Last, First, Patronymic], departing for [country] for . . . [period of time]. . . .

    1. To participate in the work of . . . [Name of Symposium, Colloquium] . . .
in the city of _____ from _____ [date] _____
to _____ [date] _____.

    2. In conversations with foreign scientists propagate widely the achievements of Soviet science and the successes of socialist construction in the USSR, the peaceable policy of our government, and the resolutions of the XXV Congress of the CPSU.

    3. Explain and popularize the ideas of the new Constitution of the USSR, and should the question of "human rights" be brought up, adhere to our policies as these are set forth in our central press organ.

    4. In speeches and conversations abide only by those facts which have been published in our open press and have been authorized for publication abroad.

    5. Inform the Soviet Embassy about your arrival in . . . . [country] . . . .
and about all subsequent movements within that country.

    6. Should you be asked to appear on radio or television, or to write an article in the local press, you must coordinate with the Soviet Embassy.

    7. Upon return home, within two weeks submit a report on your assignment to the UNSS* of the Academy of Sciences of the USSR.

Acting Director of the Institute of   _____
the Academy of Sciences of the USSR   (signature)

mats and two journalists *personae non grata* from among the 185 expulsions recommended by its counterintelligence service, the Territorial Surveillance Directorate. This represented the largest setback to USSR espionage since the comparable British action mentioned above. Two years later, Britain expelled 25 Soviet diplomats and officials as a result of a defection by the KGB station chief in London, a man named Oleg A. Gordievskii. The United States expelled 85 USSR intelligence officers in October 1986.[12]

The Soviets have developed various countermeasures to cope with a defection, the objective being to obscure the case and alert contacts who then may have time to disappear. The KGB immediately draws up a "damage assessment" in order to neutralize possible repercussions. Files at headquarters in Moscow are scrutinized to establish which documents the defector had signed out and which consequently might be compromised. Collective responsibility may dictate punitive measures against family, friends, colleagues, and those who had recommended the individual for employment.[13] In addition, officers serving abroad and known by the defector are recalled to Moscow, since they would be considered to have lost their cover. Many such operatives are destined to be used again, but only in countries where they had not served before and after a "cooling-off" period.

DIPLOMATS AS SPIES

It is estimated that at least one-fourth to as many as one-third of all Soviet officials serving abroad work for the KGB or GRU, the civilian and military intelligence agencies, respectively. Of the approximately 1,000 Soviet and 3,000 East European officials, U.N. employees, students and others in the United States, about one-third is estimated to be full-time intelligence officers. Even the others are required to collect information on at least a part-time basis. During the past several years,

NOTES: This form illustrates quite clearly the situation of a scientist in the USSR, in this case one who was granted permission to travel on a scholarly assignment abroad. Even a Soviet scientist's acceptance of the Nobel Prize would be considered an assignment and, therefore, prior to embarking on a trip to Stockholm, he or she must sign a form like the one above.

*The *Samizdat Bulletin* indicates that this may be the Office of International Scientific Relations. Michael I. Taksar in "Soviet Visitors to the U.S.A.," (unpublished manuscript of 18 November 1982) notes on page 11 that this is "presumably [an] acronym for one of the divisions of the Department of External Relations."

SOURCE: *Samizdat Bulletin*, no. 91, November 1980; translated and reprinted from *Russkaia*

TABLE 5.1
EXPULSION OF SOVIET OFFICIALS, 1981–1985

	1981	1983	1985
Africa	2	1	13
Asia/Pacific	6	41	5
Europe	*	82	39
Middle East	9	*	*
Western Hemisphere	10	11	*
Total	27	135	57

*No expulsions publicly announced.
SOURCES: U.S. Dept. of State, "Expulsion of Soviet Representatives from Foreign Countries, 1970–81," *Foreign Affairs Note* (Washington, D.C., February 1982); ibid., January 1983; ibid., January 1984; ibid., January 1986.

from among the USSR diplomats stationed throughout the world, the number of those announced to have been expelled for espionage has varied (see Table 5.1), with many unreported cases.

It is also well known that Eastern bloc intelligence officers flagrantly abuse their 492 U.N. Secretariat positions and ignore the formal pledge they sign to surrender all allegiance to their respective governments, as already mentioned in the previous chapter. According to former USSR citizen Arkadyi Shevchenko, who had served as under–secretary general at the United Nations, there is "very substantial penetration" by Soviet intelligence services at the U.N. Shevchenko disclosed that a special assistant to former Secretary General Kurt Waldheim had been a KGB officer. Similar allegations have been made against Vladimir Kolesnikov in that same position[14] since June 1985. The same secret police affiliation reportedly applies to Geli Dneprovskii, chief of personnel since 1979 at United Nations headquarters in Geneva. This man has authority to place Soviet and East European officials into key positions. Once filled, such jobs have become part of a virtual "preserve," with vacated posts subsequently occupied by other Eastern bloc nationals.

Dneprovskii's control over personnel allows free access to confidential files on all United Nations employees in Switzerland, an asset for recruitment of sympathizers. About 133 of the 429 Soviet citizens on the permanent staff at U.N. agencies in Geneva have been identified as KGB or GRU operatives. At the United Nations mission in New York, three members of the USSR delegation were arrested by the FBI for espionage. Two received sentences of 50 years in prison. The third man, protected by diplomatic immunity, was expelled from the United States. Those imprisoned were later exchanged for five Soviet dissidents jailed in the USSR, none of whom had worked for American intelligence. Ilia Dirkelov, former press attaché at World Health Organization headquarters in Geneva (which has been called the nerve center of Soviet espionage in Europe), took files along when he defected to Britain. Moscow immediately recalled a large number of intelligence officers from Western Europe, tending to confirm the importance of the documents he had brought with him.[15]

It is the Federal Republic of Germany, however, where most Soviet and East European intelligence officers are concentrated. At least 407 individuals with diplomatic cover have been identified as KGB or GRU officers (about 30 recently were expelled at one time), and another 30,000 are estimated to be "illegals" working clandestinely.[16] France has approximately 1,000 communist spies with diplomatic or other cover, half of them from East European countries. Some 53 espionage cases came before Paris courts between 1963 and 1971, involving East German, Czechoslovak, Polish, Romanian, Yugoslav, and Soviet citizens. Italy has an estimated 250 intelligence officers from the USSR and Eastern Europe, all carrying diplomatic passports. Clandestine services from the bloc greatly enhance Soviet operational capabilities, at negligible expense to the latter.

AGENTS OF INFLUENCE

A French journalist, Pierre Charles Pathé, was arrested in Paris on charges of disseminating Soviet propaganda. In the process of exchanging documents for money, he was caught with his controller, Igor A. Kuznetsov, a second secretary in the USSR permanent delegation to UNESCO. Pathé had worked from 1960 to 1978 by publishing two newsletters and various articles under pseudonyms. One of the publications, called *Synthesis* and financed by the USSR, reached almost three-fourths of the deputies and half the senators in parliament as well as other opinion makers in France.[17]

More recently, a Greek newspaper called *Ethnos* was established in 1981 reportedly with KGB financing. The publisher is accused of serving as an agent of influence for the Soviet Union. His paper has a circulation of 200,000 copies, the largest in Athens. It has described the USSR as the "world's first peace bloc," Solidarity leader Lech Walesa in Poland as an "agent of the CIA," and President Reagan and his assistants as "paranoid monsters." Correspondents for *Ethnos* in the United States and Britain reportedly are communists.[18] The foregoing case represents another example of an individual who promotes the objectives of the USSR without attribution to the latter.

The long-range nature of Soviet intelligence operations can be seen from the cases of four British subjects, three of them recruited as students at Cambridge. All attained high government positions and only in the broad sense of the term could be called "agents of influence." Harold A. R. Philby served at one time as liaison between MI-6 (British foreign intelligence) and the CIA. In mid-1980 he escaped from the West and was decorated in Moscow for "more than 40 years of difficult but honest work."[19] The others were diplomats Donald Mac-Lean and Guy Burgess, who fled to the USSR before Philby did. All three men hated the system in England and willingly betrayed it. Their recruiter, Anthony Blunt, had been a respected art scholar and member of MI-5 (British counterintelligence) during the Second World War. A knighthood was canceled after his involvement with the KGB had become public knowledge.[20]

Stanislav A. Levchenko, a former Soviet intelligence officer who defected to the United States, had directed "agent of influence" operations during 1975–1979 while ostensibly a *Novoe vremia* (New Times) correspondent in Tokyo. He identified eight Japanese, among them three prominent politicians of the socialist party, who knowingly or unwittingly helped the KGB. An official in the Norwegian foreign ministry, Arne Treholt, was convicted in 1985 for giving the Soviets copies of documents stolen from his own government and from NATO. He also used his position to influence other officials and his country's Labor Party.[21]

LOWER-LEVEL RECRUITMENT

Neither high-ranking diplomats nor clerks seem to be immune to KGB blandishments. Blackmail is used frequently as a technique of recruitment. Not long after arriving at the British embassy, John W. C. Vassall went to a party in Moscow given by one of the local Soviet employees. He became drunk and was photographed while engaging in a homosexual act. Threatened with exposure, Vassall began abstracting documents from the naval attaché's office for the KGB. Back in London, he continued this espionage work at the naval intelligence division and fleet section of the Defense Ministry. Vassall was arrested after eight years of spying.[22]

Americans, especially those with problems or grudges, represent targets of the KGB. Money is the bait. U.S. Army enlisted man Robert Glenn Thompson was recruited by a Soviet intelligence officer in West Berlin after an incident over which he had been demoted and denied a transfer. He was used to recommend other potential recruits. Sergeant Jack Dunlop was known to like women and fast cars. Approached in Moscow, he took money for classified documents stolen later from National Security Agency headquarters in the United States. Dunlop committed suicide. Lieutenant Colonel William H. Whalen, while attached to the Joint Chiefs of Staff, received a monthly stipend from the Soviet embassy in Washington, D.C.[23]

A 23-year-old CIA watch officer, William F. Kampiles, was arrested in August 1978 after selling to the KGB a stolen reconnaissance satellite manual. Many other classified documents found their way to Moscow through a teletype encoding machine operator at a private company, including messages to CIA headquarters and the National Security Agency.[24] David H. Barnett, a former CIA officer, received a sentence of eighteen years in prison for selling secrets to the KGB. He had been paid over a three and a half year period for names of CIA undercover agents and several foreign collaborators as well as details of at least one high-priority operation. Less successful was the attempt to infiltrate FBI counterintelligence, frustrated by the arrest and conviction in mid-1986 of a special agent and earlier of two refugees from the USSR who had received instructions from the Soviet consulate-general in San Francisco. Over the past three years, about 30 Americans were arrested for espionage and 110 Soviet-bloc "diplomats" were expelled from the United States.[25]

NATO is another important target, and informants are sought within the organization itself as well as among member state delegations. Georges Paques, deputy NATO press secretary, had worked for USSR intelligence from 1944 onwards while serving in eleven different French ministries. NATO financial controller Nahit Imre, caught photographing secret documents for the Romanian secret service, received extradition to Turkey. A translator, Francis Roussilhe, was arrested with classified documents by Belgian police. When NATO moved its headquarters to a suburb of Brussels, the Soviets built a $25 million auto assembly plant nearby. The factory came equipped with radio antennae and monitoring devices to intercept NATO telephone communications.[26]

Much more difficult are USSR intelligence operations against the People's Republic of China. Although speculation exists that the late Lin Biao (officially reported to have been killed in an airplane crash while fleeing to the Soviet Union) may have had clandestine links with

Moscow,[27] most KGB and GRU espionage remains at a relatively low level. There is some border infiltration by Turkestani natives into Sinkiang and probably crossings into Inner Mongolia by agents from the Mongolian People's Republic. According to Hu Yaobang, general secretary of the Chinese Communist Party, during one year some 200 Soviet spies were reportedly arrested by his security authorities. The PRC foreign ministry in mid-1986 accused the Soviet Union of conducting at least 30 surveillance flights over China.[28]

SUPPORT FOR COUPS AND TERRORISM

It is known that the KGB does not restrict itself merely to information-gathering efforts or agent of influence operations. Evidence of Soviet support for coups and terrorist activities is abundant. USSR policy in this regard tends to function simultaneously at three levels. There is (1) overt endorsement of "national liberation movements" through the media; (2) covert encouragement of support by front organizations; and (3) spreading of disinformation by condemning terrorist activity, while simultaneously financing and training its forces[29] (see Table 5.2).

President Ahmed Sekou Touré of Guinea discovered that Soviet intelligence officers had been plotting with the local teachers' union to overthrow his regime. He expelled USSR Ambassador Daniil Solod. Touré was fortunate in that he had become aware of such activities during his years in France as a member of the communist-dominated trade union organization, Confederation Général du Travail.

Less experienced was the late Kwame Nkrumah of Ghana. A popular revolt took place during his visit to Mainland China, and he never regained power. The new government discovered an East German state security officer named Jürgen Krüger directing an espionage school at Accra under the cover name National Scientific Research Laboratory. With access to all Ghanaian classified materials, he had been routinely passing them on to Moscow. Documentary evidence[30] indicates that the USSR planned to use the country as a base for subversion throughout black Africa. The new government of Ghana expelled more than 1,100 Soviet advisors in the aftermath of these discoveries.

An attempt to subvert a Latin American government came to light when authorities in Mexico City declared the USSR ambassador, along with four of his senior diplomats, *personae non grata*. A Mexican citizen named Fabricio Gomez Souza had been recruited by Soviet intelligence and received a four-year scholarship, along with 30 other students

TABLE 5.2
MAJOR TERRORIST AND "REVOLUTIONARY" GROUPINGS
IN WESTERN EUROPE

Acronym	Name	Target
ARC	Caribbean Revolutionary Alliance	France
BMG/RAF	Baader-Meinhof Group/Red Army Faction	West Germany
DEV/GENC	Federation of Turkish Revolutionary Youth	Turkey
EOKA-B	National Organization of Cypriot Fighters	Cyprus
ETA-M	Basque Fatherland and Freedom Military Front	Spain
ETA-PM	Basque Fatherland and Freedom Political-Military Front	Spain
FLB	Brittany Revolutionary Front	France
FLNC	Corsican National Liberation Front	France
FRAP	Anti-Fascist and Patriotic Revolutionary Front	Spain
GRAPO	1st of October Group of Anti-Fascist Resistance	Spain
HK	People's Liberation	Turkey
INLA	Irish National Liberation Army	Ireland
IRA	Irish Republican Army	Ireland
MAR	Revolutionary Action Movement	Italy
MLAPU	Marxist-Leninist Armed Propaganda Unit	Turkey
NAP	Armed Proletarian Nuclei	Italy
NAR	Nucleus of the Armed Revolution	Italy
PIRA	Provisional Irish Republican Army	Ireland
PL	Front Line	Italy
RB	Red Brigades	Italy
RRF	Red Resistance Front	Netherlands
RZ	Revolutionary Cells	West Germany
TPLA	Turkish People's Liberation Army	Turkey
TPLP/F	Turkish People's Liberation Party/Front	Turkey
TWPLA	Turkish Workers' and Peasants' Liberation Army	Turkey
2JM	2 June Movement	West Germany
UFF	Ulster Freedom Fighters	N. Ireland
UPC	Union of the Corsican People	France

SOURCE: CIA, National Foreign Assessment Center, *A Guide to Political Acronyms,* series PA 79–10474, October 1979, p. 11.

from his country. They studied at the Patrice Lumumba University in Moscow, then headed by KGB Major General Pavel Erzin. Three separate contingents of Mexicans, about 50 in all, later were trained in guerrilla warfare by the North Koreans. These groups came together in Mexico to form the Movimiento de Acción Revolucionaria, which began preparing a terrorist campaign under USSR direction. However, all members of the movement were arrested before they could develop any popular support.[31]

Only a few months later, President Ja'far Numairi was ousted briefly in the Sudan. Thirty-eight of his supporters were shot to death. The Soviet-inspired revolution collapsed after only three days. About 2,700 local communists were rounded up and their leaders executed. Advisers and technicians had arrived from the USSR in the Sudan several years before to help build port facilities and assist with counterinsurgency operations against the black guerrilla movement in the south. President Numairi revealed that the communist-inspired coup had received support and direction from the Soviet and Bulgarian embassies. He expelled the third-ranking USSR diplomat as well as the Bulgarian ambassador.[32]

The coup against and execution of President Salim Rabay' Ali in South Yemen received support and most probably direction from Moscow. Soviet naval ships and Cuban-piloted aircraft bombarded Aden. Since then some 2,000 East Germans have been given control over security in the People's Democratic Republic of (South) Yemen, and it appears to have become the first Arab state with a Marxist-Leninist orientation.[33] (See Chapter 10 for the abortive January 1986 coup that apparently caught the USSR by surprise.)

In Afghanistan, Soviet armed forces entered Kabul allegedly at the invitation of communist President Hafizullah Amin at the end of December 1979, surrounded his headquarters, and killed him as well as all members of his family and government. The USSR continues to maintain a "limited contingent" of more than 165,000 troops to support the puppet regime of Mohammed Najibullah, under the (rather thin) pretext of stemming United States and Chinese aid to rebel opposition forces. Soviet occupation troops have used chemical and biological warfare techniques, as well as saturation bombing attacks on civilian populations, to suppress the Moslem freedom fighters.[34]

On occasion, East European rather than direct Soviet assistance goes to terrorists like those in the outlawed Irish Republican Army. Acting on a tip, police in the Netherlands stopped a DC-6 aircraft that had arrived from Czechoslovakia under charter by a Belgian company. Although the cargo manifest indicated London as its destination, the flight plan included a refueling stop in Amsterdam and Ireland as the final destination. A search revealed 116 wooden crates containing anti-tank rocket launchers, mortars, grenades, machine guns, rifles, and ammunition. Western intelligence agencies reportedly have traced many connections among Japanese, Palestinian, Turkish, Basque, and other terrorist movements.[35] The Soviet decision to support international groups dedicated to terror reportedly was made as far back as the 1966 Tricontinental Conference in Havana.

USSR encouragement of the notorious terrorist "Carlos" (Ilich Ramírez Sánchez) is well known. Raised by a prominent Venezuelan communist family, he studied at Lumumba University in Moscow. West European intelligence has established that "Carlos" had been recruited by the KGB and serves as a link with international terrorist groups. Military training reportedly is provided for such groups at camps throughout the Middle East and Africa as well as in Cuba and the USSR. Soviets, Cubans, East Germans, and North Koreans provide the instruction. Major coordinating agencies for this network of terrorist schools include the GRU and the DGI (Dirección General de Intelligencia, that is, Cuban intelligence), the latter operating under direct Soviet control.[36]

On the issue of training, one Western specialist has written the following:

> The Palestine Resistance has been wholly armed by the Soviet Union since 1968. At least one in every ten of its guerrilla fighters and officers has been trained inside the Soviet Union or its East European satellites (not to mention North Korea, where some twenty-five hundred guerrillas were trained in the early days). The others were either trained in Cuba or had the benefit of expert Cuban instruction in *fedayeen* camps from Algeria and Libya to Syria, Lebanon, and South Yemen.[37]

According to defectors, more than 1,000 Palestinians alone already have gone through Soviet bloc training camps. The USSR military academy near Simferopol in the Crimea has graduated terrorists from such groups as Al Fatah, Popular Front for the Liberation of Palestine, and the Palestine Liberation Front. The official representative of the PLO at the United Nations reportedly confirmed that Palestinians receive arms, money, and training from the Soviet Union. Libyan defectors in Western Europe cite the existence of nearly twenty terrorist camps in their country under Cuban and East German control. Extensive military and guerrilla courses are given at schools located in Bulgaria, Czechoslovakia, East Germany, Hungary, and the USSR itself.[38]

DISINFORMATION AND MURDER

Activities of the above type are supplemented by other intelligence-related operations called "active measures," which, according to a Department of State report, include "a broad range of deceptive techniques—such as use of front groups, media manipulations, disinformation, forgeries, and agents of influence—to promote Soviet foreign policy goals and to undermine the position of USSR opponents."[39] Several of these have been dealt with earlier in this chapter as well as in the previous one. Long-term goals of Soviet active measures include the following:

1. to influence world public opinion against any foreign military, economic, and political programs perceived to threaten USSR objectives;

2. to demonstrate that the United States is "aggressive," "colonialist," and "imperialist";

3. to split the NATO alliance and discredit governments which cooperate with it;

4. to demonstrate that U.S. policies are incompatible with those of the Third World;

5. to discredit and weaken Western intelligence efforts, especially the CIA;

6. to undermine the West's political resolve in protecting its interests against Soviet encroachments.[40]

During the 1980s, many forgeries to promote the above objectives have surfaced throughout the world. Examples of falsified messages include the following: a bogus memo from the deputy secretary of state to the U.S. ambassador in Greece, suggesting American support for a military coup to preserve NATO bases; a letter to King Juan Carlos of Spain purportedly from President Reagan, naming royal advisors who were against that country's entry into the Western alliance; a forged memo from the Department of State about CIA contacts with the former president of Afghanistan, Hafizullah Amin. Other examples include a fake speech by the U.S. ambassador to the United Nations on American policy toward India; a forged West German government document accusing the United States of plotting to overthrow the regime in Ghana; another forgery from the American embassy in Nigeria, ordering the assassination of that country's leading presidential candidate; a bogus AFL-CIO letter and a falsified National Security Council memorandum "proving" United States responsibility for the troubles in Poland; a forged note to the defense minister of Austria from the U.S. ambassador; and a "secret document" showing that President Reagan had authorized deployment of 48 nuclear weapons on Iceland in case of war. Disinformation reportedly costs the USSR some $4 billion per year. [41]

In an address to the American Bar Association, U.S. Attorney General William French Smith disclosed that the KGB had mailed racist letters (allegedly from the Ku Klux Klan) before the 1984 Summer Olympics to more than twenty African and Asian countries threatening their athletes. None stayed away from the Los Angeles games. The envelopes were postmarked in northern Virginia or Prince George's County, Maryland, both easily accessible to Soviet intelligence officers from their embassy in Washington, D.C. Linguistic and forensic analysis proved beyond any doubt that the letters had been manufactured and mailed by the KGB. Toward the end of that same year, Soviet media continued to publish reports accusing the United States of having instigated the murder of Mrs. Indira Gandhi.

Finally, assassination of political opponents by the KGB, and more recently by a client secret service in Eastern Europe, has continued as state policy. Soviet intelligence officer Bogdan Stashinskii liquidated two anti-communist Ukrainian leaders in Munich. Lev Rebet and Stefan Bandera were both killed with the same cyanide spray gun at different times. The assassin, decorated personally by then KGB chief Aleksandr N. Shelepin, balked at a third assignment and surrendered to West German police. He received an eight-year prison sentence as an "accomplice" to murder.[42] Attacks on Bulgarian émigrés occurred in both London and Paris. Georgi Markov and Vladimir Kostov, two ex-members of the communist party in their native country, became victims of assassination attempts. The former died from the effects of a ricin-filled metallic pellet fired from an umbrella; the latter survived a similar attempt in Paris.[43] These attacks had been carried out by the Bulgarian intelligence service, most probably with KGB permission.

As a matter of fact, strong circumstantial evidence indicates that the USSR ordered the assassination of Pope John Paul II because of his influence on the Solidarity movement in Poland. A citizen of Turkey named Mehmet Ali Agca, who fired the shots and is now in an Italian prison, told reporters that he had been trained by the KGB in both Syria and Bulgaria. The plot presumably had the approval of secret police chief Iurii Andropov himself. State prosecutor Dr. Antonio Albano, interviewed in Rome, expressed his personal belief in the Soviet-Bulgarian connection based on the 25,000 pages of documentation in the case. Defectors from the Bulgarian state security service have revealed that the KGB decided to farm out political assassinations about ten years ago and that 400 Soviet intelligence officers help devise clandestine programs and policies in Sofia.[44]

There is no question about a Bulgarian connection in the plot to assassinate the pope. Italian magistrate Dr. Ilario Martella devoted nineteen months to a careful investigation that included testimony by a former Bulgarian diplomat, Iordan Mantarov, who had informed French authorities in 1983 about the details of the plan. Finally, the state prosecutor's 78-page report the following year explicitly contends that the plot originated with and had been paid for by the "Bulgarian secret services." A total of three Bulgarians and five Turks were acquitted on 29 March 1986 "for lack of proof," although the Jesuit journal *La Civiltà Cattolica* subsequently concluded that the attack on the pope had resulted from an "international plot."[45]

The Bulgarian, Cuban, and Nicaraguan governments also have been assisting smugglers in supplying narcotics to the United States, according to Francis M. Muller, Jr., head of the U.S. Drug Enforcement Administration. As much as 10 percent of the heroin comes through Bulgaria. A deputy assistant secretary of state has testified that Fidel Castro himself and high-ranking Nicaraguan officials are involved with cocaine smuggling from Colombia into the United States.[46]

Back in the USSR the Main Intelligence Directorate (GRU) of the Soviet armed forces, under General of the Army P. I. Ivashutin, has organized about 30,000 men and women into special units called *Spetsnaz*, which are assigned to assassinate civilian and military leaders of NATO countries in time of war. They have orders to engage in other acts of terror as well as sabotage. *Spetsnaz* (that is, units with "special designation") located at Murmansk would attack targets in Norway.[47] Although assigned to military intelligence, these units are also a part of the regular armed forces, discussed in the next chapter.

NOTES

1. William Hood, *The Mole* (New York: W. W. Norton, 1982), p. 283.
2. Oleg V. Penkovskiy, *The Penkovskiy Papers* (Garden City, N.Y.: Doubleday, 1965), p. 411; Hood, *Mole*, pp. 284–87.
3. Arnold Beichman and Mikhail S. Bernstam, *Andropov* (New York: Stein & Day, 1983).
4. Alexander G. Rahr, "Chebrikov Replaces Fedorchuk as Head of KGB," *Radio Liberty Research Bulletin* (Munich), 12 January 1983; RL 25/83; *Pravda*, 27 December 1983; Moscow radio, 19 April 1984; ibid., 7 March 1986.

5. Named after the first head of the secret police. I. A. Doroshenko et al., *Feliks Edmundovich Dzerzhinskii: Biografiia* (Moscow: Politizdat, 1983). See also "A Felix for Russia," *The Economist*, 26 October 1985, p. 51. The KGB employs more than 700,000 individuals, according to Philip Taubman in the *New York Times*, 14 September 1986.

6. John Barron, *KGB Today: The Hidden Hand* (New York: Reader's Digest Press, 1983), pp. 444–51.

7. U.S. Congress, House, Permanent Select Committee on Intelligence, Subcommittee on Oversight, *Hearings on Soviet Active Measures*, 97th Cong., 2nd sess., 1982, p. 235. See also Ladislav Bittman, *The KGB and Disinformation* (Washington, D.C.: Pergamon-Brassey's, 1985), esp. pp. 35–69.

8. International Institute of Strategic Studies, *The Military Balance, 1985– 1986* (London: 1985), p. 30.

9. Maj. Gen. Charles Andrew Willoughby, *Shanghai Conspiracy* (New York: Dutton, 1952), documents this case. His information came from captured Japanese files.

10. According to his tombstone, this man had been born William Henry Fisher in England, the son of Russian émigrés (*New York Times*, 27 August 1972).

11. John Barron, *KGB: The Secret Work of Soviet Secret Agents* (New York: Bantam Books, 1974), pp. 413–15. For a "defector" who returned to Moscow, see the case of Vitaliy S. Yurchenko in *Insight*, 18 November 1985, p. 79; *New York Times*, 10 August 1986.

12. William F. Buckley, *Inside the KGB*, transcript of 9 June 1983 *Firing Line* program with authors John Barron and Arnaud de Borchgrave (Columbia, S.C.: Southern Educational Communications Association, 1983), p. 13. See also Thierry Wolten, *Le KGB en France* (Paris: Bernard Grasset, 1986); *Wall Street Journal*, 13 September 1985, p. 27; *New York Times*, 25 October 1986; R.K. Bennett, "Expelled," *Reader's Digest*, January 1987, pp. 47–52.

13. A new law, Article 13–1 of the Soviet penal code, against revealing any official information to foreigners appeared in *Vedomosti Verkhovnogo Soveta SSSR*, no. 3 (18 January 1984): 91–93, which would seem to reinforce such sanctions. It was supplemented by Article 380, ibid., no. 22 (1 July 1984).

14. Barron, *The Hidden Hand*, p. 240. FBI director William H. Webster in ABA Law and National Security, *Intelligence Report* 7, no. 12 (December 1985): 7, on numbers; U.S. Senate, Select Committee on Intelligence, *Soviet Presence in the U.N. Secretariat* 99th Cong., 1st Sess. (Washington, D.C.: GPO, 1985); Thomas E. L. Dewey, "Soviet Espionage at the United Nations," *Heritage Foundation Backgrounder* (Washington, D.C., 30 April 1986), p. 2; *Wall Street Journal*, 3 October 1986, p. 24.

15. *Facts on File*, 4 May 1979, p. 317; *San Francisco Chronicle*, 5 May 1980.

16. Heinz Vielain in *Welt am Sonntag* (Hamburg), 13 February 1983. See also "KGB Program für deutsche Urlauber," *Epoche* 9, no. 96 (10 September 1986); 13–15; *Bild* (Hamburg), 16 September 1986, pp. 1 and 4.

17. Thierry Wolton, *Le KGB en France,* pp. 221–28.

18. *Wall Street Journal,* 19 June 1984, p. 30; *New York Times,* 15 May and 1 July 1986, for the court case that overturned a libel sentence against the accuser of *Ethnos'* cooperation with the KGB.

19. *Izvestiia,* 15 July 1980. For backgrounds and activities of these individuals, see Douglas Sutherland, *The Fourth Man* (London: Secker & Warburg, 1980). The Philby case is discussed in detail in Robert J. Lamphere, *The FBI-KGB War* (New York: Random House, 1986), pp. 228–47.

20. *New York Times,* 6 January 1980. Blunt died three years after the public disclosure (ibid., 29 March 1983). MacLean's death in Moscow came two weeks earlier, according to *Izvestiia,* 12 March 1983, p. 6.

21. U.S. House, Permanent Select Committee on Intelligence, *Soviet Active Measures,* pp. 138–69; interview in *Der Spiegel,* 14 February 1983, pp. 122–33; and John Barron, "The Spy Who Knew Too Much," *Reader's Digest,* June 1983, pp. 130, 207–14; Bittman, *The KGB and Soviet Disinformation,* pp. 61–64, for other examples; and "Agent of Influence," in *Disinformation,* no. 3 (Summer 1986): 10.

22. Lyman B. Kirkpatrick, Jr., "Soviet Espionage," in Kirkpatrick and Howland H. Sargeant, *Soviet Political Warfare Techniques* (New York: National Strategy Information Center, 1972), p. 21; Jeffrey Richelson, *Sword and Shield* (Cambridge, Mass.: Ballinger, 1986), p. 85.

23. Kirkpatrick, *Warfare,* p. 28.

24. Robert Lindsey, *The Falcon and the Snowman* (New York: Simon & Schuster, 1979), relates the story of Christopher Boyce and John Lee, who cooperated in delivering these materials, stolen from the TRW aerospace company, to the Soviet embassy in Mexico City.

25. This number includes the 25 spies at the U.N. and 55 from Washington, D.C., as well as San Francisco, expelled in October 1986. John Barron, "Why We Are Easy Prey for Spies," *Reader's Digest,* March 1986, pp. 49–54; *Insight,* 23 June 1986, pp. 6–15; *New York Times,* 15 July 1986 and 15 October 1986; *Wall Street Journal,* 23 October 1986, p. 8; *New York Times,* 17 December 1986, for Pelton case.

26. Barron, *Secret Work,* pp. 27–28 and 198; Kirkpatrick, *Warfare,* p. 30.

27. Yao Ming-le, *The Conspiracy and Death of Lin Biao* (New York: Knopf, 1983), claims that Lin Biao had been assassinated by Mao's body guards and that the son, Lin Liguo, died in the airplane crash.

28. Hu is quoted in *Far Eastern Economic Review* (Hong Kong), 23 June 1983, p. 13. Beijing radio, 16 March 1982, in *FBIS,* 23 March 1982, warned the Chinese population that Soviet espionage had increased. See *Insight,* 28 July 1986, p. 39, for the PRC protest.

29. Samuel T. Francis, *The Soviet Strategy of Terror* (Washington, D.C.: Heritage Foundation, 1981), p. 34; Roberta Goren, *The Soviet Union and Terrorism*

(London: Allen & Unwin, 1984), pp. 194–99; Hesh Kestin, "Terror's Bottom Line," *Forbes,* 2 June 1986, pp. 38–40.

30. Ghana, Ministry of Information, *Nkrumah's Subversion in Africa: Documentary Evidence of Nkrumah's Interference in the Affairs of Other African States* (Accra-Tema: State Publishing Corporation, n.d.). It is conceivable but not probable that these activities remained unknown to Nkrumah.

31. Barron, *Secret Work,* pp. 317–39.

32. Richard F. Staar, ed., *1972 Yearbook on International Communist Affairs* (Stanford: Hoover Institution Press, 1972), pp. 289–93.

33. John Duke Anthony, "People's Democratic Republic of Yemen," in ibid., 1984, pp. 70–74; Robert W. Stookey, "Yemen" in Stookey, ed., *The Arabian Peninsula* (Stanford: Hoover Institution Press, 1984), pp. 96–107; Stephen Page, *The Soviet Union and the Yemens.* (New York: Praeger, 1985).

34. Anthony Arnold, *Afghanistan's Two-Party Communism* (Stanford: Hoover Institution Press, 1983), pp. 127–34; Thomas T. Hammond, *Red Flag over Afghanistan* (Boulder, Colo.: Westview Press, 1984), pp. 97–104; *The Military Balance, 1985–1986,* p. 22.

35. Claire Sterling, *The Terror Network* (New York: Holt, Rinehart & Winston, 1981). The FBI reportedly has documented the KGB role in supporting extreme terrorist factions in the United States, according to Eugene H. Methvin, "Terror Networks, U.S.A.," *Reader's Digest,* December 1984, p. 114. See also William H. Webster, "Terrorism as a Crime," *FBI Law Enforcement Bulletin:* 55, no. 5 (May 1986): 11–13.

36. Herbert Romerstein, *Soviet Support for International Terrorism* (Washington, D.C.: Foundation for Democratic Education, 1981); U.S. Department of State, "Terrorism: Overview and Developments," *Current Policy,* no. 744 (Washington, D.C.: 13 September 1985). The PLO has had a diplomatic mission in the USSR for more than ten years, according to Moscow radio, 16 June 1986; *FBIS,* 18 June 1986, pp. H 1–2.

37. Sterling, *Terror Network,* p. 292. See also Elbridge Durbrow and Charles J. V. Murphy, "Terrorism and Wars of National Liberation," *Situation Report* 3, nos. 3–4 (Washington, D.C., Security and Intelligence Fund, Summer 1982 and Spring 1983); U.S. Dept. of Defense, "Soviet Support to Terrorism," *Soviet Military Power* (Washington, D.C., March 1986), pp. 124–28.

38. William J. Casey, "Speech to Commonwealth Club in San Francisco," 3 April 1984, p. 4 of transcript; U.S. Department of State, "International Terrorism," *Gist,* August 1985; Thomas L. Friedman, "Loose-Linked Network of Terror," *New York Times,* 28 April 1986.

39. U.S. Department of State, "Soviet Use of Active Measures," *Current Policy* no. 761, 18 September 1985. Some 15,000 individuals work on these projects in Moscow, according to Richard H. Shultz and Roy Godson, *Dezinformatsia: Active Measures in Soviet Strategy* (McLean, Va.: Pergamon-Brassey's International Defense Publishers, 1984), pp. 155–57.

40. U.S. Congress, House, Permanent Select Committee on Intelligence, *Soviet Active Measures*, p. 33.

41. Shultz and Godson, *Dezinformatsia*, pp. 155–57; *U.S. News & World Report*, 20 August 1984, p. 36; *New York Times*, 18 November 1984; Stockholm radio, 5 December 1984, in *FBIS* the following day; *Washington Post*, 29 December 1985, p. B7; *Insight*, 1 December 1986, pp. 26–29; Gary Thatcher in *Christian Science Monitor*, 11 December 1986, for more recent forgeries.

42. Karl Anders, *Mord auf Befehl* (Tübingen/Neckar: Schlichtenmayer, 1963).

43. Harry Rositzke, *KGB: The Eyes of Russia* (New York: Doubleday, 1981), p. 114; Georgi Markov, *The Truth That Killed* (London: Weidenfeld & Nicolson, 1983).

44. Paul B. Henze, *The Plot to Kill the Pope* (New York: Scribner's, 1983), pp. 153–80. See also Claire Sterling, *The Time of the Assassins* (New York: Holt, Rinehart & Winston, 1983); and David Shiflett, "Solving the Plot to Kill the Pope," *Reader's Digest*, October 1984, pp. 83–89, at p. 86. See also Z. M. Rurarz, "A KGB Role in Polish Priest's Murder?" *Wall Street Journal*, 2 November 1984, p. 22, which discusses the killing of Father Jerzy Popieluszko by the secret police in Poland. Sterling in *New York Times*, 21 November 1986, discusses the Bulgarian connection.

45. Antonio Albano, *Report of State Prosecutor's Office* (Rome, Italy: Appeals Courts, 28 March 1984), p. 76 of the English translation; *New York Times*, 8 June 1986, for the acquittal and quotations from the Jesuit journal. See also "Italian Judge Doubts Bulgarian Alibi," *New York Times*, 12 November 1986, p. 3.

46. "Drugs and Communist Connection," *New York Times*, 13 September 1984, p. 9; "Communist Connections in the Global Drug Trade?" *Christian Science Monitor*, 20 December 1983, p. 18; *Castro and the Narcotics Connection: The Cuban Government's Use of Narcotics Trafficking to Finance and Promote Terrorism* (Washington, D.C.: Cuban American National Foundation, 1983); Voice of America editorial broadcast on 23 September 1984, reflecting views of the U.S. government.

47. Former GRU major, Viktor Suvorov, *Inside the Aquarium* (New York: MacMillan, 1986), pp. 31–40, discusses Spetsnaz. See also U.S. Department of Defense, *Soviet Military Power* (Washington, D.C.: March 1986), p. 72; James Markham in the *New York Times*, 2 November 1986; *Washington Times*, 12 November 1986, p. 3A.

6

MILITARY STRATEGY

USSR attitudes toward military strategy differ fundamentally from those of Western leaders and military experts. In the Soviet view, the objective is defined as a "program of action for ensuring military-technical superiority over the armed forces of the probable enemies."[1] Principles are determined by the political leadership, that is, the Defense Council, which receives advice from the highest-ranking military officers. Mikhail S. Gorbachev, general secretary of the CPSU since March 1985, also holds the position of Defense Council chairman.[2]

A country's strategic doctrine may be influenced by its geographic location, the characteristics of its people, as well as its economic resources, ideology, and foreign policy objectives. Taking all these elements into account, Soviet military strategists actively study the nature of future war, how to prepare for different types of conflict, means of organizing the armed forces, and methods for conducting warfare. As expressed succinctly by a former USSR defense minister, "We have never and will never hide the basic fundamental provisions of our military doctrine. They are expressed with utter clarity in the policy of the communist party and the Soviet government and in the status of our armed forces."[3]

The composition of the ten-man Defense Council during peacetime reportedly includes five Politburo members (Gorbachev, Ligachev, Ryzhkov, Shevardnadze, Chebrikov) and Deputy Prime Minister and Military-Industrial Commission Head Iu. D. Masliukov. The High Command, apart from the defense minister, Sokolov, is represented by only three other military officers: Marshals S. F. Akhromeev (chief-of-staff) and V. G. Kulikov (Warsaw Pact commander), as well as General of the Army A. D. Lizichev (chief of the Main Political Directorate).[4] The existence of this body, which is similar to the U.S. National Security Council, was revealed in early 1976, shortly before Brezhnev's promotion to the rank of marshal became officially known.

Another source lists a core of six members of the Defense Council in wartime: the CPSU general secretary, the defense minister, the chief of the General Staff, the KGB head, the USSR prime minister, the Gosplan chairman, plus others as required.[5] The basic difference between this list and the "peacetime" list is that the former includes Masliukov, who directs the government's military-industrial commission. In addition, the second list includes the chief of Gosplan, N. V. Talyzin, currently a first deputy prime minister.

The Defense Council is also mentioned in the 1977 constitution as the successor of two previous organs (the Supreme Military Council at the Defense Ministry and the Defense Committee of the Soviet government) and apparently now performs the functions of both. Its mandate remains to develop the armed forces on the basis of wartime experience, to coordinate national defense, and to expand the military potential of the country.[6]

There seems to be some disagreement among American scholars concerning Soviet military doctrine. One critic has discerned at least six Western schools of thought regarding the interpretation of USSR strategy—"primitive," "convergent," "neo-Clausewitzian," "Talmudic," "imperial," and "eclectic"—which suggests that single-factor models may not be too useful. However, at the most basic level, one should always be careful to distinguish between real Soviet military writers and journalists, even those among the latter who ostensibly advise CPSU politicians, yet whose chief function frequently is in fact to influence (and mislead) the informed elites of the West.[7]

TYPES OF WARFARE

It is safe to say that military thinking in the USSR revolves around certain major themes. Soviet commentators divide world conflicts into several categories: "general" wars; "national liberation" or civil conflicts; low intensity or geographically limited wars; and what Western strategists would call "police actions." A war becomes classified on the basis of its political nature, the class structure of the belligerent powers, the size of the military conflict, and the means used in the application of armed force.[8]

According to Soviet strategy, a conflict can be either just or unjust, and USSR military doctrine claims to support only just wars. The conclusion to be drawn from this point is that *any* conflict in which Moscow participates is just *by definition*. The same holds true for wars between "socialist" (that is, communist) and capitalist countries: they are always just on the communist side. The most just conflicts of all are those fought in defense of the Soviet Union. It is claimed that no political compromise will be allowed and that, in such a case, all resources at the disposal of the state are to be employed for this purpose.[9] Moreover, USSR strategy emphasizes that retribution will be taken against all defeated countries and/or coalitions.

From the Soviet point of view, there are four types of international class conflict: wars between two diametrically opposed social systems (that is, capitalist and socialist), national liberation struggles, civil strife, and wars between capitalist states. The size of a military conflict may range from local to worldwide in extent. It is the latter to which Moscow assigns highest priority, although USSR strategy recognizes that a global war can escalate from a more limited one. Because of this danger, advance preparation remains the first priority throughout the Eastern bloc.[10] In a world war, Soviet resources will be used to destroy "imperialism" (that is, the Western democracies) as a system. The USSR develops all of its weapons, nuclear and non-nuclear, with such an eventuality in mind. As a result, the evolution of weapons simply follows advances in technology. Radical changes are not encouraged.[11]

The USSR Versus the United States

From the Soviet standpoint, the principal means used in a global or world war would involve strategic nuclear forces in general and ICBMs in particular, as these are capable of attaining objectives directly. However, USSR strategy emphasizes that ultimate victory requires effective and wide-scale employment of other branches of the armed forces: ground, air, navy, anti-air and anti-missile defense, as well as civil defense. Furthermore, large reserves for all categories are necessary to support front-line troops and, hence, the national economy itself is structured for total mobilization. Indeed, even in peacetime, the Soviet economy appears to be almost, if not already, on a war footing.

USSR strategists emphasize that it is imperative, under conditions of general or world war, that Moscow strike first. This, according to

Soviet strategy, is by far the best way to seize the strategic initiative.[12] In other words, success will result from the application of surprise and pre-emption. Principal land targets are located throughout the continental United States and Western Europe. Other objectives would include severing maritime lines of communication between those two areas in the Atlantic as well as others in the Pacific; damaging or destroying Western intelligence-gathering capabilities, which are not limited to satellites; and generally confronting the United States and its allies with a series of *faits accomplis,* whereby escalation of the war would be to Soviet advantage.

Peripheral theaters of military operations include western, northwestern, southwestern, southern, and far eastern so-called TVDs. The Atlantic, Arctic, Indian, and Pacific oceans are also designated as individual theaters of military operations. The USSR navy currently has forward bases in Angola, Cuba, Ethiopia, Vietnam, and South Yemen.[13] It is building one at São Tomé and Principe.

Warsaw Pact Versus NATO

Soviet strategy in an attack against Western Europe would be partly dictated by geography. The three main strategic invasion routes include the northern plain, the Fulda gap, and the Hof corridor from East Germany, where the largest concentration of forces is stationed. The five USSR divisions in Czechoslovakia since the August 1968 occupation of that country, along with other Soviet divisions deployed in Hungary and Poland, would add considerable military power to assault formations moving West.[14] It is probable that a violation of Austria's neutrality would occur. At the same time, the USSR must assume that Southern Europe and the Balkans might become a NATO target, if Warsaw Pact troops support the main drive towards the English Channel.

A successful occupation of Western Europe by the East would destroy the main forces of NATO, deny the United States a beachhead for counterattack, acquire resources to substitute for those lost in the event of a retaliatory strike with nuclear weapons against the Soviet homeland, and provide a possible safe haven for Warsaw Pact troops. All of this is based on the assumption that the administration in Washington, D.C., would be reluctant to attack NATO territory with nuclear missiles—an attack that would have the effect of destroying Western Europe in order to save it.

Nonetheless, the foregoing scenario would require USSR reinforcements to cross Eastern Europe, the northern tier of which may no longer be considered by the Soviet military to be entirely reliable. It has been reported, for example, that the USSR stores nuclear munitions in East Germany, Czechoslovakia, and Poland[15] but does not allow access to these warheads by these or other members of the Warsaw Treaty Organization. Whether the Czechs and Slovaks would fight willingly on behalf of their occupation power remains doubtful. Events since 1980 seem to indicate that Polish troops also could be unreliable, and the East Germans most probably are not trusted by the Soviets. The southern tier[16] poses even more complicated problems, since Yugoslavia has never belonged to the Warsaw Pact.

Other Conflicts

The USSR looks upon wars of "national liberation" as low-risk opportunities for expanding its influence while avoiding the danger of direct confrontation with the West. Indeed, the latter has been the loser in all such struggles to date, whether by limiting its intervention or by a kind of default. Over a period of only six years, Ethiopia (1974), South Vietnam (1975), Angola and Mozambique (1975), Afghanistan (1979), and Nicaragua (1980) fell successively into the hands of totalitarian ruling groups closely aligned with the USSR. The East had hopes to score a similar victory in El Salvador. Leaders in Moscow have watched as the West squandered manpower, money, and prestige where modern weapons could not be employed effectively. According to a former USSR defense minister: "In its foreign policy initiatives, the Soviet state actively . . . supports the national liberation struggle . . . in whatever distant region of our planet it may appear"[17] (see Table 6.1).

It is noteworthy that lower-intensity or geographically limited conflicts have occurred in 150 instances during the first four decades after World War II, yet only one escalated into a major confrontation between the superpowers.[18] That took place in October 1973 during a worldwide United States alert, when it became known that USSR armed forces had threatened to intervene if Israel refused to halt its offensive against Egypt. Moscow did not dispatch any troops and possibly never intended to do so.

According to Soviet military writers, war even in Central Europe may remain "limited" as long as NATO does not use *tactical* nuclear weapons. In practice, however, nuclear escalation would almost certainly take place. Warsaw Pact maneuvers—including ones as far back as 1965, code-named "October Storm"—have included scenarios with simulated battlefield nuclear explosions triggered by both sides.[19]

In USSR strategy, a police action represents the lowest level of

TABLE 6.1
MAJOR SOVIET EQUIPMENT DELIVERED TO THE THIRD WORLD, 1980–1985

	Total	Near East and South Asia	Sub-Saharan Africa	Latin America	East Asia and Pacific
Tanks/self-propelled guns	5,015	3,600	630	505	280
Light armor	8,095	6,565	1,000	280	250
Artillery	7,145	3,810	2,050	895	390
Major surface combatants	39	26	4	4	5
Minor surface combatants	145	27	21	49	48
Submarines	9	7	0	2	0
Missile attack boats	37	16	9	6	6
Supersonic aircraft	2,085	1,340	340	135	270
Subsonic aircraft	130	120	5	0	5
Helicopters	1,040	695	190	80	75
Other combat aircraft	440	250	70	40	80
Surface-to-air-missiles	14,020	10,400	1,890	1,300	430

SOURCES: U.S. Department of Defense, *Soviet Military Power, 1986* (Washington, D.C.: GPO, 1986), p. 131.

conflict, where Moscow expects little or no resistance. Such was the case when, fulfilling their "international duty," Soviet armed forces suppressed East Germany (1953), Hungary (1956), Czechoslovakia (1968), and most recently Afghanistan (1979–present). Formal ideas of sovereignty and national independence will not prevent the USSR from intervening where communist party rule is threatened by so-called counterrevolutionaries (which is why the Soviets invaded Hungary but held back in Poland that same year). It is the concept of the inviolability of communist party rule that lies at the heart of the so-called "Brezhnev Doctrine," discussed in Chapter 1. The foregoing examples also illustrate the fact that to date the Soviets have never launched an attack unless they have had an overwhelming chance for success.

SOVIET MILITARY CAPABILITIES

As mentioned in the foregoing, all five military services would participate in a coordinated arms offensive: Strategic Rocket, Ground, Air, Navy, and Air Defense forces. According to authoritative information,[20] the USSR has 5.9 million citizens in uniform, including border guard, internal security, railroad, and construction troops. Between 1.7 and 2.0 million young men are called up for two or three years of active duty annually (depending on the branch), and the same number are subsequently discharged into the reserve forces. As a consequence, Soviet reserves total more than 25 million trained men.

Strategic Rocket Forces

The Strategic Rocket Forces (SRF) comprise 300,000 men, plus some 50,000 civilians. Commanded by Marshal Iu. P. Maksimov, in the mid-1980s they were servicing 1,398 on-line ICBM launchers as well as more than 600 medium-range launchers, including almost 450 of the SS-20 variety with three multiple independently targeted (MIRV) warheads each as well as refire capabilities of at least one reload per launcher. The SS-20 can be upgraded to intercontinental-range, either by off-loading the MIRVs or adding a third booster. Six such SS-20s were test-fired, with dummy warheads from a complex near Kirov, along a polar trajectory toward the United States and destroyed over the Barents Sea. The majority of these launchers are positioned in the western parts of the USSR, facing NATO, with the remaining 162 deployed along the Chinese frontier.[21]

The Soviets have sought to achieve their goal of limiting damage to the USSR chiefly by deploying superior strategic *offensive* forces capable of pre-emptively destroying or neutralizing the power of all principal adversaries. In addition, Moscow has developed extensive air and missile defense systems. They are designed to defeat the *residue* of enemy nuclear forces not eliminated by pre-emptive offensive nuclear strikes. Before acquiring a comprehensive anti-ballistic missile system, the USSR maintains a civil defense program, including shelters, to protect the top political leadership as well as other key (10 to 20 percent of the total) population segments. Preference is given to those workers essential for continuation of economic activity during the war and for the post-attack recovery period.[22]

During the remainder of the 1980s, Soviet ICBM accuracy can be expected to improve (although it appears precise enough for military purposes already), as will target flexibility and discrimination. Through the end of the decade, MIRVed strategic missiles should be able to destroy any undefended fixed target in the United States with a single warhead. A second would also normally be used to increase certainty of success. This means, in effect, that the USSR should be able to destroy more than 90 percent of all American ICBM forces in their pre-launch configuration.[23] The United States continues to lack any comparable "counterforce" capability against Soviet ICBMs.

Even if one were to set aside the disparity between USSR and U.S. counterforce capabilities, the Soviet Union would still possess superiority in all indices of strategic power through the end of the 1980s. In recent years it has become more and more apparent that both the SALT I and SALT II agreements, the latter unratified by the U.S. Senate, succeeded more in providing an institutional justification for the USSR drive toward superiority than in controlling or reversing it. The unsettling fact remains that if deterrence were to fail in the current decade and war break out, it would be to Soviet advantage to attack U.S. forces directly and without any warning.[24] Trends in the strategic buildup have been the product of deliberate decisions taken quite consciously by the USSR leadership (see Figure 6.1). For many years, the Soviet Union was depicted by a large number of Western commentators and strategists as technologically unsophisticated regarding the nuances of war in the nuclear age. This turns out to have represented a preconception without any basis in fact. During the mid-1960s, decision makers in Washington, D.C., formulated a nuclear posture designed above all to avoid conflict. The hope was that their Moscow counterparts would reciprocate. Instead, the Kremlin deliberately chose to develop weapons commensurate with a war-fighting posture.[25] Many U.S. leaders believed that by engaging the USSR in forums such as SALT, Western negotiators could help reverse the Soviet war-fighting and war-survival orientation. This expectation never achieved fulfillment.

Ground Forces

The army, the largest service in the Soviet military establishment, is commanded by Gen. E. F. Ivanovskii and comprises 1,995,000 men. It is organized into 7 airborne, 51 armored, and 141 motorized rifle divisions. Only half of these 199 major units are at full strength, yet they dispose of approximately 52,600 tanks and 77,500 armored personnel carriers, fighting vehicles, and scout cars, as well as 33,000 artillery pieces and 1,500 nuclear capable surface-to-surface missile launchers, not to mention anti-aircraft or mobile surface-to-air missile systems organic to all ground divisions. The latter fall into three categories of combat readiness: (1) three-fourths to full strength, completely equipped; (2) between half and three-quarters manned, with all fighting vehicles; and (3) below half-strength, with some obsolescent equipment.[26]

Deployments include 31 divisions in Eastern Europe (20 in East Germany, 2 in Poland, 4 in Hungary, and 5 in Czechoslovakia), with a total of 16,500 tanks and 565,000 men. All these forces are at category-one readiness. Military districts in the European parts of the Soviet Union have 65 divisions, about half in category one. In addition, there are 16 divisions in the central USSR strategic reserve, 30 divisions in the south (most of the latter probably would be in category three), and some 52 divisions along the Sino-Soviet border (all in categories one or two). The remaining 6 divisions are in Afghanistan, probably at full strength. USSR ground forces are also stationed abroad, outside of Eastern Europe, in more than 21 countries (see Table 6.2).

The Soviet Group of Forces in Germany (SGFG) disposes of 380,000 troops with 10,500 tanks (not counting those held in reserve), about 2,400 fighting vehicles, and 1,200 aircraft. The Third Assault Army alone has 55,000 men, about 1,200 tanks and 1,100 fighting vehicles, in addition to new battlefield missiles (SS-21, -23, and -22) and artillery. The SS-22, deployed starting in early 1984, has a range of about 950 kilometers, which equals that of the Pershing II missile, about which Western pacifists raise such objections. However, the Soviet 500 kiloton warhead is twice the size carried by the U.S. model.[27] The central core of SGFG comprises 200 battalion-size combat groups. These forces could achieve several breakthroughs simultaneously. The Soviet order of battle in East Germany has not changed since the late

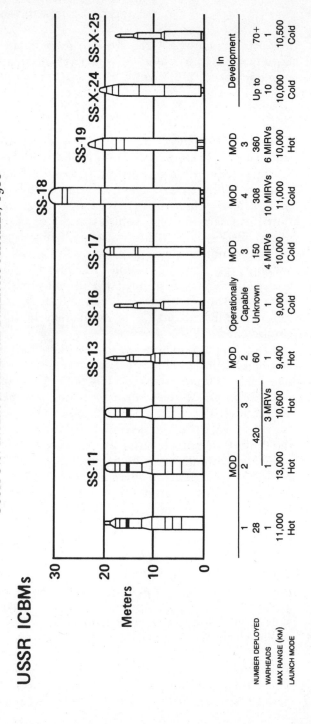

FIGURE 6.1

USSR/U.S. INTERCONTINENTAL BALLISTIC MISSILES, 1986

U.S. ICBMs

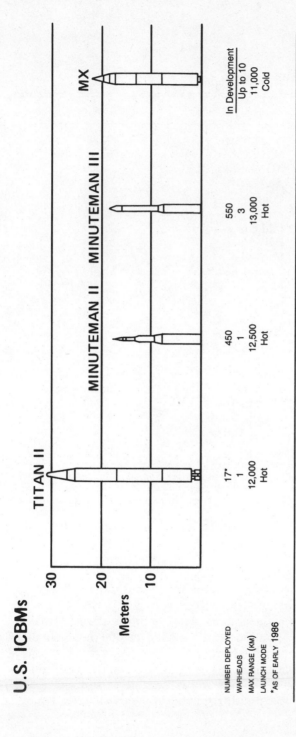

	TITAN II	MINUTEMAN II	MINUTEMAN III	MX
NUMBER DEPLOYED	17*	450	550	In Development
WARHEADS	1	1	3	Up to 10
MAX RANGE (KM)	12,000	12,500	13,000	11,000
LAUNCH MODE	Hot	Hot	Hot	Cold

*AS OF EARLY 1986

SOURCE: U.S. Department of Defense, *Soviet Military Power, 1986* (Washington, D.C.: GPO, 1986), p. 26.

TABLE 6.2
SOVIET ARMED FORCES ABROAD, 1986

	Country	Number
1.	Afghanistan	118,000[a]
2.	Mongolia	65,000
3.	Algeria	1,000
4.	Angola	1,500
5.	Congo	100
6.	Cuba	8,000
7.	Ethiopia	1,500
8.	India	200
9.	Iraq	600
10.	Kampuchea	200
11.	Laos	500
12.	Libya	2,000
13.	Mali	200
14.	Mozambique	300
15.	Nicaragua	50
16.	Peru	160
17.	Syria	4,000
18.	Vietnam	2,500
19.	Yemen, North	500
20.	Yemen, South	1,500
21.	Africa (rest)	900
Total		208,710[b]

NOTES: [a]Some 50,000 additional airborne troops, stationed on adjoining Soviet territory, are used as a quick reaction force on raids inside Afghanistan.
[b]This total does not include the 565,000 Soviet troops in East Germany, Czechoslovakia, Hungary, and Poland.
SOURCE: International Institute for Strategic Studies, *The Military Balance, 1986–1987* (London, 1986), p. 46.

1960s, except for internal reorganization and a consistent yet substantial increase in firepower combined with a reduction in the portion of forces qualifying as support elements. Each motorized rifle division now disposes of eighteen battalions and a total of 12,000 men—smaller than a NATO division yet much stronger.

A successful Warsaw Pact offensive is predicated on the assumption that forward deployed NATO units will be unable to stop an attack without large-scale and rapid reinforcement. Western alliance deployments still reflect to some extent zones of occupation agreed upon in 1945, as devised by the Allied Control Commission, rather than current logistic and tactical requirements. The Soviet offensive strategy would be one of envelopment, probably attempting to split the northern and southern zones with the Third Assault Army.

The first objective of such an offensive might be to seize or destroy American nuclear weapon stockpiles maintained in West Germany. Physical occupation of as much territory as possible would follow, in order to prevent any rapid reinforcement and to encourage political disintegration. In contrast to Western thinking, there exists no "short war" versus "long war" controversy in Soviet military thought. A briefer conflict is preferred,[28] although capabilities for a protracted struggle are in place. If attained, strategists in Moscow reason, a quick victory might preclude expansion of the conflict to other theaters, such as northeast Asia or in the area between eastern Turkey and the Soviet republic of Armenia. However, the emphasis given to modernizing USSR ground forces should be evidence enough of determination to prosecute a long war, if necessary.

Warsaw Pact forces require a minimum of maneuver prior to attack. Hence, the West may be relying on questionable assumptions with regard to the warning that will be available before an Eastern offensive. It is not clear whether NATO will even have sufficient time for mobilization. What is more, Soviet leaders can assume relatively soberly that the Americans will not be the first to use nuclear weapons, unless faced with imminent defeat at the conventional level. The East's use of such weapons, meanwhile, would necessitate rapid dispersal of Western anti-tank forces, putting NATO at a serious disadvantage. This in turn could influence the main directions of a Warsaw Pact attack, leading to a new allocation of tactical resources, more use of artillery and of chemical weapons, and prosecution of the general ground offensive at the highest possible rates of speed.[29]

The Air Forces

The 570,000-man Soviet Air Force under Marshal A. N. Efimov is divided into three components: long-range, frontal, and transport aviation. Frontal aviation, the most important one, disposes of sixteen air armies, four of which are deployed throughout Eastern Europe and the others allocated to the twelve most important military districts. About 5,900 combat aircraft plus 4,000 interceptors and 2,830 armed helicopters belong to these forces. Military transport includes approximately 600 aircraft and is augmented, both in peace and war, by the civilian airline Aeroflot, which currently maintains more than 1,400 passenger planes.

Not content with an output of about 600 new MiG-23 "Floggers" per year and doubling the production of Sukhoi-24 "Fencers," the USSR is turning out the Sukhoi-25 "Frogfoot" and the MiG-25 "Foxbat" as well as three new fighters equipped with look-down shoot-down radar.[30] Soviet aircraft deployed in the central region of Europe have improved markedly. They possess several times the weapons delivery and range of earlier models. These new developments have given frontal aviation the means to attack targets throughout all of Western Europe. Just as important, the current USSR rate of military aircraft production is almost twice that of the United States.[31] Long-range strategic aviation includes about 125 Bear and 45 Bison bombers, 300 Backfires, and the new Blackjack, which became operational in 1987.

General Naval Forces

The Soviet Navy, commanded by Fleet Admiral V. N. Chernavin, totals 480,000 men and includes a naval air arm of 1,185 planes, naval infantry (16,000 marines in five brigades), rocket and coastal artillery troops as well as four special forces (*Spetsnaz*) organized into twenty independent units. It has 1,469 surface combat ships, 62 intelligence collection vessels, about 371 submarines, and 331 auxiliaries for a grand total of 2,233 units afloat and in reserve. In addition, since 1975 the USSR has been deploying new classes of heavy cruisers—the latest being nuclear-powered, the largest non-carrier surface combatants ever built—as well as anti-submarine warfare ships. The first of eight large aircraft carriers is under construction, with a length of approximately 1,000 feet and space for 60 to 70 fighter planes. The latest cruise missile–firing attack submarine "Oscar" is about twice the size of any U.S. equivalent and is believed to have a titanium hull. The new Soviet ballistic missile–firing "Typhoon" displaces 27,000 tons or almost 50 percent more than the American "Trident" submarine.[32]

One of the four USSR fleets is on the Baltic Sea and consists of 45 submarines, about 185 surface ships, and 260 aircraft. Most of the naval schools are located in Leningrad, along with a major shipbuilding facility. The Black Sea fleet has 35 submarines, some 230 surface vessels, and 450 planes. A squadron of 40 to 50 additional ships in the Mediterranean is assigned from there. The most rapid expansion during the post–World War II era has occurred in the Pacific fleet. By the mid-1980s, it had grown to include 90 submarines, about 295 surface ships, and 510 aircraft. Between 20 and 25 of the ships are stationed at Cam Ranh Bay in Vietnam. The Northern fleet is somewhat smaller, consisting of approximately 247 surface ships and 425 aircraft. Primary strength lies in its 141 submarines. In the event of a global conflict with the United States, all of these Soviet fleets would have breakout difficulties in reaching the open oceans. The Northern fleet, however, has relatively less of a problem due to its access to the Barents Sea. An explosion in mid-1984 at Severomorsk on the Kola peninsula reportedly destroyed two-thirds of that fleet's surface-to-air and surface-to-surface missiles, killing several hundred persons.[33]

Air Defense Forces

The last of the five Soviet military services is Air Defense, which has 531,000 men (a significant increase over a two-year period) under Marshal A. I. Koldunov. Recent organizational changes may have placed these troops under operational control of the various military districts or groups of forces in Eastern Europe. The one exception to this structure is the Moscow Air Defense District. Apart from the 64 "Galosh" anti-ballistic missile (ABM) launchers with nuclear warheads in four complexes and eight sites around Moscow (now being upgraded to 100 ABM X-3 launchers), this branch disposes of 4,000 aircraft, some 9,600 surface-to-air missile launchers (with 14,000 launcher rails) in about 1,200 fixed sites, and approximately 7,000 warning systems, including satellites and early warning/ground control intercept radars. A new ABM system is reportedly being emplaced at Krasnoiarsk in Central Asia.[34] This development represents a treaty violation, discussed in Chapter 12.

Civil Defense

The USSR maintains two widespread shelter programs as far down as the city/rural/industrial level, with 1,500 hardened command post facilities within 120 kilometers of Moscow, providing accommodations for at least 175,000 high-ranking officials. The system has been assigned four basic missions: preparing for a possible nuclear attack, protecting the population, safeguarding national economic resources, and providing post-attack recovery and rescue operations.[35] Since 1961, civil defense has been under the control of the Defense Ministry and now encompasses both military as well as civilian components. There are an estimated 150,000 permanent staff in the various republics working in civil defense activities under a deputy defense minister,

General of the Army A. T. Altunin. The number of civilians engaged in similar duties probably totals several hundred thousand, both full-time and part-time. Sixteen million individuals could be mobilized for these tasks during wartime.[36]

In the Soviet view, post-attack recovery is essential to war planning and will play a key role in determining the winner of a nuclear war. To prepare for such a possible conflict, the USSR has dispersed and hardened many industrial sites; revised urban planning; made preparations to decontaminate agricultural areas; and stockpiled essential resources. Many deep bunkers and blast shelters can be found in USSR cities. The Soviet approach to nuclear conflict, therefore, definitely emphasizes "assured survival," as opposed to "assured destruction." Civil defense represents an integral component of overall USSR strategic preparedness. Combined with superior strategic offensive forces and a more dynamic strategy, it does demonstrate a commitment to war preparation and war survival unmatched by any country in the world.

Other Forces

To all of the foregoing must be added the paramilitary units. These include about 350,000 KGB border troops and 350,000 Internal Affairs Ministry, or MVD, domestic security personnel (uniformed police). Neither is subordinate to the Defense Ministry. Both, nevertheless, are considered to be parts of the Soviet armed forces in time of war.[37] The best units from the Red Army historically had been assigned to the border guards. As a result, they were the first to be attacked in June 1941 by German troops. Currently, they are equipped with a full panoply of modern weapons.

A civilian military training organization called DOSAAF (Volunteer Society for Cooperation with the Army, Air Force, and Navy) provides instruction to youth fifteen years of age and older at schools and workers' centers. It claims a membership of more than 80 million, some 5 million of whom are instructors and activists, organized into 330,000 units. A two-year long cycle of war games recently included participation by nearly 30 million adolescent boys and girls in the Young Pioneers (eight to fifteen years of age) who were given a taste of war, using blank ammunition. DOSAAF is headed by Admiral of the Fleet G. M. Egorov, suggesting that it plays an important role in the military-educational system.[38]

FUTURE PROSPECTS

The Saliut-7 space station continues to orbit the earth, with efforts directed toward deployment in 1990 of structures housing up to twelve persons. The Cosmos 1267 satellite has been identified by experts as a prototype that could serve the function of a building block for space stations larger than the current one, which weighs 660,000 pounds. Several years ago the former director of U.S. Air Force intelligence, Major General George Keegan, warned that eight out of every ten Soviet space launches were military in nature and that the Saliut station represented a huge orbiting military workshop. Saliut 7 has been joined since February 1986 by the Mir space station, which is 56 feet long and has five docking ports.[39]

Keegan is convinced that the USSR began working on a charged particle beam weapon some 20 to 25 years ago and had built an experimental facility at Semipalatinsk in south-central Asia, where Soviet scientists reportedly invented a "nuclear device to generate a giant electrical pulse" that could totally neutralize the American strategic deterrent if perfected. The chief of U.S. Air Force research and development, Lieutenant General Kelly Burke, has predicted that the USSR would be capable of building an operational laser weapon that could disable American space satellites. Reports indicate that a Soviet hunter-killer space vehicle had caught up with a target satellite over Eastern Europe and damaged it. The USSR has been conducting such experiments successfully since 1977, according to unclassified U.S. Department of Defense publications. As a result of these Soviet advances, the same sources report that "most [American] military systems are vulnerable to damage and require survivability enhancements."[40]

Although trends are difficult to project with any degree of absolute accuracy, it is now apparent that Kremlin decision makers have at least the capability to implement offensive options, depending upon where they place their priorities. During the period from 1971 through 1980, Soviet outlays for defense were at least 40 percent higher than those of the United States. During calendar year 1985, the USSR spent the equivalent of almost $400 billion (up from $155 billion for 1970) on its military—still 25 percent higher than the United States figure of $290 billion for 1986–1987, as voted by Congress.[41] The uniformed personnel strength of Soviet armed forces exceeds 5.9 million men, or more than twice the American level. All of this has been accomplished with a GNP only slightly over half that of the United States. What the future holds, of course, is a preponderance of USSR military capability during the late 1980s and potentially beyond.

Whether or not the Soviets decide to pursue a more openly aggressive policy against the West, and specifically NATO, will depend upon the decision makers in the Kremlin. However, it is unsettling to recall that in October 1962 during the Cuban missile crisis the USSR found itself close to a nuclear war with the United States, even though it suffered from gross inferiority both in strategic and conventional forces. One thing is clear: Soviet participation in the arms control process in particular and detente in general has done nothing to change the USSR's strategic doctrine. This doctrine continues to emphasize counterforce, war fighting, and war survival more than simple deterrence.

All military production decisions in the Soviet Union, with regard to both strategic and general purpose forces, have been directed at rendering inconceivable a nuclear retaliatory strike by the United States. With its preponderance of military power, the USSR political leadership wants to assure itself that the West will never risk a direct attack on its own initiative. Certainty of this condition will then enhance Moscow's international political status and create the opportunity for further expansion along its extensive frontiers that commenced toward the end of the Second World War in Eastern Europe. With a military procurement level[42] of $55 to $60 billion per year from 1976 through 1982, which has increased by 5 to 10 percent annually since then, a large surplus of older equipment remains available for shipment abroad. This plays an important role in Soviet foreign trade, the subject of the next chapter.

NOTES

1. Marshal A. A. Grechko, "Military Superiority," in *Sovetskaia voennaia entsiklopedia* Vol. 2 (1976), p. 258; cited in William T. Lee and Richard F. Staar, *Soviet Military Policy Since World War II* (Stanford: Hoover Institution Press, 1986), p. 30. The basic text still remains V. D. Sokolovskii, *Voennaia strategiia,* 3rd rev. ed. (Moscow: Voenizdat, 1968).

2. Probable membership of the Supreme High Command appears in table 2 of Lee and Staar, *Soviet Military Policy,* p. 55.

3. *Krasnaia zvezda,* 7 April 1976.

4. U.S. Department of Defense, *Soviet Military Power, 1986* (Washington, D.C.: GPO, 1986), p. 15.

5. Ellen Jones, *The Red Army and Society* (Boston: Allen & Unwin, 1985), pp. 6–7.

6. Harriet Fast Scott and William F. Scott, eds., *The Soviet Art of War: Doctrine, Strategy and Tactics* (Boulder, Colo.: Westview Press, 1982), provide excerpts from Soviet writings on these subjects.

7. Douglas M. Hart, "The Hermeneutics of Soviet Military Doctrine," *Washington Quarterly* 7, no. 2 (Spring 1984): 77–88, discusses the six schools; Peer H. Lange, "Soviet Military Doctrine and the West," *Europa Archiv* 39, no. 6 (25 March 1984): 179–86, makes the last point.

8. A. A. Grechko, *Vooruzhennye sily sovetskogo gosudarstva* (Moscow: Voenizdat, 1974), p. 319. See also John J. Dziak, *Soviet Perceptions of Military Power* (New York: National Strategy Information Center, 1981), especially pp. 39–58.

9. N. V. Ogarkov, "Military Strategy," *Sovetskaia voennaia entsiklopediia* (Moscow: Voenizdat, 1979), 7:555–65. See also his article "Defense of Socialism," *Krasnaia zvezda*, 9 May 1984, pp. 2–3, which may have contributed to Ogarkov's transfer from chief-of-staff to commander of the Western theater of military operations. Removed on 6 September 1984, he was reported in the new post by U.S. Department of Defense, *Soviet Military Power, 1986* (Washington, D.C.: March 1986), p. 19.

10. V. G. Kulikov, *Kollektivnaia zashchita sotsializma* (Moscow: Voenizdat, 1982).

11. H. F. Scott and W. F. Scott, *The Armed Forces of the USSR*, 3rd rev. ed. (Boulder, Colo.: Westview Press, 1984), pp. 63–65.

12. Joseph D. Douglass, Jr., and Amoretta M. Hoeber, *Soviet Strategy for Nuclear War* (Stanford: Hoover Institution Press, 1979), pp. 89–107.

13. *Soviet Military Power, 1986,* pp. 11–14 and 60–63; Charles W. Jones, "Soviet Access to Port Facilities," in Bruce W. Watson and Susan M. Watson, eds., *The Soviet Navy* (Boulder, Colo.: Westview Press, 1986), pp. 276–86.

14. U.S. Secretary of Defense, "The NATO–Warsaw Pact Balance," *Annual Report to the Congress: Fiscal Year 1987* (Washington, D.C.: GPO, 1986), pp. 61–63; Stephen J. Cimbala, "Soviet Blitzkrieg in Europe," *Strategic Review* 14, no. 3 (Summer 1986), pp. 67–75.

15. According to an unidentified senior U.S. official, the USSR has had nuclear weapons in Eastern Europe since at least 1980 (*Baltimore Sun*, 2 June 1983). See also *Soviet Military Power, 1986*, p. 91 for a NATO–Warsaw Pact comparison.

16. Ivan Volgyes, *The Political Reliability of the Warsaw Pact Armies: The Southern Tier* (Durham, N.C.: Duke University Press, 1982), especially pp. 41–59 for Romania; Teresa Rakowska-Harmstone et al., *Warsaw Pact: The Question of Cohesion*, Vol. 3 (Ottawa, Canada: Department of National Defence, March 1986), esp. pp. 291–340 and 404–68 on Bulgaria and Hungary.

17. A. A. Grechko, "The Leading Role of the CPSU in Building the Army of a Developed Socialist Society," *Voprosy istorii KPSS* 16, no. 5 (May 1974): 39. See also Stephen T. Hosmer and Thomas W. Wolfe, *Soviet Policy and Practice Toward Third World Conflicts* (Lexington, Mass.: D.C. Heath, 1983), pp.

129–33; Elizabeth K. Valkenier, "Revolutionary Change in the Third World: Recent Soviet Reassessments," *World Politics* 38, no. 3 (April 1986): 415–34.

18. The figures are from United Nations, *Disarmament Fact Sheet,* no. 38 (May 1985), p. 4, which gives a total of 71 countries involved.

19. Richard F. Staar, *Communist Regimes in Eastern Europe,* 4th rev. ed. (Stanford: Hoover Institution Press, 1982), pp. 277–78.

20. International Institute for Strategic Studies, *The Military Balance, 1985–1986* (London, 1985), p. 21; U.S. Department of Defense, *Soviet Military Power 1986,* pp. 8–9 and 103.

21. See William Kucewicz in *Wall Street Journal,* 5 September 1984, p. 30, for the test-firing; *The Military Balance, 1985–1986,* p. 21, for numbers.

22. H. F. Scott and W. F. Scott, *The Soviet Control Structure: Capabilities for Wartime Survival* (New York: Crane, Russak, 1983), pp. 121–28; Lee and Staar, *Soviet Military Policy,* pp. 51–53.

23. "The Soviets nevertheless now probably possess the necessary combination of ICBM numbers, reliability, accuracy and warhead yield to destroy *almost all* of the 1,047 U.S. ICBM silos, using only a portion of their own ICBM force" [italics added] *(Report of the President's Commission on Strategic Forces* [Washington, D.C.: GPO, 1983], p. 4). See also Lee and Staar, *Soviet Military Policy,* pp. 183–84, for accuracy of Soviet ICBMs.

24. Samuel T. Cohen and Joseph D. Douglass, Jr., "Selective Targeting and Soviet Deception," *Armed Forces Journal International* 121, no. 1 (September 1983): 95–101. See also "What If Soviet Silos Are Empty," *Wall Street Journal,* 18 July 1986, p. 18, by the same co-authors.

25. Norman Polmar, *Strategic Weapons: An Introduction,* rev. ed. (New York: Crane, Russak, 1982), pp. 27–35; Lee and Staar, *Soviet Military Policy,* pp. 61–78.

26. *The Military Balance,* p. 22.

27. Ibid., p. 22.

28. See P. H. Vigor, *Soviet Blitzkrieg Theory* (London: Macmillan, 1983), pp. 185–205, for a possible scenario.

29. North Atlantic Treaty Organization, *NATO and the Warsaw Pact: Force Comparisons* (Brussels: NATO Information Service, 1984), pp. 7–10. The USSR has four types of chemical agents in its stockpile, which totals 350,000 tons at seven centers. See also U.S. Department of Defense, *Soviet Military Power, 1986,* pp. 72–76; Brad Roberts, "Chemical Weapons: A Policy Overview," *Issues in Science and Technology* 2, no. 3 (Spring 1986): 103–14.

30. *Soviet Military Power, 1986,* pp. 76–79; *The Military Balance, 1985–1986,* pp. 23–24.

31. Organization of the Joint Chiefs of Staff, *United States Military Posture FY 1987* (Washington, D.C.: The Pentagon, 1986), p. 52.

32. *Soviet Military Power, 1986*, pp. 5 and 81–87. The classic treatise on the USSR navy is by S. F. Gorshkov, *Morskaia moshch' gosudarstva*, 2nd rev. ed. (Moscow: Voenizdat, 1979). See also Bryan Ranft and Geoffrey Till, *The Sea in Soviet Strategy* (London: Macmillan, 1983); "Soviet Naval Activities: 1977–1984," *NATO Review* 33, no. 1 (February 1985): 17–20; Captain J. E. Moore, RN, ed., *Jane's Fighting Ships 1986–87* (London: Jane's Publ. Co., 1986).

33. *The Military Balance, 1985–1986*, pp. 24–26. *Soviet Military Power, 1986*, pp. 8–9 and 12–14; explosion reported by *Jane's Defence Weekly* and discussed by Drew Middleton in *New York Times*, 11 July 1984. For the Kola Peninsula base complex, see *Aftenposten* (Oslo), 23 August 1986, p. 10.

34. *Soviet Military Power, 1986*, pp. 15, 33–34; *The Military Balance, 1985–1986*, p. 23; Defense Intelligence Agency, *Force Structure Survey* (Washington, D.C.: May 1986).

35. Central Intelligence Agency, *Soviet Civil Defense*, series NI 78–10003, July 1978; Capt. John F. Troxell, "Soviet Civil Defense and the American Response," *Military Review* 63, no. 1 (January 1983): 36–46; *Soviet Military Power, 1986*, p. 53.

36. *The Military Balance, 1985–1986*, p. 22.

37. Scott and Scott, *Armed Forces of USSR*, pp. 236–39; *The Military Balance*, p. 30.

38. *Sovetskii patriot* (Moscow), 26 June 1983; *The Military Balance*, p. 30; "Plenum of DOSAAF," *Krasnaia zvezda*, 22 November 1985, p. 3; D. Volkogonov, "Defense of Socialism and Military-Political Education," *Pravda*, 15 August 1986, pp. 2–3.

39. U.S. Congress, Office of Technology Assessment, *Salyut: Soviet Steps Toward Permanent Human Presence in Space*, OTA-TM-STI-14, December 1983, pp. 21–39; Thomas Y. Canby, "Are the Soviets Ahead in Space?" *National Geographic:* 170, no. 4 (October 1986), pp. 420–58.

40. U.S. Joint Chiefs of Staff, *United States Military Posture for FY 1984* (Washington, D.C.: GPO, 1983), pp. 9–29; U.S. Department of Defense, *Soviet Military Power, 1986*, pp. 45–47.

41. Transcript of Defense Intelligence Agency background briefing for reporters at the Pentagon, 13 June 1984, p. 5; William T. Lee, "Soviet Military Spending Is Growing," *National Security Record*, no. 91 (May 1986): 5; *New York Times*, 19 October 1986, p. 17, for the U.S. defense budget.

42. The Defense Intelligence Agency briefing, cited in Note 41 above, revealed these procurement figures. See also Brian Field, "Soviet military expenditure estimates: Meaning and measurement," *NATO Review* 34, no. 4 (August 1986), pp. 28–31. William T. Lee (see note 41) states that total USSR defense spending has reached 17 percent of gross national product or more than 2½ times the U.S. share of its GNP. Boris Rumor, *Christian Science Monitor*, 24 September 1986, reports that investment for armed forces' machinery production will be increased by 80 percent during the current (1986–1990) five-year planning cycle.

7

FOREIGN TRADE

Commercial relations with other countries always have served as an instrument of Soviet foreign policy and continue to perform that same function today. The objective of trade is not simply to make money but to enhance the USSR's economic power and influence throughout the world. As Khrushchev once explained to a group of visiting U.S. senators: "We value trade least for *economic* reasons and most for *political* reasons as a means for promoting better relations between our countries" (italics added).[1] Within the East European bloc, the USSR has aimed at achieving total integration of the various economies—a goal that has met with resistance. Trade with developed capitalist states, meanwhile, has chiefly involved purchase of food or technology, either on credit or in return for cash obtained from the sale of natural resources. It has been conditioned at all times by the Soviet Union's relative lack of hard currency and its domestic economic problems. In the Third World, the USSR has used trade mainly to promote its foreign policy objectives, even when this involves dealing at times with governments it condemns.

The Soviets also have curtailed or cut off trade with certain foreign countries on several occasions in order to penalize them.[2] This happened with Iceland in 1948, when that country's government showed an inclination to become a charter member of NATO. The total embargo against Yugoslavia (1949), following its expulsion from the Cominform, is well known. Wool imports from Australia were eliminated in 1954 after that country granted political asylum to a defecting Soviet intelligence officer. Exports to Mainland China were cut back drastically in 1965 following the withdrawal of USSR technicians during the previous years. More recently (1980), the Soviet Union temporarily stopped deliveries of petroleum to Romania because of statements by President Nicolae Ceauşescu in effect equating Eastern missile deployments in Central Europe with those of NATO.

FOREIGN TRADE DECISIONS

Although several other Soviet governmental agencies are involved in making decisions, in addition to the Ministry of Foreign Trade (under B. I. Aristov since October 1985), only the following ones will be mentioned here: Gosplan (the State Economic Planning Committee), the State Committee for Science and Technology, the Finance Ministry, Gosbank (the State Bank), and the State Committee for Foreign Economic Relations.

Gosplan prepares targets for the five-year planning cycle. Its chairman since 1985, N. V. Talyzin, directs about 5,000 employees[3] and also serves as head of the coordinating committee for integration of the Eastern bloc member state economies via the Council for Mutual Economic Assistance (CMEA), which is discussed in the next chapter. The foreign trade department, one of 67 such units at Gosplan, compiles actual trade and payments plans.

The State Committee for Science and Technology, under G. I. Marchuk from 1980 to 1986, was responsible for negotiating technical cooperation agreements with foreign governments and business firms. These usually include exchanges of information and of specialists who are assigned the task of obtaining Western technology. Machinery, equipment, patents, and licenses all remain within the purview of this state committee.[4]

The Ministry of Finance and the State Bank have joint responsibilities, with the latter providing the funds. The Bank board chairman since 1986, V. V. Dementsev, reportedly is subordinate to the finance minister (B. I. Gostev since 1985), even though both officials are members of the Council of Ministers. The government's budget is presented to the Supreme Soviet by the finance minister once a year. Gosbank monitors fulfillment of plans, especially monetary transactions between domestic firms, through the specialized Bank for Foreign Trade, which in 1985 had a balance of 56 billion rubles.[5]

Finally, the State Committee for Foreign Economic Relations, under Ia. P. Riabov during 1983–1984, administers the Soviet overseas aid program. It coordinates export of complete industrial plants, including nuclear powered ones, as well as of petroleum and natural gas. Pipelines for the latter do not extend beyond the borders of CMEA member states in Central Europe. There is some indication that Riabov, a secretary of the Central Committee from 1976 to 1979 and later first deputy chairman of Gosplan, received orders to eliminate corruption from the foreign trade bureaucracy. During this period, the chairman as well as the imports director of Technopromexport, which administers technical assistance for Soviet power plants built abroad, were executed because of "systematically taking large bribes."[6] Riabov became a deputy premier and was succeeded by M. A. Sergeichik, who retired in November 1985 to make place for K. F. Katushev.

EASTERN EUROPE AND THE BLOC

Trade with the other ten members of CMEA more than doubled during the past two five-year planning cycles. For calendar year 1985, it comprised almost half the Soviet total. Five of the ten CMEA members showed a negative balance of trade with the USSR. The disparities for Mongolia and Vietnam were especially large. (See Table 8.2) Soviet trade figures do not include statistics on the export of weapons or other military supplies.

CMEA was established in January 1949 on Stalin's orders, most probably with the aim of attaining economic self-sufficiency for the bloc. East Germany became a member the next year, followed by Mongolia (1962), Cuba (1972), and most recently Vietnam (1978). Yugoslavia remains an associate member, Albania dropped out in December 1961, and China never joined this organization. A comprehensive plan for economic integration was adopted in 1971, although implementation has fallen well short of the announced goal.[7] The CMEA summit conference, held at Moscow during mid-November 1986, reportedly did not solve many of the key problems (see Chapter 8).

Not only is the Soviet Union's economy overwhelmingly larger than that of all other CMEA members combined, but the East European governments are dependent upon raw materials and energy from the USSR. For example, during 1985 the Soviet compared with the East

European share of the bloc's total output ran as follows: 31.1 million versus 6.8 million barrels (per day) of crude oil equivalent; 155.0 versus 59.3 million metric tons of crude steel; 1,545 versus 473 billion kilowatt-hours of electricity; and 131 versus 58 million metric tons of cement. That same year, the East European regimes owed the USSR at least 13 billion rubles.[8] Traditional colonialism used to involve deliveries of raw materials to the metropole, which sent its dependencies manufactured products in return. The Soviet Union has reversed these procedures; its East European client states provide Moscow with semi-finished goods or even complete factories in exchange for raw materials and energy.

Two CMEA banks finance these exchanges as well as the various cooperative investments that have been launched over the years. The International Bank for Economic Cooperation, with some 4.4 billion transferable rubles plus 1.6 billion equivalent in convertible currency (end of 1985), issues short-term trade credits and is responsible for clearing accounts among members. The International Investment Bank, although its assets totaled only 2.4 billion transferable rubles (1985), provides funds for individual as well as joint projects. Both banks have borrowed large amounts of hard currency from Western financial institutions.[9]

Reflecting the world market, prices for Soviet raw materials delivered to Eastern Europe increased by 200 percent during calendar year 1977 alone. The rise primarily affected oil, deliveries of which probably remained at the same level during 1981–1985 as earlier or may have declined. Former USSR Prime Minister Aleksei Kosygin had promised Eastern Europe 20 percent more energy in the course of the above-mentioned five-year period. However, most of it has come in the form of natural gas and electricity, rather than petroleum. An ambitious program of building nuclear power plants also has been launched. Despite all these measures, Soviet trade subsidies to the six East European CMEA member states, according to one source, had increased to an estimated $21.7 billion for the year 1980.[10] These figures probably do not subtract USSR economic exploitation (see Chapter 8 for more details).

Joint CMEA ventures have resulted in completion of the *druzhba* (friendship) oil pipeline, the *bratstvo* (brotherhood) natural gas pipeline, and the *mir* (peace) electric power grid connecting Eastern Europe with the Soviet Union. Other projects under way involve nuclear energy as well as extraction of raw materials, with labor and construction costs being shared among CMEA members. Several of the East European states import grain from the USSR, which purchases it in turn from the West.

In general, some 40 billion rubles in exports (raw materials comprised 70 percent) went to CMEA member states from the USSR during 1985 and only 37.6 billion worth of goods came back. The bloc has had to reduce imports from Western industrialized countries because hard currency loans have become more difficult to obtain. The decline amounted to 28 percent during the first half of the 1980s, and in the case of Poland it dropped by 51 percent.[11]

EAST-WEST TRADE

Over the period from 1976 through 1980, Soviet trade with industrially developed countries amounted to 30.1 percent of its total, declining to just over 26 percent during 1985 and a trade gap of $2 billion. The United States was in sixth place; in 1978, at the height of detente, it had been third (after the Federal Republic of Germany and Japan). The USSR's largest trade deficits were with Japan, Canada, and the United States, in that order (see Table 7.1). Western countries, especially Argentina, Australia, Canada, and the United States,[12] have shipped large amounts of grain and soybeans to the Soviet Union, which experienced in 1985 its seventh successive year of shortfall. During the 1970s, it is estimated that the USSR spent about $40 billion for such agricultural imports. More than one-fifth of all grain traded on the world market during twelve months in 1984, that is, about 45 million metric tons, was purchased by the Soviet Union, at a cost of more than $7 billion. Soviet agricultural output, which grew at an annual rate of 2.2 percent during the 1950s and at only 1 percent during the 1960s, had been declining during the late 1970s and early 1980s. No official figures on grain harvests were released until Chernenko finally announced that 190 million metric tons were brought in during 1983, despite the "bad weather." The U.S. Department of Agriculture estimates that the 1986 harvest will bring in only 180 million metric tons or 70–75 million below Moscow's target.[13]

The same inefficiency is evident in Soviet livestock farming, where during 1985 some 43 million cows produced only 98 million tons of milk, compared with the 106 million tons of milk produced by fewer than 25 million cows owned by farmers of the European Economic Community. The peak Soviet beef production to date reached just 17 million tons from 121 million head of livestock, compared with 23 million tons from only 78 million head in Western Europe. Meat output per million pigs in the USSR[14] is only about two-thirds of that in West Germany or the United States.

In order to obtain the foreign exchange needed to purchase food

TABLE 7.1
LARGEST WESTERN TRADE PARTNERS, 1985
(IN MILLIONS OF RUBLES)

	Country	Exports	Imports	Balance
1.	West Germany	3,991.5	3,094.0	897.5
2.	Finland	2,299.1	2,686.6	− 387.5
3.	Italy	2,467.6	1,325.0	1,142.6
4.	France	2,174.4	1,603.2	571.2
5.	Japan	928.0	2,286.9	−1,358.9
6.	United States	326.1	2,376.4	−2,050.3
7.	Great Britain*	1,217.8	683.8	534.0
8.	Canada	17.8	949.0	− 931.2
9.	Australia	13.7	532.1	− 518.4

*Despite this rather substantial trade, the USSR gave the British coal miners' trade union more than $1 million in assistance during a strike, according to union officials (*Wall Street Journal,* 20 November 1984, p. 37). Gorbachev announced in London a target of a 40 to 50 percent bilateral trade increase over the next few years (*FPI International Report* 12 March 1986, p. 7).
SOURCES: Insert to *Vneshniaia torgovlia,* no. 3, 1985; "Soviet Foreign Trade by Groups of Countries," *Foreign Trade* (Moscow), no. 3, March 1986.

from the West, Eastern Europe and the Soviet Union at times engage in the practice of "dumping" low-priced items and services to disrupt foreign markets. The Federal Republic of Germany has accused Hungary, Poland, and Yugoslavia of offering certain pharmaceuticals at 39 to 47 percent less than their own domestic cost of production. In addition, visitors to the USSR are routinely "fleeced" not only through the artificial and arbitrary exchange of $1.48 for one ruble but also by the exorbitant hotel costs, several times higher than the price local citizens are charged. Due to cut-rate Soviet freight charges, three American shipping companies (Pacific, Far East, and United States lines) have been driven out of business.[15]

Combined with this are the pricing practices of the Soviet merchant fleet, which according to Lloyd's Register of Shipping is the sixth largest in the world, with a total 23.5 million gross tons. It earns foreign currency as a third-flag carrier and has undercut Liner Conference rates by up to 40 percent. At a 1982 meeting in Moscow, representatives of five West European governments (Germany, Britain, France, Netherlands, and Belgium) heard Soviet officials agree to restrict shipping activities on certain routes.[16] Whether this will actually be done is another question.

Despite such practices, the USSR has been able to obtain more than

$50 billion worth of high technology from the West over the past decade. According to testimony by Dr. Jack Vorona, assistant director for science and technology at the Defense Intelligence Agency, the 1973–1974 sale of 164 miniature precision ball bearing machines enabled the USSR to develop heavy multi-warhead intercontinental ballistic missiles at a more rapid rate than would otherwise have been possible. Military trucks now in Afghanistan were produced by the supposedly civilian Kama River plant, built with $1.5 billion worth of Western technology.[17] The automated foundry, engines, production line, and computer all came from the United States, which had been reassured that none of the output would be given to the Soviet armed forces.

Legal technology transfer has taken the forms primarily of agreements for scientific cooperation, licensing arrangements, turnkey projects, coproduction ventures, and three-party or even multilateral schemes.[18] J. Fred Bucy, president of Texas Instruments and chairman of a U.S. Defense Science Board task force on the export to the USSR of American technology, testified before a Senate panel that "transfer of militarily significant technology has been of major proportions."[19] However, the United States during 1981 ranked only ninth among Western countries contributing to this outflow, as shown in Table 7.2.

Shipments to the Soviet Union over the past ten years have included semiconductors, computer hardware and software, and chemical processes in all fields, not only from the United States but also from Western Europe and Japan. NATO members (except Iceland) and Japan belong to a Coordinating Committee on Multilateral Export Controls, or CoCom, which supervises trade in 125 categories of industrial items. Militarily significant products require unanimous approval prior to export, but less important technology can be shipped to the USSR and Eastern Europe after simple notification of other CoCom members. Total trade between members of the two blocs during 1983 totaled $75 billion, some of it in the "high-tech" field, with credits continuing to flow from West to East.[20]

According to American defense officials, there has been "large-scale leakage of this technology to the East," as a result of USSR espionage or theft and also because of "gaping holes in the CoCom structure." Indeed, the same individuals reported that the USSR has adapted Western technology to "in excess of 150 Soviet weapons systems." These U.S. officials, who attended a CoCom meeting in Paris, spoke of about 20,000 USSR personnel stationed abroad and involved in the acquisition, both legal and illegal, of high technology from the West. Some 1.4 billion are spent each year to obtain such information by Soviet and bloc intelligence agencies.[21]

TABLE 7.2
LEADING SOVIET HIGH-TECH SUPPLIERS, 1981

Country	Millions of dollars	Percentage of World Industrial Sales
1. West Germany	501.8	28.9
2. Japan	366.0	21.1
3. France	204.7	11.8
4. Italy	156.3	9.0
5. Finland	121.8	7.0
6. Britain	93.6	5.4
7. Switzerland	80.0	4.6
8. Sweden	77.3	4.5
9. United States	56.5	3.3
10. Austria	30.4	1.8
11. Denmark	17.9	1.0
Total	1,706.3	

SOURCE: U.S. Department of Commerce, as cited in "Stemming Flow of High-Tech to East," *Christian Science Monitor*, 22 April 1983, pp. 1 and 12.

In their efforts to obtain Western technology, Moscow focuses especially on computers, microelectronics, fiber optics, and lasers. These items can be diverted with relative ease after leaving the United States through one of approximately 300 air, sea, and highway exit points. During one year, about 45 diversion cases had been discussed within an interagency committee in Washington, D.C. Among these, only 36 were brought to the attention of foreign governments. Administrative penalties could be imposed in twelve instances, and criminal proceedings instituted against only four individuals. Two computer systems plus parts, valued at approximately 180,000 British pounds sterling, were seized before shipment from England to the Soviet Union. Boxes had been labeled "pipe setting equipment."[22]

Another recent case involved two computers, Digital Equipment Corporation VAX 11–782 models, powerful enough to guide long-range missiles. One was seized in West Germany and the other (weighing 30 tons) in Sweden before being transshipped to the USSR. Both were returned to the United States by the respective customs authorities. The equipment had been purchased legally and sent first under license to a front organization in the Republic of South Africa by a German citizen who operated 77 such fronts. A federal judge in the United States subsequently fined a Swedish firm $3.1 million for illegally exporting American strategic materials to the Soviet Union over a three-year period.[23]

The interesting aspect is that a considerable amount of advanced technology has been obtained by the East on credit from the West. Soviet and East European debts at the end of 1985 totaled more than $113 billion, as shown in Table 8.4. The problem of Poland is most acute, with the $2.5 billion due on the principal in 1981 having been postponed to 1986. The same procedure was followed in 1982 (over $2 billion), delaying repayment until 1987. Finally, in 1983 an additional $1 billion had to be rescheduled. Some 500 Western banks are involved as Polish creditors.[24]

With only $32 billion in annual hard currency earnings, some two-thirds of which had come from sales of petroleum and natural gas, the USSR received about $4.5 billion in credits during 1985 from the West. The rest came from hidden borrowing in the interbank market through Soviet-owned financial institutions in Paris (Banque Commerciale pour l'Europe du Nord), London (Narodnyi Bank), Frankfurt (Ost-West Handelsbank), and others in Luxembourg, Zurich, Vienna, and Singapore. Roughly $5 billion in Western deposits are held by these USSR banks, whose managers are foreign nationals to obscure Soviet ownership.[25]

THE NATURAL GAS PIPELINE

Completely ignoring previous experience and its own embargo on high-technology items, the Carter administration approved sale to the USSR of 200 bulldozers produced by the Caterpillar Tractor Company and especially configured for laying pipe, only two weeks after having lost the election. When completed in 1990 at an estimated cost of $14 billion, this pipeline will carry 40 billion cubic meters of natural gas each year from Siberia to both East and West Europe. It will extend some 4,000 kilometers across the USSR, through Czechoslovakia, and into the Federal Republic of Germany. Consequently, West Germany will increase its dependence upon Soviet natural gas from the current level of 3 percent to a projected 30 percent, while France's imports will climb from 5 percent also to 30 percent of total French consumption. During 1985 already, Bavaria and West Berlin will receive—or not receive—95 percent of their gas from the Siberian pipeline.[26]

When the project is completed, the USSR will be in a position to threaten to or even stop deliveries as a means of exercising political pressure. Such a reduction in deliveries to Western Europe actually occurred in January 1981, when major Soviet natural gas supply cut-backs took place because of alleged "technical difficulties" with the existing pipeline. Moreover, the USSR has used the oil weapon against its own allies on at least two occasions: Cuba in 1967 and Romania in 1980. In both cases, the communist leaders of these respective countries were proving to be recalcitrant.[27] Would there be any hesitation to use the same approach against a non-communist government? Moscow television announced on 29 October 1984 that Soviet ships would stop supplying Britain any kind of fuel during the coal miners' strike in that country. Five days later TASS disavowed such "Western fabrications."

Crude oil—some of which comes from Saudi Arabia and Libya as payment for arms—and natural gas already had provided the Soviet Union with more than $20 billion per year in hard currency earnings until prices dropped during 1985–1986. Apart from that, the USSR can sell much of its 350 tons per year of gold production to the West in exchange for hard currency. Exports of platinum and polished diamonds might bring in as much as several hundred million dollars more per annum. However, income from precious metals, although substantial, cannot be compared with that from natural gas in the future. Between 1970 and 1984 the percentage of Soviet hard currency earnings on energy exports is estimated to have risen from 25 to 80 percent, with gas sales steadily increasing. However, in 1986 USSR hard currency earnings were half of what they had been two years earlier and one-third less than the year before.[28]

It is worth noting that even construction of the natural gas pipeline depended decisively on Western technology. Only the General Electric (GE) Company could produce the special rotor for turbine engines required in the Soviet pipeline. An engineering group in France, Alsthom-Atlantique, purchased the plans from GE and was able to make the device. The Reagan administration attempted for a time to prevent delivery of the turbines to the USSR by invoking trade sanctions under U.S. law against the French firm. Even before the sanctions had been lifted, other West European companies also proceeded to deliver key components to the Soviet Union. Nuovo Pignone of Italy began to supply nineteen compressor stations and 57 turbines. West Germany's AEG-Kanis benefited from a $1 billion credit line extended by a consortium of West European banks, which offered an additional half billion dollar equivalent. The John Brown Company in the United Kingdom also shipped turbines to the USSR. Gaz de France and Ruhrgas in the Federal Republic of Germany even contracted to pay an amount for Soviet natural gas, linked to the basic oil price of $34 per barrel, a figure $5 above the OPEC established level.[29]

THIRD WORLD

Soviet trade with the lesser developed countries, although it had doubled in the course of an earlier five-year plan (1975–1980), still represented only 12.2 percent of total turnover in 1985. The largest amount is with India, followed by Argentina, with which, owing mainly to purchases of wheat, the Soviet Union registered more than a one billion ruble negative trade balance in 1985 (see Table 7.3). Other substantial deficits occurred in commercial transactions with Libya. Trade with Iran showed a surplus, probably because of the war against Iraq. However, total commerce, involving 102 Afro-Asian and Latin American countries, decreased by 0.4 percent to approximately 17.3 billion rubles.[30]

Some of the favorable trade balances are misleading, because certain partners obviously lack the means to pay. This is the case with Angola and Ethiopia, both of which have become tied economically to the USSR through credits and military assistance. Dramatic increases have taken place in trade with Afghanistan, up 100 percent, since the invasion of that country in December 1979 by the Soviet army. The People's Democratic Republic of (South) Yemen ships almost nothing to Moscow but does provide valuable military bases for the USSR at Aden and on the island of Socotra.

On most occasions, Soviet trade with the Third World is designed to parallel political objectives and to help extend USSR influence. When it really needs a given product, however, Moscow will deal with any type of government. Examples include rubber imports from Malaysia as well as agricultural commodities from countries like Argentina, Brazil, and the United States.

It has been suggested that the USSR may hope to gain control over certain strategic raw materials throughout the Third World[31] and might even proceed to establish a cartel similar to the Organization of Petroleum Exporting Countries (OPEC). The United States government lists 93 minerals as being critical. Of this total, the USSR has to import only six. Over a long period of time, it had sold chromite, manganese, and platinum to the West. During the past several years, however, these exports dropped by 50 percent or more, and the Soviet Union has actually begun to purchase these minerals as well as titanium, vanadium, lead, beryllium, tantalum, and lithium from the Third World.[32] The USSR has negotiated more than several dozen technical/economic aid agreements alone or through CMEA with lesser developed countries where strategic minerals are located (see Table 7.4).

TABLE 7.3

SOVIET TRADE WITH SELECTED LESSER DEVELOPED COUNTRIES, 1985
(IN MILLIONS OF RUBLES)

	Country	Exports	Imports	Balance
1.	India	1,572.6	1,499.6	73.0
2.	Argentina	62.4	1,229.9	−1,167.5
3.	Libya	83.4	877.8	− 794.4
4.	Afghanistan	550.2	323.0	227.2
5.	Iraq	267.5	556.7	− 289.2
6.	Egypt	282.3	302.8	− 20.5
7.	Syria	319.5	188.8	130.7
8.	Brazil	70.3	380.0	− 309.7
9.	Algeria	132.3	272.9	− 140.6
10.	Iran	203.8	144.1	59.7
11.	Ethiopia	280.1	34.6	245.5
12.	Nigeria	149.1	41.0	108.1
13.	South Yemen	142.9	8.4	134.5
14.	Angola	94.0	2.5	91.5

SOURCE: Insert to *Foreign Trade* (Moscow), no. 3, March 1986.

In addition, the Soviet Union has offered to participate over the years in joint development projects designed to provide it with access to the following: *alumina* from Greece, Guyana, Indonesia, Jamaica, and Turkey; *bauxite* from Guinea and India; *natural gas* from Afghanistan and Iran; *oil* from Syria and Iraq; and *phosphates* from Morocco.[33] In certain instances, the USSR purchases raw materials of which it possesses a surplus, apparently to deny the West access to a given source and to build up its own strategic reserve stockpile.

The Eastern bloc is not self-sufficient in cobalt, and the Soviet Union bought up large quantities from Zaire just before the 1978 invasion of that country by Cuban-trained mercenaries. The latter invasion represented the second attempt by Cuba, acting as Soviet proxy, to seize the ore-rich province of Katanga. In 1980, the USSR agreed to deliver $85 million worth of arms to Zambia in return for cobalt. Zimbabwe (formerly Rhodesia) is the world's main supplier of chrome. Since the Soviets have also been a major producer in the past of both cobalt and chrome, they might be in a position to establish a cartel in cooperation with Zaire and/or Zimbabwe at some future date.[34]

The outlook for Western access to strategic minerals would become

TABLE 7.4
SOVIET IMPORT DEPENDENCE, 1980–1985

Mineral	Percentage Imported	Source	Reported Production Source
Fluorspar	52	Kenya (54%), Morocco (36%), Thailand (19%)	All
Molybdenum	51	U.S. (15%)	U.S.
Bauxite	35	Guinea (70%), Yugoslavia (18%) Greece (12%)	All
Alumina	38	Hungary (44%), Jamaica (18%), Guyana (13%), U.S. (13%), Italy (8%), Turkey (4%)	All except Italy
Cobalt	15	Cuba (45%), Zaire (40%)*, France, Belgium, United Kingdom (5%)	Cuba, Zaire
Tungsten	26	China, Mongolia (20%), Australia and West (80%)	All
Antimony	19	Turkey (72%), Yugoslavia (26%) China (2%)	All
Tin	30	United Kingdom (67%), Malaysia (22%), Bolivia (10%) Vietnam (1%)	All
Nickel	0	Cuba (concentrate/100%)	
Lead	8	Yugoslavia, North Korea, United Kingdom, Peru	All

*Estimate for 1980 only.

SOURCES: James A. Miller et al., eds., *The Resource War in 3-D* (Pittsburgh, Pa.: World Affairs Council of Pittsburgh, 1980), p. 47; Central Intelligence Agency, *Handbook of Economic Statistics, 1986* (Washington, D.C.: Directorate of Intelligence, September 1986), figure 15, p. 17.

even more critical, should the USSR ever exercise influence over the Republic of South Africa to the extent that it does in neighboring Angola and Mozambique. The combination of those three countries as potential suppliers of raw materials would provide the Soviet Union with access to the following percentages of world production: 94 percent of *platinum,* 67 percent of *chrome,* 62 percent of *manganese,* 72 percent of *gold,* 70 percent of *vanadium,* 26 percent of *fluorspar,* 47 percent of *asbestos,* and 43 percent of *uranium.*[35] The implications of such a development are both obvious and ominous.

FOREIGN ASSISTANCE

Within the Third World, six countries make up a group called "special friends" of the USSR: Cuba, Vietnam, Mongolia (all members of CMEA), Afghanistan (a CMEA "observer" currently occupied by Soviet troops), and Laos and Cambodia (virtual satellites of Vietnam). The first four are given about 90 percent of all Soviet aid to the Third World. Together the six probably received almost $7 billion in assistance during calendar year 1984 (see Table 7.5).

Non-communist recipients of aid, which accounts for the remaining few percentage points in terms of money value, paid back to the Soviet Union during the past several years in capital and interest more than they received over that same period of time. Aid promised to various countries by the USSR sometimes fails to materialize and, since 1954 in fact, less than half the offers have been delivered to Third World countries. A British study[36] concluded that the actual amount of Soviet aid to non-communist governments during the five years from 1976 through 1980 totaled only $8 billion, as opposed to the $45 billion claimed by Moscow.

Cuba's share of USSR largesse has amounted to one-fourth of that island nation's gross national product. For 1984, economic aid to Ha-

TABLE 7.5
SOVIET ECONOMIC ASSISTANCE TO SPECIAL FRIENDS, 1980–1984
(IN MILLIONS OF DOLLARS)*

	Country	1980	1982	1984
1.	Cuba	3,465	4,665	4,620
2.	Vietnam	1,050	1,015	1,040
3.	Cambodia	134	82	n.a.
4.	Laos	50	100	n.a.
5.	Mongolia	835	870	785
6.	Afghanistan	276	286	237
	Totals	5,810	7,018	ca. 6,682

*Excluding military aid.

SOURCES: U.S. Department of State, *Soviet and East European Aid to the Third World, 1981,* Publication No. 9345, February 1983, pp. 17–19; U.K., Foreign and Commonwealth Office, Economic Service (International Division), *Soviet, East European and Western Development Aid, 1976–1982,* Foreign Policy Report No. 85 (London, May 1983), p. 22; Central Intelligence Agency, *Handbook of Economic Statistics, 1986* (Washington, D.C.: Directorate of Intelligence, September 1986), tables 79 and 82, pp. 112 and 115.

vana from Moscow may have amounted to $4.6 billion, or about $12 million per day (more than one dollar per head of population). On top of that comes Soviet military assistance, free of charge, totaling about $700 million per annum. Two-thirds of the economic aid involves balance of payments support, and the other one-third goes for development projects. The USSR also pays five times (38 cents a pound) the world market price (7.6 cents in May 1986) for Cuban sugar, even though it does not require any of the latter for its own domestic consumption.[37] At the same time, petroleum is delivered to Cuba at less than OPEC charges, that subsidy alone having totaled $100 million in 1984.

Vietnam received over $1 billion worth of economic assistance during 1984, plus $775 million free of charge in military aid and $350 million for additional project support. Thousands of Vietnamese are sent to work in the USSR and Eastern Europe, their labor charged against repayment of debts. Moscow continues to supply Hanoi with about 1.5 million tons of petroleum per year at a price below world levels. The USSR raised the cost considerably in 1981, forcing Hanoi to reduce imports of other goods. The oil subsidy still amounted to about $7 million in 1982. Roughly 200,000 tons of Soviet foodstuffs were delivered to Vietnam during that year.

In contrast with Cuba and Vietnam, Afghanistan does not receive any free USSR military equipment. During 1983, arms deliveries cost Afghanistan $150 million, exclusive of maintenance provided for Soviet troops in country. Moscow's aid commitments over the past 30 years now total more than $3.2 billion, of which something more than half had been disbursed by the end of 1984. Much of the aid includes commodities such as petroleum, foodstuffs, and textiles. The USSR imports 95 percent of Afghanistan's natural gas at below world market prices and is also believed to resell the latter's produce (olives, nuts, raisins, honey) at a profit in Eastern Europe.

During 1984 Soviet project assistance to its oldest satellite, Mongolia, totaled $785 million. The money was earmarked for construction of a copper-molybdenum ore-dressing complex at Erdenet. Ulan Bator also had received a $10 million annual subsidy in the form of low prices for petroleum imported from the USSR. Bordering on the People's Republic of China, Mongolia provides a huge base for Soviet troops stationed in that country.

Aid to Laos, mainly in the form of commodity grants as well as assistance for some projects, reached $100 million in 1982. The USSR also delivered some oil at below market prices and paid for a certain amount of petroleum imported by Laos from other countries. Cambodia received about $82 million, mainly in Soviet vehicles and machinery, during 1982. However, the USSR has not contributed to the United Nations humanitarian program for that country; Moscow's aid seems devoted rather to propping up the Heng Samrin regime.

Although the USSR and other communist-ruled states in Eastern Europe contribute about one-tenth of all economic aid received by the Third World, they outperform the West in military assistance. During 1985 the Soviet Union ranked first with $9.4 billion in the value of arms transfer agreements, as compared to $5.3 billion for the United States. The East Europeans supplied $2.8 billion worth of weapons on their own, with other communist regimes like China exporting the same amount, for a total of $15 billion.[38]

The USSR has been able to exploit the impact of its foreign assistance program in the past also by becoming involved with projects that have high visibility. Building the Aswan dam in Egypt and the Bokaro steel plant for India are prime examples of a technique that maximizes foreign policy returns with showplace projects that had been turned down earlier by the United States.[39]

Of greater long-range significance probably are the 400 or more Soviet and East European multinational companies with financial investments in 23 countries outside the bloc. Examples include a partnership selling Hungarian coal technology to the United States, a company from Poland with equity in 30 West European firms, a Czechoslovak-owned enterprise in Canada with branches in South America, and a forklift truck plant in Bulgaria, which has attempted to purchase its French competitor.[40] Soviet leaders are only too aware of both the economic and strategic value of such multinational companies. Relations between the USSR and its client regimes in Eastern Europe are the topic of the next chapter.

NOTES

1. Quoted in the *New York Times*, 16 September 1955, p. 48.

2. H. Stephen Gardner, *Soviet Foreign Trade: The Decision Process* (Boston, Mass.: Kluwer-Nijhoff, 1983), p. 27; Marshall I. Goldman, *USSR in Crisis* (New York: W. W. Norton, 1983), p. 138.

3. Gardner, *Soviet Foreign Trade*, p. 43.

4. Ibid., p. 47.

5. *Foreign Trade*, no. 4 (Moscow), April 1985, p. 9. The Gostev and Dementsev appointments were announced by Moscow radio on 14 December 1985 and 10 January 1986, respectively.

6. *New York Times,* 14 January 1984.

7. Richard F. Staar, *Communist Regimes in Eastern Europe,* 4th rev. ed. (Stanford: Hoover Institution Press, 1982), pp. 300–24.

8. Central Intelligence Agency, Directorate of Intelligence, *Handbook of Economic Statistics, 1986,* series CPAS 86–10002, September 1986, table 3, p. 25. Jan Rostowski in *CPE Current Analysis* (13 November 1985), cited by Philip Hanson, "Prospects for Soviet-Western Trade," *Radio Liberty Research,* 9 April 1986, RS 150/86, p. 2.

9. Gardner, *Soviet Foreign Trade,* p. 54; V. Liakin, "Economic Review," *Ekonomicheskaia gazeta,* no. 22 (May 1986): 20; *1986 Europa Yearbook* (London: Europa, 1986), p. 166.

10. Jan Vanous and Michael Marrese in *Wall Street Journal,* 15 January 1982, p. 22.

11. U.S. Department of Commerce, "Report on East-West Trade and Finance," cited by Gabriel Partos, "East Europe's Trade with the West," *BBC Current Affairs Talks,* 23 May 1986. no. 52/86.

12. The grain embargo, imposed by his predecessor because of the invasion of Afghanistan, was lifted in April 1981 by President Reagan. Prior to the embargo, the United States had been supplying about 70 percent of Soviet grain imports, which have dropped to 20 percent (*New York Times,* 17 May 1983). The U.S. share of world grain and soybean trade has declined from 62.6 to 52.0 percent over the preceding five years (*Wall Street Journal,* 15 November 1984).

    In an attempt to entice the USSR to fulfill its grain import agreement, the U.S. government offered 3.85 million metric tons of wheat, which will be subsidized at $20 per ton (Keith Schneider in the *New York Times,* 16 August 1986). The 1985 trade deficit is from ibid., 17 December 1986.

13. Chernenko speech on the harvest in *Pravda,* 3 March 1984, p. 1. Central Intelligence Agency and Defense Intelligence Agency, *The Soviet Economy Under a New Leader,* a report submitted to the Joint Economic Committee of Congress, 19 March 1986, p. 41, gives the 1985 harvest figures. The 1986 projections and target are from U.S. Department of Agriculture, *USSR: Situation and Outlook Report,* May 1986, RS–86–3, pp. 14–15.

14. *Handbook of Economic Statistics, 1986,* Tables 161, 163, 164 on pp. 196 and 198. The Common Market in Western Europe sold the USSR 175,000 tons of frozen beef, from its surplus of 800,000 tons, at less than one-third the original cost of production (*Daily Telegraph* [London], 21 September 1985, p. 36). Some 110,000 tons of butter, also at low prices, were delivered the following year (*Bild* [Hamburg], 4 September 1986).

15. *Business Eastern Europe* 10, no. 16 (17 April 1981): 22; Curtis Cate, ed., *The Challenge of Soviet Shipping* (New York: National Strategy Information Center, Inc.), pp. 6–9.

16. *Financial Times* (London), 25 March 1982; *Sea Power* 28, no. 5 (15 April

1985): 185; U.S. Department of Transportation, *A Statistical Analysis of the World's Merchant Ships* (Washington, D.C.: GPO, 1985), p. iv.

17. Central Intelligence Agency, *Soviet Acquisition of Western Technology*, September 1985, p. 3. See also Roger W. Robinson, Jr., "Soviet Cash and Western Banks," *The National Interest*, no. 4 (Summer 1986), pp. 37–44.

18. Eugene Zaleski and Helgard Wienert, *Technology Transfer Between East and West* (Paris: OECD, 1980), p. 113. See also Gardner, *Soviet Foreign Trade*, p. 29.

19. Cited by Carl Gershman, "Selling Them the Rope," *Commentary* 63, no. 4 (April 1979): 42. See also "High-Tech Hemorrhage from U.S. to Soviet Union," in *U.S. News & World Report*, 7 May 1984, pp. 47–48, and CIA, *Soviet Acquisition of Western Technology*, September 1985, p. 34, passim.

20. *The Economist*, 7 January 1984, p. 64. See also U.S. Department of State, "Controlling Transfer of Strategic Technology," *Gist*, April 1986, p. 2.

21. Felix Kessler, "U.S. Urges Bar on Technology Sales to Soviets," *Wall Street Journal*, 6 October 1982; *Soviet Acquisition of Western Technology*, September 1985, table 2, pp. 9 and 10; Bundesministerium des Innern, "Das 'Rote Buch' oder wie die UdSSR westliche Technologien beschafft," Bonn: 1985, mimeographed.

22. Statement by Frank C. Conahan, director, International Division, General Accounting Office, before the U.S. Senate, Committee on Banking, Housing, and Urban Affairs, Subcommittee on International Finance and Monetary Policy, *Hearings on Functions of the Treasury and the Export Administration Act*, 97th Cong., 1st sess., 1981, pp. 21–47 at pp. 37–39; London radio, 31 May 1983, as cited in *FBIS*, 1 June 1983.

23. *Wall Street Journal*, 28 April 1984; Richard N. Perle, "Strategic Impact of Technology Transfer," in Robert L. Pfaltzgraff, Jr., and Uri Ra'anan, eds., *East-West Trade and Technology Transfer* (Cambridge, Mass.: Institute for Foreign Policy Analysis, 1986), p. 22; and *Wall Street Journal*, 28 July 1986, p. 19, for a case involving sensitive equipment stopped in Vienna, Austria.

24. *New York Times*, 14 June 1983; *Wall Street Journal*, 10 January and 19 March 1984, 18 March 1986.

25. Roger W. Robinson, Jr., "Financing the Soviet Union," *Wall Street Journal*, 10 March 1986. The author served on the National Security Council staff, 1982–1985.

26. *The Economist*, 22 May 1982, p. 66; see *Wall Street Journal*, 20 November 1984, p. 32, for Bavaria and West Berlin. During 1984, some 15 percent of the natural gas used by France came from the USSR, according to ibid., 7 June 1985, p. 25. Beginning in mid-1987, Turkey will receive Soviet gas through a pipeline from Bulgaria, according to Sofia radio, 23 July 1986; *FBIS*, 27 July 1986, p. C1.

27. Jeffrey G. Barlow, "NATO: Restoring American Leadership," *The Heritage Foundation Backgrounder*, no. 132 (Washington, D.C., 11 February 1981), p.

17; *The Economist,* 22 May 1982, p. 66; Richard F. Staar, "Soviet Relations with Eastern Europe," *Current History* 83, no. 496 (November 1984): 353–56 and 386–87.

28. See *The Times* (London), 19 July 1982, on gold sales ($4.6 billion); *New York Times,* 11 and 26 April 1983, on figures for other precious metals and minerals ($375 million); *Wall Street Journal,* 10 May 1984, p. 30, for percentages; ibid., 7 September 1984, p. 29, on oil for weapons; Henry S. Rowen and Vladimir G. Treml, ibid., 21 May 1986, on the drop in hard-currency income; ibid., 18 August 1986, p. 4.

29. *New York Times,* 1 April 1983. Gaz de France negotiated a price reduction of 5 to 10 percent and a delivery growth slowdown, according to the *Wall Street Journal,* 7 June 1985, p. 25.

30. *Vneshniaia torgovlia,* no. 5 (1986), p. 5.

31. James Arnold Miller, Daniel I. Fine, and R. Daniel McMichael, eds., *The Resource War in 3-D: Dependency, Diplomacy, Defense* (Pittsburgh, Pa.: World Affairs Council of Pittsburgh, 1980), pp. 37–56. See also John R. Thomas, *Natural Resources in Soviet Foreign Policy* (New York: National Strategy Information Center, 1985), esp. pp 47–49.

32. John P. Hardt, "Soviet Non-Fuel Minerals Policy: The Global Context," *Journal of Resource Management and Technology* 12, no. 1 (January 1983): 57–62; Table M-6, "U.S. Net Import Reliance on Metals and Minerals," *Sea Power* 28, no. 5 (15 April 1985).

33. Gardner, *Soviet Foreign Trade,* p. 30. See also M. Ryzhkov, "USSR Cooperation with Developing Countries in Recovery of Mineral Resources," *Vneshniaia torgovlia,* no. 7 (July 1986): 21–25.

34. Peter Vanneman and Martin James, "Soviet Coercive Diplomacy," *Air Force Magazine* 64, no. 3 (March 1981): 122. See also Robert England, with Bill Gertz, "Metals More Precious than Diamonds," *Insight,* 30 September 1985, pp. 52–55.

35. James A. Miller, *Strategic Minerals and the West* (Washington, D.C.: American African Affairs Association, 1980), p. 58; James E. Sinclair and Robert Parker, *The Strategic Metals War* (New York: Arlington House, 1983), especially pp. 66–77; U.S. Congress, Office of Technology Assessment, *Strategic Materials* (Washington, D.C.: GPO, May 1985), p. 409; "Pondering the Cost of Sanctions," *Insight,* 14 July 1986, pp. 8–12.

36. United Kingdom, Foreign and Commonwealth Office, Economic Service (International Division), *Soviet, East European and Western Development Aid, 1976–1982,* Foreign Policy Report No. 85 (London, May 1983), p. 3.

37. Three-quarters of Cuban sugar production goes to the Soviet bloc (*Wall Street Journal,* 3 August 1984, p. 20). The USSR sugar subsidy in 1984 totaled $3.4 billion according to CIA, *Handbook of Economic Statistics, 1986,* table 82, p. 115.

38. Richard F. Grimmett, "Trends in Conventional Arms Transfers to the Third World by Major Supplier, 1978–1985," *Congressional Research Service*

Report, no. 86–99 F (Washington, D.C.: 9 May 1986), p. 6. See also U.S. Arms Control and Disarmament Agency, *World Military Expenditures and Arms Transfers, 1985,* August 1985, Table A, p. 42.

39. Gardner, *Soviet Foreign Trade,* pp. 27–28.

40. Carl H. McMillan, "Soviet and East European Participation in Business Firms and Banks Established in the West: Policy Issues," unpublished paper presented at a symposium sponsored by the NATO Economics Directorate in Brussels, 6–8 April 1983. See also "Joint Ventures Encouraged by Soviet Bloc," *Washington Times,* 15 November 1984, p. A-9, for other details.

It is interesting to note that the USSR may request membership in both the International Monetary Fund and the World Bank, using these organizations to obtain credibility for loans from the international credit markets. It is estimated that the Soviet hard-currency debt will exceed $50 billion by the end of 1990 (*Wall Street Journal,* 15 August 1986, p. 20; ibid., 25 August 1986, p. 6).

The CPSU Central Committee adopted a resolution, allowing some 20 ministries/departments and 70 of the largest associations/enterprises to engage directly as of 1 January 1987 in export/import operations (*Pravda,* 24 September 1986, p. 1). About 15 American companies have proposed joint ventures to USSR authorities (*New York Times,* 29 November 1986).

★ PART III ★

REGIONAL POLICIES

8

POLICIES TOWARD EASTERN EUROPE

The last colonial empire in the world today, the Soviet Union, is faced with mounting problems among its dependencies in Eastern Europe.[1] A facade of political unity exists; alliance war games take place on schedule, and the most recent multiyear economic plans are being implemented. And yet the winds of change seem evident. During the past, Soviet leaders have ordered armed forces to invade several countries within their sphere of direct influence in order to turn back efforts at political liberalization. Such intervention has occurred, directly or indirectly, about once in every decade since the Second World War: Hungary (October–November 1956), Czechoslovakia (August 1968), and Poland (December 1981). In this last country, the establishment of an indigenous military dictatorship and the proclamation of martial law functioned as a surrogate for Soviet military occupation.

In contrast to Brezhnev, who summoned East European leaders individually to Oreanda in the Crimea every summer for audiences[2] with this *de facto* head of the "socialist commonwealth of nations," Gorbachev sees each one of these viceroys individually at his office in the Kremlin. The February 1984 and March 1985 funerals of Andropov and Chernenko provided all sides with an opportunity to become acquainted, and the periods before and during the economic summits offered time for more extended talks.

THE MAVERICK STATES

One East European client regime has appeared to be a continual aggravation to Soviet decision makers, namely, Romania. The month before Andropov died, Andrei Gromyko stopped off in Bucharest. The visit seems to have been prompted by a statement of Nicolae Ceauşescu to the effect that both the United States and the USSR should remove their intermediate-range nuclear missiles from Europe.[3] The previous visit of the Soviet foreign minister, four years earlier, had been occasioned by Romania's abstention from the United Nations' vote calling for withdrawal of foreign (that is, Soviet) troops from Afghanistan.

Gromyko returned to Moscow in January 1984 with a joint Soviet-Romanian statement embodying the revised position that NATO should dismantle its 41 newly deployed ground-launched cruise and Pershing II ballistic missiles. Ignored this time were the 284 Soviet triple-warhead SS-20s already in place and targeted against Western Europe. By coincidence (or perhaps as a reward), the USSR reportedly[4] promised to deliver 1.5 million tons of coal and 1.8 billion cubic meters of natural gas to Romania during that calendar year.

At a state dinner in the Kremlin five months later, Chernenko is alleged to have told Ceauşescu that a few possibilities still existed to further develop bilateral relations in the political, ideological, economic, cultural, and other fields between the two countries. However, the final communiqué made no mention of Romania's decision to participate in the Los Angeles Summer Olympics, as the only bloc member (together with Yugoslavia from Eastern Europe) not supporting the Soviet boycott. Other loyal client regimes (Bulgaria, Cuba, Czechoslovakia, East Germany, Hungary, North Korea, Mongolia, Poland) joined the USSR in hosting different types of international sports competition during August in their own respective countries.[5]

However, it took new Soviet leader Gorbachev only about fourteen months to bring Ceauşescu back into line with a "Long-Term Program for Development of Economic, Scientific and Technical Cooperation Between the USSR and Romania Through the Year 2000." Signed in Moscow on 16 May 1986, it even provides for coordination of central planning and foreign trade. The latter is of special importance because Soviet oil deliveries are made in return for agricultural products. During mid-October 1986, E. A. Shevardnadze met with Ceauşescu just before the Warsaw Pact foreign ministers convened at Bucharest.[6]

Romania, of course, had long adopted a maverick stance toward its Soviet patron; developments in Poland, on the other hand, are both novel and unique. To date, there has been nothing comparable in any other East European state. The political situation during 1980–1981 completely undermined the basis for governmental authority in Warsaw. The regime reached the point where it must have considered the independent Solidarity trade union a real constraint upon its freedom of action, especially in the economic sphere, where the latter succeeded in obtaining broad concessions from the communist government.

That constraint appeared to represent the basic reason for USSR uneasiness and for the propaganda barrage aimed at Warsaw from other East European capitals, which Moscow most probably had a hand in orchestrating. Worried by reports of Soviet troop concentrations along the country's borders, then Polish communist party leader Stanislaw Kania asserted in mid-March 1981 that Poland "is and will be an ally of the Soviet Union." Only two weeks later, the official CPSU daily newspaper launched a strong attack[7] on the "anti-socialist" elements that had organized a meeting at Warsaw University and allegedly criticized the Marxist system. And according to Moscow, the local Polish communist party organization had made no attempt to refute this criticism. It is unknown exactly what Foreign Minister Gromyko discussed during his July 1981 visit in Poland. The communiqué made no direct reference to liberalization.

Because of its geographic location within the staging area for the second echelon of Warsaw Pact troops facing North Atlantic Treaty Organization countries, the western region of Poland is of significant military importance to the USSR. In case of war, Soviet naval infantry would move out from the Baltic coast for assaults against the Danish islands and the West German port city of Kiel. According to American military analysts,[8] Warsaw Pact commander-in-chief Marshal Viktor G. Kulikov reportedly had attempted to convince Brezhnev to invade and occupy Poland because of the above considerations.

Yet in the event of such a takeover, USSR occupation authorities most probably would have been faced with a general strike. Indigenous troops and/or police, it was thought at the time, probably could not be relied upon to maintain foreign-imposed martial law over an essentially hostile population of 36 million. The national character of the Poles is anything but passive, and Soviet soldiers would make easy targets for urban guerrillas operating in the manner of Poland's efficient anti-German underground *Armia Krajowa* (Home Army) during World War II. Assassination of puppet officials, attacks upon military patrols, disruption of railroad traffic—not to mention the oil and natural gas pipelines crossing Poland en route to East Germany—sabotage of defense plants, and flooding of coal mines in Silesia are a few examples of what Moscow might have anticipated. In the end, probably because of the foregoing considerations and possibly also because of U.S. efforts during the crisis,[9] the USSR did not invade.

Rather than risk this kind of chaos, Kremlin decision makers applied psychological pressure to contain the free trade union movement in Poland. During mid-1981, Western intelligence indicated that readiness of Soviet troops along Polish borders was reduced to a point where as many as three days would have been required before an invasion could be launched, compared with a few hours during the previous "high alert" period.[10] This may have been simply a case of deception, in view of what followed.

The local communist regime's indigenous armed forces in effect became the surrogate occupation authority for the USSR. Invoking martial law on 13 December 1981, the government of Poland implemented a plan that had been drawn up under the supervision of Army General A. F. Shcheglov, who headed the 800-member Soviet military mission in Warsaw. By that time, the *de jure* ruling Polish United Workers' (communist) Party had lost all credibility and most of its membership.[11] Economic power, and hence political authority, appeared to be gravitating toward the 10 million strong urban and rural *Solidarność* labor unions.

Nineteen months of military rule under General Wojciech Jaruzelski (first party secretary, premier, defense minister, commander-in-chief of the armed forces, and junta chairman) officially ended on 21 July 1983. However, many of the martial law controls became permanently institutionalized through additions to the penal code, after the ban on Solidarity as a legal organization. Regime spokesmen admitted to holding only 190 political prisoners (non-government estimates placed the total at between 4,000 and 5,000). The last 225 were released under the September 1986 amnesty. At the same time, police visited about 3,000 others known to be in contact with the political underground and warned them to cease this support. The militarization of Poland, however, may not be repeated in any other bloc country, because of the way in which such an act removes all appearance of legitimacy from communist ideology.[12]

In the course of his speech to the tenth congress of the Polish United Workers' Party in Warsaw on 30 June 1986, Gorbachev declared that the crisis of the late 1970s and early 1980s in Poland had involved a protest against "distortions of socialism." On the other hand,

to attack the socialist system, attempt to subvert it from the outside, to tear away this or that country from the socialist community—means to encroach not only on the will of the people but also on the entire postwar settlement and, in the last analysis, on peace.[13]

Earlier in the address, Gorbachev stated that "socialist conquests are irreversible," meaning presumably that the USSR would fight to protect them.

WARSAW TREATY ORGANIZATION

The Warsaw Pact, or Warsaw Treaty Organization (WTO), forms the basis of Soviet military control over East bloc countries and provides the USSR with the wherewithal to intervene if local communist authority appears in jeopardy. The Pact includes all East European states except Yugoslavia and Albania. The USSR predominates militarily and politically: it supplies two-thirds of the Pact's conventional as well as all of its nuclear capabilities. In addition, most of the advanced weapons systems and equipment comes from Moscow. The highest alliance military commanders, WTO chiefs-of-staff, and representatives in member-country defense ministries always have been career Soviet officers. The USSR's distrust of its allies also manifests itself in the weakness of Pact organizational integration. In peacetime, the unified command supervises only combat readiness and participation in joint maneuvers.

The treaty that created the alliance was signed in Warsaw on 14 May 1955, although East German armed forces did not become part of WTO until the following January. Albania left the organization *de facto* in 1961; it announced formal withdrawal after the Soviet invasion of Czechoslovakia seven years later.[14] The Chinese discontinued sending observers to maneuvers in 1962. The northern tier states (Czechoslovakia, East Germany, and Poland) have received better equipment than other Pact members. Of these three countries, only East Germany spends almost as much per capita on defense as does the USSR (see Table 8.1).

One thorough study of the northern tier concludes that because of radically different institutional histories of the Czechoslovak, East German, and Polish military forces, the Soviets would face serious constraints in attempting to deploy these Pact armies in combination against the West. Even individual national interests of the different countries are at odds. Coalition warfare would be difficult, and only a surprise Pact offensive against NATO might create the necessary momentum to pull the northern tier armed forces along.[15] Indeed, the latter are not completely reliable, even for domestic repression. Under

TABLE 8.1
WARSAW PACT ARMED FORCES, 1986

| Country | MANPOWER | | | EQUIPMENT | | | EXPENDITURES | |
	Army	Air	Navy	Tanks	Combat Aircraft (incl. helicopters)	Vessels (incl. subs)	Defense Budget 1986 (billion $)	Est. GNP 1985 (billion $)
Bulgaria	105,000	35,000	8,500	1,950	300	86	1.656	40.0
Czechoslovakia	145,000 (80,000)	56,000	—	3,500	468	—	4.426	96.0
East Germany	123,000 (380,000)	40,000	16,000	2,800 (1,600 storage)	407	142	6.865	126.0
Hungary	83,000 (65,000)	22,000	—	1,360	167	—	2.440	48.4
Poland	295,000 (40,000)	88,000	19,000	3,570	687	163	6.874	149.0
Romania	150,000	32,000	7,700	1,430	378	180	1.327	90.0
USSR	1,991,000* (excluding long-range Air Force)	453,000	451,000	54,200	5,150 (tactical only)	1,960	23.400	1,765.0

*Only 565,000 are located in Central and Eastern Europe, as given in parentheses. Total includes Soviet forces also in the Western military districts of the USSR proper that would reinforce those deployed against NATO.

SOURCES: International Institute for Strategic Studies, The Military Balance, 1986–1987 (London, 1985), pp. 31–54.

martial law in Poland, when the military actually ruled as a Soviet proxy, motorized "ZOMO" citizens' militia (police) units rather than regular army troops were brought in to quell disturbances.

The East European members of WTO provide lines of communication and logistic support between the USSR proper and its forward military deployments facing NATO. Status-of-forces agreements exist for this reason with Czechoslovakia (which has 80,000 Soviet troops), East Germany (380,000), Hungary (65,000), and Poland (40,000). Only the Bulgarians and Romanians have no such arrangements.[16]

The WTO maneuvers take place in several segments in the spring, summer, and fall of each year. Units from the central tier (Czechoslovakia, Hungary, USSR) held joint tactical exercises on the territory of Hungary during February 1986. Headquarters staffs and only token contingents of reservists participated in movements conducted on maps, testing command and control as well as cooperative action. (Since 1964 the Romanians have refused to allow any foreign armed units on their national territory but instead send staff officers to observe them in other Pact countries.) Five days of maneuvers by 25,000 Czechoslovak, Hungarian, and Soviet troops took place during 8–12 September 1986 under the code name "Friendship-86" on the territory of Czechoslovakia. For the first time since 1979, NATO observers were invited to watch the last two days of these war games.[17]

Arrangements exist to place the armed forces of WTO member states under direct Soviet military command, in the event of a war with NATO. Romania probably would resist such an attempt. It is known that elite units from other East European armies have been selected and already integrated with the second echelon, behind forward deployed USSR troops. None of the client states, however, is allowed to produce enough weapons for its own national army. Furthermore, those East European officers who aspire to flag rank must be graduates of Soviet military schools and speak Russian, according to a recent study funded by the Canadian government.

Even after more than 30 years of Moscow-supplied training and indoctrination, East European armed forces are neither loyal to the USSR nor efficient. If NATO troops were to cross the frontiers into Warsaw Pact territory, the Canadian report argues that this would "trigger a collapse of the communist regimes there . . . with repercussions in the western borderlands of the Soviet Union."[18] The USSR rules the alliance by dividing it. Elite units within WTO armies are detached and placed under Soviet military command, as mentioned above. Finally, penetration of all Pact armed forces by security police has been extensively developed.

Despite these controls, or perhaps because of them, there seems to have been a noteworthy lack of enthusiasm for emplacement of new Soviet battlefield nuclear missiles in both East Germany and Czechoslovakia. All three countries announced simultaneously on 24 October 1983 that preparatory work had begun for deployment of "operational tactical missile complexes" in response to the planned introduction of new intermediate-range nuclear forces (INF) into Western Europe by NATO at the end of the year. U.S.-Soviet negotiations, of course, were still being conducted in Geneva when the bloc statement was issued.[19]

Regardless of the fact that talks were still under way and that Western INF deployments were scheduled to be completed over a five-year period, the first SS-22 appeared in East Germany already during January 1984. The SS-21 and SS-23 missiles had been emplaced in advance of the October announcements mentioned above, as part of a long-range modernization program, even though the East European regimes must have felt uncomfortable with these developments. All three weapons systems carry either conventional or nuclear warheads. TASS revealed in mid-May 1984 that the German Democratic Republic had agreed to accept additional "enhanced range theater missile complexes" that would be kept "strictly within the limits necessary for maintaining the balance of forces and neutralizing" the NATO threat.[20]

Two years later, the WTO Political Consultative Committee convened during 10–11 June 1986 at Budapest and issued an appeal to all European countries. It called for reductions in ground and tactical air forces "from the Atlantic to the Urals," starting with 100,000–150,000 on each side within one year or two. By the early 1990s, the Warsaw Pact and NATO would each have 500,000 fewer troops.[21] The Mutual and Balanced Force Reduction Talks cover only Central Europe and have achieved no agreement, since they started in October 1973, which should be considered regarding the above proposal.

COUNCIL FOR MUTUAL ECONOMIC ASSISTANCE

The Soviet Union also maintains substantial day-to-day economic leverage throughout the bloc. The Council for Mutual Economic Assistance (CMEA) was established by the USSR for Eastern Europe, supposedly as a response to the Marshall Plan.[22] Membership has been discussed in Chapter 7. Other "fraternal" governments, like those in

Afghanistan, Angola, Ethiopia, Kampuchea, (North) Korea, Laos, Mozambique, and (South) Yemen, send observers to meetings. Cooperation agreements have been signed by CMEA with Finland, Mexico, Iraq, and Nicaragua.

Almost 70 percent of all East European iron ore requirements, 93 percent of the coal, and 68 percent of the petroleum are supplied from within CMEA. Admittedly problems exist: inadequate efficiency, a low degree of assimilation of new equipment, rising prices of raw materials and energy from outside the bloc, shortages of manpower, bad weather conditions and misuse of assets through waste.[23]

Soviet spokesman Oleg T. Bogomolev, director of the Institute on the Economics of the World Socialist System, warned East European CMEA members that by 1990 they will be forced to import half their energy needs from outside the bloc. In addition to cutting back oil deliveries to between 71 and 72 million tons per year, the USSR announced increases in its prices for 1983 to $27 and for 1984 to $29 per barrel, which approximated the OPEC level.[24] The drop in world petroleum prices during 1985 and 1986 did not help Eastern Europe, because it has no surplus foreign exchange. Some of the loss of oil supplies may be made up from electricity generated by nuclear power plants, now under construction, and increased deliveries of natural gas from the Soviet Union.

At their thirty-third council session, all CMEA members from Eastern Europe, including Yugoslavia, agreed to produce equipment for the construction of nuclear power stations on Soviet territory. The first of these plants, planned for completion in 1984, should have had a 4,000 megawatt capacity. Each major contributor to the project (Czechoslovakia, East Germany, Poland, Romania, and Yugoslavia) will receive electricity through the year 2003, in proportion to individual investment.[25] A second plant, with the same capacity, should be ready by 1990; it remains unclear which countries will contribute to this one. The disaster at Chernobyl in 1986 has not affected these plans. Two additional projects are scheduled for joint construction inside the Soviet Union. Apart from petroleum, the USSR already is supplying natural gas from Orenburg to East Europe via a 2,677 kilometer pipeline, at its planned annual capacity of 15.5 billion cubic meters, almost half of what the region receives from the USSR. By 1990, the total may reach 65 bcm per year.

The CMEA council met for its 41st session during 17–18 December 1985 in Moscow. It discussed coordination of economic plans for the next five-year period (1986–1990), cooperative ventures in automation, the unified electric power system, and adopted a fifteen-year

"Comprehensive Program for Scientific and Technical Progress." Delegations of member states were headed by prime ministers.[26] These individuals also must have attempted to address deteriorating economic conditions.

Financial problems have developed throughout Eastern Europe, as a result in part of the worldwide recession that occurred during the late 1970s and early 1980s and of the slowdown in the Soviet economy. The USSR has been supplying energy and raw materials to other CMEA member states in return for machinery and agricultural products in quantities from the latter that have not been sufficient to even accounts. Only three East European trading partners during calendar year 1985 (Hungary, Yugoslavia, Romania) had positive financial balances with the USSR (see Table 8.2).

The Soviet intention to attempt closer integration of the various CMEA economies at the mid-1984 summit meeting in Moscow met with opposition from those governments that fear a limitation on their access to Western markets and deterioration into second-class status. East Germany wants to expand its profitable relations with the neighboring Federal Republic, and Hungary would like to continue its own modified market economy as well as closer trade relations in the West without interference. Meanwhile, however, intra-bloc trade increased from 53.4 percent (1981) to 61.1 percent (1985) of total exports and imports among CMEA members.[27] Overall national income, on the other hand, has experienced a sustained decline over the past fifteen years (see Table 8.3).

Between 12 and 14 June 1984, party-government leaders from all CMEA member states had met in Moscow for their first summit conference since April 1969. (Fidel Castro was absent, and sent a representative.) Participants agreed to coordinate their industrial planning and to cooperate in research on high technology. The concluding communiqué[28] called for production of equipment and machinery that would compare in quality as well as in technical levels with what is manufactured by the highly industrialized countries of the Western world. Emphasis was placed on electronics, microprocessors, and robots, where the lag between East and West is most evident.

Two documents were published, one political and the other economic. The declaration "On the Maintenance of Peace and International Economic Cooperation" pledged aid to the Third World, without any specific commitments. It called for United Nations' talks on international economic problems. A long-term strategy for CMEA, as outlined in the economic statement, is planned to include

1. coordination of economic planning;
2. a fifteen- to twenty-year scientific and technological program, to be prepared jointly for atomic energy, electronics, and space; and
3. improvement of specialization via direct links among government agencies and industrial plants in CMEA member states as well as promotion of cooperative research and production.[29]

Also mentioned were more frequent top-level meetings. The transferable ruble, an accounting unit in bilateral trade, will be strengthened. However, no move seems to have been made toward convertible currency. It is anticipated that prices for oil should approximate world levels in the future. The economic statement also emphasized mutual dependence. CMEA members pledged to adapt their export policies toward the Soviet market in return for energy and raw materials.

Apart from the incipient problems of satisfying future energy requirements, all countries in the East European bloc are in debt to Western financial institutions. The total amounts to more than $113 billion, most of which had been used for purchase of modern industrial plants and equipment from capitalist countries (see Table 8.4). In addition, at different times Hungary, Poland, Romania, and Yugoslavia have received "most favored nation" treatment from the United States—a status that has been extended despite an American semi-embargo against the Soviet Union[30] (see Table 8.5).

Economic relations with its East European colonial empire probably will become more strained in the future for the Soviet Union, as the latter becomes less able and/or willing to help. Over the two most recent decades, USSR subsidies to client states are estimated to have grown from $186 million (1960) to $17.8 *billion* (1980) per year. This last figure represents the equivalent in value of about 70 percent of total Soviet imports from the West.[31] Obviously, these subsidies (if indeed they are so high) cannot continue to increase at such an astounding rate or be maintained even close to the above level for an indefinite period.

Total industrial production during calendar year 1981 decreased by 1.3 percent for all of Eastern Europe. Hungary, with the New Economic Mechanism (NEM) reform, registered a small gain, while Poland dropped twelve points. In fact, the Polish situation had become so desperate that the USSR reportedly pledged to deliver $1.3 billion worth of goods during that year. According to a Yugoslav source, Poland enjoys a "special status" within CMEA like such underdeveloped

TABLE 8.2
SOVIET TRADE WITHIN CMEA, 1985
(IN MILLIONS OF RUBLES)

	Country	*Exports*	*Imports*	*Balance*
1.	East Germany	7,651.7	7,553.0	+ 98.7
2.	Czechoslovakia	6,813.3	6,587.3	+ 226.0
3.	Bulgaria	6,434.7	6,040.0	+ 394.7
4.	Poland	6,516.7	5,525.0	+ 991.7
5.	Hungary	4,560.0	4,850.1	− 290.1
6.	Cuba	3,848.7	4,140.1	− 291.4
7.	Yugoslavia	2,717.9	3,338.9	− 621.0
8.	Romania	1,948.8	2,276.5	− 327.7
9.	Mongolia	1,113.6	386.6	+ 727.0
10.	Vietnam	1,165.3	280.8	+ 884.5
	Total	42,770.7	40,978.3	+ 1,792.4

SOURCES: Insert to *Foreign Trade* (Moscow), no. 3 (March 1985).

allied countries as Cuba, Laos, Mongolia, and Vietnam. No move has been made by the Soviet Union to help Poland reduce its foreign currency debt. The latter did receive credits, however, to balance its 1984 trade account with the USSR, as a result of which 4.5 billion rubles reportedly were added to what Warsaw owed Moscow.[32]

It probably would be impossible (without Soviet permission) for any of the East European regimes to introduce radical economic reforms. However, the last Hungarian five-year plan (1981–1985) envisaged doubling investment funds for modernization of firms with export markets in the West and a limited convertibility of its currency by the end of that period. Similar objectives, of course, have been pursued in Budapest ever since 1968 under the New Economic Mechanism, albeit cautiously, so as to avoid provoking Moscow. During the period from 1982 to 1984, the International Monetary Fund advanced credits totaling more than $1 billion to Hungary.[33]

Among all bloc members, as mentioned above, the Romanians have acted with the greatest degree of independence. Ceaușescu accepted an invitation to visit the Federal Republic of Germany in mid-October 1984. On occasion, he reportedly has even demanded economic concessions from the USSR. The leaders in Bucharest, however, are careful to stress their cooperation and close ties with the Soviet Union, especially on the anniversary of the friendship treaty between the two countries. The events in Poland apparently triggered a shift in emphasis from

TABLE 8.3

PRODUCED NATIONAL INCOME IN CMEA, 1976–1990 (PROJECTED)
AVERAGE GROWTH/DECLINE
(PERCENTAGE)

	1976–1980	1981–1985	1986–1990 (projected)
Bulgaria	6.1	3.7	4.1–4.6
Czechoslovakia	3.7	1.8	3.4–3.5
East Germany	4.1	4.5	4.4–4.7
Hungary	3.2	1.4	2.8–3.2
Poland	1.6	−0.8	3.0–4.0
Romania	7.3	4.4	7.6–8.3
CMEA(7)	3.6	3.2	4.1

SOURCES: Wharton Econometric figures, as cited by *Wall Street Journal*, 1 March 1984, p. 30; David E. Albright, "On Eastern Europe: Security Implications for the USSR," *Parameters* 14, no. 2 (Summer 1984): 25. See also U.S. Congress, Joint Economic Committee, *East European Economies: Slow Growth in the 1980's*, Vol. 3 (Washington, D.C.: GPO, 1986); Gerhard Fink in *Europäische Rundschau* (Vienna) 14, no. 2 (1986), pp. 17–25.

TABLE 8.4

CMEA HARD CURRENCY DEBT TO THE WEST, 1985
(IN BILLIONS OF DOLLARS)

Country	Amount
Poland	29.3
USSR	26.4
Yugoslavia	18.8
East Germany	13.9
Romania	6.5
Hungary	11.8
Czechoslovakia	3.9
Bulgaria	3.2
Total	ca. 113.8

SOURCES: Central Intelligence Agency, *Handbook of Economic Statistics, 1986* (Washington, D.C.: September 1986), tables 20 and 49.

industrialization to food production as the first priority in Romania. Procurement prices were raised by 12 percent. Agriculture will receive more investment for large-scale irrigation projects as well as erosion control, drainage, and land reclamation. These measures were taken as a direct result of domestic strikes and demonstrations because of food shortages.[34]

Yugoslavia holds only associate membership in CMEA and has never joined the Warsaw Pact. After the death of Josip Broz Tito in May 1980, there had been speculation concerning possible Soviet use of force to bring Yugoslavia back into the bloc. This has not yet happened. Despite an official inflation rate of 96 percent and unemployment at 15 percent in 1986, the country appears to be stable, at least on the surface.[35]

There seems to be no fear in Yugoslavia of criticizing the USSR. Janez Stanic, a journalist from Slovenia, who had been stationed in Moscow for twelve years, subsequently published a book. It described pervasive Soviet censorship and showed how this resulted in misinformation concerning the outside world as well as domestic conditions. The author stated that in the USSR national minorities are subjected to "Russian hegemony." Eurocommunism, anathema to Moscow, is also publicized in Yugoslavia through frequent interviews with West European communist leaders. Discussions of alternatives to the political system even take place. However, 28 intellectual dissidents, including Milovan Djilas, were arrested at a private apartment and subsequently tried for doing just that.[36]

Only little Albania, the smallest among the East European countries, is completely hostile toward the USSR. This atmosphere could be felt at a conference dealing with the struggle against Soviet "revisionism" over the preceding two decades. Each year, the media in Moscow publish an article commemorating the 1945 establishment of diplomatic relations with Tirana. However it is doubtful that such official contact will be resumed, especially while the Albanian leadership remains ruthless in its response to even the slightest pro-Soviet activity within the country itself.[37]

THE SOVIET CRACKDOWN

An article in the official CPSU newspaper issued a strong warning to all East European regimes against "bowing to the pressure of NATO." It referred specifically to the plenary session, held in April 1969 by the Czechoslovak ruling movement's Central Committee, which ousted reformist leader Alexander Dubček. His name was not mentioned in the article. From the context, however, it could be understood all over Eastern Europe that similar "internal reactionary forces" would not be tolerated by the USSR, a grim reminder of the Brezhnev Doctrine and

TABLE 8.5
U.S. TRADE WITH CMEA STATES, 1981–1985
(MILLIONS OF DOLLARS, IMPORTS AND EXPORTS F.O.B.)

Country of Origin	IMPORTS FROM			EXPORTS TO		
	1981	*1983*	*Jan.–Aug.* *1985*	*1981*	*1983*	*Jan.–Aug.* *1985*
Bulgaria	34.1	26.0	27.6	258.2	55.2	44.0
Czechoslovakia	67.2	45.8	53.6	82.6	35.8	43.7
East Germany	47.4	41.9	70.6	295.7	90.2	37.6
Hungary	128.5	119.7	149.6	78.0	89.0	69.6
Poland	365.1	142.9	144.6	681.5	238.8	168.6
Romania	560.1	369.1	573.5	504.2	143.4	127.2
USSR	347.8	258.0	281.7	2431.6	1195.7	1,781.4
Total European CMEA	1,550.2	1,003.4	1,301.2	4,331.8	1,848.1	2,272.1
Total imports from entire world	260,981.8	187,935.4	224,758.7	233,739.1	148,959.8	143,778.8

SOURCE: U.S. Department of State, Bureau of Intelligence and Research, *Trade of NATO Countries with European CEMA Countries*, prepared by Lucie Kornei, Report no. 1184-AR, 25 October 1985, p. 19.

of the Soviet military occupation that led to the more pliable Gustav
Husak becoming Dubček's successor in Prague. The 27th CPSU Congress did nothing to dispel the "firm course" for the bloc.[38]

Along with its periodic renewals of the threat of brute force, Moscow has recently moved to change its watchdogs throughout Eastern
Europe. During 1983–1986, it replaced all seven ambassadors in the
region. In addition, the secret police had been accorded new prestige
in Bulgaria, where the interior minister was promoted to candidate
status on the local politburo and in Czechoslovakia, where his counterpart became a deputy prime minister.

Hungary witnessed its first political trial in a decade. A bookshop
operated by Laszlo Rajk (son of the communist party leader executed
in 1949) was closed down by authorities. Even official periodicals are
carefully censored. The editor of *Mozgo vilag* (The World in Motion)
was dismissed for holding deviationist views, the literary magazine *Tis-
zataj* (Tisza Region) was suspended, and the works of leading author
Istvan Csurka were banned. Possibly because of its willingness to maintain this tough internal policy against dissent, the Soviets have stood by
while Hungary has moved to legalize small private enterprises and
encourage personal initiative. A visit to Budapest by KGB chairman
V. M. Chebrikov in April 1986 preceded a crackdown on dissidents,
perhaps from concern over the forthcoming thirtieth anniversary of
the Hungarian uprising.[39]

Bulgaria seems to have the least problems with the USSR. The
movement toward greater cultural freedom, led until her death by the
leader's daughter, Lyudmila Zhivkova, seems to have been cut short
with the unexpected ouster of Aleksandr Lilov, who had been thought
of as a possible successor to Todor Zhivkov. The latter's visit to Moscow
coincided with the opening of a display celebrating "Forty Years Along
the Road of Socialist Ascent: The People's Republic of Bulgaria." It was
part of a larger exhibition on Soviet achievements. The leaders in Sofia
certainly remain more loyal to their mentors in the Kremlin than those
in any of the other East European states. Obviously bowing to Soviet
pressure, Zhivkov canceled a visit to Bonn. The July 1986 party congress in Sofia appeared to be almost a carbon copy of the one held a
few months earlier in Moscow.[40]

East Germany would appear to be the second most loyal regime.
Ties with the Soviet Union can be assessed from the fact that each is the
largest trading partner of the other (more than 15 billion rubles in
turnover during 1985) despite the disparity in populations: 16.7 million
compared with 280 million. Some 174,000 indigenous troops, together
with 380,000 "guests" from the USSR, provide the so-called German

Democratic Republic (GDR) with the world's highest concentration of military manpower and hardware per square mile.[41] It would appear doubtful that the Soviets need to tighten domestic controls here. The implicit threat of force should be sufficient to keep any internal dissent within tolerable limits.

However, the Soviet media carried open attacks on the Federal Republic of Germany for allegedly attempting to undermine the GDR's communist system and to absorb it. When the East Germans received a further offer of 950 million marks or $355 million in hard currency credits from Bonn (a similar loan had been accepted the year before), *Pravda* continued its verbal assault. East Berlin postponed indefinitely plans for Honecker to visit the Federal Republic of Germany toward the end of September 1984, although closer ties with Bonn remain the objective.[42]

East Germans are the envy of other bloc countries because only they have access, through a special trading arrangement, to the European Economic Community and to generous credits from the Federal Republic. The latter continues to purchase the freedom of political prisoners in the East (40,000 since 1962), paying between $20,000 and $60,000 per head in goods and services. Only 30 individuals were able to break through the fortified border during 1985, whereas 7,000 pensioners emigrated legally to the West. CPSU leader Gorbachev attended the ruling party's eleventh congress in April 1986, where he made the routine demand that the Federal Republic accept East Germany as an "equal, sovereign state."[43] During the fall a statue of prewar German communist leader Ernst Thälmann was unveiled in Moscow, the only such East European honored to date.

FUTURE TRENDS

It is significant that USSR military deployments throughout Eastern Europe (in Czechoslovakia, East Germany, Hungary, and Poland) have increased over the past several years in numbers of sites occupied, size of logistical support and infrastructure, troop strengths, as well as quantity and quality of weapons systems. At the same time, indigenous armed forces in these allied countries have been dispersed so that none are stationed adjacent to Soviet borders. Their equipment remains obsolescent, and some national armies have declined in size, Czechoslovakia[44] being a specific example.

Meanwhile, USSR troops reportedly have been strengthened vis-à-vis the southern and northern flanks: in Czechoslovakia and Hungary facing Austria and Yugoslavia; and in East Germany, Poland, and the

Baltic states (Lithuania, Latvia, and Estonia) facing Sweden and Finland. If this information is accurate, it would imply a fundamental change in the perceived function of Soviet armed forces within Eastern Europe. Kremlin decision makers clearly remain unworried, despite their propaganda to the contrary, about a NATO attack. They seem to be concerned more in extending their influence, probably using the threat of military power as an instrument of foreign policy, into the four neutral countries located on Warsaw Treaty Organization borders.[45]

Even though the freedom of action by individual East European countries varies, all (except Albania and Yugoslavia) are constrained by the Brezhnev and Gorbachev doctrines of limited sovereignty. This means that commitment to the "socialist system" takes precedence over each member's national interests. The USSR, of course, decides the collective interest. As long as these conditions prevail, there can be no change in Eastern Europe that might lead to a relaxation of tensions between the Soviet Union and most of its subordinate communist regimes.

In order to emphasize that a tightening of alliance bonds is taking place, a world affairs magazine in Moscow translated an article that had appeared in the Czechoslovak communist party daily. The latter expressed surprise that "some people overestimate their own 'model' for solving difficulties encountered in socialist countries," implying that certain unnamed East European regimes were unjustifiably opposed to the current hard line emanating from the Kremlin. That same month, an authoritative CPSU historical journal published a long article[46] that reinforced what the Prague newspaper had written. Gorbachev articulated similar attitudes at the tenth congress of Poland's ruling party in mid-1986.

The politburocrats in Moscow seem intent on maintaining their East European empire at any cost, even if this means applying military force to prevent its disintegration. In a time when colonialism has all but disappeared from the face of the earth, the Soviet Union gives every indication that it will continue to pursue anachronistic imperial policies. In the long run, this approach might well result in an explosion that could affect the USSR itself.[47] East-West relations in Europe, discussed in the next chapter, may have some influence on these developments.

NOTES

1. A comprehensive survey, covering 1939–1980, can be found in Jens Hacker, *Der Ostblock: Entstehung, Entwicklung und Struktur* (Baden-Baden: Nomos Verlag, 1983).

2. Over a period of five years, a total of 37 such meetings took place (*Pravda*, 20 March, 2 April, and 16 May 1981, carried details of one annual series).

3. Richard F. Staar, "Soviet Relations with Eastern Europe," *Current History* 83, no. 496 (November 1984): 353 ff. See also Vladimir V. Kusin, "Gorbachev and Eastern Europe," *Problems of Communism* 35, no. 1 (January–February 1986): 39–53.

4. *The Economist*, 11 February 1984, p. 46.

5. *Pravda*, 6 June 1984. See also Frederick Kempe, "The So-There Olympics," *Wall Street Journal*, 24 August 1984, p. 17.

6. *Pravda*, 17 May 1986, p. 1; discussion in ibid., 2 June 1986, p. 4. See also V. Andreiev, "The Priorities of Cooperation," *New Times* (Moscow), no. 34, 1 September 1986, pp. 20–21, on Soviet-Romanian economic ties; Bucharest radio, 16 October 1986, in *FBIS*, p. H 1, the following day.

7. For an excellent analysis of Soviet pressure against Poland, see Georges Mond, "Pressions sovietiques en Europe de l'est: En Pologne apres la seconde guerre mondiale," in Francis Conte and Jean-Louis Martres, eds., *L'Union Soviétique dans les relations internationales* (Paris: Economica, 1982), pp. 519–39.

8. Quoted in *New York Times*, 6 April 1981.

9. Zbigniew K. Brzezinski, *Power and Principle* (New York: Farrar, Straus & Giroux, 1983), pp. 463–68.

10. Maneuvers on Polish territory code-named "Soiuz-81" lasted 22 days, ending on 7 April, the longest in Warsaw Pact history. Soviet reservists were called up in Transcarpathia, bordering on Poland, and were told they might be required to defend the socialist community. Finally, the USSR itself conducted combined arms (ground, air, navy) exercises during 4–12 September in Belorussia and along the Baltic seacoast. See the description by Major General A. I. Skryl'nik, chief ed., *Zapad-81* (Moscow: Voenizdat, 1982).

11. Martial law plans were revealed by a high-ranking Polish defector, General Leon Dubicki, to *Wall Street Journal*, 4 June 1984, p. 24. Some 800,000 members officially left the communist party during 1980–1982, according to Józef Barecki et al., eds., *Rocznik polityczny i gospodarczy, 1981–1983* (Warsaw: PWE, 1984), p. 151. The actual number probably exceeded the above. See also Sidney I. Ploss, *Moscow and the Polish Crisis* (Boulder, Colo.: Westview Press, 1986).

12. Amnesty International, *Report* (London, 1984), pp. 293–97; A. V. Kuznetsov, "Theoretical Concepts of a Certain Policy Political Scientist," *Voprosy filosofii* (Moscow), no. 12 (1983): 27–39; Milovan Djilas, "The Militarization of the Soviet Bloc," *Wall Street Journal*, 30 May 1984, p. 31; *The Economist*, 22 December 1984, p. 36; editorial, "Freedom as Seen from Poland," *New York Times*, 23 August 1986.

13. *Pravda*, 1 July 1986, p. 1. On the amnesty, see the interview with Lech Walesa in *Le Soir* (Brussels), 15 September 1986, p. 1; and *Insight*, 20 October 1986, pp. 28–29.

14. Richard F. Staar, *Communist Regimes in Eastern Europe,* 4th rev. ed. (Stanford: Hoover Institution Press, 1982), pp. 273–74. See also North Atlantic Treaty Organization, *NATO and the Warsaw Pact* (1984), pp. 47–48, on military production and technology capabilities.

15. A. Ross Johnson et al., *East European Military Establishments: The Warsaw Pact Northern Tier* (New York: Crane, Russak, 1982), pp. 143–49. See also Daniel N. Nelson, *Alliance Behavior in the Warsaw Pact* (Boulder, Colo.: Westview Press), pp. 27–70.

16. Richard C. Martin, "Warsaw Pact: Force Modernization," *Parameters* 15, no. 2 (summer 1985), pp. 3–11; Teresa Rakowska-Harmstone et al., *Warsaw Pact: The Question of Cohesion,* 3 vols. (Ottawa, Canada: Department of National Defence, 1984–1986).

17. Budapest radio, 27 January 1986; *FBIS,* 28 January 1986, p. AA-1. *Washington Post,* 11 September 1986, p. A-30; Prague radio, 12 September 1986 in *FBIS,* 19 September 1986, p. AA-2.

18. Teresa Rakowska-Harmstone et al., *Warsaw Pact* (1984), vol. I, p. xii.

19. See Robert L. Hutchings, *Foreign and Security Policy Coordination in the Warsaw Pact* (Cologne: Biost, 1985), pp. 1–6.

20. *Pravda,* 15 May 1984. A West German disarmament expert, after attending a conference in Czechoslovakia, stated that the latter and East Germany look upon the new Soviet missiles as "punishment for their countries" (Hamburg radio, 25 June 1984; *FBIS,* 26 June 1984, p. J-4).

21. *Pravda,* 12 June 1986, p. 1.

22. V. A. Menzhinskii, chief ed., *Mezhdunarodnye organizatsii sotsialisticheskikh gosudarstv* (Moscow: Mezhdunarodnye otnosheniia, 1980), p. 57; W. E. Butler, "COMECON and Third Countries," in F. J. M. Feldbrugge and W. W. Simons, eds., *Perspectives on Soviet Law for the 1980s* (The Hague: Nijhoff, 1982), pp. 243–53; letter from Novosti Press Agency to the editor of *The Economist,* 23 June 1984, p. 4.

23. *The Economist* (London), 6 July 1985, pp. 12–13, provides a table comparing energy and steel wasted in selected CMEA and West European countries.

24. *Christian Science Monitor,* 31 March 1983; *Neue Zürcher Zeitung,* 6 April 1984. See also O. T. Bogomolev, *Strany sotsializma v mezhdunarodnom razdelenii truda,* 2nd rev. ed. (Moscow: Nauka, 1986) and his interview in *Nepszabadsag* (Budapest), 13 September 1986, p. 5.

25. Information on what equipment each country will contribute appeared in *Sovetskaia Rossiia,* 19 June 1983, p. 5. Yugoslavia will participate, according to Belgrade radio, 17 April 1984; *FBIS,* 20 April 1984, p. AA 2. For percentages of electricity from nuclear power plants, ranging from zero (Poland) through 11 (USSR) to 31.6 (Bulgaria), see *New York Times,* 31 August 1986.

26. Communiqué in *Pravda,* 19 December 1985, p. 1. For a view from Czechoslovakia, see "Active Participation in the Comprehensive Program," *Rude pravo* (Prague), 11 September 1986, p. 3.

27. *Rude pravo* (Prague), 5 May 1984, p. 6; *Vneshniaia torgovlia,* no. 5 (May 1986): 4. See also Keith Crane, *The Soviet Economic Dilemma of Eastern Europe* (Santa Monica, Calif.: Rand, May 1986), R–3368–AF.

28. *Pravda,* 16 June 1984, pp. 1–2.

29. Ibid., 15 June 1984, p. 1; *Ekonomicheskaia gazeta, no.* 48 (November 1984): 20. See also Philip Joseph, ed., *Adaptability to New Technologies of the USSR and East European Countries* (Brussels: NATO Economics Directorate, 1985); Ferry de Kerckhove, "The Economies of Eastern Europe," *NATO Review:* 34, no. 3 (June 1986), pp. 16–23.

30. Poland's status was suspended in October 1982 after the Solidarity trade unions had been banned. See, however, "U.S.-Polish Relations Start to Thaw," *Los Angeles Times,* 27 March 1986, p. 16, and "West Gets Soft on Jaruzelski," *Insight,* 23 June 1986, pp. 24–25.

31. David E. Albright, "On Eastern Europe: Security Implications for the USSR," *Parameters* 14, no. 2 (Summer 1984): 30, citing Paul Marer. Other estimates, between \$16.5 and \$21.7 billion are given by Charles Wolf, Jr., et al., in *The Costs and Benefits of the Soviet Empire, 1981–1983* (Santa Monica, Calif.: Rand Corporation, 1983), table 6, p. 29. It is impossible, of course, to know the extent of Soviet economic exploitation that should be subtracted from the above figures.

   A Soviet source claims that oil had been delivered to Eastern Europe from 1976 through 1980 at less than world prices, which resulted in savings to recipients of 15 billion rubles (*Krasnaia zvezda,* 7 August 1984, p. 3).

32. Central Intelligence Agency, Directorate of Intelligence, *Handbook of Economic Statistics, 1985,* series CPAS 85–10001, September 1985, Table 8, p. 35. *Trybuna ludu* (Warsaw), 4 July 1981, claimed that the USSR already had given Poland the equivalent of \$4.2 billion in credits during the preceding year. Polish trade within CMEA reportedly had increased from 53.6 to 63.5 percent of total turnover since 1981 (Slavko Stanic over Belgrade radio, 10 May 1983; ibid., 8 June 1983, on "special status"). *Trybuna ludu,* 17 April 1984, revealed the increase in Polish debts to the USSR. One should note that these are regime figures, which may not be accurate. See also Bartlomiej Kaminski, "The Dying Command Economy: Solidarity and the Polish Crisis," *Journal of Contemporary Studies* 8, no. 1 (Winter/Spring 1985), pp. 5–35.

33. Budapest radio, 17 January 1984; *FBIS,* 18 January 1984, p. H-1. See also Gabriel Partos, *CARIS Reports* nos. 8 and 30, 6 February and 13 May 1986, for the economy and foreign trade; Warsaw radio, 9 September 1986 in *FBIS,* 10 September 1986, p. G 6, for rescheduling of debts to the West.

34. *The Economist,* 11 February 1984, p. 46; "Lasting Romanian-Soviet Friendship," AGERPRES (5 July 1986), in *FBIS,* 10 July 1986, p. H-8.

35. Jan Sejna, *We Will Bury You* (London: Sidgwick & Jackson, 1982), pp. 138–39, for the speculation; *Wall Street Journal* 8 May 1986, on the drift in the economy; *New York Times,* 14 August 1986; "Yugoslavia Declares War on Inflation," *CARIS Report,* no. 62/86, 25 July 1986.

36. *The Economist,* 17 November 1984, pp. 49–50; *Insight,* 30 June 1986, pp. 26–27.
37. Nikolaos A. Stavrou, "Origins of the Albanian Communist Movement," *Hellenic Review of International Relations* 3–4, (1983–1984): 73–113; Amnesty International, *Torture in the Eighties* (London, 1984), pp. 207–8; Natalia Bessonova, "When Rebirth Began," *New Times,* no. 2 (January 1986): 13–14.
38. *Pravda,* 17 April 1984; "Prague Party Congress Supports Status Quo," *Washington Post,* 29 March 1986, p. A-20; Sarah M. Terry, "The 27th CPSU Congress and Eastern Europe," *Radio Liberty Research,* 25 March 1986, RL 136/86.
39. "The Party Shows the Way," *Nepszabadsag,* 21 April 1984, p. 5; *Pravda,* 26 April 1986, p. 4; *Los Angeles Times,* 27 July 1986, Part I, p. 2; and "Hungarian Writer and Journal Banned," *CARIS Report* no. 67/86, 11 August 1986.
40. John D. Bell, "Bulgaria," in Richard F. Staar, ed., *1984 Yearbook on International Communist Affairs* (Stanford: Hoover Institution Press, 1984), p. 303; "Bulgaria After the 13th BCP Congress," *Pravda,* 17 July 1986, p. 4; commentary on relations with Bulgaria over Moscow radio, 9 September 1986; *FBIS,* 11 September 1986, p. F1.
41. Central Intelligence Agency, *The World Factbook, 1986* (Washington, D.C.: June 1986), CR WF 86-001, pp. 80 and 226; International Institute for Strategic Studies, *The Military Balance, 1985–1986,* pp. 26 and 33.
42. *Pravda,* 27 July and 2 August 1984; *The Economist,* 13 October 1984, p. 52. See also Federal Republic of Germany, *Zahlenspiegel, BRD/DDR: Ein Vergleich* (Bonn: September 1985).
43. Ernest Gill, "Foreigners in Their Own Land," *New York Times Magazine,* 16 February 1986, p. 46; "Gorbachev's Message to East Germans," *CARIS Talk,* no. 43/86 18 April 1986; "DDR-Grenzsperranlagen," *Innere Sicherheit,* no. 2 (12 May 1986): 23–24; *Pravda,* 4 October 1986, pp. 1–2.
44. Four motorized rifle divisions and one infantry regiment of Czechoslovak troops were demobilized after the August 1968 Soviet invasion (Phillip A. Karber, "The Competition in Conventional Forces Deployed in Central Europe, 1965–1980," in Uwe Nerlich, ed., *The Soviet Asset: Military Power in the Competition over Europe* [Cambridge, Mass.: Ballinger, 1983], pp. 37–38).
45. M. A. Lunderius, "Detente and Foreign Military Presence in Europe," unpublished paper, pp. 9–11. The author, a citizen of Sweden, had been employed with the Stockholm International Peace Research Institute (SIPRI).
46. "Of the National and the International," *Rude pravo,* 10 April 1984, translated in *New Times* (Moscow), no. 16 (April 1984): 12–14. See also O. V. Borisov, "Alliance of a New Type," *Voprosy istorii KPSS,* no. 4 (1984): 34–49; Jens Hacker, "Political Change in the Soviet Union Since Brezhnev and Its Effects on Eastern Europe," *Journal of East and West Studies* 15, no. 1 (Spring/Summer 1986), pp. 231–44.

47. John Van Oudenaren, *The Soviet Union and Eastern Europe: Options for the 1980s and Beyond* (Santa Monica, Calif.: Rand Corporation, March 1984), pp. 73–90, for a long-term prognosis; Vladimir V. Kusin, "Gorbachev and Eastern Europe," *Problems of Communism* 35, no. 1 (January–February 1986): 39–53; Ivan Volgyes, "Troubled Friendship or Mutual Dependence?" *Orbis* 30, no. 2 (Summer 1986), 343–53.

9

EAST-WEST RELATIONS
IN EUROPE

Viewed from Moscow, the small peninsula of Western Europe appears as the mere edge of a vast Eurasian landmass almost completely dominated by the USSR. Western Europe's population, however, remains much larger than that of adjacent Eastern Europe and also more competent in the application of advanced technology as well as in the pursuit of basic research and development. Because of their enormous capacity to produce wealth, the West Europeans represent the most important immediate target of Soviet foreign policy.

LONG-RANGE OBJECTIVES

USSR objectives have military, economic, and political ramifications that overlap. The basic prerequisite for achieving Soviet goals is withdrawal of U.S. troops from Western Europe, especially from the Federal Republic of Germany. If this should occur, decision makers in Moscow probably would concentrate on subverting the remainder of NATO as well as the European Economic Community and, with that accomplished, could be in a position to dictate a fundamental realignment of political forces.

In the unlikely event that American troops are withdrawn unilaterally or, even less conceivably, as a result of an agreement at the Mutual and Balanced Force Reduction negotiations in Vienna, the Soviets would hope for a collapse of the North Atlantic alliance. If the Warsaw Treaty Organization (WTO) were to be dissolved as a symbolic part of the bargain, this would still leave in place the web of twenty-year bilateral treaties that bind all of the WTO states in Eastern Europe to the USSR.

After the hypothetical breakup of NATO, the Soviet Union most probably would attempt to frustrate establishment of an independent European nuclear force. Moscow certainly would make a sustained effort to block any UK–France cooperation that could enhance their individual deterrent forces. Indications of such a future approach can be seen from earlier Soviet demands[1] that the nuclear delivery systems of these two countries be counted in the INF and/or START negotiations (1981–1983) and at first in the new talks since 12 March 1985 with the United States at Geneva.

The final stage in this process might well involve unilateral disarmament throughout all of Western Europe, after the two Germanys already had done so and been declared neutralized as well as non-aligned within a Central European "nuclear free" zone. One is reminded here of the historic struggle between Rome and Carthage for control over the Mediterranean, which resulted in the latter's population being exterminated or reduced to slavery.[2] Alternating between the carrot of "detente" and the frequently brandished club of its growing military might (made more credible by the suggestion that the United States may be unwilling or unable to defend its allies), Moscow most assuredly keeps its ultimate objective of domination over Western Europe firmly in mind.

The economic "weapon" remains no less important in future Soviet–West European relations. For example, France during 1985 had a 571 million ruble deficit in its trade with the USSR.[3] Some 83 percent of French imports from the Soviet Union consist of oil and natural gas. Delivery of the latter accelerated after completion of the pipeline between Urengoi and the border of West Germany. It now operates at full capacity. Annual deliveries for the Federal Republic of Germany will amount to 10.5 billion cubic meters; France and Italy to 8 billion each; Belgium and the Netherlands to 5 billion each; Austria to 3 billion; and Switzerland to around one billion. If, as may happen, the second planned natural gas pipeline is not built, the Soviet Union will earn less than $5 billion per year from sales, estimated to total only 20 billion cubic meters, or half the originally anticipated volume for Western Europe. Italy, for example, renegotiated[4] its agreement down to 4.4 billion cubic meters from a previous level of 8 billion.

Dependence upon fuel from the USSR may be dangerous, as mentioned already in Chapter 7, especially if Moscow decides to suspend deliveries at various points because of what the Soviets like to call "technical difficulties." Even though the chairman of Ruhrgas, A.G., the privately owned utility in West Germany, is quoted as stating that the USSR has been a reliable supplier of natural gas since 1968, the fact is that Moscow did cut off petroleum supplies to Romania in 1980, when that country assumed a foreign policy stance not to Soviet liking. Still, the growth of East-West trade continues. Mannesmann, A.G., a West German company making steel products, has been negotiating with the USSR, which wants coal-processing equipment in order to develop reserves in southern Siberia. Finally, the Soviet Union is expected to apply for membership in both the International Monetary Fund and the World Bank in order to qualify for large loans.[5]

Along with its economic warfare, the USSR can be expected to continue exercising whatever political leverage it has in Western Europe. Lenin had taught that the Soviets must exploit basic "contradictions" or conflicts throughout the industrialized world, not only those of workers versus capitalists but also those among "imperialist" countries themselves. Such conflicts are plentiful in the West and could conceivably become the basis for a radical domestic realignment of political forces within certain West European states, resulting in a decoupling of the United States from its NATO allies.

At one time, Soviet decision makers no doubt hoped that local communist parties and agents of influence as well as terrorist organizations might play a part in this process. The communist movement in Europe has become fragmented, however, with pro-Moscow groups standing little chance of participating in coalition governments or even influencing them when they do gain access to and share power. Only in the case of Finland can the USSR still prevent a non-cooperative candidate from running for the presidency or a local politician from standing for parliament.[6] By contrast, until they resigned in 1984, the three communist cabinet members in the socialist government of France had exercised little, if any, significant influence on the foreign policies of President François Mitterrand.

As for the future, it is conceivable that a neutralized Federal Republic of Germany could be susceptible to political pressure. During his last visit to Bonn, the late Leonid I. Brezhnev actually threatened his hosts with USSR military power. It must be remembered that an overwhelming Warsaw Pact force is concentrated on the territory of the neighboring German Democratic Republic (GDR). Such intimidation certainly may have an effect in the future, to the degree that Western Europe undertakes unilateral disarmament.

The language of such Soviet threats to NATO countries is exceedingly explicit. Scandinavian members of the North Atlantic alliance were told that they would "burn in the fire of a nuclear war [fought] in the name of 'Atlantic Solidarity.'" The 1983 election of Helmut Kohl, the USSR said, could result in West Germany "ascending a nuclear gallows." Similarly, deployment of U.S. ground-launched cruise missiles would convert all of Italy into "a Pompeii." Despite such unambiguous nuclear blackmail, the foreign ministers of Italy, Spain, the Federal Republic of Germany, and the president of France himself all visited Moscow during the initial two months of Chernenko's incumbency as party-state leader. A similar "pilgrimage" has taken place since March 1985, when Gorbachev became CPSU general secretary.[7]

Side by side with these open threats, the Soviet-directed "active measures" network has been attempting to destabilize NATO member governments by supporting indigenous terrorists. Money from Czechoslovakia went to the Baader-Meinhof terrorist gang in the Federal Republic of Germany (FRG). Moscow maintains active ties with the terrorist Basque ETA in Spain. And weapons from the USSR have found their way to the Irish Republican Army in Northern Ireland as well as to the Red Brigades in Italy. During 1985 about 40,000 East Germans emigrated legally to the FRG, and over the first eight months of 1986 the same number of "refugees" from the Middle East came into West Berlin from the GDR. How many terrorists were among them is not known.[8]

It is likely that the Soviets envision the assimilation of Western Europe occurring in stages, beginning with the neutralization of various countries, leading perhaps to formation of a commonwealth of "socialist" satellite states, and finally culminating in the establishment of a single integrated communist regime under USSR guidance. Whether or not Kremlin leaders have a specific blueprint in mind, Moscow can be depended upon to take advantage of opportunities and of any power vacuum that may occur if the United States were to withdraw from the continent.

SHORT-TERM OBJECTIVES

Almost all of the proposals offered by the USSR and its East European client states (as well as the non-ruling-communist parties from Western Europe) at the 24–26 April 1967 conference in Karlovy Vary, Czechoslovakia, and initially resisted by the West, were in fact accepted by the latter within the ensuing eight years. These original demands had included the following:[9]

1. recognition of *de facto* existing borders in Europe;
2. acceptance of two sovereign and equal German states;
3. a ban on nuclear weapons for the Federal Republic of Germany;
4. acknowledgment that the 1938 Munich agreement had been invalid *ab initio*;
5. a treaty renouncing the use or threat of force by all European states;
6. diplomatic recognition of East Germany and of West Berlin as separate independent political entities;
7. abrogation of the ban on the communist party in the Federal Republic of Germany; and
8. conclusion of a non-proliferation treaty as a step toward halting the arms race.

The Soviet invasion of Czechoslovakia in August 1968, only sixteen months after the Karlovy Vary conference, interrupted the beginning of a thaw in East-West relations. Yet by the end of the following year, the United States government had decided to ignore the military occupation of this supposedly "independent" country and to initiate strategic arms limitation talks with the USSR.

THE HELSINKI FINAL ACT

In 1973 the West began to make preparations for a Conference on Security and Cooperation in Europe (CSCE) after obtaining agreement from the East that both the United States and Canada would participate, that access to the USSR and Eastern Europe would be liberalized (the four-power protocol on Berlin had been signed in 1972), and that talks on Mutual and Balanced Force Reductions would begin in Vienna. The CSCE discussions formally opened with preliminary proceedings at the foreign ministers' level. The working phase lasted almost two years, and the Final Act was approved by 35 heads of government on 1 August 1975 at Helsinki.[10]

In retrospect, the outcome appears to have been one-sided. The West had hoped to create the necessary conditions for arms control, to increase cooperation, and to promote human rights in the East. In the end, none of these goals was achieved. Eastern objectives, by contrast, included *de jure* recognition of postwar borders in Europe, acquisition of advanced technology through trade, strengthening the appearance of detente, and improvement of conditions for unilateral Western disarmament. All of these, except for the last, were attained, although Washington later issued an official statement to the effect that USSR annexation of the Baltic states had not been recognized by the United States government.

From the start, moreover, the Helsinki accords were violated by the East. The most blatant transgression occurred in December 1979 when Soviet troops invaded Afghanistan. At least six of the basic principles agreed upon (sovereign equality, non-use of force, inviolability of frontiers, territorial integrity, non-intervention in internal affairs, and self-determination) were ignored completely by Moscow and are being violated as of this writing.

Less than a year after the USSR had occupied Afghanistan, the second CSCE review conference convened in November 1980 at Madrid (the first had been held in Belgrade during 1977–1978). It continued well into 1983 because of disagreements over wording of the final communiqué. The process revealed, in the American view,[11] a "serious decline in the necessary good faith compliance with the provisions of the Final Act on the part of a number of important signatories, including the Soviet Union."

Although USSR behavior thus far appears not to have been modified in the slightest by the Helsinki agreement, talks on confidence-building measures between East and West were undertaken again at Stockholm and on peaceful settlement of disputes at Athens in January and March 1984, respectively. More discussion of human rights occurred during 1985 at Ottawa and on reunification of families from 15 April to 26 May 1986 at Berne.[12] The process continues at the third CSCE review conference, which opened on 4 November 1986 at Vienna.

The Conference on Confidence- and Security-Building Measures and Disarmament in Europe (CDE) included delegations from the same 35 governments that participated in the original meeting at Helsinki and both follow-on assessments. Within a week after CDE had convened, the NATO alliance proposed to discuss the following in detail: (1) exchange of information on the organization and location of armed forces, (2) exchange of annual plans for military activities, (3) at least 45 days' advance notice of significant maneuvers, (4) presence of observers at such war games, (5) monitoring and verification of compliance with agreements reached by the CDE, and (6) improved communications.[13]

In contrast to these specific proposals, then Foreign Minister Gromyko indicated at the CDE opening session that the East wanted broad agreements on "no first use" of nuclear weapons, "non-aggression," limitation of defense budgets, a ban on chemical weapons, and nuclear free zones in Europe. In exchange, the Soviet spokesman offered a promise to elaborate on limits and prenotification of military maneuvers at some point in the future.[14] The USSR proposal amounted, in essence, to a general statement of intent rather than a specific basis for negotiations. In an attempt to break the stalemate, the American delegation head spent two days in Moscow at the end of April 1984 in meetings also attended by his Soviet counterpart. President Reagan, when addressing the parliament of Ireland, offered to accept the USSR proposal for a renunciation of force agreement if the latter would make concessions on confidence-building measures. TASS immediately rejected the compromise.[15]

Almost four months after the CDE talks had begun, the Soviet Union presented its formal proposal, put forward by that government alone and not in the name of other Warsaw Pact members. (One reason for the USSR's unilateral performance may have been that Romania had submitted its own outline on 25 January 1984, the day after NATO made its offer.) The USSR suggested the following general confidence-building measures without any further details:

1. limitation of military exercises to a *certain* numerical level;
2. prior notification of *major* military maneuvers;
3. prior notification of *major* movements and transfers;
4. development of the *existing* practice of inviting observers to major military maneuvers; and
5. *adequate* forms of verification. [Italics added.]

Two years later, a *Pravda* headline stressed "The Need for Good Will" on the part of the West, which suggested that there might not be any Soviet concession. The USSR chief delegate stated during the following month: "We could . . . agree to the conduct of on-site inspection." The negotiations at Stockholm ended in September 1986, with a compromise agreement that probably will not lead to any genuine confidence-building measures.[16]

CONVENTIONAL FORCE REDUCTIONS

Objectives have differed also at the Mutual and Balanced Force Reduction (MBFR) talks in Vienna, which began in October 1973 and include twelve Western and seven Eastern delegations. The reluctance with which they agreed to participate gave the Soviets an advantage from the beginning. In the course of the talks, the USSR has sought to solidify the favorable correlation of armed forces in Central Europe, has taken advantage of Western concessions, and has attempted to exploit as well as create differences among the NATO allies.

The West had offered in December 1975 to withdraw 1,000 theater nuclear warheads, a total of 54 aircraft (F-4s), and 36 Pershing I missile launchers, as well as 29,000 American troops if the East removed an entire 68,000 man Soviet tank army with its full complement of 1,700 tanks. No satisfactory response ever came from the East. It continued to propose that each side reduce troops by the same percentage, which actually would have increased ratios in favor of the already overwhelming Warsaw Pact preponderance.

Reductions do not make any sense, of course, unless agreement can be reached on figures for existing manpower. In order to obtain such data from the East, NATO negotiators agreed not to consider the four Soviet divisions stationed in Hungary. The Eastern count of Warsaw Pact ground forces issued in mid-1976 amounted to 120,000 less than the lowest Western estimate. Eight years later, that discrepancy had risen to approximately 180,000 ground troops.[17] If air force manpower is added, the total becomes 210,000 (see Table 9.1). No progress has been made in the MBFR negotiations as of this writing, despite the fact that both sides have submitted proposals in treaty form plus additional modifications.

The NATO draft agreement of mid-July 1982 included a major concession: individual reductions would be specified upon signature of a single comprehensive treaty, something that the East had insisted upon from the start of the talks. It would have seemed to be the Soviet turn to clear up the data problem and/or to agree upon a set of Western-proposed confidence-building and associated measures that include verification.[18] The USSR and its allies do not appear to want an agreement at this time, since it would require them to reduce their ground forces by 270,000 men, compared with approximately 90,000 for NATO, in order to bring the two sides to genuine parity.

One approach has been suggested to solve this data discrepancy—namely, concentrating on residual troop levels after reductions have taken place. This would imply that the East might be willing to take out more than a quarter of a million men, if these reductions were not watched by Western observers, and then allow inspection of the 700,000 ground troop residual force in the reduction area (East Germany, Poland, Czechoslovakia).[19] Obviously, such a resolution of the problem would require subsequent intrusive verification measures, including mandatory on-site inspection, hitherto resisted by the Soviet Union.

TABLE 9.1

DISPARITY BETWEEN FORCES OF EASTERN AND WESTERN DIRECT
PARTICIPANTS IN THE REDUCTION AREA (MBFR) 1 JANUARY 1981

	ACCORDING TO NATO ESTIMATES		
	NATO estimate for WTO forces	*Western figures for NATO forces*	*Disparity*
Ground	960,000	790,000	*170,000
Air	230,000	200,000	30,000
Total	1,190,000	990,000	*200,000
	According to Warsaw Pact Data		
	Eastern figures for WTO forces	*Western figures for NATO forces*	*Disparity*
Ground	800,000	790,000	10,000
Air	180,000	200,000	−20,000
Total	980,000	990,000	−10,000

NOTE: *A more recent source (see note 17 for this chapter) raises each of these figures by 10,000 men.
SOURCE: U.S. Delegation to MBFR, *Mutual and Balanced Force Reductions,* June 1983, appendix to a mimeographed and unclassified report from Vienna, Austria.

After criticizing the comprehensive Western proposal for almost a year, the East did submit in June 1983 a new draft treaty of its own. This document concentrates on monitoring final ceilings and not the reductions themselves, as alluded to above. Among the associated measures proposed by the Warsaw Pact is one, with the "opportunity to carry out on-the-spot checks, provided certain conditions are observed."[20] This deliberately vague formulation is not intended to imply mandatory inspection.

The long recess between mid-December 1983 and mid-March 1984, after the East had reversed its previous decision not to agree on a date for resumption of the talks, had been utilized by the Western delegations to prepare a compromise proposal. This document cleared the NATO Council and could be submitted to the East on 19 April 1984 along the following lines:[21]

1. data to be exchanged only on ground combat and combat support forces;
2. this information should fall within an acceptable range of Western estimates [that is, no precise agreement necessary];

3. initial token Soviet and U.S. reductions;
4. satisfactory verification of remaining forces; and only then,
5. a full agreement on data.

In return, the Warsaw Pact was asked to accept the associated measures proposed as far back as December 1979 by the West. The East had raised the possibility of a trade-off between data and verification on many occasions in the past. However, on 7 June 1984, the East rejected the NATO attempt at breaking the deadlock in MBFR.

Other proposals were presented during 1985. In February the USSR offered to remove 20,000 of its troops if the U.S. took out 13,000 from the respective reduction areas, with a freeze on the remainder. Only "three or four" observation points would be allowed on each side. The West responded in December, proposing withdrawal of 11,500 Soviet and 5,000 American soldiers; a collective no-increase commitment for three years; and verification measures, including 30 annual on-site inspections. Rather than attempt to negotiate the differences, Gorbachev complicated matters at the 11th East German communist party congress on 18 April 1986 by offering an extended reduction area "from the Atlantic to the Urals," which would involve withdrawing 500,000 men from each side. In December 1986, NATO accepted the area extension.[22]

Thus there appears to be little cause for optimism as the Vienna talks enter their fourteenth year. An agreement reducing the massive concentration of conventional armed forces in Central Europe should be advantageous for both sides. Obviously, the East does not think so and prefers to retain its conventional superiority, which can be used for political blackmail also in the future (see Table 9.2). A change of venue or format of the talks will not affect that.

INTERMEDIATE-RANGE NUCLEAR FORCES

Despite the fact that the USSR announced on 6 May 1978 its acceptance of military parity as a principle, there has been a steady and constant build-up of its intermediate-range nuclear forces (INF) since that time. As of late 1986, Soviet INF forces included 112 SS-4 single warhead launchers plus about 441 mobile triple warhead SS-20s. Some 270 of the latter are targeted against Western Europe. The first INF salvo could deliver almost 1,000 nuclear warheads. Each launcher reportedly stocks at least one but probably more refire missiles that also hold three SS-20 warheads each.[23]

TABLE 9.2
NATO–WARSAW PACT FORCE COMPARISON, 1986

Category	NATO	Warsaw Pact
1. Total military (incl. navy)	4,500,000	6,000,000
2. Division equivalents	121	202
3. Main battle tanks (armament, 90 mm or above)	24,250	49,000
4. Anti-tank guided weapon launchers	22,580	33,000
5. Artillery mortars (tubes, 100 mm or above)	18,350	41,000
6. Armored vehicles	41,500	74,000
7. Attack helicopters	1,250	950
8. Transport/support helicopters	6,000	1,950

SOURCE: U.S. Department of Defense, *Soviet Military Power, 1986* (Washington, D.C.: The Pentagon, March 1986), p. 91.

Perhaps anticipating these developments, NATO agreed upon the "dual track" decision in December 1979, that is, to modernize its own weapons' systems through deployment of 572 Pershing IIs and ground-launched cruise missiles (GLCMs), both types with one warhead each, while supporting U.S. negotiations for an INF arms control agreement with the Soviet Union. Deployment was scheduled to begin in December 1983 and continue through 1988, barring successful attainment of a treaty between the United States and the USSR.

In February 1982, the U.S. delegation submitted a draft agreement embodying the "zero option," which envisaged non-deployment of any new Pershings or GLCMs, if the Soviets eliminated all of their intermediate-range missiles, of which they possessed a monopoly. The USSR responded by claiming that a balance already existed and proposed that the sides reduce their totals to 300 each. It modified this later by suggesting a level equal to the combined total of British and French ballistic missiles. The latter are not assigned to NATO and, in any event, represent strategic rather than intermediate-range systems. At the time, Defense Minister Dmitrii F. Ustinov warned[24] that the USSR would retaliate directly against the United States and those NATO countries which accepted INF deployments.

This blackmail approach registered only limited success. The Federal Republic of Germany, after the March 1983 elections, reaffirmed that it would accept 110 Pershing II and 96 Tomahawk ground-launched cruise missiles. Another 160 of the latter would be placed in the United Kingdom and 110 in Italy. Only 48 each were to go into Belgium and the Netherlands.[25] The first nine Pershing IIs were deployed in West Germany at the end of December 1983, more than a month after the Soviets had walked out of the Geneva talks. During the same time, England and Italy installed sixteen GLCMs each. Because no agreement had been reached at Geneva, almost all of the NATO allies have accepted the new U.S. weapons systems. The latter will not redress the balance completely but did convince the USSR to resume negotiations in March 1985 (see Table 9.3 and Figure 9.1).

The missile controversy has been attended by "peace demonstrations" in the Federal Republic of Germany[26] and elsewhere throughout Western Europe. These protests were largely spearheaded by what could be termed the generation of 1968, which began in the mid-1970s to occupy positions of influence in government, education, and the churches. One conspicuous group in this movement are the co-opted anti-industry and apolitical ecologists. The West German parliament, or *Bundestag,* now includes 27 members (from a 520 total) of these so-called Greens, whose avowed aim is destruction of the political system. The Soviets have proven extremely efficient in exploiting such indigenous developments for their own purposes; however, the demonstrations seem to have lost their momentum.[27]

WEST-EAST TECHNOLOGY TRANSFER

The huge quantities of weaponry at the disposal of the USSR and its allies have been offset to a certain extent by NATO technological superiority. In some areas, the development gap between West and East may even be widening. Introduction of "smart" weapons, especially with the use of micro-electronics and computers, soon will revolutionize the battlefield. The NATO Defense Planning Council adopted new guidelines in early November 1984, the "Follow-on Forces Attack," to hit enemy reinforcements up to hundreds of miles beyond the East-West border by exploiting the new technology.[28]

That the Soviet Union is most desirous of obtaining this "high-tech" knowledge can be seen from the activities by KGB Directorate "T," which disposes of approximately 300 intelligence specialist officers stationed abroad to direct the effort. These men operate out of USSR embassies, trade missions, and export-import companies designed for the acquisition of advanced technology as well as for industrial espionage and theft. More than half of the 135 expulsions of Soviet "diplo-

TABLE 9.3
INF DEPLOYMENTS: USSR AND U.S. PERSPECTIVES ON THE BALANCE, 1983

Soviet Assessment			
WESTERN SYSTEMS		SOVIET SYSTEMS	
System	*Number*	*System*	*Number*
United States			
Fighter-bombers		Land-based missiles	
F-111s	172	(SS-20s, SS-5s, SS-4s)	496
FB-111s	65	Submarine missiles	18
F-4s	246	Medium-range bombers	
A-6s & A-7s	240	(Backfire/Badger/Blinder)	461
United Kingdom			
Polaris missiles	64		
Vulcan bombers	55		
France			
Land-based missiles	18		
Submarine missiles	80		
Mirage-4 bombers	46		
Total	986	Total	975

American Assessment			
U.S. SYSTEMS		SOVIET SYSTEMS	
F-111 fighter-bombers	164	SS-20s	378
F-4s	265	SS-4s & SS-5s	350
A-6s & A-7s	68	SS-12s & 22s	100
FB-111s (U.S.-based for		TU-26 Backfire bombers	45
use in Europe)	63	TU-16 Badgers &	
Pershing I	9	TU-22 Blinders	350
GLCMs	32	SU-17, SU-24, & MiG-27	
		fighter-bombers	2,700
		SS-N-5s	30
Total	601	Total	3,953

NOTE: The USSR includes third-country missile and bomber systems in its overall count. Soviet inclusion of French and British strategic systems in the NATO balance is incorrect and therefore misleading. French forces are totally independent of the NATO nuclear deterrent, and France does not participate in NATO's integrated military command. While the U.K. participates in the integrated command, its SLBMs are clearly strategic deterrent forces.

SOURCE: U.S. Department of Defense, "Soviet Claims on the Nuclear Balance in Europe," *Background Paper* (Washington, D.C., 1983), pp. 6–9.

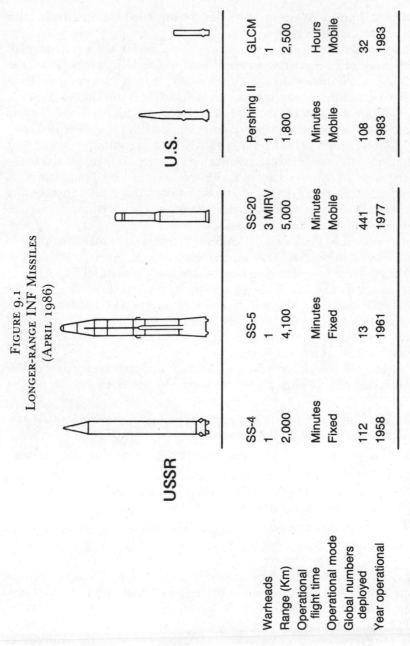

FIGURE 9.1
LONGER-RANGE INF MISSILES
(APRIL 1986)

	USSR				U.S.	
	SS-4	SS-5	SS-20		Pershing II	GLCM
Warheads	1	1	3 MIRV		1	1
Range (Km)	2,000	4,100	5,000		1,800	2,500
Operational flight time	Minutes	Minutes	Minutes		Minutes	Hours
Operational mode	Fixed	Fixed	Mobile		Mobile	Mobile
Global numbers deployed	112	13	441		108	32
Year operational	1958	1961	1977		1983	1983

SOURCES: U.S. Department of Defense, Joint Chiefs of Staff, *Military Posture, FY 1985* (Washington, D.C.: GPO, 1984), p. 35; *Soviet Military Power, 1986*, p. 37.

mats" from various Western countries during 1983 resulted from such activities (see Table 5.1).

In August of that year, seven people were fined by the government of Switzerland for re-exporting strategic computer equipment via France to Warsaw Pact countries. In the same month, British customs officials at Dover seized computer parts destined for the USSR and labeled "typesetting equipment." Toward the end of the year, machines on their way to Czechoslovakia were also stopped in the United Kingdom. The two powerful Digital Equipment Corporation VAX 11–782 computers, capable of guiding ballistic missiles, were confiscated en route via South Africa to the Soviet Union by West Germany and Sweden (mentioned in Chapter 5). During calendar year 1986, at least forty of the latest-model engineering work stations were diverted to Eastern Europe. They are used for design of memory chips and microprocessors.

As previously discussed, in order to curtail such illegal shipments and ordinary theft, NATO (minus Iceland) and Japan established in 1949 at Paris the Coordinating Committee for Multilateral Export Controls, known as CoCom. This group has drawn up three lists for military, atomic energy, and dual-use items or commercial goods with military applications.[29] It has been mentioned already that CoCom reviews license requests from companies in its fifteen member states and attempts to harmonize enforcement.

During the 1980s, according to the U.S. undersecretary of state for security assistance, science and technology, the Soviet Union is

1. increasing the selective search for critical components that affect performance of its weapons;
2. concentrating on production equipment and technology rather than end-products;
3. giving the East European intelligence services an even greater role in individual espionage; and
4. stepping up acquisition of American technology outside U.S. borders.[30]

It is obvious that technology and equipment from Western Europe and/or North America contribute directly to USSR military programs, saving research and development costs, revealing the directions of NATO planning, and thus assisting in development of countermeasures. If reverse engineering is achieved, series production from copies can be initiated. Items with dual civil/military application also may benefit the Soviet economy. Even personal computers are in use by NATO

for battlefield communications and management.[31] These are some of
the reasons CoCom has revised its export controls on computers.

FUTURE PROSPECTS

After the Soviets had failed in their blatant threats to prevent the initial
modernization of NATO intermediate-range nuclear forces, they broke
off negotiations with the United States at Geneva. The USSR most
probably will continue to use whatever means remain at its disposal to
subvert the American commitment to Western Europe. Walking out of
the talks denied it a propaganda forum that had been utilized rather
successfully, often in violation of the agreement to maintain confidenti-
ality regarding what went on behind closed doors.

Soviet representatives also made a habit during these negotiations
of deceiving Western public opinion, if not the NATO governments.
Thus, in March 1982, Moscow announced a unilateral moratorium on
further deployment of INF missiles in the European part of the USSR.
Two months later, a government spokesman explained what this
meant: no further preparations for deployment would take place.
However, between March and December 1982, four additional SS-20
sites were completed—while the Geneva talks were in progress—which
added more than 100 warheads to the Soviet arsenal.[32]

As in the MBFR negotiations, moreover, the East was less than
honest when it released INF figures. The data comparisons of arsenals,
made public by the USSR, were based upon numbers of launchers and
not warheads, thus undervaluing the three-warhead SS-20 (Pershing
and ground-launched cruise missiles carry only one warhead each). In
addition, unmentioned by the Soviets were the SS-22s now stationed in
East Germany,[33] which have a range of 1,000 kilometers and can hit
targets throughout most of France and Britain.

By demanding that sea-based missiles and ICBMs of the United Kingdom and France be considered as part of the Western INF total, the USSR
in effect counted the same forces twice, since provisions had already been
made in *strategic,* as opposed to intermediate-range, negotiations to an-
swer Soviet concerns about these weapons. In addition, when adding the
totals, the Soviets failed to count their own "Fencer" bomber, capable of
delivering nuclear ordinance, as well as SS-12 (also excluded was the
follow-on SS-22, mentioned above) land-based mobile missiles.[34]

One must consider also the qualitative improvements in Soviet INF
weapons systems and what this means. Accuracy has been improved by
one-sixth in the SS-20 versus the SS-4. The latter can only be used

effectively against "soft" civilian sites, whereas the former is capable of destroying hardened military targets. The potential for a first strike by the USSR is in place. As a consequence, Western Europe will remain militarily inferior and vulnerable if the Soviet Union's definition of national security is accepted. None of this, meanwhile, seems to have affected the decisions by European, Canadian, and Japanese banks to provide the Soviet Union with $4.5 billion in new loans, despite the fact that the latter at that time already owed more than $28.7 billion to the West. Almost two-thirds of this amount has been subsidized by tax-payers.[35] Soviet foreign policy vis-à-vis the Third World projects a different image, as discussed in the next chapter.

NOTES

1. Jean-Louis Arnaud's interview with USSR General Iurii Lebedev, pub-lished by *Le Matin* (Paris), 20 July 1983, pp. 3–4.
2. Walter F. Hahn, "Disarmament: An Ancient Story," *Strategic Review* 10, no. 3 (Summer 1982): 9–10.
3. "Soviet Foreign Trade by Countries," *Foreign Trade* (Moscow), no. 3, March 1986. The record sale of 4 billion francs worth of French steel products oc-curred that same year (Paris radio, 23 May 1985; *FBIS,* 24 May 1985, p. K2).
4. *New York Times,* 27 May 1983, for original sales estimates; *Wall Street Jour-nal,* 29 May 1984, p. 26, for revised figures. However, the $64 billion contract for Norwegian natural gas deliveries to Western Europe over the next twenty years should lessen reliance on the USSR, according to ibid., 12 August 1986, p. 30.
5. *The Economist,* 15 September 1984, pp. 88–89, on the coal project; *Wall Street Journal,* 15 August 1986, p. 20, for IMF and World Bank. See also Iu. V. Andreev and V. N. Shenaev, eds., *SSSR–Zapadnaia Evropa* (Moscow: Mezhdunarodnye otnosheniia, 1986).
6. "Finlandized Germany?" *Wall Street Journal,* 2 March 1983. Soviet trade with Finland ranked high during 1985, with a turnover of almost 5 billion rubles (*Foreign Trade* [Moscow], no. 3, March 1986).
7. For Soviet threats, see *Washington Post,* 23 May 1984. During 1983–1984, the USSR and West German foreign ministers held six meetings (ibid., 22 May 1984). For the superlatives used by President Mitterand to describe Gorbachev, see *Le Monde* (Paris), 12 July 1986, p. 1.
8. Claire Sterling, *The Terror Network* (New York: Holt, Rinehart & Winston, 1981), pp. 286–97; *New York Times,* 1 September 1985; ibid., 21 July 1986; Hamburg radio, 18 September 1986, in *FBIS* for same date, p. J-2.
9. *Information Bulletin* (Prague: Peace and Socialism Publishers), nos. 8–10, 1967. See the discussion by Richard V. Allen, ed., *1968 Yearbook on Interna-*

tional Communist Affairs (Stanford: Hoover Institution Press, 1969), pp. 753–57.

10. United States Embassy, Helsinki, *News Release,* 1 August 1975.

11. U.S. Congress, Commission on Security and Cooperation in Europe, *Implementation of the Final Act to the Conference on Security and Cooperation in Europe: Findings and Recommendations Seven Years after Helsinki,* 97th Cong., 2nd sess., 1982, Committee Print, provides excellent coverage. Quotation is from the letter of transmittal. See also U.S. Department of State, *Implementation of Helsinki Final Act* (October 1985–April 1986), 10th Semiannual Report, published in July 1986.

12. *CSCE Digest* (Washington, D.C.), June 1986; Michael H. Armacost, "The CSCE Process," *Current Policy,* no. 813 (25 March 1986); Vojtech Mastny, *Helsinki, Human Rights, and European Security* (Durham, N.C.: Duke University Press, 1986), pp. 333–48.

13. Conference on Confidence- and Security-Building Measures and Disarmament in Europe, *Confidence- and Security-Building Measures (CSBMs) Proposed by the Delegations of Belgium, Canada, Denmark, France, Federal Republic of Germany, Greece, Iceland, Italy, Luxembourg, Netherlands, Norway, Portugal, Spain, Turkey, United Kingdom, United States of America* (Stockholm: U.S. Delegation to CDE, 24 January 1984), series CSCE/SC.1, pp. 2–4.

14. See, e.g., O. N. Bykov, *Mery doveriia* (Moscow: Nauka, 1983), pp. 71–72, who listed these same measures one year before the conference opened in Stockholm.

15. Moscow radio, 27 April 1984; *FBIS,* 30 April 1984, p. AA-1, for the Moscow meetings; *Wall Street Journal,* 5 June 1984, p. 31, for the speech in Dublin and rejection by TASS.

16. Conference on Confidence- and Security-Building Measures and Disarmament in Europe, *Confidence- and Security-Building Measures in Europe: Proposals of the Soviet Union* (Stockholm: U.S. Delegation to CDE, 8 May 1984), series CSCE/SC.4, pp. 4–5.

   Almost one year after the CDE talks started, the USSR agreed to the establishment of working groups to examine specific proposals (Moscow radio, 3 December 1984; *FBIS,* 4 December 1984, p. AA2). See also *Pravda,* 19 July 1986; ibid., 26 September 1986, p. 4. Part V of "Key Sections of Document at Stockholm Meeting," *New York Times,* 22 September 1986, mentions only three inspections per year in the agreement.

17. U.S. Department of State, "Arms Control: MBFR Talks," *Gist,* May 1986, p. 2.

18. Richard F. Staar, "The MBFR Process and Its Prospects," in Staar, ed., *Arms Control: Myth Versus Reality* (Stanford: Hoover Institution Press, 1984), pp. 47–58. See also by the same author, "Soviet Deception at MBFR," in Brian D. Dailey and Patrick J. Parker, eds., *Soviet Strategic Deception* (Lexington, Mass.: Lexington Books, 1987), pp. 261–72.

19. U.S. Congress, House, Committee on Foreign Affairs, Subcommittee on

International Security and Scientific Affairs, *East-West Troop Reductions in Europe: Is Agreement Possible?* 98th Cong., 1st sess., 1983, pp. 14–16.

20. Interview with head of the Soviet delegation, as reported in the communist party newspaper *Volksstimme* (Vienna), 2 July 1983. See also Michael Alexander, "MBFR-Verification Is the Key," *NATO Review* 34, no. 3 (June 1986), pp. 6–11.

21. Wilfried Aichinger, "Die Wiener Truppenabbauverhandlungen: Eine Bestandsaufnahme," *Österreichische Militärische Zeitschrift* 22, no. 3 (May–June 1984): 189–95; Carnes Lord, "The MBFR Mystery," *The American Spectator* 19, no. 6 (June 1986): 14–15.

22. *Los Angeles Times,* 15 February 1985; *Gist,* May 1986, pp. 1–2; *Horizont* (East Berlin), no. 6 (June 1986): 9; *Christian Science Monitor,* 12 December 1986.

23. U.S. Department of Defense, *Soviet Military Power, 1986* (Washington, D.C.: GPO, 1986), p. 37; Michael R. Gordon in the *New York Times,* 21 September 1986, for numbers of launchers.

24. *Pravda,* 31 July 1983.

25. The Netherlands government postponed deployment because of its weakness vis-à-vis the domestic political opposition. After Prime Minister Ruud Lubbers visited Moscow, the USSR attempted unsuccessfully to continue talks that would reverse the decision (*NTC Handelsblad,* 1 November 1985, p. 3). Subsequently, deployment was announced.

26. David Gress, *Peace and Survival: West Germany, the Peace Movement, and European Security* (Stanford: Hoover Institution Press, 1985).

27. Gerhard Wettig, "The Western Peace Movement in Moscow's Longer View," *Strategic Review* 12, no. 2 (Spring 1984): 44–54. At their congress, the Greens called for withdrawal from NATO and abolition of all nuclear power stations, according to the *New York Times,* 21 May 1986. They conduct regular talks with the CPSU, according to Hamburg radio, 21 April 1986; *FBIS,* 22 April 1986, p. J6; *Pravda,* 15 November 1986, p. 4.

28. General Bernard W. Rogers, SACEUR, "Follow-on Forces Attack: Myths and Realities," *Parameters* 15, no. 2 (Summer 1985): 75–79; Manfred Woerner, "A Missile Defense for NATO Europe," *Strategic Review* 14, no. 1 (Winter 1986): 13–19; Stephen J. Cimbala, "Flexible Targeting and War in Europe," *Armed Forces & Society* 12, no. 3 (Spring 1986): 383–400.

29. U.S. Department of State, "Controlling Transfer of Strategic Technology," *Gist,* April 1986.
Despite these controls by CoCom, the USSR Military-Industrial Commission has been drawing up lists of desired technological secrets totaling over 3,500 each year and obtaining more than one-third from the West. Report by the U.S. Senate Select Committee on Intelligence, cited by the *New York Times,* 18 October 1986, p. 16.

30. William Schneider, Jr., "Statement to the Federal Bar Association," Newton, Mass., 29 March 1984, mimeographed transcript, p. 9.

31. Central Intelligence Agency, *Soviet Acquisition of Militarily Significant Western Technology: An Update* (Washington, D.C.: September 1985).

32. U.S. Department of State, *INF Arms Reduction and Modernization Issues* (March 1983), p. 41. See also John Cartwright and Julian Critchley, *Cruise, Pershing and SS-20* (London: Brassey's Defence Publishers, 1985).

33. *The Economist,* 11 February 1984, p. 17, includes a map. The SS-22 (range, 550 miles) has been augmented by the SS-23 (range, 300 miles) and the SS-21 (range, 75 miles), according to the *New York Times,* 2 March 1986, p. 4.

34. For the Soviet propaganda line on West European INF deployments "as first-strike weapons," see Lt. General M. Proskurin's article in *Krasnaia zvezda,* 14 August 1984, p. 3.

35. "Financing the Soviet Empire," *National Security Record,* no. 90 (April 1986): 2; Judy Shelton, "Another Soviet Swindle," *Wall Street Journal,* 16 September 1986, European edition.

10

THE THIRD WORLD

Although an overwhelming majority of former colonies in the under-developed part of the world have attained political independence, the USSR claims that these new states must break foreign investment links with the industrialized capitalist countries in order to achieve complete economic freedom. According to Soviet ideology,[1] such freedom can be attained only in association with the so-called socialist (that is, com-munist-ruled) governments.

The lesser developed countries (LDCs) comprise approximately two-thirds of the world's 159 self-governing political units, occupy some 40 percent of global land area, and account for almost half of the total population. The Soviet Union is acutely conscious of the strategic importance of these states. Their vast holdings of raw materials, their ability to exercise economic leverage through an oil embargo, their influence in the United Nations and other international organizations such as the Group of Seventy-Seven, and their proximity to maritime choke points (23 of 31 trade channels essential to the United States and to the free world) all figure critically in the Soviet approach to LDCs.[2]

The USSR itself does not openly emphasize this aspect of relations with lesser developed countries. When Libyan dictator Moammar Qad-dafi visited Moscow, he was told by Brezhnev himself that the USSR adheres to a "code of conduct," which allegedly includes:[3]

1. recognition of the right of each people to decide its domestic affairs without outside interference;

2. strict respect for territorial integrity and inviolability of frontiers;

3. unconditional recognition of the right of each African, Asian, and Latin American state to equal participation in international life;

4. complete and unconditional recognition of sovereignty of these states over their natural resources; and

5. respect for the status of non-alignment chosen by the majority of African, Asian, and Latin American states.

None of the foregoing has corresponded to reality, since all five points have been violated overtly and covertly by every single Soviet leader since Lenin.

CATEGORIES OF LDCs

Two months earlier Brezhnev spoke of certain governments in the Third World that had taken the "revolutionary-democratic path" toward socialist development. They included at the time "Angola, Ethiopia, Mozambique, Afghanistan, and the People's Democratic Republic of [South] Yemen."[4] The late CPSU general secretary next listed similar developments within these countries: the gradual "liquidation" of imperialist monopolies, the upper middle class, and feudal lords; the curbing of foreign capital; the transition to economic planning; the creation of "cooperatives" (that is, collective farms) in rural areas; an "anti-imperialist" (that is, anti-Western) foreign policy; and the growth of a strong "revolutionary" party.

Brezhnev also cited a second group of states, which were said to be among the "genuinely independent" countries and to have strong "anti-imperialist" governments or "revolutionary parties." Examples included Syria, India, Iran, and Iraq. He mentioned that in the Iranian case, under the banner of Islam, the progressive struggle could be swept away by "counterrevolutionary mutinies." The ultimate outcome was dependent on "the real content of a particular movement."[5]

The so-called non-aligned movement includes states in both of these categories. When it met for its sixth summit conference at Havana in September 1979, the movement had a total of 95 members and 21 observers. Romanian and Yugoslav delegates prevented adoption of a Cuban resolution proclaiming the USSR as the "patron" of the movement. Several months later, in January 1980, when the U.N. General Assembly considered a resolution calling for withdrawal of foreign (that is, Soviet) troops from Afghanistan, 57 non-aligned states voted in favor, 24 abstained, and only 9 opposed it. (On 5 November 1986, the full United Nations vote on this matter registered 122 for, with 11 abstentions, and 20 against the motion.)

At the seventh non-aligned summit conference, held from 7 to 12 March 1983 in New Delhi, participating delegations had increased to 101 full members, nineteen countries with observer status, and 26 guests. The seat for Kampuchea remained vacant. A final declaration emphasized the movement's independence from all blocs. The text attacked the Republic of South Africa's "destabilization attempts" in the region. It also condemned Israel as well as the United States regarding the Middle East. Strong anti-American language appeared in the section on Nicaragua and El Salvador.

The eighth non-aligned conference took place from 1 to 7 September 1986 at Harare, Zimbabwe. It attracted 28 Asian, 50 African, 18 Latin American, 3 European, and 1 Oceania heads of state plus leaders from the PLO and SWAPO. At least 32 of the members were openly aligned with Moscow. (See Table 10.1.) Observers represented several other governments, and national or international organizations. Muammar Qaddafi called the movement "useless," and the Iran-Iraq war led to disagreements. Most of the members voted against South Africa as well as the United States.[6]

The developing countries in Africa, Asia, Latin America, and the Middle East have received considerable attention from USSR foreign policy makers since the early 1960s. A theoretical framework, within which so-called "national liberation" movements operate, also has been elaborated upon by USSR ideologists. The economic basis for revolutions in the Third World is the alleged conflict between independence and "imperialist monopoly." This and other contradictions can only be resolved in alliance with the "world socialist system" (that is, the communist-ruled states). The latter, it is claimed, represents a natural ally of the Third World.[7]

However, in order to achieve convergence with the so-called world socialist system, a national liberation movement must overcome several obstacles:

1. resistance by local bourgeois and petit-bourgeois elements;
2. anti-communist "prejudices" among certain groups in the liberation movement itself;

3. narrow-minded nationalist leaders who maneuver between the two camps; and

4. subversive activities of the "imperialists," who are aided by Beijing.

It had been stated by a CPSU apparatus worker already in early 1970 that the above difficulties could be resolved and that the national liberation movement "can gain victory only in alliance with the other major revolutionary force—the world socialist system."[8]

In other words, the revolution allegedly will not succeed on a global basis without eliminating the basic contradiction or conflict between the two worldwide systems—defined by Soviet ideologues as "socialism" versus "imperialism." In the USSR view, the capitalist economy will become undermined by the proliferation of national liberation movements, which, in turn, will accelerate the revolutionary process. However, this is only one factor, allegedly neither decisive nor predominant, among those operative during the future world transition from capitalism to socialism.[9]

According to Soviet theory, a small number of developing countries already has chosen the "non-capitalist path." Their leaders will move toward "scientific socialism," that is, communism, after the temporary "national front" alliance with "anti-imperialist" elements runs its course. In 1978, only nine countries were definitely stated[10] to be in this category; by 1986 the number had increased to twenty-four (see Table 1.3). Of course, the policies and/or leaderships in such countries may change and thus move the process either forward or back.

As an example, the abortive coup in Indonesia (1965) and subsequent developments resulted in its loss of the above designation. Cuba was promoted to "socialist" status on the basis of personal remarks in 1962 by Fidel Castro, only two years after its revolution. Ghana left the progressive path following the ouster of Kwame Nkrumah (1966). Formerly non-capitalist Iraq remains in an uncertain status with the Ba'th party ruling and communists since 1975 in and out of the government. The most dramatic reversal occurred during 1972 in Egypt. Mali (1968) and Somalia (1977) also "regressed" in Soviet terms. With all three countries, the USSR has lost influence. One of the problems facing the Kremlin has to do with the high proportion of rural inhabitants[11] among the working populations in many Third World countries, estimated to account for up to 80 percent of the total. Hence, in the absence of a large industrial proletariat, there is the need for an alliance that would mobilize the rural majority throughout these underdeveloped regions of the world.

TABLE 10.1
NON-ALIGNED SUMMIT PARTICIPANTS, HARARE, 1986

Members

1.	Afghanistan	26.	Ecuador	51.	Liberia	76.	Saudi Arabia
2.	Algeria	27.	Egypt	52.	Libya	77.	Senegal
3.	Angola	28.	Equatorial Guinea	53.	Madagascar	78.	Seychelles
4.	Argentina			54.	Malawi	79.	Sierra Leone
5.	Bahamas	29.	Ethiopia	55.	Malaysia	80.	Singapore
6.	Bahrain	30.	Gabon	56.	Maldives	81.	Somalia
7.	Bangladesh	31.	Gambia	57.	Mali	82.	SWAPO
8.	Barbados	32.	Ghana	58.	Malta	83.	Sri Lanka
9.	Belize	33.	Grenada	59.	Mauritania	84.	Sudan
10.	Benin	34.	Guinea	60.	Mauritius	85.	Suriname
11.	Bhutan	35.	Guinea-Bissau	61.	Morocco	86.	Swaziland
12.	Bolivia	36.	Guyana	62.	Mozambique	87.	Syria
13.	Botswana	37.	India	63.	Nepal	88.	Tanzania

14. *Burkina Faso*
15. *Burundi*
16. *Cape Verde*
17. Central African Republic
18. Chad
19. Colombia
20. Cameroon
21. Comoros
22. *Congo*
23. *Cuba*
24. Cyprus
25. Djibouti

38. Indonesia
39. Iran
40. Iraq
41. Ivory Coast
42. Jamaica
43. Jordan
44. *Kampuchea*
45. Kenya
46. *Korea (DPR)*
47. Kuwait
48. *Laos (PDR)*
49. Lebanon
50. Lesotho

64. *Nicaragua*
65. Niger
66. Nigeria
67. Oman
68. Pakistan
69. *PLO*
70. Panama
71. Peru
72. Qatar
73. Rwanda
74. St. Lucia
75. *São Tomé & Principe*

89. Togo
90. Trinidad & Tobago
91. Tunisia
92. Uganda
93. Vanuatu
94. *Vietnam*
95. Yemen, Arab Republic
96. *Yemen, PDR*
97. *Yugoslavia*
98. Zaire
99. Zambia
100. Zimbabwe

Italics denote Soviet alignment.
SOURCE: *New York Times*, 4 September 1986; AP dispatch from Harare.

"National" or "revolutionary democracies" have similar characteristics. According to a professional apparatus worker in the CPSU Central Committee, they include the following:[12]

1. rapid growth of the state sector and limitation on private enterprise;

2. nationalization of foreign capital investments;

3. undermining the influence of landlords and the middle class;

4. introduction of one-party, "anti-imperialist" dictatorships;

5. reforms in labor, agriculture, and industry;

6. "friendly relations with the Soviet Union and other socialist states."

This last condition is actively fostered by the USSR and its dependencies. The Soviet Union claims that it allocated 1.4 percent of GNP to build 3,800 industrial and other economic projects already commissioned on the basis of agreements signed with 70 governments in Africa, Asia, and Latin America. An estimated 122,745 Soviet and East European plus 19,045 Cuban economic and military technicians served in underdeveloped countries during 1985 for periods of one month or more.[13]

SUB-SAHARAN AFRICA

One of the more spectacular Moscow schools and training establishments, mentioned in Chapter 4, is the University of the Friendship of Peoples named after Patrice Lumumba, who had been a leader in the Congo. According to the official Soviet press agency, by 1975 approximately 5,600 individuals had received diplomas and 450 had completed postgraduate courses.[14] The Soviet interest in Africa is long-standing. Already in 1959, an Association for Friendship with the Peoples of Africa had been launched in Moscow. Nonetheless, although the USSR maintained trade relations with 31 countries south of the Sahara, the above organization almost a decade subsequent to its establishment had counterparts in only seven of these: Congo (Brazzaville), Ethiopia, Mali, Nigeria, Senegal, Somalia, and Uganda.[15]

It is interesting to note that only after fifteen years of experience did the Soviet Union finally seem to have grasped some of the realities concerning Africa. An authoritative article in the leading Moscow journal devoted to the Third World recognized that "nationalism, religious superstition and attachment to private property and also patriarchal and peasant ideas of social justice—these are what distinguish many radical non-proletarian revolutionaries . . . from Marxists."[16] Another study, edited by the then director of the Africa Institute at the USSR Academy of Sciences, indicated that the Soviets have become aware of the errors they had made between 1960 and 1970. This volume divides African political parties into three types: Marxist-Leninist, revolutionary-democratic, and bourgeois or pro-bourgeois.[17]

Parties of the first category as of 1970 were said to be "active" in Algeria, Lesotho, Morocco, Nigeria (Socialist Workers' and Farmers' Party), Réunion, Senegal, South Africa, the Sudan, and Tunisia. According to this source, virtually all had been banned and forced to operate underground. It then went on to cite the "revolutionary-democratic" ruling parties in Algeria (not Marxist-Leninist), Congo (Brazzaville), Egypt, Guinea, and Tanzania as "reliable detachments." The national liberation movements in Angola (independent, 11 November 1975), Guinea-Bissau (independent, 12 September 1974), and Mozambique (independent, 25 June 1975) were viewed at the time as short-term prospects.

The means by which nationalist movements are transformed into avowedly communist ones is never explained. Presumably, dedicated agents[18] would infiltrate for the purpose of revolutionizing the former. Applying a Marxist analysis, unafraid of contradictions, Solodovnikov's book on the political parties of Africa defined the single-party system as progressive in revolutionary-democratic states, but one that "suppresses democratic freedoms" in pro-Western countries.[19]

One lesson learned by the USSR prior to the decade of the 1970s, presumably due to the many expulsions of its diplomats, is that Africans resent heavy-handed interference in domestic affairs, which for the Soviets had been the order of the day. A good example involved Guinea, where USSR ambassador Daniil S. Solod became *persona non grata* after attempting to organize local schoolteachers and overthrow the government of Ahmed Sekou Touré. A decade later, however, Guinea under the same leader was marching in the vanguard of progressive forces on the African continent. The rift between Moscow and Conakry apparently had been healed, at least for the time being, although Touré finally became disenchanted with Moscow.[20] Already during 1983, Guinea's repayments on loans reportedly exceeded earnings from bauxite delivered to the Soviets. The death of Touré and subsequent coup by the military during early April 1984 altered relations with the USSR. This fact probably accounts for the subsequent movement of the Soviet airbase from Guinea to the islands of São Tomé and Principe, whose leader visited Moscow at the end of that year. In 1986, Guinea still was considered to have a "socialist" orientation.

Moscow has made its greatest gains in Ethiopia. The only political movement, named the Commission for Organizing the Party of the Working People of Ethiopia, transformed itself into the Ethiopian Workers' Party (EWP) at a founding congress in September 1984. According to the leader, Colonel Mengistu Haile Mariam, the EWP will become "the sole instrument to effect the realization of communism." Some 2,500 "technicians" from the USSR and Eastern Europe have been guiding the development of the new economic and political structure, which already includes a National Central Planning Committee. At the end of July 1986, a high-level CPSU delegation visited Addis Ababa.[21]

The main potential threat to Soviet influence in competition for leftist loyalties throughout Africa are the Chinese communists. If the latter support a liberation group in Africa, it is condemned by Moscow as dissident. Praise is lavished on such groups as FRELIMO in Mozambique, PAIGC in Guinea-Bissau, and MPLA in Angola, all of which rely on Soviet assistance. The Chinese reportedly have been criticizing Soviet aid as ineffective and identifying the "Russians" with previous European colonizers who also happened to have been Caucasian. In this connection, the Parti Africain de l'Indépendance in Senegal, described as tropical Africa's first Marxist movement, split into pro-Beijing and pro-Moscow factions. Many adherents to the latter ended up in prison. The Sino-Soviet dispute thus has made the situation more complex, since the USSR is forced to cope with competition not only from the "imperialist" West but also from Mainland China[22] and a brand of communism from a lesser developed country.

BETWEEN THE MAGHREB AND INDIA

The two states that the Soviets claim led the Arab anti-imperialist movement in the early 1970s were Algeria and Syria, because they "officially adhered to a socialist orientation." Iraq, Libya, and South Yemen at that time only strove "to place their natural riches at the service of the people."[23] They still represent, in Moscow's eyes, an important part of the Arab national liberation movement. Obviously, among the countries that occupy the area between North Africa and India, it is in these five countries that the USSR has had the most success.

Moscow's strategy in the Middle East has been more complicated than in Africa, due primarily to the Arab conflict with Israel.[24] The USSR presumably hopes that tension will not lead to war, which, in turn, might result in yet another Arab defeat, unless its own troops were to become involved. This last contingency carries with it the risk of escalation, should the United States in turn support Israel.

Originally the Kremlin's attention had been centered around Cairo, even though then Foreign Minister Gromyko gave USSR support for a separate Palestinian state at the time of the November 1974 Arab "summit meeting" in Morocco. The high point in Soviet-Egyptian relations came earlier, toward the end of May 1971 when Presidents Nikolai Podgornyi and Muhammad Anwar Sadat signed a fifteen-year treaty, the first of its kind in the Arab world (see Table 10.2). The twelve articles included provisions for economic and military assistance. Article 7 stipulated that both sides "will contact each other without delay in order to concert their positions with a view to removing a threat that has arisen or re-establishing peace."[25]

However, earlier that same month, a purge had eliminated six ministers (housing, information, interior, electric power, presidential affairs, and war) from the Egyptian cabinet. Their arrests followed soon after expulsion from office of Vice President Ali Sabry, leader of a radical pro-Soviet faction in Cairo. Reportedly,[26] this man and Interior Minister Shaarawi Gomaa had established a secret organization within Sadat's ruling Arab Socialist Union that, if successful, would have transformed it into a "vanguard party" and led to a "dictatorship of the proletariat."

Despite this setback for the USSR, the treaty became duly ratified within just over one month, and President Sadat subsequently visited Moscow. The joint communiqué[27] spoke of "measures aimed at further strengthening the military might of Egypt." Prior to this agreement, it was estimated that the Soviet Union already had delivered to Cairo about $2.5 billion in weapons since its 1967 defeat in the war against Israel. However, less than nine months later, some 20,000 USSR military advisers were ordered out of Egypt. Despite the inconclusiveness of the fourth Arab-Israeli war in October 1973 and Cairo's dissatisfaction with Moscow, relations between the two capitals improved to the extent of rescheduling debts in 1975 and new USSR deliveries of military equipment. This occurred after Sadat had publicly criticized the USSR for not having replaced the arms destroyed in the most recent round of fighting.[28] However, relations between Egypt and the Soviet Union have improved recently under Sadat's successor, Hosni Mubarak, and after a three-year break the two countries in late September 1984 exchanged ambassadors again.

TABLE 10.2
TREATIES OF FRIENDSHIP AND COOPERATION IN THE THIRD WORLD, 1971–1986

	Country	Date	Place	Duration (years)	Abrogated
1.	Egypt	27 May 1971	Cairo	15	15 March 1976
2.	India*	9 August 1971	New Delhi	20	
3.	Iraq	9 April 1972	Baghdad	15	
4.	Somalia	11 July 1974	Mogadishu	20	13 November 1977
5.	Angola	8 October 1976	Moscow	20	
6.	Mozambique	31 March 1977	Maputo	20	
7.	Vietnam*	3 November 1978	Moscow	25	
8.	Ethiopia*	20 November 1978	Moscow	20	
9.	Afghanistan*	5 December 1978	Moscow	20	
10.	Yemen, South*	25 October 1979	Moscow	20	
11.	Syria	8 October 1980	Moscow	20	
12.	Congo	13 May 1981	Moscow	20	
13.	Yemen, North	9 October 1984	Moscow	20	
14.	Mali	18 July 1986	Moscow	**	
15.	Burkina Faso	12 October 1986	Moscow	**	
16.	Benin	25 November 1986	Moscow	**	

*These five countries were ranked at the time within the lowest ($265 or less) annual per capita income category among all LDCs by the World Bank (*Washington Post*, 14 May 1978).

**Called declarations on further development of friendship and cooperation, these may be preliminary steps toward formal treaties.

SOURCES: *Pravda*, 28 May 1971, 10 August 1971, 10 April 1972, 13 July 1974, 9 October 1976, 2 April 1977, 4 November 1978, 21 November 1978, 6 December 1978, 26 October 1979, 9 October 1980, 14 May 1981, 11 October 1984, 20 July 1986, 13 October 1986, 28 November 1986; "Egypt breaks off Soviet pact," *Facts on File, 1976*, p. 193; "Somalia Expels Soviets, Cubans," ibid. *1977*, p. 874.

Kremlin leaders also cultivate other Arab governments, even those that do not profess socialism. The late Premier Kosygin traveled to Morocco and was received by King Hassan II. The latter accepted an invitation to visit the USSR. None of these amenities interrupted Soviet deliveries of heavy mortars and SAM-6 antiaircraft missiles to the Polisario guerrillas in the southwestern Sahara. However, about 100 Moroccans are studying in Moscow, and trade between the two countries has increased recently. The president of the People's Democratic Republic of Algeria visited the USSR, and both governments signed several agreements on cooperation. A few months later, a Soviet delegation traveled to Algeria for a meeting of the intergovernmental standing commission on economics, science, and technology.[29]

The premier and defense minister of the People's Democratic Republic of Yemen (PDRY), Ali Nasir Muhammad, spent ten days in the Soviet Union. Subsequently, all PDRY debts to the USSR were canceled. Fleet Admiral Sergei Gorshkov visited the country, presumably to survey base facilities at Aden and anchorages off the island of Socotra. In the mid-1980s, the PDRY has moved solidly into the Soviet orbit, so that regular political and military consultations take place in Moscow. A coup d'etat in January 1986 overthrew President Ali Nasir, whose successor, Haidar Abu Bakr al Attas, had been in Moscow during most of the fighting. Approximately 10,000 persons were killed and USSR influence was re-established.[30] Five years after the PDRY had done so, North Yemen also signed a treaty of friendship and cooperation with the USSR (see Table 10.2). However, ruler Ali Abdullah Saleh may be able to maintain his independence from Moscow due to discovery of 300 million barrels in oil reserves. He owes the USSR some one billion dollars for military equipment and in mid-1986 received the same high-level Soviet delegation that had visited South Yemen.

More than just another communiqué was involved when the Soviet Union signed a fifteen-year treaty of friendship and cooperation with Iraq. Article 4 attacks colonialism, imperialism, and Zionism. Article 9 mentions strengthening defense capability, which Moscow had been helping Baghdad to do already for more than a decade. An economic agreement followed the treaty, with provisions for the refining and marketing of Iraq's nationalized petroleum by the USSR. It was disclosed subsequently that the Soviets would construct an oil refinery at Mosul as well as a pipeline from Baghdad to Basra. Agreements under which the USSR will build a nuclear reactor and supply about $2.5 billion in arms on credit appeared to signal support for Iraq in its war against Iran. Gorbachev reaffirmed these policies when he met with President Saddam Husayn at the end of 1985 in Moscow.[31]

Syria also has been receiving assistance and, in contrast to Egypt, did not expel its Bloc economic and military advisors (totaling about 5,500 during 1985). The first arms deal concluded with Moscow in 1972 provided Damascus with surface-to-air missiles. Ten years later, after Israel had destroyed Syrian air defenses, the USSR quickly supplied more advanced SS-21 weapons systems. Alignment with Moscow could be seen in mid-1983, when President Hafiz al-Asad refused to speak with U.S. special envoy Philip C. Habib. On the other hand, CPSU Politburo member G. A. Aliev spent four days in Damascus the following spring and returned with a communiqué that reaffirmed the close cooperation between the two countries. Trade between Syria and the Soviet Union has increased fourfold over the past ten years. In mid-1986, Gorbachev promised to continue sending arms.[32]

Relations with a non-Arab country in the Middle East clearly show the USSR's adaptability to changed circumstances. The late Shah Mohammed Riza Pahlevi personally had experienced Soviet efforts to detach Iran's northern provinces after World War II and yet later entered into many economic agreements with Moscow. Already in 1969, the USSR had extended credits to Teheran for purchase of trucks, armored personnel carriers, and light anti-aircraft guns. A steel mill at Isfahan and a natural gas pipeline were soon under construction. Another agreement included a Soviet polyisoprene factory, prefabricated housing plants, and additions to the steel mill. After the fall of the Shah, the USSR ordered the local communist (Tudeh) party to support the Ayatollah Khomeini. It also warned the new regime of the coming attack by Iraq and even began supplying Iran with weapons.

Despite arrests of Tudeh leaders in February 1983 and dissolution of their movement three months later, the USSR still maintains 1,200 military advisors in the country. It claims that 160 projects have been built or are under construction. The then First Deputy Foreign Minister Georgii Kornienko visited Teheran in early February 1986 and agreed to resume Aeroflot flights as well as establish a joint economic commission. About one-fifth of all imports, especially from Europe, cross Soviet territory en route to Teheran.[33]

A different kind of adaptability has been evident vis-à-vis Afghanistan, where the Soviets first gave assistance to Muhammad Zahir Shah's development plan. The monarch lost his throne in July 1973, during a visit to Europe. The coup placed in power Mohammed Daoud, whose revolutionary program received support from the indigenous communist rank and file. During the next five years, however, the new government turned away from the USSR and began diversifying the sources of its foreign aid. Soviet leaders most probably saw their influence declining. Another coup in April 1978 led to the murder of Daoud as well as his family and the beginning of communist rule in Afghanistan. Since the end of the following year, about 120,000 Soviet troops (plus others across the border) have occupied the country and are engaged in military activities against a strong guerrilla movement. Armed forces loyal to the puppet regime have dropped from 80,000 to 30,000 men, and some 4.5 million refugees have fled to neighboring countries.[34]

At the other side of the Middle East lies India, and here the USSR has scored an impressive gain by removing that state from among the objectively non-aligned countries of the world. Two decades ago, the Soviet Union mediated successfully and brought about the Tashkent agreement (1965) between Pakistan and India. No noncommunist head of government had visited Moscow more frequently than the late Prime Minister Indira Gandhi. Economic assistance to India from the USSR through the end of 1985 totaled the equivalent of more than $4.4 billion.[35]

It may have been President Richard M. Nixon's announcement that he would visit Beijing, but more probably the approaching showdown with Pakistan over Bangladesh, that decided the Indian leaders to sign a twenty-year friendship treaty with the USSR. Initialed at New Delhi by the respective foreign ministers, the pact received ratification within a record nine days. Subsequent developments would seem to indicate that the Soviet Union gave India both essential military equipment and diplomatic support in the war against Pakistan and subsequent proclamation of independence by Bangladesh.

Article 9 of the treaty,[36] which is directed against Pakistan as well as China, calls for "immediate consultations with a view to taking appropriate effective measures" in the event of a threat or an actual attack. Ambiguity in language makes it difficult to establish whether the agreement is a military alliance. India considers itself non-aligned and certainly has more justification to claim such a status than countries like Cuba, Ethiopia, or Vietnam. This does not prevent the Soviet Union from apparently being its best friend. An arms deal between India and the USSR in 1981 came to a total of $2.5 billion. Two years later, an agreement allowed New Delhi to begin producing fighter aircraft, including the advanced MiG-29 and MiG-31, during the late 1980s. In early 1984 then Defense Minister Ustinov, accompanied by a retinue of 66 generals and admirals, visited India and agreed that the USSR would sell more jets, warships, missiles, army equipment, and electronic surveillance systems. The new prime minister, Rajiv Gandhi, who succeeded his assassinated mother, visited Moscow in May 1985 and received $1.5 billion in credits. His foreign trade minister signed an agreement at the end of that year which envisages a two and one-half times greater commercial volume during 1986–1990 than in the previous five years.[37]

LATIN AMERICA

As if mesmerized by the orthodox requirement for an industrial proletariat, only the vanguard of which can exercise a dictatorship in theory, Soviet writers welcome the growth of the working class in any part of the world. Latin American countries experienced an increase of more than 50 percent in this population category from 1960 through the end of 1975. Their working class reportedly totaled 18.7 million people (or almost one-fifth of the labor force) by that year. Singled out as the first example in the Western hemisphere of a successful revolution is Cuba, which the Soviets present as a model for the liberation struggle.[38] Yet for many years, the upsurge in revolutionary activity throughout Latin America predicted by USSR commentators encompassed only the short-lived Popular Unity (socialist plus communist) rule in Chile and the continuing anti-imperialist developments under the current regime in Peru.[39] More recently, however, Nicaragua joined the category of "Marxist-Leninist" regimes.

Fidel Castro has an almost obsessive hatred of the United States and pledged support for all "genuine" revolutions in Latin America, promising that the Cubans would aid consistently and decisively any such process carried out in a Latin American country. During 1985, Soviet economic aid to that Caribbean island rose to over $4.6 billion, or about one-quarter, of the country's gross national product. Millions more came from the six East European regimes.[40] Havana's debt to Moscow has been rescheduled with payments beginning in 1986 and extending over a 25-year period. Most probably, it will never be collected.

Soviet specialists are planning the development of the Cuban sugar industry through 1990. Being itself one of the world's largest producers, the USSR obviously did not need all of the 3.7 million metric tons of sugar (half of which could be exported) that it bought from Havana in 1985 and for which it paid Havana five times the market rate. In fact, the Soviet Union is known to have resold the surplus for hard currency at less than the world price.[41] In return for their assistance, the Soviets have access to naval and air base facilities on the island. They also station a combat brigade there. Cuban mercenaries have acted as surrogates for the USSR in many countries of Africa.

In Chile, meanwhile, a major breakthrough for Soviet influence on the continent of Latin America seemingly had occurred after election of Salvador Allende as president of that country in 1970 with the support of the indigenous communists. Moscow moved cautiously in this case, nonetheless, offering at first only $50 million in hard currency credit for imports from the USSR. Another equivalent sum in rubles had been set aside for the financing of industrial and construction projects. Total credits[42] soon amounted to $385 million from both the USSR and Eastern Europe.

Following the military coup that overthrew the Allende regime during September 1973, *World Marxist Review* published an analysis of what had gone wrong. Several mistakes were cited: (1) the press had not been curtailed soon enough; (2) Allende moved too slowly within both political and economic arenas; (3) the communists should have forced rapid confiscation of private enterprise; (4) soviets [councils] of workers and peasants were unavailable to function as pressure groups; (5) occupation of farms and factories by the radical left undermined potential support; and (6) penetration of the armed forces did not extend deeply enough to prevent the coup.[43]

Less than six years later, on 19 July 1979, the Sandinistas came to power in Nicaragua and established the first Marxist-Leninist regime in Central America. Eliminating all opposition, by 1986 they hosted between 7,000 and 9,000 Cubans, Russians, East Germans, Bulgarians, Libyans, PLO members, and other terrorists (including 3,000 to 3,500 military or security advisors). An additional 5,000 to 6,000 Cubans are present as teachers and construction or health workers. The *modus operandi* devised by Castro for consolidating Latin American communist forces was followed in Nicaragua:[44] unification of the extreme left, establishment of a broad coalition including sympathetic non-communist elements, use of the latter to isolate the target regime on the right, and Soviet bloc aid.

All five top Sandinista leaders received their training after 1960 in Havana. One of them, the current minister for economic planning, Henry Ruiz, spent two full years in Moscow at Lumumba University. He is the only cabinet member who speaks Russian. Approximately 1,000 young Nicaraguans are currently studying in the USSR. Soviet-made AK-47 assault rifles are seen almost everywhere throughout Nicaragua. Indeed, through calendar year 1986, the Soviet Union will have delivered $1.5 billion in aid (about $750 to $800 million is military) since the Sandinistas seized power. Freighters arriving from the

TABLE 10.3
COMMUNIST ECONOMIC AND MILITARY TECHNICIANS IN THE THIRD
WORLD,* 1985

	USSR AND EASTERN EUROPE		CHINA	
	Economic	Military	Economic	Military
Total	122,745	18,375	46,820	395
Africa	78,830	9,280	8,380	240
North Africa	64,150	3,915	1,975	20
Algeria	17,150	615	450	20
Libya	44,000	3,300	50	n/a
Mauritania	50	—	400	—
Morocco	2,325	—	75	—
Tunisia	625	—	1,000	—
Sub-Saharan Africa	14,680	5,365	6,405	220
Angola	2,475	1,050	150	100
Congo	2,350	70	35	10
Ethiopia	—	2,600	—	—
Gabon	15	—	100	—
Ghana	70	—	60	—
Guinea	620	70	75	—
Guinea-Bissau	210	85	150	—
Kenya	95	—	125	—
Madagascar	170	75	625	—
Mali	505	50	250	5
Mozambique	1,400	950	150	—
Niger	25	—	125	—
Nigeria	4,880	50	100	—
Rwanda	10	—	600	n/a
São Tomé and Principe	150	150	15	—
Senegal	50	—	100	—
Sierra Leone	10	—	35	—
Somalia	—	—	1,000	20
Sudan	105	20	400	5
Tanzania	110	90	550	—
Zambia	315	100	100	—
Other	1,115	40	1,660	80
East Asia	255	—	115	—
Europe	10	—	225	—
Latin America	1,465	260	200	—
Bolivia	40	—	—	—

Brazil	120	—	—	—
Colombia	60	—	60	—
Nicaragua	695	160	—	—
Peru	90	100	10	—
Uruguay	10	—	—	—
Other	450	—	130	—
Middle East	34,200	6,260	37,425	115
Iran	1,500	1,200	—	—
Iraq	15,625	1,300	17,000	50
North Yemen	650	310	6,000	—
South Yemen	3,250	1,100	—	—
Syria	5,500	2,300	15	—
Other	7,675	50	14,410	65
South Asia	7,985	2,575	475	40
Afghanistan	5,225	2,025	—	—
Bangladesh	95	50	100	40
India	1,600	500	—	—
Nepal	15	—	225	—
Pakistan	955	—	100	—
Sri Lanka	90	—	50	—
Other	5	—	—	—

*Minimum estimates of number present for a period of one month or more. Numbers are rounded to nearest 5.

SOURCES: CIA, *Handbook of Economic Statistics, 1986*, series CPAS 86–10002, September 1986, pp. 124–25.

USSR during ten months of 1986 had delivered 18,700 tons of arms, a record amount.[45]

The 75,000-man Nicaraguan army, under training by Cubans, now has the following heavy equipment: tanks, armored personnel carriers and reconnaissance vehicles, howitzers, anti-tank guns, mortars and rocket-propelled grenade launchers, transport aircraft, helicopters, anti-aircraft guns, surface-to-air missiles, and machine guns. In addition to foreign economic debt obligations of $5.3 billion, the Sandinista regime owes the Soviet Union about $1.7 billion for arms.[46]

The enormous quantity of weapons shipped to Nicaragua would suggest that the USSR is using the country for stockpiling military equipment in anticipation of a protracted struggle throughout Central America and the Caribbean. A similar operation had been envisaged for the island of Grenada, where the New Jewel Movement seized power on 13 March 1979. Within six months, the regime had been recognized by the USSR. Four years later, the dictatorship could boast

TABLE 10.4
SELECTED LATIN AMERICAN GROUPS ALLIED WITH CUBA

Country	Name of Group
Argentina	Montoneros
	People's Revolutionary Army (ERP)
Chile	Communist Party of Chile (PCCH)
	Movement of the Revolutionary Left (MIR)
Colombia	Communist Party of Colombia (PCC)
	Revolutionary Armed Forces of Colombia (FARC), guerrilla group of PCC
	April 19 Movement (M-19)
	National Liberation Army (ELN)
Costa Rica	Popular Vanguard Party (PVP)
	People's Revolutionary Movement (MRP)
	Costa Rican Socialist Party (PSC)
Dominican Republic	Dominican Communist Party (PCD)
El Salvador	Farabundo Martí Front of National Liberation (FMLN)
	Armed Forces of National Resistance (FARN)
	Communist Party of El Salvador (PCES)
	Popular Liberation Forces (FPL)

	Popular Revolutionary Army (ERP)
	Central American Revolutionary Workers' Party (PRTC)
Grenada	New Jewel Movement
Guatemala	Guatemalan National Revolutionary Unity (URNG)
	Guatemalan Party of Labor
	Guerrilla Army of the Poor (EGP)
	Armed People's Organization (ORPA)
	Rebel Armed Forces (FAR)
Honduras	National Unified Directorate (DNU)
	Popular Liberation Movement (MLP)
	Morazanista Front of National Liberation (FMLN)
	Honduran Communist Party (PCH)
Nicaragua	Sandinista Front of National Liberation (FSLN)
Uruguay	Communist Party of Uruguay (PCU)
	National Liberation Movement (MLN-Tupamaros)

SOURCES: R. Daniel McMichael and John D. Paulus, eds., *Western Hemisphere Stability: The Latin American Connection* (Pittsburgh, Pa.: World Affairs Council of Pittsburgh, 1983), pp. 109–10; Richard F. Staar, ed., *1986 Yearbook on International Communist Affairs* (Stanford: Hoover Institution Press, 1986), pp. 46–58.

1. a Marxist-Leninist ruling party, headed by a Soviet-style polit-
    buro;
2. an army and militia larger than the combined total of all its
    non-communist neighbors;
3. complete control of the media;
4. mass organizations to compel support for the regime; and
5. a tight and growing internal security apparatus.[47]

All of the foregoing had been accomplished with guidance from the
large Soviet and Cuban embassies on the island, and with additional
help by other communist bloc representatives.

By 1985 the indigenous military build-up would have resulted in an
army of eighteen battalions, or up to 10,000 men, giving Grenada the
largest armed forces per head of population (111,000) in the world.
Secret agreements with the Soviet Union, Cuba, and North Korea
specified delivery of exactly 10,000 rifles and 20,000 sets of uniforms,
plus enough heavy weapons to equip the projected eighteen battalions.
Czechoslovakia also had delivered ammunition, although the Cubans
served as intermediaries for all shipments.[48]

Before these agreements could be fully implemented, a struggle for
power developed within the New Jewel Movement. A Stalinist-style
leader, Bernard Coard, seized control of the party from Maurice
Bishop, who was placed under house arrest. After the latter's execution
(together with more than one hundred of his supporters) on 19 October 1983, a Revolutionary Military Council under army chief Hudson
Austin announced a shoot-on-sight curfew. Six days later, a combined
U.S.-Caribbean force landed on Grenada. All Cubans, Libyans, North
Koreans, Soviets, East Germans, and Bulgarians were expelled from
the island. By 15 December most of the American combat troops had
been withdrawn, leaving only 270 U.S. marines and several hundred
soldiers from six Caribbean countries on the island.[49]

The situation in El Salvador has developed along more complicated
lines, mainly because of that country's proximity to Nicaragua. Soon
after seizing power, the Nicaraguan Sandinistas began training guerrillas from other Central American states. During November 1980, encouraged by Castro, five insurgent factions in El Salvador united to form
the Farabundo Martí Front for National Liberation (FMLN). Honduras,
without its knowledge, would be used for transit of guerrillas and arms.
In 1980 alone, an estimated 800 tons of weapons were committed to the
struggle by the Cuban/Soviet bloc.[50] However, the Salvadoran guerrillas'
"final offensive" in early 1981 did not achieve success.

Despite the surge in arms deliveries to the insurgents by air, sea, and land, more than 80 percent of eligible Salvadorans voted on 28 March 1982 for a constituent assembly that repudiated the extreme left. The murder and alleged suicide a year later in Managua, Nicaragua, of leaders from the largest Salvadoran insurgent group made clear the guerrillas' immediate source of support. According to the U.S. undersecretary of defense for policy, "nearly 80 percent of the ammunition and other 'consumable' material used by the guerrillas in El Salvador is provided by Nicaragua." Direct presidential elections on 25 March 1984 again showed that the overwhelming majority of Salvadorans supported a democratic process. They were among the most carefully overseen in history, some 29 foreign countries sending observers. By mid-1986, the guerrillas had lost half of their members and were down to about 5,000—facing some 52,000 government troops.[51]

The remaining three governments on the Central American isthmus have not remained immune to Cuban and Soviet revolutionary efforts. In early 1982, a Guatemalan guerrilla leader held a press conference at Havana to announce unification of four main groups in his country. Terrorists have been trained by the Sandinistas and sent into Honduras. Nicaragua provides weapons for similar organizations operating in Costa Rica that are supported also by Cuba. Moscow has been delivering more than 65,000 tons of military equipment per year to Havana for destabilization activities throughout the Central American region[52] (see Table 10.4). Soviet leader Gorbachev has scheduled visits to Mexico, Argentina, Brazil, and Cuba during the spring of 1987.

It is obvious that "national liberation" movements could not sustain themselves without Soviet bloc assistance in training, weapons, and logistics. Although they claim to be fighting for social justice and/or independence, in reality their objective remains establishment of totalitarian regimes, which by definition would be anti-United States. The USSR has achieved only mixed results from the pursuit of similar basic policies throughout East Asia, as discussed in the next chapter.

NOTES

1. A. A. Gromyko, ed., *Aktual'nye problemy otnoshenii SSSR so stranami Afriki* (Moscow: Mezhdunarodnye otnosheniia, 1985); A. E. Bobin et al., eds., *Razvivaiushchiesia strany v sovremennom mire* (Moscow: Nauka, 1986).

2. U.S. Congress, House of Representatives, Committee on Foreign Affairs, Subcommittees on Europe and the Middle East and on Asia and Pacific Affairs, *Report on Soviet Policy and United States Response in the Third World,*

97th Cong., 1st sess., 1981, Committee Print, p. 28. See also Seth Singleton, "Defense of the Gains of Socialism: Soviet Third World Policy in the mid-1980s," *Washington Quarterly* 7, no. 1 (Winter 1984): 102–15; Harry Gelman, "The Soviet Union in the Third World," *Occasional Paper* (Santa Monica, Ca.: Rand, March 1986), OPS-006.

3. Moscow radio, 29 April 1981; *FBIS,* 30 April 1981.

4. Speech to the Twenty-sixth CPSU Congress in Moscow (*Pravda,* 24 February 1981).

5. Ibid. See also R. A. Ul'ianovskii, "National Liberation and Its Relation to Nationalism," *Novaia i noveishaia istoriia,* no. 2 (March–April 1982): 3–22.

6. Reports from Harare in *Pravda,* 3 and 4 September 1986, p. 5; Tony Hawkins in the *Christian Science Monitor,* 8 September 1986; special report in *Izvestiia,* 9 September 1986, p. 5.

7. Boris Ponomarev speech in *Pravda,* 22 April 1980. See also Elizabeth Kridl Valkenier, *The Soviet Union and the Third World* (New York: Praeger, 1983); Alvin Z. Rubinstein, "A Third World Policy Waits for Gorbachev," *Orbis* 30, no. 2 (Summer 1986), pp. 355–64.

8. K. N. Brutents, "A Growing Revolutionary Force," *Pravda,* 23 January 1970. See also the book he edited with others, *Sotsialisticheskaia orientatsiia osvobodivshikhsia stran* (Moscow: Mysl', 1982).

9. Gleb Starushenko, "Chosen Path," *New Times* (Moscow), no. 40 (October 1980): 18–20. See also Joseph G. Whelan, "The Soviet Union in the Third World, 1980–1982," *Congressional Research Service Report,* no. 83–2105 (Washington, D.C., 30 November 1983), pp. 29–87, for other Soviet writers on the subject.

10. E. Primakov, "Certain Problems of the Developing Countries," *Kommunist,* no. 11 (July 1978): 81–82. See Iu. V. Irkhin, *Revoliutsionnyi protsess v stranakh sotsialisticheskoi orientatsii* (Moscow: Izdatel'stvo Universiteta druzhby narodov, 1985), for more recent information.

11. See L. V. Goncharev, ed., *Agrarnye preobrazovaniia v stranakh Afriki na sovremennom etape* (Moscow: Nauka, 1982), for problems with transformation of agriculture in Africa.

12. R. A. Ul'ianovskii in *Pravda,* 3 January 1968.

13. *Za rubezhom,* no. 47 (15–21 November 1985): 8; see Table 10.3; Moscow radio, 8 July 1986, in *FBIS,* 11 July 1986, p. R-13, quoting K. Katushev on GNP percentage; CIA, *Handbook of Economic Statistics, 1986,* table 90, p. 124.

14. TASS report, "Loyalty to Lenin's Behest," *Pravda,* 18 February 1975. A KGB Major general, Pavel Erzin, served as the first deputy rector.

15. V. G. Solodovnikov, "The Soviet Union and Africa," *New Times* (Moscow), no. 21 (28 May 1969): 9; economic and technical cooperation agreements have been signed with 37 LDCs in Africa, according to Moscow radio, 24 June 1986 (*FBIS,* 24 June 1986, p. J-2).

16. P. N. Andreasyan, "Contradictions and Criteria of Non-capitalist Development," *Narody Azii and Afriki* 20, no. 2 (March–April 1974): 41.

17. V. G. Solodovnikov et al., *Politicheskie partii Afriki* (Moscow: Nauka, 1970). See also Iu. A. Iudin, ed., *Partii v politicheskoi sisteme* (Moscow: Nauka, 1983), especially chapter 1 by V. E. Chirkin, pp. 5–35.

18. A current illustration is Joe Slovo, chairman of the South African Communist Party, who is identified as commanding *Umkhonto we Sizwe* (Spear of the Nation), the ANC military organization. See also Bureau of Information, *Talking with the ANC* (Pretoria: Government Printer, June 1986), for the interlocking directorate; and John R. Silber in *The Wall Street Journal*, 9 October 1986, editorial page.

19. Even the armed forces are considered progressive in certain states of Africa. Z. Sh. Gafurov, *Natsional'no-demokraticheskaia revolyutsiia i armiia* (Moscow: Nauka, 1983) and E. I. Dolgopolov, *Sotsial'no-politicheskaia rol' armii osvobodivshikhsia stran* (Moscow: Voenizdat, 1986).

20. Thomas H. Henriksen, "Introduction to Africa and Middle East," in Richard F. Staar, ed., *1983 Yearbook on International Communist Affairs*, p. 4.

21. Quoted in the *Christian Science Monitor*, 15 February 1984; U.S. Department of State, *Warsaw Pact Economic Aid to Non-communist LDCs, 1984* (Washington, D.C.: May 1986), table 15, p. 16. See also *Pravda*, 26 July 1986, p. 4, on the Soviet delegation; Francis Fukuyama, *Moscow's Post-Brezhnev Reassessment of the Third World* (Santa Monica, Calif.: Rand, February 1986), R-3337-USDP; and N. I. Gavrilov, ed., *10 let efiopskoi revoliutsii* (Moscow: Nauka, 1986).

22. A good example is the 1,100 mile railroad built by 15,000 Chinese workers between Dar es Salaam in Tanzania and the rich copper deposits of Zambia. A new international airport was constructed by the People's Republic of China on Mauritius. For more recent activities, see Thomas H. Henriksen, "The USSR and Africa: Challenge and Prospects," *Survey* 27, no. 118/119 (Autumn/Winter 1983): 260–72. For competition in arms sales, see *The Economist*, 17 November 1984, pp. 40 and 45. China promised African countries 155,000 tons in cereal food aid compared with 7,500 by the Soviet Union, according to ibid., 20 July 1986.

23. N. Iakubov, "The Soviet Union and the Arab East," *Mezhdunarodaia zhizn'*, no. 8 (August 1974): 27–37; Michael J. Dixon, "The Soviet Union and the Middle East," *Congressional Research Service Report*, no. 83–2295 (Washington, D.C., 12 December 1983); Karen Brutents interview published by *Al-Watan* (Kuwait), 6 January 1986; *FBIS*, 9 January 1986, pp. H3–15, for USSR policy in the region.

24. Note the strong propaganda against Israel in the book by A. I. Filatova, ed., *Belaia kniga* (Moscow: Iuridizdat, 1985), published by the Anti-Zionist Committee of Soviet Society together with the Association of Soviet Jurists.

25. "Treaty of Friendship and Collaboration Between the Union of Soviet Socialist Republics and the United Arab Republic," *Pravda*, 28 May 1971.

26. Mohamed Heikal, *The Road to Ramadan* (New York: Quadrangle Press, 1975), pp. 122–39. Editor of *Al Ahram,* the author had been a confidant of President Sadat at the time.

27. Moscow radio, 13 October 1971; *FBIS,* 14 October 1971.

28. For Sadat's explanation of the ouster of Soviet advisors, see *New York Times,* 20 July 1972; Cairo radio, 24 February 1975, broadcast the criticism (*FBIS,* 25 February 1975); *New York Times,* 2 February 1977, on Soviet replacement of aircraft engines and spare parts.

29. John Damis, *Conflict in Northwest Africa* (Stanford: Hoover Institution Press, 1983), pp. 45–103 for background; *Pravda,* 27 August 1984, concerning the students and trade relations; *New York Times,* 15 August 1985, pp. 1 and 8, on weapons for Polisario; Moscow radio, 28 March 1986, in *FBIS,* 1 April 1986, p. H-1; *Pravda,* 26 June 1986, p. 4, about Algeria.

30. The two defense ministers met, according to Moscow radio, 7 August 1984; *FBIS,* 8 August 1984, p. H-1. For background, see Mark N. Katz, *Russia and Arabia* (Baltimore: Johns Hopkins University Press, 1986), pp. 61–102, on South Yemen; *Pravda,* 5 June and 23 July 1986, for talks held in Moscow and Aden, respectively; ibid., 8 September 1986, p. 5, for names of killed leaders; Moscow radio, 29 October 1986, in FBIS, p. H-3, 30 October 1986, for a new agreement.

31. *Pravda,* 20 March 1984; *Wall Street Journal,* 31 May 1984, p. 27; *Pravda,* 9 September 1984, p. 4, and 17 December 1985, p. 1. According to the U.S. Department of State, the East European regimes are selling weapons to Iran (*New York Times,* 2 October 1986).

32. *Pravda,* 14 March 1984; Moscow radio, 28 July 1984, *FBIS,* 30 July 1984, p. H-5; *Pravda,* 15 and 16 October 1984, for Asad's visit to Moscow; *New York Times,* 29 May 1986, for the Gorbachev promise; *CIA, Handbook of Economic Statistics, 1986,* table 90, p. 125, for bloc advisors.

33. *Izvestiia,* 25 December 1983; *Christian Science Monitor,* 5 June 1984; Teheran radio, 4 February 1986, in *FBIS,* 5 February 1986, p. D1; *Handbook, 1986,* op. cit., for advisors; Moscow radio, 7 October 1986, in *FBIS,* 17 October 1986, p. H 1. See also *New York Times,* 10 December 1986, on USSR-Iran relations.

34. Thomas T. Hammond, *Red Flag over Afghanistan* (Boulder, Colo.: Westview Press, 1984), pp. 49–94. For the Soviet view, see M. Ia. Koval'zon, ed., *Teoriia revoliutsii: Istoriia i sovremennost'* (Moscow: Izdatel'stvo Moskovskogo universiteta, 1984), pp. 125–39. On military operations, see Joseph J. Collins, *The Soviet Invasion of Afghanistan* (Lexington, Mass.: Lexington Books, 1986), pp. 144–152; *New York Times,* 29 July 1986, p. 1, for troop estimates; ibid., 9 August 1986, for refugees; ibid., 17 October 1986, p. 27, for Pakistan's dilemma; ibid., 13 December 1986, p. 1, for Soviet casualties.

35. For specific years, see United Kingdom, Foreign and Commonwealth Office, Economic Service (International Division), *Soviet, East European, and*

Western Development Aid, 1976–82, Foreign Policy Report, no. 85 (London, May 1983). The total comes from CIA, *Handbook of Economic Statistics, 1986,* table 79, p. 112.

36. "Treaty of Peace, Friendship and Cooperation between the USSR and the Republic of India," *Pravda,* 10 August 1971.

37. Details on the military agreement, see *New York Times,* 10 March 1984. The latest credits are given in ibid., 8 December 1985, p. 2E; and the new five-year agreement was announced by *Pravda,* 24 December 1985, p. 4. See also *Insight,* 18 August 1986, p. 43, on the MIG-29 and *Pravda,* 28 November 1986, for declaration signed at Delhi by Gorbachev.

38. V. I. Ermolaev, *Iz istorii rabochego i kommunisticheskogo dvizheniia v Latinskoi Amerike* (Moscow: Mysl', 1982); V. V. Volskii, chief ed., *Kapitalizm v Latinskoi Amerike* (Moscow: Nauka, 1983); Kenneth N. Skong, Jr., *Cuba as a Model and a Challenge* (Washington, D.C.: Cuban-American National Foundation, 1984); Aleksandr Serikov commentary on 1985 events in Latin America over Moscow television, 29 December 1985, in *FBIS,* 6 January 1986, pp. K 4–5. See also Tad Szulc, "Fidel Castro's Years as a Secret Communist," *New York Times Magazine,* 19 October 1986, pp. 47ff.

39. Since the early 1970s, the Peruvian government has received more than one-half billion dollars worth of Soviet military equipment (report from Lima in the *Washington Times,* 12 June 1984, pp. 1 and 12). At the same time, a ship with more than 3,000 pieces of military hardware from East Germany destined for the "Shining Path" guerrillas in Peru was stopped by Panamanian authorities (*National Review,* 18 July 1986, pp. 15–16; *New York Times,* 31 August 1986).

40. Robert Rand, "Soviet Union Forcing Allies to Aid Cuba," *Radio Liberty Research Bulletin,* no. RL 35/48 (Munich, 18 January 1984); Central Intelligence Agency, *Handbook of Economic Statistics, 1986,* September 1986, p. 115; *New York Times,* 29 July 1986, reported from Havana that payments on the $3.5 billion debt to the West had been stopped.

41. International Sugar Organization, *Sugar Yearbook, 1985* (London, July 1986), p. 58; *The Economist,* 14 January 1984, p. 34; CIA, *The Cuban Economy,* series ALA 34–10052, June 1984, pp. 35 and 37. See also A. D. Bekarevich, ed., *Kuba: Stroitel'stvo sotsializma* (Moscow: Nauka, 1983), p. 10, which estimates annual Cuban sugar production for 1981–1985 at between 8.4 and 8.8 million tons. By 1986, the world price of sugar was 7.6¢ per pound (U.S. Agricultural Department, *Sugar and Sweetener* [Washington, D.C.: Economic Research Service, June 1986], p. 10).

42. U.S. Department of State, *Soviet and East European Aid,* p. 18.

43. René Castillo, "Lessons and Prospects of the Revolution," *World Marxist Review* 17, no. 7 (July 1974): 83–95; and part 2 in no. 8 (August 1974): 107–16. Ten caches of buried weapons, including 3,383 used M-16 rifles (from Vietnam), 117 Soviet rocket launchers, two million rounds of ammunition, about 2,000 rocket-propelled grenades, and tons of explosives were

found by Chilean authorities (*Wall Street Journal,* 16 September 1986, p. 34; *New York Times,* 19 October 1986, p. 9).

44. U.S. Department of State and U.S. Department of Defense, *Background Paper: Central America,* 27 May 1983, pp. 3–4, and their *The Challenge to Democracy in Central America* (Washington, D.C.: June 1986), pp. 17–36. See also *La Vanguardia* (Barcelona), 31 July 1984, pp. 3, 8–9, for transcript of a speech given at a closed meeting in Managua by leading Sandinista ideologist Bayardo Arce; and Daniel Ortega Saavedra's seventh anniversary speech over Managua radio, 19 July 1986, in *FBIS,* 21 July 1986, pp. 10–20.

45. Stephen Kinzer and John Cushman in *New York Times,* 10 July and 29 October 1986. Timothy Ashby, *The Bear in the Back Yard* (Lexington, Mass.: Lexington Books, 1987), forthcoming, gives details on specific arms deliveries.

46. Keith Bradsher, "The Americas," *Wall Street Journal,* 7 August 1986, p. 17, for debt figures; Alan M. Field, "Yes, They Have No Bananas," *Forbes,* 25 August 1986, pp. 76 and 80.

47. *Pravda,* 13 September 1979, for recognition; U.S. Department of State and U.S. Department of Defense, *Grenada: A Preliminary Report,* 16 December 1983, p. 8. See also *Pravda,* 24 October 1986, p. 5, for current assessment.

48. Ibid., pp. 18–26. The original agreements are reproduced here.

49. Ibid., p. 1. For an analysis of the captured documents, see U.S. Department of State, *Lessons of Grenada* (Washington, D.C.: February 1986), Publication 9457. The trial of Bishop's seventeen accused murderers is described by Joseph Treaster, *New York Times,* 28 July 1986. See also "The Tragedy of Grenada," *Pravda,* 18 August 1986, p. 5.

50. U.S. Department of State and U.S. Department of Defense, *The Challenge to Democracy in Central America,* pp. 47–56. See also K. A. Khachaturov, *Latinskaia Amerika: Ideologiia i vneshniaia politika* (Moscow: Mezhdunarodnye otnosheniia, 1983), pp. 37–52, for the Soviet view of El Salvador.

51. Fred C. Iklé to U.S. Congressman Mickey Edwards, dated 18 April 1984 (copy of letter released by the latter); *Wall Street Journal,* 30 July 1986, p. 22.

52. U.S. Department of State and U.S. Department of Defense, *Background Paper,* pp. 10–16; *The Challenge to Democracy in Central America,* pp. 57–64.
    Secretary of State Shultz, in a speech to Organization of American States representatives at Guatemala City, accused the USSR, Cuba, and Nicaragua of distributing U.S. weapons left behind in Vietnam to guerrilla groups in Chile, Colombia, El Salvador, Guatemala, Honduras, Jamaica, and other countries in Latin America (*Washington Times,* 12 November 1986, p. 6A).

11

THE USSR IN EAST ASIA

USSR foreign policy suffered a major failure on the mainland of China, where Soviet military assistance had played a significant role in helping the Chinese communists to defeat their Nationalist opponents. All of the arms and munitions taken by the Red Army after the Japanese surrender in Manchuria were given to Mao Tse-tung's troops. It would have seemed that ideological solidarity between the two largest communist-ruled states should have prevailed. This did not happen.

The People's Republic of China (PRC) allowed its 30-year friendship treaty with the USSR to expire, despite the fact that the agreement included provisions for almost automatic extension.[1] Mao Tse-tung had spent eight weeks in Moscow negotiating this agreement in 1949–1950, and he subsequently appeared at the Kremlin as an honored guest during the fortieth anniversary of the Bolshevik revolution in 1957. Since then, however, ideological, political, and territorial differences had led to a situation where some observers did not exclude the possibility of war between the two countries, despite the fact that both were ruled by communist parties.

SINO-SOVIET RELATIONS

The genesis of the disagreement over ideology apparently predated the 1957 visit by Mao to the USSR. Khrushchev's speech at the Twentieth

USSR FOREIGN POLICIES AFTER DETENTE

CPSU Congress on 14 February 1956 included the statement that many kinds of revolutionary transformation were possible, even by means of democratic elections and attainment of a parliamentary majority. This formulation appeared again in the documents adopted by the 1957 and 1960 Moscow world conferences of communist parties. The Chinese voiced their disagreement in an article, published by the official *People's Daily*,[2] to the effect that "Marxism has always openly proclaimed the inevitability of violent revolution."

Dispute over Nuclear War

Another subject of early disagreement involved war with the use of nuclear weapons. In the same speech, cited above, Khrushchev had stated that "the world was faced with either peaceful coexistence or the most destructive war in history; there is no third way . . . war is not fatalistically inevitable." Beijing again replied in its party newspaper, refusing to admit that any qualitative change had occurred in the nature of modern warfare due to these new weapons of mass destruction. It subsequently issued a press release that included the following: "The atomic bomb is a paper tiger which U.S. reactionaries use to scare people. [T]he outcome of war is decided by the people, not by one or two new types of weapons."[3]

Only two days after Khrushchev's ouster from power, on 16 October 1964, the PRC exploded its first atomic bomb at Lop Nor. A hydrogen warhead test took place less than three years later. It was described by the *Liberation Army Daily* as a victory for Maoist thought over its enemies. At least 30 nuclear explosions,[4] including an underground one, took place through the end of 1985. For obvious reasons, the non-proliferation treaty always has been opposed by Beijing. A Soviet historian wrote that Chinese nuclear strategy had evolved "from total disregard to strenuous development for their own hegemonist purposes," in three stages:

> The first (1945–53) was characterized by underestimating the signifi-cance of nuclear weapons. During the second period (from the end of the Korean war to the 1960s), Chinese military theorists admitted that "science has developed further with the emergence of nuclear missile weapons." Mao Tse-tung stated in 1956 at a closed conference of leading party personnel: "We should not only have more aircraft and guns but also the atomic bomb. We cannot do without it." The third stage in Beijing's nuclear strategy commenced during the early 1960s, when Chinese leaders steered a course toward an accelerated buildup of their own nuclear missile potential.[5]

According to U.S. Department of Defense information, a PRC medium-range ballistic missile became operational in 1966, and an intercontinental-range missile (ICBM) underwent its first test about ten years later.[6]

The nuclear weapons program has continued, and Beijing was believed by another source in 1986 to have had a deployed force capable of reaching all parts of the Soviet Union. About 120 land-based ICBMs and medium-range launchers plus three missile-firing submarines reportedly were operational at that time. The PRC will be able to target all of its weapons systems against the USSR, whereas the latter must aim most of its own arsenal against NATO and the continental United States (see Table 11.1).

In the meantime, the People's Liberation Army has been conducting military maneuvers with simulated nuclear explosions in the north and northwest of Mainland China. Approximately 200,000 troops took part in one such exercise[7] held in the Xinjiang-Uighur Autonomous Region, which borders on the People's Republic of Mongolia, the oldest Soviet dependency.

Although it received membership in the International Atomic Energy Agency and previously allowed a visit by the director general in August 1983, the PRC's attitude toward any restraint over nuclear weapons' development has been negative. Moscow called on Beijing to join in sponsoring an international freeze on the level of such arsenals. The latter replied that it would reduce its own stockpile only after both superpowers had cut theirs by one-half.[8]

The regular PRC armed forces number about 2.9 million men, and Mainland China shows increasing interest in acquiring Western military technology. Britain has delivered aircraft engines, artillery and fire-control equipment, as well as radar. Computers, helicopters, transport planes, and air-defense radar systems in the near future may come from the United States and Western Europe. Officially released annual expenditures for Chinese defense totaled over $6 billion or more than one-fourth of the 1986 budget.[9] These figures exclude pay and allowances for troops as well as other items. In addition, the estimates may be understated, since Chinese pricing methods differ from those in the West.

Ideological Differences

Another problem in the dispute between Moscow and Beijing centers on the evaluation of Stalin. Condemnation of that man by Khrushchev in his February 1956 secret speech came as a surprise to the Chinese. The latter have continued to praise Stalin as heir to Lenin and the last true Marxist-Leninist leader of the USSR. Even before Khrushchev's

TABLE 11.1
STRATEGIC BALANCE: USSR-CHINA, 1986

	Soviet Union	China
Intercontinental ballistic missiles (ICBMs)	1,398	2 DF-5, 5-MT warhead 4 DF-4, 3-MT warhead
Submarine-launched ballistic missiles (SLBMs)	983 in 77 subs	*2 subs with 12 JL-1 (1 × 2 MT warhead) 4 subs ordered (perhaps 12 planned)
Intercontinental-range strategic bombers	160	None
Intermediate- and medium-range ballistic missiles (IRBMs & MRBMs)	IRBMs & MRBMs: some 553 deployed (perhaps 382 in western USSR, rest in central and eastern USSR) About 171 new SS-20s (each with 3 independently targetable warheads) deployed against China	IRBMs: 60 DF-3, 2-MT MRBMs: some 50 DF-2, 20-KT

Medium-range bombers	510 (about 140 Backfire)	120 H-6 medium bombers; 3,000 km combat radius
Ballistic missile defense	32 ABM-1B Galosh range over 320 km warheads nuclear, presumably MT range. 8 sites & 4 complexes around Moscow. Those available at Central Asian test site also effective against Chinese ICBMs.	Ballistic missile EW phased-array radar complex

NOTE: *The PRC released a photograph of its first nuclear-powered submarine, reproduced in the *San Francisco Chronicle*, 4 January 1987, p. A-20.

SOURCE: International Institute for Strategic Studies, *The Military Balance, 1986–1987* (London, 1986), pp. 36–46, and 142–45.

ouster in October 1964, the Soviet press had compared Mao with Stalin, specifically in terms of purging loyal communists, the personality cult, and the use of force. After the fall of Khrushchev, perhaps in an attempt to slow down the rehabilitation of Stalin, certain writers in the USSR slanted their criticism of Mao to make it clear that both men had been equally evil.

For their part, the Chinese leaders took the initiative even earlier in the quarrel, when they issued the 29 October 1958 resolution calling for establishment of communes and an accelerated transition to communism. In this regard, they appeared to be inviting invidious comparisons with Moscow. Khrushchev replied personally[10] at the Twenty-first Extraordinary CPSU Congress, claiming first place for the USSR in the building of communism. The new party program set 1980 as the target year, when "the present generation of Soviet people shall live under communism." Furthermore, it was stressed that the "state of the whole people" already had replaced the dictatorship of the proletariat in the USSR.[11] These formulations obviously displeased the Chinese.

Almost two years after Khrushchev's fall from power, Beijing elevated the thoughts of Mao in August 1966 from national to worldwide significance, with the attendant claim to ideological leadership over the international communist movement. Obviously, taking offense at this, the new CPSU leader Brezhnev went so far as to label the Great Cultural Revolution in China a "counterrevolution." After that, many articles appeared in Moscow that criticized Beijing for deviating from Marxist doctrine. The weekly *Novoe vremia* (New Times) even linked Maoism with Trotskyism and anarchism as well as defining it as an "anti-proletarian," counterrevolutionary ideology "of the infuriated petty bourgeoisie."[12]

While accusing the Chinese of following "a political course aimed at consolidating great power–nationalistic aims in the field of foreign policy and strengthening their interconnection with a hegemonistic, anti-Soviet domestic policy," one writer complained that about 2,500 items derogatory to the USSR had been published during 1981 in the communist party daily newspaper *Renmin Ribao* alone. Moscow radio continued to broadcast regular series of programs about friendship for the "people," emphasizing the difference between the latter and the regime that rules from Beijing. However, the speech by Gorbachev on 28 July 1986 in Vladivostok included proposals for improving Sino-Soviet contacts.[13]

Inter-state Relations

Government-to-government contacts are separate from inter-party affairs. They have had as their foundation the already mentioned 1950 treaty of friendship, alliance, and mutual assistance. The agreement envisaged military aid against Japan or an ally of that country (meaning the United States). However, the Soviet Union maintained occupation troops in both Port Arthur as well as Darien until 1955 and subsequently continued to station about 20,000 politico-military advisors in other parts of the PRC. A secret 15 October 1957 defense technology agreement was repudiated unilaterally, when the USSR refused to transfer a sample atomic bomb and related technical data to the Chinese.[14]

For almost five years diplomatic relations between the two countries remained at the chargé d'affaires level, following mutual withdrawal of ambassadors. The Soviet embassy at Beijing withstood a siege lasting three weeks in February 1967, during which time personnel venturing outside the compound were manhandled by demonstrating Chinese. The appointment of V. S. Tolstikov as ambassador to the PRC in September 1970 ostensibly signified a return to normalization. He had been first secretary of the CPSU Leningrad region during the preceding eight years. On the other hand, the seating by the United Nations of a Mainland Chinese delegation in the fall of 1971 has given the PRC a worldwide forum to publicize its differences with the Soviet Union. In July 1978 I. S. Shcherbakov replaced Tolstikov, and in April 1980 a new PRC ambassador arrived in Moscow to fill a vacancy that had existed for eleven months. The current Soviet envoy, O. A. Troianovskii, arrived in April 1986 to present his credentials.[15]

Economic Relations

Part of the Sino-Soviet dispute is undoubtedly economic. Moscow promised Beijing through 1959 a total equivalent to $3.8 billion in financial support for construction of 291 projects, of which only 198 were completed. By 1955, the Chinese already had a trade deficit with the USSR, amounting to about $1 billion. Two years later, the debt had reached $2.4 billion. Between 1960 and 1970, annual trade turnover declined from almost 1.5 billion to less than 42 million rubles. It increased in 1975 to 200 million and in 1980 to 340 million. However, the 1981 level was down 40 percent from the preceding year, and trade in 1982 did not reach the 1980 level. It doubled after that during each of the following two years (see Table 11.2). An example of early Chinese resentment against the Soviet Union can be seen from the following published complaint:[16]

> It was unreasonable for China to bear all expenses of the Korean War. During World War I and II, the U.S. lent funds to its allies. After-

ward, some countries repudiated their debt, while the U.S. waived some claims. The Soviet loan is repayable in full within ten years. This time is too short and, moreover, interest must be paid. I propose an extension to 20 or 30 years. When the USSR liberated our northeast [that is, Manchuria], it dismantled machinery equipment in our factories. Was there compensation? Will there be repayment?

The mere fact that this appeared in the official communist party daily newspaper indicates that such sentiments must have been shared within the top leadership at Beijing.

However, during 1985 Sino-Soviet trade turnover totaled more than 1.6 billion rubles and reached its highest level in 25 years. The Central Asian frontier between the two countries has been opened at several points for commercial exchange, although these new border crossings remain closed for travel by individuals. At the same time, the Mongolian People's Republic began to expel about 8,000 Chinese citizens who had lived there for generations. A deputy foreign minister from the PRC arrived in Ulan Bator for talks on improving relations.[17]

The Border Dispute

Another matter under protracted discussion between the two governments involves the frontier. The 4,500 mile border remains divided by Mongolia. A seemingly fixed landmark is the Amur River, separating Chinese Manchuria from the Soviet Far East. It was here that pitched battles occurred over which country owned certain islands. Clashes also took place along the Mongolian-Chinese border as late as the end of 1974, in the course of which about 30 casualties were sustained by both sides.[18] One of the most potentially volatile areas is located between Soviet Central Asia and the Xinjiang-Uighur region inside the PRC. The populations on both sides of the frontier are Turkic and remain distrustful of Russians as well as Chinese.

Border incidents began in 1962, when some 5,000 Uighurs and Kirghiz fled from the Ili Valley in the PRC to the USSR. Interestingly enough, Moscow subsequently charged the Chinese communists with more than 5,000 frontier violations in that one year.[19] The PRC in turn accused the Soviets of instigating 4,189 incidents during the ensuing five-year period. In an interview given to a Japanese socialist party delegation, Mao stated: "About 150 years ago, the area east of Lake Baikal became Russian territory; since then, Vladivostok, Khabarovsk, Kamchatka, *et alia* have been Soviet territory. We have not yet presented our account for this list."[20] Although negotiations on border

TABLE 11.2
SOVIET-CHINESE TRADE, 1960–1986
(IN MILLIONS OF RUBLES)

Year	Turnover	Exports	Imports	Balance
1960	1,498.7	735.4	763.3	−27.9
1965	375.5	172.5	203.0	−30.5
1970	41.9	22.4	19.5	+ 2.9
1975	200.6	92.8	107.8	−15.0
1980	340.0	190.8	149.6	+41.2
1981	176.8	82.6	94.2	−11.6
1982	223.5	120.1	103.4	+16.7
1983	488.2	255.6	232.6	−23.0
1984	977.8	467.9	509.9	−42.0
1985	1,605.0	779.0	826.0	−47.0
1986	est. 2,400.0*			

*Estimate is based upon the 10 July 1985 agreement to exchange 12 billion rubles in goods during 1986–1990 (*Vneshniaia torgovlia*, no. 3, March 1986, p. 10).

SOURCES: USSR, *Vneshniaia torgovlia za 1960 god* (Moscow: Statistika, 1961), p. 9, and the same for subsequent years; *Vneshniaia torgovlia*, no. 3 (March 1981) and ibid., March 1982, March 1983, March 1984, and March 1986, p. 9.

problems began in 1969, they were conducted for almost a decade without any apparent progress. Political talks on state-to-state relations suddenly ended in December 1979, when the Chinese said that it would not be appropriate to continue because the USSR invaded Afghanistan.

Even before then, during the previous year, Beijing had accused Soviet border troops of crossing the Ussuri River and attacking PRC citizens. According to the official news agency, Hsinhua, a USSR helicopter and eighteen boats carrying about 30 troops penetrated several miles into Chinese territory. Approximately fourteen PRC citizens allegedly were harassed, beaten, and dragged to the river, according to this source. The TASS news agency replied that USSR border guards had been "pursuing a dangerous criminal," mistakenly crossed the border, and that reports of Soviet aggression against Chinese civilians were "pure fabrication."[21]

Another incident began, according to Beijing, when a four-man USSR military patrol forded the Ergun River in a remote region of Heilongjiang province in northeast China and tried to kidnap a local herdsman, who was killed in the process. One USSR soldier was shot in an exchange of fire, as the invaders retreated across the river. The

PRC claims that as many as 54 divisions or one million Soviet troops are poised along its border. At least that many Chinese soldiers reportedly face them, according to the USSR. Premier Zhao Ziyang had affirmed that the PRC will stage an active struggle against Moscow "hegemonism"[22] throughout the world.

Only in October 1982 were government-to-government negotiations resumed at the level of deputy foreign minister. They take place twice a year. The Chinese have made three demands: (1) reduction of USSR troops along their common border in Mongolia, (2) an end to support by Moscow for Vietnam's occupation of Kampuchea, and (3) withdrawal of Soviet armed forces from Afghanistan.[23] Despite the death of Brezhnev within weeks after resumption of PRC-USSR talks, the new leader Andropov indicated that he would follow his predecessor's policy vis-à-vis Mainland China. The Soviets apparently were unwilling to meet any of the three demands mentioned above.

The ninth round of talks, held in Beijing during October 1986, did not result in any progress on the issue of the 171 or more SS-20s in the Far East, USSR troops along the PRC border, and the Soviet armored divisions totaling 75,000 men in Mongolia. The other two problems— Vietnamese forces in Kampuchea and the USSR occupation of Afghanistan—could not be resolved either. (CPSU leader Mikhail Gorbachev made it clear in his July 1986 speech at Vladivostok that the number of Soviet troops along the Chinese border go far beyond "reasonable sufficiency.") It was agreed to meet at Moscow in February 1987. A special Soviet envoy had signed an agreement for an exchange of engineers and technicians.[24]

VIETNAM AND CAMBODIA

A major issue in the conflict between the two communist giants has involved their respective attitudes toward Southeast Asia in general and Vietnam in particular. Before his ouster, it is possible that Khrushchev may have decided to disengage from the Indochinese problem. His successor Brezhnev, however, reasserted Soviet interest in the region. Perhaps he thought, as Khrushchev possibly did, that North Vietnam would never win its war, but he probably felt that the USSR could not leave opposition to American "imperialism" by default to China alone. The late Prime Minister Kosygin spent the first half of February 1965 in Beijing and Hanoi. A secret letter sent to the PRC on 17 April of that year requested transit rights for some 4,000 Soviet troops to be sent by rail to Vietnam, establishment of two airfields with 500 USSR

ground personnel in southwest China, and an air corridor for unre-
stricted flights to and from Hanoi. The response from Beijing came
three months later in the following words: "Frankly speaking, we do
not trust you. We and other fraternal countries have learned bitter
lessons in the past from Khrushchev's evil practice of control under
cover of aid. We cannot accept your control. Nor will we help you
control others."[25]

A subsequent Chinese statement on 3 May 1966 condemned the
USSR for its policy of detente in Europe, which allegedly had enabled
Americans to transfer troops from the Federal Republic of Germany to
South Vietnam. It also denied allegations concerning obstruction of
Soviet military shipments crossing Mainland China by railroad to Ha-
noi and suggested that the USSR could use sea routes, perhaps in the
hope that this would precipitate a confrontation with the United States.
Charges that Beijing had stolen two anti-aircraft guided missile
launchers were denounced as slander, and Moscow in turn was accused
of collusion with Washington. This dispute died down in 1975 after
American troops had been withdrawn from South Vietnam.

Four years later, a controlled Chinese invasion of Vietnam was
described by Deputy Premier Deng Xiaoping as a punitive action "intended to teach the Vietnamese that their adventurism in Cambodia
[Kampuchea] would not pay, even with assurances of Soviet support."
Moscow's restraint was explained after it had become clear that the
Vietnamese were standing their ground against the Chinese. According
to a USSR official:[26] "We did not intervene when the U.S. was bombing
Vietnam during the last war, and that was a real provocation. Why
should we intervene now?" The Soviet-Vietnamese treaty calls for consultations in the event that either party is threatened. Such meetings
have taken place between Hanoi's ambassador in Moscow and a Soviet
deputy foreign minister, as well as through other official channels.
However, both Mainland China and Vietnam were criticized by other
communist parties for engaging in war and acting in an "imperialist"
manner. According to an unconfirmed USSR tally, 57 of the 80 movements that took a position condemned Beijing rather than Hanoi.[27]

Regardless of the alleged impact on other communist parties, the
PRC continues to support the ousted Kampuchean regime, whose
guerrillas are fighting against Vietnamese occupation troops. A long
article in the CPSU daily newspaper accused Beijing of providing assistance to those guilty of genocide against the Cambodian people. During the spring and summer of 1984, border skirmishes continued along
the Sino-Vietnamese border. Two years later, the Chinese were firing
mortar and artillery shells into northern Vietnam. The USSR, for its

part, supports Hanoi both verbally and financially. The PRC, according to Prince Norodom Sihanouk, offered Vietnam aid to rebuild the economy, if it withdraws from Kampuchea.[28]

CHINA AND EASTERN EUROPE

Up to 1958, only Albania among the other fourteen communist-ruled states had been aligned with Mainland China. Tirana repeatedly came under attack during the early 1960s by USSR propagandists as a symbol for the PRC, which, in turn, directed criticism at Belgrade as a surrogate for Moscow. The thirtieth "liberation anniversary" celebrated by the Albanian communists in November 1974 attracted many pro-Beijing splinter movements, including small delegations of exiles from Poland and Yugoslavia[29] (see Table 11.3). In Eastern Europe only the governments of Romania and Yugoslavia had consistently maintained good relations with the PRC.

These two countries were visited during the latter part of August 1978 by Chinese Communist Party leader Hua Guofeng, who was seeking to counter USSR influence. In Romania, he attacked Soviet "hegemonism." Both sides signed a joint statement[30] that pledged increasingly to expand and deepen bilateral ties as well as to oppose "all forms of domination." The subsequent week-long visit to Yugoslavia by Hua emphasized reconciliation between these two ruling parties.

Relations have remained friendly. Hua Guofeng attended the funeral of Tito, calling the deceased a "farsighted, experienced and tested politician . . . a real visionary."[31] The press in Yugoslavia devotes considerable space to Sino-Soviet affairs, with a pro-Chinese bias. Beijing is praised for returning to the international arena, while Moscow is criticized for its dogmatic ideas. During a recent two-year period about 260 visits of various types took place between Mainland China and Yugoslavia, some 40 of which involved high-level government contacts. Five other East European countries (Bulgaria, Czechoslovakia, East Germany, Hungary, and Poland) have agreed to upgrade PRC factories in return for agricultural and light industry products.[32] The extent of foreign trade can be seen in Table 11.4. In 1985, it totaled more than $2.6 billion.

Premier Zhao Ziyang spent five days each during July 1986 in Romania and Yugoslavia, still the most friendly regimes in Eastern Europe. Both governments had signed long-range (1986–1990) commodity exchange agreements with China. Yugoslav engineers are helping build a 280-kilometer modern railroad track in the PRC.[33] The

Soviet Union cannot prevent its "allies" in Eastern Europe from improving relations with the Chinese, because that is exactly what the USSR is attempting to do with more than 60 delegations traveling to the PRC during 1985. Top communist party leaders from Poland and East Germany, Wojciech Jaruzelski and Erich Honecker, visited Beijing in September and October of the following year.

RELATIONS WITH NORTH KOREA AND JAPAN

The communist leadership in Pyongyang, North Korea, avoided taking sides in the Sino-Soviet dispute. It has supported neither the puppet regime in Afghanistan nor the Vietnamese involvement in Kampuchea. However, the shooting down of the South Korean civilian airliner by the USSR on 1 September 1983 (for other attacks, see Table 11.5) appears to have triggered a Pyongyang rapprochement with Moscow. Shortly afterward, in a demonstration of their own cold-bloodedness, three North Korean army officers set off a powerful bomb at Rangoon, killing four Burmese and seventeen high-ranking South Korean officials who were on a government visit in Burma.[34]

North Korean ruler Kim Il-sung traveled by train in May 1984 to Moscow, his first trip since 1967 (he had been to Beijing in 1975), and held three rounds of talks with Chernenko. He reportedly asked for new jet fighters and support against the "Washington-Tokyo-Seoul bloc" as well as PRC "hegemonism," to which he had referred publicly only a few weeks earlier. Moscow, in addition to delivering twenty to thirty MiG-23s, has financed North Korea's largest iron and steel works and a new port at Najin that provides the USSR with naval facilities.[35]

North Korea became the thirteenth country to withdraw from the Los Angeles Summer Olympics, which must have pleased the Soviet Union. Obviously, the latter is in a position to supply more substantial economic and military aid than the Chinese communists. Furthermore, Kim reportedly resented the PRC attitude toward Seoul. The communist Chinese formerly had accepted, without consulting Pyongyang, a Japanese proposal that Korean residents of the Mainland be allowed to visit their relatives in South Korea. Although they do not have diplomatic relations, Beijing and Seoul also conduct trade. However, the North Korean prime minister subsequently spent five days at Beijing to discuss economic relations. Kim Il Sung visited Moscow toward the end of October 1986 and met with Gorbachev.[36]

The USSR also is disturbed by the rapprochement between the

TABLE 11.3
PRO-CHINESE COMMUNIST ORGANIZATIONS

Argentina	Communist Party (Marxist-Leninist) of
	Communist Vanguard of
	Revolutionary Communist Party of
Australia	Communist Party (Marxist-Leninist) of
Austria	Communist League
	Austrian Marxist-Leninist Party
	Austrian Revolutionary Workers Association
	Communist League of Vienna
Bangladesh	Communist Party (Marxist-Leninist) of
Belgium	Communist Party (Marxist-Leninist) of
Bolivia	Communist Party (Marxist-Leninist) of
Brazil	Communist Party of
Britain	Communist Federation (Marxist-Leninist) of
	Communist Federation of Britain/East London Marxist-Leninist Association
	Communist Unity Association (Marxist-Leninist)
Burma	Communist Party of
Canada	Canadian Communist League (Marxist-Leninist)
	Canadian Marxist-Leninist Group "In Struggle"
Ceylon	Communist Party of
Chile	Revolutionary Communist Party of
Colombia	Colombian Marxist-Leninist League
	Marxist-Leninist League of
	Communist Party (Marxist-Leninist) of
Denmark	Communist League (Marxist-Leninist) of
Dominican Republic	"June 14" Revolutionary Movement, Political Committee of Red Line of
	Red Banner
	Voice of Proletariat
	Workers Party of the
	Bandera Proletaria (possibly Red Banner/Voice of Proletariat combination)
Ecuador	Communist Party (Marxist-Leninist) of
Faroe Islands	Marxist-Leninist Organization of
Finland	Marxist-Leninist Groups of
France	Marxist-Leninist Communist Party of
	Marxist-Leninist Revolutionary Communist Party of
	Marxist-Leninist Communists of L'Humanité Rouge
	Marxist-Leninist Communists of (probably a renaming of L'Humanité group, above)

Germany	Communist Party of
	Communist Party (Marxist-Leninist) of
	Communist League of
	Communist Party, "New Unity" (Marxist-Leninist)
	Workers Union for Reconstruction of Communist Party
	Communist Workers Union of
Greece	Communist Party (Marxist-Leninist) of
	Organization of Greek Marxist-Leninists
	Organization of Marxist-Leninists of
	Revolutionary Communist Movement of
Guadeloupe	Workers Party of
Haiti	Haitian Workers' Party
Honduras	Communist Party (Marxist-Leninist) of
Iceland	Communist Party (Marxist-Leninist) of
	Communist League of Union (Marxist-Leninist)
Indonesia	Communist Party of
Italy	Communist Party (Marxist-Leninist) of
	Marxist-Leninist Organization of
	Party of Socialist Revolution of
	Organization of Communists (Marxist-Leninist) of
	"Consciousness of Workers"
	"Proletarian Ideology"
	Italian (Marxist-Leninist) Communist Party
	Red Star Marxist-Leninist Revolutionary Front of
	Coordinating Committee for Unity of Marxist-Leninists
	Laborers Movement for Socialism
Japan	Japanese Communist Party (Left)
	Japanese Workers' Party
Korea	South Korean Revolutionary Party for Unification
Luxembourg	Communist League of
Malaya	Communist Party of
Malaysia	Communist Party of
Netherlands	Marxist-Leninist Communist Unitarian Movement of
	Marxist-Leninist Communist Unity Movement of
	Marxist-Leninist League of
	Marxist-Leninist Party of
	Socialist Party of
	League of Dutch Marxist-Leninists
	League of Marxist-Leninists
	Communist Workers Organization
	Breda Communist Group (Marxist-Leninist)

TABLE 11.3 *(continued)*
PRO-CHINESE COMMUNIST ORGANIZATIONS

New Zealand	Communist Party of
North Kalimantan	Communist Party of
Norway	Norwegian Workers' Communist Party (Marxist-Leninist), Working Committee of
Paraguay	Communist Party of
Peru	Communist Party of
	Peruvian Communist Party
Philippines	Communist Party of
Poland	Communist Party of
Portugal	Communist Party (Marxist-Leninist) of
	Portuguese Communist Party (reconstituted)
Réunion	Marxist-Leninist Communist Organization
San Marino	Communist Party (Marxist-Leninist) of
Spain	Labour Party of
	Spanish Workers' Revolutionary Organization
	Spanish Communist Party (Marxist-Leninist)
Sri Lanka	Communist Party (Marxist-Leninist) of
Suriname	Communist Party of
	People's Party
Sweden	Communist Party of
	Marxist-Leninist Union of Struggle
	Swedish Communist Party
	Clarte Federation
	Groups for Communist Unity
Switzerland	Marxist-Leninist Communist Party
Thailand	Communist Party of
Uruguay	Uruguayan Revolutionary Communist Party
	Communist Party of
	Revolutionary Communist Party
U.S.A.	Revolutionary Communist Party
	October League
	Organizing Committee for a Marxist-Leninist Party
Venezuela	Party of Venezuelan Revolution
Yugoslavia	Communist Party of

NOTE: Some of the above may have fused or disbanded.

SOURCES: Richard F. Staar, ed., *Yearbook on International Communist Affairs* (Stanford: Hoover Institution Press), published annually in June; *Beijing Review,* various issues.

TABLE 11.4
PRC TRADE WITH EASTERN EUROPE, 1985
(IN MILLIONS OF DOLLARS)

	Exports to	Imports from	Trade Balances
Czechoslovakia	161.9	242.6	−80.7
East Germany	65.4	186.5	−121.1
Hungary	61.6	113.4	−51.8
Poland	120.3	177.3	−57.0
Romania	336.7	515.2	−178.5
Yugoslavia	20.9	133.1	−112.2

SOURCE: CIA, Directorate of Intelligence, *China: International Trade* (Washington, D.C.: GPO, July 1986), EA CIT 86-001, tables 2, 3, 4 on pp. 3, 5, and 7.

PRC and Japan, because its own relations with the latter have deteriorated since 1980. By that time Tokyo already had become convinced that Moscow would not honor its 1956 promise to return two of the four South Kuriles, occupied at the end of the Second World War. Since then the Soviets have deployed 10,000 ground troops and about forty MiG-23 jet fighters as well as SSC-1 Sepal missiles on Etorofu, one of the islands in the chain.[37]

By stationing 171 of its SS-20 intermediate-range nuclear missile launchers and perhaps 100 Backfire bombers in the Far East, the USSR is attempting to intimidate Japan. Meetings at the ambassadorial and deputy of even foreign minister level have not resolved any of the problems between the two countries. The Japanese unilaterally renounced the means to project military power in their 1946 constitution, so they pose no threat to the Soviets. The invasion of Afghanistan and 1981–1983 martial law in Poland, however, did result in Japanese economic sanctions against the USSR. Export-Import Bank credits were stopped and new enterprises canceled or delayed by Tokyo. Only a few remaining old projects are still being pursued: coking coal mines in southern Yakutia, oil and gas development on Sakhalin, and a forestry venture. During 1985 commercial exchange increased only moderately. Subsequent negotiations resulted in a 1986–1990 trade agreement.[38]

Toward the end of 1982 the Japanese public had learned about extensive Soviet intelligence activities against its country from KGB defector Stanislav Levchenko, mentioned in Chapter 5. He revealed that 40 percent of all TASS correspondents in Japan belonged to the KGB and that another 10 to 15 percent were GRU officers. Levchenko claimed to have recruited about 200 local informants, including a

TABLE 11.5
SOVIET ATTACKS ON FOREIGN AIRCRAFT, 1950–1983

	Date	Description of Attack	Casualties/Injuries
1.	8 April 1950	U.S. Navy Privateer bomber with ten on board disappears over the Baltic. U.S. says plane was brought down by Soviets.	*
2.	6 November 1951	U.S. Navy plane lost over international waters off Siberia after Soviet planes fire on it.	Crew of ten missing.
3.	29 April 1952	Soviets attack French commercial airliner.	Two passengers injured.
4.	13 June 1952	U.S. reconnaissance plane missing after interception by Soviet planes over Japan.	*
5.	16 June 1952	Soviet jets down unarmed Swedish military plane over international waters in the Baltic.	Seven crewmen rescued.
6.	7 October 1952	U.S. B-29 bomber with crew of eight disappears over northern Japan after taking Soviet fire.	*
7.	10 March 1953	U.S. Air Force jet fighter shot down by two Soviet MiGs in Germany.	No casualties.
8.	12 March 1953	Soviet MiGs down British bomber above Elbe River Valley at the East-West frontier of Germany.	Five crewmen die.
9.	15 March 1953	U.S. reconnaissance plane attacked by MiG about 25 miles from Soviet border.	Shots exchanged, but neither is hit.
10.	29 July 1953	U.S. B-50 bomber shot down by MiGs over the Sea of Japan.	*Sixteen crewmen presumed killed.

#	Date	Event	Outcome
11.	22 January 1954	U.S. reconnaissance plane over Yellow Sea attacked by eight MiGs.	No casualties.
12.	12 March 1954	Two U.S. military planes flying near Czechoslovak border on training flight attacked by MiG.	Both land safely.
13.	3 June 1954	Belgian transport carrying livestock fired upon over Yugoslavia by MiG fighter.	One crewman killed, two injured.
14.	4 September 1954	U.S. Navy plane shot down by Soviet jets 30 miles off Siberian coast.	One dead.
15.	7 November 1954	American reconnaissance plane shot down over northern Hokkaido, Japan.	One American killed.
16.	10 May 1955	Eight American fighter planes on patrol over international waters near North Korea attacked by MiGs.	No casualties.
17.	22 May 1955	U.S. Navy patrol bomber attacked by Soviet aircraft near St. Lawrence Island in Bering Sea.	Seven in crew injured.
18.	27 June 1958	Unarmed American military transport, diverted from its course by storm, shot down over Soviet Armenia.	No casualties.
19.	2 September 1958	C-130 transport aircraft shot down over Armenia near Turkish border.	*Seventeen Americans presumed killed.
20.	7 November 1958	Soviet MiGs fire on U.S. Air Force reconnaissance jets over Baltic and Sea of Japan.	
21.	16 June 1959	U.S. Navy patrol plane attacked by Soviet-made MiG over Sea of Japan.	One crewman injured.
22.	1 May 1960	Soviets down U.S. reconnaissance plane piloted by Francis Gary Powers.	U-2 pilot captured, jailed.

TABLE 11.5 (*continued*)
SOVIET ATTACKS ON FOREIGN AIRCRAFT, 1950–1983

	Date	Description of Attack	Casualties/Injuries
23.	1 July 1960	American RB-47 shot down over Barents Sea near Kola Peninsula.	Four of six on board die.
24.	20 November 1963	Soviets down Iranian plane after it strays over Russian border and flies back into Iran.	
25.	28 January 1964	U.S. Air Force jet trainer shot down over East Germany.	Three Americans die.
26.	10 March 1964	American bomber downed by Soviets after it strayed across East German frontier.	No deaths.
27.	20 April 1978	South Korean airliner flying from Paris to Seoul fired at when it crosses over Soviet territory.	Two passengers killed, thirteen injured.
28.	July 1981	Argentine cargo plane crashes after colliding with pursuing Soviet plane in Armenia.	
29.	1 September 1983	South Korean passenger aircraft flying from Anchorage to Seoul shot down as it leaves Soviet territory.	All passengers and crew killed (269).

*In these five cases, 57 U.S. airmen may have survived the crashes. The Soviet government has denied having any information about the missing crew members (Foreign Press International, *FPI International Report* [New York], 26 October 1984, p. 3).
SOURCE: *U.S. News & World Report*, 12 September 1983, p. 25.

former labor minister and an ex-chairman of the Socialist Party.[39] These revelations have had a negative impact on the image of the USSR. They probably influenced the Japanese decision to continue sanctions, even after the respective foreign ministers met during March 1984 in Moscow. Visits by the USSR foreign minister, E. A. Shevardnadze, to Tokyo in January and by his counterpart, Sintaro Abe, to Moscow during May–June 1986 seemed to be in preparation for talks about a peace treaty.[40] All of these developments bear on Soviet relations with the United States, which are dealt with in the next chapter.

NOTES

1. The treaty was signed on 14 February 1950 and published in *Pravda* the following day. The Chinese announced in advance that it would not be extended. See Harry Gelman, "Soviet Policy Toward China," *Survey* 27, no. 118/119 (Autumn–Winter 1983): 165–74.

2. *Renmin Ribao* (People's Daily), 31 March 1960. Compare also Lin Biao, "Long Live the Victory of the People's War," *Hongqi* (Red Flag), 3 September 1965.

3. "Long Live Leninism!" editorial, *Renmin Ribao*, 16 April 1960; quotation from PRC government statement, issued by New China News Agency, 1 September 1963, and cited in U.S. Consulate General, *Current Background* (Hong Kong), no. 712 (4 September 1963).

4. Michael R. Gordon in the *New York Times*, 25 March 1986, with a table listing nuclear tests, 1945–1985; the PRC has announced it will no longer test above ground.

5. B. Gorbachev, "Beijing's Nuclear Ambitions," *Krasnaia zvezda*, 25 January 1981. Citing unidentified foreign press reports, this article states that the PRC possessed twelve nuclear reactors as well as fourteen accelerators and more than ten processing and enrichment facilities at that time.

   For a PRC source, see Nie Rongzhen, "How China Develops Its Nuclear Weapons," *Beijing Review* 28, no. 17 (29 April 1985): 15–17.

6. James R. Schlesinger, Secretary of Defense, *Annual Defense Department Report for Fiscal Year 1976* (Washington, D.C.: GPO, 1976), pp. II–16 and –17.

7. David Chen in *South China Morning Post* (Hong Kong), 7 July 1982, p. 8. For maneuvers reportedly in a radioactive and chemical or bacteriological environment, see *Insight*, 13 October 1986, p. 38.

8. *Washington Post*, 28 July 1983. Between 1970 and early 1986, the PRC has orbited eighteen satellites according to *New Times* (Moscow), no. 38, 29 September 1986, pp. 20–21.

9. International Institute for Strategic Studies, *The Military Balance, 1986–*

46 USSR FOREIGN POLICIES AFTER DETENTE

1987, p. 142. Manpower cuts are planned, according to the *New York Times,* 4 January 1985. For U.S. military high-tech sales to the PRC, see ibid., 9 April 1986, p. A-3. A defense budget of six billion dollars for 1985 is given by *Insight,* 2 June 1986, p. 25.

10. *Pravda,* 28 January 1959.

11. Ibid., 2 November 1961. The PRC subsequently proclaimed what it calls a "people's democratic dictatorship," akin to the "state of the whole people" in the USSR.

12. See, e.g., I. Gudoshnikov and G. Sergeeva, "Maoists' Revision of the Marxist-Leninist Foundations of the Communist Party," *Partiinaia zhizn',* no. 24 (December 1974): 60–68; editorial "Beijing Changes Tactics," *Novoe vremia,* no. 51 (December 1980): 10–12; O. Drugov, "Proletarian Internationalism: Traditions and the Contemporary Period," *Partiinaia zhizn',* no. 12 (June 1984): 13–22.

    A spokesman for the State Statistical Bureau in Beijing revealed that "over 10 million people had died of unnatural causes, due to man-made factors and serious natural disasters" during the Great Cultural Revolution from 1959 through 1962. American demographers estimate the number to have been three or more times higher. This "natural disaster" is comparable to the mid-1930s purge in the USSR (*Washington Times,* 13 September 1984, p. 11A).

13. Oleg Borisov, "The Situation in the PRC," *Far Eastern Affairs* (Moscow) 36, no. 3 (1982): 13. Moscow television, 28 July 1986; *FBIS,* 29 July 1986, pp. R14–15, for Gorbachev's references to the PRC.

14. This is not mentioned by O. Ivanov, "Contrary to the Chinese People's Interests: On the History of Soviet-Chinese Relations," *Mirovaia ekonomika i mezhdunarodnye otnosheniia,* no. 8 (August 1974): 39–51. However, the Chinese announcement in early 1958 that they would develop their own nuclear weapons is significant in this respect. See also Nie Rongzhen, op. cit., p. 17.

15. John L. Scherer, ed., *USSR Facts and Figures Annual* (Gulf Breeze, Fla.: Academic International Press, 1986), 10: 25; Hong Kong radio, 29 April 1986, in *FBIS,* 30 April 1986, p. B-1. See also B. Borisov, "Resolving Important Tasks," *Pravda,* 1 October 1986, p. 4, on the improvement of Sino-Soviet relations.

16. *Renmin Ribao,* 14 July 1957, as translated in *Current Background* (Hong Kong), no. 470, 26 July 1957. Radio Peace and Progress, 26 October 1984; *FBIS,* 29 October 1984, p. B-1, broadcast a long commentary in Mandarin about Soviet military aid to the PRC during the Korean War.

17. Rome radio, 27 June 1983; *FBIS,* 28 June 1983. ANSA dispatch from Frunze, Kirghizia, USSR, in *New York Times,* 26 June 1983; *Foreign Trade* (Moscow), no. 3, March 1986, insert; *New York Times,* 10 August 1986, on PRC-Mongolian talks.

18. *Daily Telegraph* (London), 17 December 1974.

19. *Pravda,* 21–22 September 1963. It is interesting to note that the Politburo reportedly in 1969 discussed a nuclear strike against China, according to Arkady N. Shevchenko, *Breaking with Moscow* (New York: Knopf, 1985), p. 286.

20. *Asahi Shimbun* (Tokyo), 1 August 1964. The Chinese claim to 1.5 million square kilometers of territory, annexed by tsarist Russia and held by the USSR, was rejected again almost 20 years later in *Novoe vremia* (Moscow), no. 15 (April 1984): 23–25.

21. Hsinhua, 11 May 1978; TASS, 12 May 1978.

22. *Beijing Review,* 9 March 1981, gave Soviet troop estimates; *Washington Post,* 7 October 1980, carried the quotation. The actual figures are 810,000 PRC and 720,000 USSR troops along the border, according to *Christian Science Monitor,* 27 January 1984, or at least 600,000 Soviet soldiers, according to the *New York Times,* 1 August 1986.

23. Dieter Heinzig, "Entspannung zwischen Moskau und Peking," *Europa Archiv* 12, no. 8 (25 April 1983): 244, quoting Deng Xiaoping. See also John F. Burns, "Chinese Rebuff Soviets," *New York Times,* 17 April 1986, where a PRC spokesman repeated the three obstacles and called a summit "unrealistic."

24. Moscow radio, 22 March 1986, in Mandarin; *FBIS,* 24 March 1986, pp. B1–2. See also *Pravda,* 22 March 1986, p. 4; *Izvestiia,* 24 October 1986, p. 6. First Deputy Premier I.V. Arkhipov conducted the talks in Beijing. Gorbachev speech is cited in Note 13 above.

25. Hsinhua, 14 July 1965.

26. Cited in *Asian Wall Street Journal* (Hong Kong), 15 March 1979.

27. Ibid. See also Douglas Pike, "Soviet-Vietnamese Relations," in U.S. Congress, House, Committee on Foreign Affairs, Subcommittees on Europe and the Middle East and on Asia and Pacific Affairs, *Hearings on the Soviet Role in Asia,* 98th Cong., 1st sess., 1983, pp. 205–12; *Far Eastern Economic Review,* 27 September 1984, pp. 56–57. See also Pao-min Chang, *The Sino-Vietnamese Territorial Dispute* (New York: Praeger, 1986), pp. 82–94.

28. *Pravda,* 22 December 1983. The current regime in Kampuchea claims that its predecessor, headed by Pol Pot, had killed 2.7 million individuals between 1975 and 1979 (*New York Times,* 21 May 1984).

    Hanoi radio claimed that starting on 11 January 1986 the Chinese fired 19,000 shells at targets along the border, according to an AP dispatch from Bangkok in *New York Times,* 18 February 1986. Vietnam's "international debt" to Kampuchea is described in *Pravda,* 30 May 1986, p. 5; Sihanouk is quoted in the *New York Times,* 7 August 1986. See also *Pravda,* 3 December 1986, p. 4.

29. Nicholas C. Pano, "Albania," in Richard F. Staar, ed., *1975 Yearbook on International Communist Affairs* (Stanford: Hoover Institution Press, 1975), p. 11.

30. *Scinteia* (Bucharest), 22 August 1978.

31. Quoted in *Vjesnik* (Zagreb), 10 August 1980.

32. *Ekonomska politika* (Belgrade), 6 October 1980; *Far Eastern Economic Review*, 26 May 1983, pp. 29–30; *Renmin Ribao*, 19 May 1984; *Tongil Ilbo* (Tokyo), 9 December 1984, as given in *FBIS*, 10 December 1984, p. E1.

33. Bucharest radio, 6 July 1986, in *FBIS*, 16 July 1986, pp. H 1–3, for the joint communiqué; Belgrade radio, 9 July 1986, in *FBIS*, 14 July 1986, pp. I 3–4, for commentary.

34. United Nations General Assembly, Thirty-ninth Session, Agenda Item 128, "The Bomb Attack at the Martyr's Mausoleum in Rangoon," *Report on the Findings by the Enquiry Committee and the Measures Taken by the Burmese Government*, A/39/456/Add.1, 27 September 1984.

35. *The Economist*, 5 May 1984, p. 32; *Pravda*, 26 May 1984; *Washington Times*, 20 June 1984. See also the *Wall Street Journal*, 16 June 1986, p. 13, for more details on Soviet military relations with North Korea.

36. Free Press International, *International Report* 4, no. 10 (9 May 1984): 1–2, quoting *Tongil Ilbo*, a daily for Koreans residing in Japan. On the visit by Prime Minister Kang Song-san to the PRC, see ibid., no. 17 (15 August 1984): 4. Trade figures are given by *The Economist*, 2 November 1985, pp. 76–77. A four-day visit to Pyongyang by USSR Foreign Minister Shevardnadze resulted in a communiqué that lined up the North Koreans with most Soviet positions (*Pravda*, 24 January 1986, p. 5; and ibid., 28 October 1986, p. 1).

37. Tetsuya Kataoka, "Japan's Northern Parent," *Problems of Communism* 33, no. 2 (March–April 1984): 1–16; for the build-up on Sakhalin and Kamchatka, see *Insight*, 26 May 1986, p. 31; *Far Eastern Economic Review*, 21 August 1986, pp. 38–39; Richard H. Solomon and Masataka Kosaka, *The Soviet Far East Military Buildup* (Dover, Mass.: Auburn House, 1986), pp. 40–55.

38. Galina Orionova, "Cheerless Prospects for Soviet-Japanese Economic Cooperation," *Radio Liberty Research Bulletin*, no. RL 100/84 (Munich, 1 March 1984), pp. 2–4; V. Korionov dispatch in *Pravda*, 1 August 1984, p. 4, on the sanctions; *Vneshniaia torgovlia*, no. 6 (June 1986): 14, on the trade agreement.

39. U.S. Congress, House, Permanent Select Committee on Intelligence, Subcommittee on Oversight, *Hearings on Soviet Active Measures*, 97th Cong., 2nd sess., 1982, p. 153; *Japan Times*, 12 and 17 December 1982.

40. *Pravda*, 20 January 1986, p. 5; ibid., 31 May 1986, p. 1. However, note a statement in Japan by the visiting deputy chairman of the Soviet-Japan Society that the USSR view on the four islands off Hokkaido has not changed (Tokyo radio, 19 March 1986; *FBIS*, 19 March 1986, p. C 1).

    See also the message from USSR Prime Minister N. Ryzhkov to Soviet and Japanese participants in "round table" discussions (*Pravda*, 1 December 1986, p. 1).

12

SOVIET-AMERICAN
RELATIONS

President Richard M. Nixon's visit to Moscow in May 1972—the first ever by an American chief executive—seemingly opened the way to improved relations between the Soviet Union and the United States. Almost exactly twelve years earlier, President Dwight D. Eisenhower's invitation had been canceled by Khrushchev, ostensibly because of the shooting down of an American U-2 reconnaissance plane over Soviet territory.

Prior to 1953, it would have been inconceivable for a United States president to visit the USSR (see Table 12.1). Stalin believed that the conflict between the two camps of communism and capitalism remained irreconcilable and ultimately would lead to war. His foreign policy moves reflected this dogma. Attempts to force American troops out of Berlin took the form of a blockade. An uprising in Greece was staged in an attempt to secure Soviet access to the Mediterranean. However, the ensuing Greek civil war precipitated the articulation in March 1947 of the Truman Doctrine, which promised U.S. aid to governments faced with external threats or domestic subversion. Shifting his emphasis to the Far East, the USSR leader successfully brought the Chinese into the Korean War as "volunteers" against the United States during the early 1950s.

Three years after Stalin's death, the Twentieth CPSU Congress in

February 1956 heard Khrushchev denounce the two-camp image and inevitability of war concept. In their place, he called for "peaceful coexistence" as a means to catch up with and then overtake the United States. Khrushchev actually rivaled Stalin in brinksmanship: the Soviet Union acted provocatively in Berlin (1958), the Congo (1960–61), and Cuba (1962). The last gambit almost resulted in a nuclear conflict between the two superpowers. It also probably contributed to Khrushchev's removal two years later.

The collective leadership that succeeded Khrushchev apparently decided to concentrate its resources on military power and an arms race that it had a chance of winning, provided the United States could be convinced that the Soviet Union desired no more than "parity." Interestingly, the new leader Brezhnev told the CPSU Central Committee in 1968 that military parity had already been reached. A few months later, he proclaimed the following:[1]

Our party and the Soviet government will use all means and possibilities to push back the aggressive policy of [U.S.] imperialism and to create an international situation favorable in the highest degree to the interest of building socialism and communism, and furthering national and social liberation of all nations.

As the United States withdrew from its various outposts throughout the world, the USSR would attempt to fill each vacuum that emerged.

ARMS CONTROL

This objective, to replace America on a global basis, shaped the Soviet approach to arms negotiations. In 1946, while it still enjoyed a monopoly on nuclear weapons, the United States made an offer to destroy its stockpile and transfer all fissionable material to international control under a veto-free body.[2] The USSR rejected this approach and instead proposed a general treaty banning nuclear weapons. Two years later, the U.N. General Assembly endorsed the American plan. After exploding their first atomic bomb, the Soviets withdrew from United Nations' disarmament commissions. Again in 1957, the West proposed a comprehensive disarmament plan that received U.N. endorsement. The USSR also withdrew from these negotiations.[3]

However, an American suggestion to study a test ban in May of the following year was accepted by the Soviet Union. After opening a conference on the subject that fall, both superpowers announced a morato-

TABLE 12.1
SUMMIT MEETINGS, 1943–1986

	Date	Participants	Place
1.	28.11.–1.12. 1943	Roosevelt, Churchill, Stalin	Teheran
2.	4–11.2. 1945	Roosevelt, Churchill, Stalin	Yalta
3.	17.7.–2.8. 1945	Truman, Churchill/Attlee, Stalin	Potsdam
4.	18–23.7. 1955	Eisenhower, Eden, Faure, Bulganin	Geneva
5.	25–27.9. 1959	Eisenhower and Khrushchev	Camp David, Md.
6.	3–4.6. 1961	Kennedy and Khrushchev	Vienna
7.	23–25.6. 1967	Johnson and Kosygin	Glassboro, N.J.
8.	22–29.5. 1972	Nixon and Brezhnev	Moscow
9.	18–25.6. 1973	Nixon and Brezhnev	Washington, D.C.
10.	27.6.–3.7. 1974	Nixon and Brezhnev	Moscow and Yalta
11.	23–24.11.1974	Ford and Brezhnev	Vladivostok
12.	30.7.–1.8. 1975	Ford and Brezhnev	Helsinki
13.	15-18.6. 1979	Carter and Brezhnev	Vienna
14.	19–21.11. 1985	Reagan and Gorbachev	Geneva
15.	11–12.10. 1986	Reagan and Gorbachev	Reykjavik

SOURCE: *Facts on File*, vols. 3–39 *passim;* Gordon R. Weihmiller, *U.S.-Soviet Summits, 1955–1985* (Lanham, Md.: University Press of America, 1986); Richard F. Staar, comp., *The Summit and the Peace Process* (Stanford: Hoover Institution, 1986); for reports by the two principals, see text of President Reagan's address over television in the *New York Times*, 14 October 1986, p. 4, and General Secretary Gorbachev's speech in *Pravda*, 15 October 1986, pp. 1–2.

rium on testing. A ten-member disarmament group resumed negotiations in March 1960 at Geneva. The USSR and four of its East European client states offered typically vague proposals about largely undefined "general and complete disarmament" while rejecting Western counterproposals for verification and mandatory compliance. All five communist delegates walked out of these negotiations in June, even after revised proposals had been offered by both sides. The Soviet Union broke the three-year moratorium on testing (without any prior notification), when it began a series of forty tests during September 1961, including a mammoth 50-megaton device exploded in the Arctic.

A new eighteen-member disarmament committee convened in March 1962 but could not reach any agreement. It took the Cuban missile crisis to obtain a partial nuclear test ban agreement, negotiated within a ten-day period. The resulting Treaty of Moscow, signed on 5 August 1963 by the United States and the USSR, allows only for underground explosions, which subsequently were limited to 150 kilotons. Early the following year, the United States again took the initiative and proposed a nuclear non-proliferation treaty. The ouster of Khrushchev in mid-October 1964, detonation of the first Chinese atomic bomb two days later, and the tensions along the Sino-Soviet border may have been factors in the subsequent USSR decision to make limited agreements.

Thus, at the end of 1966 the United Nations endorsed an American-Soviet ban on weapons of mass destruction in space and in mid-1968 approved the concept of a nuclear non-proliferation treaty.[4] However, it was not until November 1969, and three years after the United States had offered to discuss a strategic arms limitation treaty (SALT), that talks on the latter opened with the USSR. Meanwhile, an agreement was signed in February 1970 that banned nuclear weapons from the seabed, followed a month later by ratification of the treaty on nuclear non-proliferation. Significantly, with the exception of the April 1972 convention[5] outlawing bacteriological warfare (BW), no agreement has been reached to date that theoretically eliminates any kind of weapon from the arsenal of the major powers.

Even in this last case, there is no evidence that the USSR has disposed of its BW weapons. To the contrary, an accident at a secret biological weapons installation near Sverdlovsk resulted in an anthrax epidemic that killed approximately 1,000 inhabitants of the area. The Soviet government has admitted neither this nor that it is preparing to wage bacteriological warfare.[6] On the other hand, the U.S. representative to the 40-nation disarmament conference at Geneva invited all delegates to an army base at Tooele, Utah, where American chemical weapons were being destroyed. The USSR representative ridiculed the invitation, suggesting it had been made only because the United States had other things to hide. He did not accompany the other diplomats who made the trip to observe the destruction process.[7]

SALT I AND II NEGOTIATIONS

The SALT talks began with preparatory sessions at Helsinki and formally opened in April 1970 at Vienna. Soviet chief ideologist Mikhail Suslov reportedly told a group of visiting Japanese socialists in Moscow that the USSR government had rejected a comprehensive agreement, proposed by the United States, on limitation of missile systems. He then voiced hope for a more restricted agreement.[8] A year later, Moscow sent diplomatic notes to the five nuclear powers suggesting an exchange of views on the whole range of arms control issues. Even the French, who had expressed readiness to participate, looked upon the proposal as merely a propaganda gesture. The United States saw no reason to divert attention from the SALT negotiations, which resumed in July 1971 at Helsinki.

After 23 months of secret talks, two agreements were signed in Washington, D.C., on measures to lessen the risk of war due to accidental or unauthorized use of nuclear weapons and on improving direct communications via satellite between the United States and the USSR.[9] Finally, during President Nixon's visit to Moscow, a five-year interim agreement was reached on 26 May 1972 that placed *upward* limits on land-based and sea-launched strategic missiles, submarines carrying the latter, as well as anti-ballistic missile (ABM) systems.[10] The treaties did not reduce these weapons systems but instead established ceilings that proved high enough to accommodate strategic programs that the Soviets already had under way.

At the same time, a statement on "Basic Principles of Relations Between the USSR and the United States" was agreed upon and published in the Soviet Union. It pledged both sides to avoid military confrontation and prevent a nuclear war. Efforts to obtain unilateral advantage, directly or indirectly, were recognized as being inconsistent with the objectives of the declaration. Renunciation of the use or threat of force was recognized as the prerequisite for peaceful relations between the two countries.[11]

In June of the following year, when Brezhnev came to Washington, D.C., both governments agreed not to use force or the threat thereof when such action might escalate from conventional to thermonuclear war. A protocol to the ABM treaty, signed on 3 July 1974, reduced the number of ABM systems permitted from two to one for each side. President Gerald R. Ford's trip to Vladivostok resulted in a joint statement on 24 November 1974, enumerating certain provisions that should appear in a future SALT II agreement.[12]

Again, however, the Soviet Union refused to reduce its growing nuclear arsenal. Under the Vladivostok accord, the number of strategic delivery vehicles (including those carried by intercontinental bombers) held by each side could total 2,400 or some 300 more than the United States had proposed. Of these, only 1,320 might be fitted with multiple warheads. Carried over from the 1972 interim agreement were provisions for a limit of 300 (within the 2,400 total) on the largest and heaviest Soviet SS-9 and SS-18 missiles, a ban on new silo construction, and a restriction on increases in the size of existing silos to 15 percent.

It was hoped that details could be agreed upon by negotiators within a short period of time.

In early 1975 talks resumed at Geneva, based on the general framework of the Vladivostok accord. Disagreement centered on two major issues: how to classify cruise missiles and whether the new Soviet "Backfire" bomber would be counted, like the American B-52, in the 2,400 total for strategic delivery systems. In March 1977, at President Carter's direction, Secretary of State Cyrus Vance proposed significant reductions in ceilings agreed upon at Vladivostok, with the Backfire and cruise missile issues to be deferred until SALT III. Both proposals were rejected categorically by the USSR at a press conference in Moscow,[13] the first that Foreign Minister Gromyko had ever given.

Negotiations continued on several levels. President Carter, Vance, and Gromyko met in Washington during September 1977. Other high-level meetings were held at Moscow over both of the next two years. SALT delegations from the United States and the Soviet Union continued their sessions in Geneva to work out the language on those issues where agreement "in principle" had been reached at the ministerial level. The completed SALT II agreement was signed on 18 June 1979 by President Carter and Supreme Soviet presidium Chairman Brezhnev in Vienna.[14]

In the fall of 1979, the Carter administration did not have the necessary votes to obtain U.S. Senate approval for the SALT II treaty. A setback came when the Armed Services Committee voted ten to zero, with several abstentions, that the agreement did not contribute to the national security of the United States. The Soviet invasion of Afghanistan at the end of December 1979 further reduced the prospects for SALT II, and President Carter finally requested that the treaty be tabled. The new Republican administration indicated[15] that it would enter into strategic arms reduction talks (START) with the Soviet Union before the end of its first year in office.

THE START TALKS

During a commencement address at Eureka College in early May 1982, President Reagan announced that the United States would propose at the strategic arms negotiations in Geneva to reduce both Soviet and U.S. nuclear arsenals by one-third, so that each side would have approximately 5,000 warheads.[16] This represented a new departure, because neither SALT I nor II had provided for cutting back on stockpiles of weapons. At the same time, the United States suggested that the number of missile launchers be reduced to 850 for each side in its offer of a new draft treaty.

The authoritative Soviet response from the new leader, Iurii Andropov, came toward the end of the year and called for an immediate freeze on all new strategic weapons as well as reduction over an eight-year period of ICBM and SLBM missile launchers to 1,800 for each side,[17] a relatively small cut. The proposed freeze obviously was designed to stop development of the MX missile, B-1 bomber, and Trident II submarine in the United States. Soviet weapons systems, already in production, would not have been affected.

To place the START talks into context, one should recall that during the preceding ten years, the USSR had deployed or developed 21 new strategic systems. By contrast, the United States had discontinued the B-1 bomber, closed down its Minuteman production line canceling 100 ICBMs, deactivated ten Polaris submarines with 160 missiles, and begun disassembling 54 Titan I ICBM launchers. This unilateral reduction of strategic forces had been undertaken in good faith with some hope that the Soviets would eventually reciprocate. No such USSR response was forthcoming. As Secretary of Defense Harold Brown told Congress in 1979: "We build, they build. We stop building, they build"[18] (see Table 12.2).

The last American proposal at the START talks, offered on 25 October 1983, was based on the "build-down" concept. For each new fixed ICBM warhead, two old ones would be destroyed; submarine-launched missiles would be converted on a two-for-three ratio and mobile ICBMs on a one-for-one basis. The United States also indicated a willingness to reduce the number of bombers carrying air-launched cruise missiles and SLBMs on Trident II submarines in return for a reduction in number of the large SS-18 ICBMs. Moscow reacted negatively to this approach. It insisted that Andropov's offer be accepted and that both sides work from the USSR rather than the American draft treaty.

On 8 December 1983, after a 35-minute meeting in Geneva, the chief USSR negotiator told his U.S. counterpart (Ambassador Edward L. Rowny) that he could not set a resumption date for the next round of talks. He explained that Moscow wanted to review the issues that had surfaced during the negotiations. The United States delegation expressed its regrets that Round VI would not begin early the following year. In a long interview with the CPSU daily newspaper, the new leader Konstantin Chernenko explicitly stated that strategic arms con-

TABLE 12.2
STRATEGIC OFFENSIVE FORCES
1 JANUARY 1986

United States		Soviet Union	
	ICBMs		
17	Titan	SS-11	450
450	Minuteman II	SS-13	60
550	Minuteman III	SS-17	150
1,017		SS-18	308
		SS-19	360
		SS-25	45
			1,373
	SLBMs		
288	Poseidon (C-3)	SS-N-5	39
360	Trident I (C-4)[a]	SS-N-6	304
648		SS-N-8	292
		SS-N-17	12
		SS-N-18	224
		SS-N-20[a]	80
		SS-N-X-23	32
			983
	Bombers		
167	B-52G	Bear	130
96	B-52H	Bison	30
61	FB-111	Backfire[b]	270
3	B-1B		
327			430
	Approximate Totals		
Delivery Vehicles		*U.S.*	*USSR*
Missiles		1,665	2,356
Bombers		327	430

NOTES: [a]Includes SLBMs potentially carried on Trident and Typhoon SSBNs on sea trials.
[b]Includes Backfire aircraft, assigned to both Soviet strategic air force and naval aviation.
SOURCE: U.S. Department of Defense, Joint Chiefs of Staff, *Military Posture, FY 1987* (Washington, D.C.: GPO, 1986), p. 19.

trol talks would not be resumed.[19] When a derogatory cartoon appeared in *Pravda* on 15 October 1983 showing President Reagan's face for the first time, it could have been a signal that the USSR would break off arms control negotiations in Geneva.

THE INF TALKS

Intermediate-range Nuclear Force (INF) negotiations between the United States and the Soviet Union commenced after the U.S. offered a proposal, called the "zero option," in November 1981 to eliminate *all* such land-based missiles.[20] Two years earlier, Chancellor Helmut Schmidt from the Federal Republic of Germany had initiated a request through NATO that American ground-launched cruise (GLCM) and Pershing II ballistic missiles be deployed in Western Europe to counter the growing number of SS-20 launchers being produced by the USSR.

Soviet deployment of this triple-warhead, reloadable mobile weapons system had begun in 1977, at the height of detente. About 260 launchers were already operational when the INF talks started in Geneva; another 100 were added over the two years of the negotiations. While this buildup continued in the East, not only USSR negotiators but also Kremlin leaders stated repeatedly between 1979 and 1986 that parity or equality existed on both sides (see Figure 12.1). It should be noted that the range of the SS-20 is three times that of the American single-warhead Pershing II, of which there will only be 108 at the end of 1988 when all are in place.[21]

The U.S. "zero option" was rejected at Geneva. Instead the USSR offered to reduce its missiles and bombers to a total of 300, if the Americans, British, and French did likewise and if no new deployments were made. Neither France nor the United Kingdom were participants in the INF negotiations; both of their deterrents remain outside of NATO; and their nuclear weapons are strategic rather than intermediate in range.

After fifteen months of talks, the United States presented an interim proposal. It envisaged substantial cuts in Pershing II and GLCM deployment, if the Soviet Union would simply reduce its INF missiles to equal numbers on a global basis, which would include those targeted against East Asian countries. Gromyko called the offer unacceptable, only five days after it had been presented.

When negotiations resumed in May 1983, the United States made a third proposal that would allow any number of missiles between zero and 450, with parity for the two sides. The USSR refused to engage in a discussion even of this rather flexible approach and rejected the American initiative.

Finally, on 26 October, Soviet leader Andropov proposed a reduction of SS-20 launchers aimed at Western Europe to "about 140," which he claimed would almost equal the number of British and

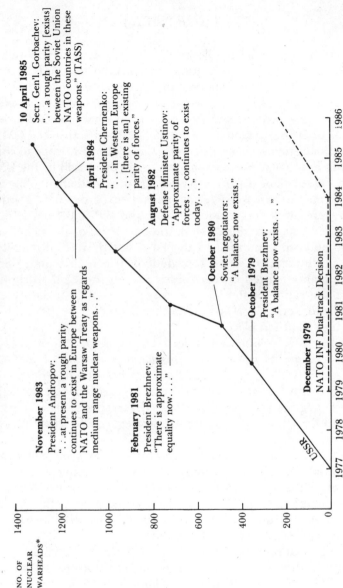

FIGURE 12.1

LONGER-RANGE INF MISSILE WARHEADS, 1977–1985

10 April 1985
Secr. Gen'l. Gorbachev:
". . . a rough parity [exists]
between the Soviet Union
NATO countries in these
weapons." (TASS)

April 1984
President Chernenko:
". . . in Western Europe
. . . [there is an] existing
parity of forces."

August 1982
Defense Minister Ustinov:
"Approximate parity of
forces . . . continues to exist
today. . . ."

November 1983
President Andropov:
". . . at present a rough parity
continues to exist in Europe between
NATO and the Warsaw Treaty as regards
medium range nuclear weapons. . ."

October 1980
Soviet negotiators:
"A balance now exists."

February 1981
President Brezhnev:
"There is approximate
equality now. . . ."

October 1979
President Brezhnev:
"A balance now exists. . . ."

December 1979
NATO INF Dual-track Decision

USSR

NO. OF
NUCLEAR
WARHEADS*

1400
1200
1000
800
600
400
200
0

1977 1978 1979 1980 1981 1982 1983 1984 1985 1986

*Includes Soviet SS-20s; U.S. Pershing II and ground-launched cruise missles.

SOURCES: U.S. Department of Defense, Joint Chiefs of Staff, *Military Posture, FY 1985* (Washington, D.C.: GPO, 1984), p. 78; interview with Chernenko in *Pravda*, 9 April 1984, p. 1; TASS communique, reported in the *Washington Post*, 11 April 1985; JCS, *Military Posture FY 1987* (Washington, D.C.: 1986), p.31; W.T. Lee and R.F. Staar, *Soviet Military Policy Since World War Two* (Stanford, Ca.: Hoover Institution Press, 1986), Table 31, pp.150–151.

French warheads. This was a simple misrepresentation. The 300 French and British warheads would have been "matched" under the Andropov proposal by 420 Soviet warheads (each SS-20 launcher carries three warheads). Moreover, the USSR offer ignored the roughly 100 SS-20s then targeted against Asia—which because of their mobile launchers could be relocated to the European theater on short notice. Simultaneously, *Pravda* announced that new "tactical" missiles (SS-21, -22, and -23) would be placed in East Germany and Czechoslovakia[22] if the Pershing IIs and GLCMs were deployed.

As the first ground-launched cruise missiles arrived in England on 14 November 1983, the United States offered to cut its INF deployment from 572 to 420 warheads if the USSR would reduce to the same number—that is, 140 launchers multiplied by three warheads each. Senior U.S. government officials indicated that the offer was merely "illustrative," meaning negotiable. TASS rejected the proposal even before it had been transmitted to the Soviet delegation at Geneva. A week before *Pravda* had printed a second cartoon of President Reagan, this time showing former Nazi propaganda minister Josef Goebbels whispering in his ear.[23]

After a session that had lasted for less than half an hour, U.S. Ambassador Paul H. Nitze announced on 23 November that "the present round of negotiations has been discontinued [by the USSR] and no date has been set for a resumption." At a subsequent press conference, he declared the Soviet action to be "as unjustified as it is unfortunate."[24] Chernenko later stated repeatedly that the INF talks would be resumed only after the Pershing IIs and GLCMs had been withdrawn from Western Europe. However, in his interview with *Pravda* on 2 September 1984 he left the matter ambiguous, suggesting that if the United States were to first stop all testing of an anti-missile system and sign an ASAT treaty on Soviet terms, the USSR might resume other arms control negotiations.

Even before Chernenko died the following spring, an agreement had been made to commence bilateral talks on nuclear and space weapons. They started in Geneva the day after Gorbachev's election as the new party leader, that is, 12 March 1985. The Soviets used the new forum to announce a series of old proposals:

1. a moratorium on SS-20 deployments until November 1985, when the Dutch would decide whether to accept cruise missiles;

2. a ban on nuclear tests from August through December, if the U.S. government were to do likewise;

3. a "Star Peace" proposal at the United Nations for an international space organization; and

4. a 50 percent reduction in strategic nuclear weapons by both sides, suggested in October.

This public relations campaign or "megaphone diplomacy" continued through the November 1985 summit itself. Although no agreement could be reached on arms control, except to accelerate the talks, the two sides decided to resume exchange programs, establish consulates in New York and Kiev, provide for a communications' link between Tokyo and Khabarovsk for air safety, and hold another summit before the end of 1986 in the United States. It proved impossible to find common ground on regional issues or human rights.[25]

EXCHANGE AGREEMENTS

The early 1970s had brought so-called detente, and with it came the acceleration of exchange programs between the United States and the Soviet Union. A general understanding on contacts, exchanges, and cooperation signed in 1973 by President Nixon and Chairman Brezhnev extended the validity of the agreements to six years from the two envisioned in the original (1958) pact. Eleven others went into effect between 1972 and 1974 for the following:[26]

1. science and technology

2. environmental protection

3. medical science and public health

4. space

5. agriculture

6. world oceans

7. transportation

8. atomic energy

9. artificial heart research and development

10. energy

11. housing and other construction.

During the second half of the 1970s, the pattern of U.S.-USSR exchanges reflected the growing tension between the two countries. President Ford postponed several visits of delegations concerned with housing and energy (1976) as a protest over Cuban mercenaries in Angola. Two years later, President Carter imposed a similar ban on high-level contacts because of legal proceedings in the USSR against Anatolii B. Shcharanskii and because of other human rights violations. By early 1980, all high-visibility exchanges with the Soviet Union had been suspended in response to the invasion of Afghanistan.

These exchanges unfortunately had failed to produce the expansion of civil liberties in the USSR or the freer flow of ideas hoped for in the early days, especially after the August 1975 Helsinki accord. The academic side continued to be plagued with problems of non-reciprocity and lack of access, even at the height of detente. A Twentieth Century Fund study concluded:

> Americans are still largely restricted to Moscow, Leningrad and a few other cities, while Soviets travel freely throughout the U.S. Access to archives and laboratories is frequently denied Americans, while Soviets in the U.S. have the same access to resources as Americans. The KGB still harasses Americans and especially their Soviet associates, while legitimate Soviet participants have not reported harassment by an American police agency.[27]

If only limited progress could be achieved in the SALT II negotiations, the reverse had been true for cultural relations. The sixteenth consecutive year of this exchange covered 1979–1980 and included performing groups, graduate students as well as junior faculty, and professors. A new category of environmental problems was added, with delegations from both sides being sent to study oceanography, pollution, management systems, social security, agricultural economics, and treatment of waste water. Joint projects and exchange of information were envisaged under this agreement. Numbers of people traveling in both directions expanded from about 1,500 to more than 100,000 per annum over a twenty-year period.[28]

President Carter stopped the one-sided scientific exchanges after the invasion of Afghanistan. Pan American Air Lines had discontinued flights to Moscow as unprofitable even before this White House action. Beginning with the Moscow book fair in 1979, certain American publications were confiscated regularly and did not appear on display. That same year, an incident occurred in Tashkent, when *U.S. News & World*

Report's Robin Knight and his wife were physically mistreated by KGB thugs. During the two preceding years *Newsweek, New York Times, Baltimore Sun,* and *Los Angeles Times* reporters had been harassed. Restrictions on travel remained in force.

In 1941, as a wartime measure, the USSR had forbidden the movement of any foreign diplomat beyond a 25-mile radius from the center of Moscow by requiring two days' advance notice for areas that were not off limits because of military security. These regulations continued until April 1974, when ambassadors and their families, interpreters, and drivers no longer needed permission to visit "open" cities. However, lower-ranking diplomats still must give a day's notice for travel outside the Moscow region. Foreign correspondents, businessmen, and tourists require a stamp on their visas in order to move outside the 25-mile limit. In 1978, the government reduced the area banned to Americans by 4 percent down to one-fifth of all Soviet territory, and this still applies today.

At the end of 1986 the Soviet Union had 251 diplomats at its embassy in Washington, D.C., and consulate-general in San Francisco (compared to the same number of Americans in Moscow and Leningrad). This parity in numbers had been achieved after the United States expelled twenty-five KGB and GRU agents from the Soviet U.N. delegation in mid-October 1986—one-fourth of those who must leave over a two-year period. The USSR retaliated by ousting five American diplomats from Moscow. The U.S. then also ordered five Soviets plus fifty more to leave Washington, D.C., and San Francisco, so that the numbers henceforth would be equal. The USSR next expelled five more Americans and refused to allow 260 Soviet citizens to work at either the U.S. embassy or its consulate general.[29]

Telephones are tapped, and listening devices concealed in the walls of foreign embassies at Moscow. The United States compound experienced a fire in August 1977, which led indirectly to discovery of sophisticated electronic gear. Still publicly unexplained is the reason for Soviet low-intensity microwave bombardment of the U.S. embassy, which began in 1960, intensified up to the level of eighteen microwatts after October 1975, stopped six weeks before the June 1979 Vienna summit meeting, and resumed after mid-1983 on an intermittent basis. Despite many diplomatic protests by the United States, the radiation bombardment has continued. The new American embassy, not to be occupied until 1988, is located near the Moscow river. By contrast, the already completed Soviet compound consists of a ten-acre complex on Mount Alto, which happens to be the second-highest point in Washington, D.C., and ideal for electronic espionage.[30]

SOVIET-AMERICAN TRADE

What USSR leaders desire more than cultural exchange is trade on advantageous terms with the United States. The purchase of 1.7 million metric tons of American wheat in 1964 for about $100 million and the policy enunciated two years later by President Lyndon B. Johnson of "building bridges" were hopeful developments from the Soviet point of view. However, U.S.-USSR trade still remained in the tens of millions of dollars, as compared with the $5 billion annual American commercial exchange with Western Europe and Japan at that time. The U.S. Congress periodically extended the 1949 Export Control Act, which restricts export licenses and bans transfer of technology to "unfriendly countries." Another earlier obstacle had been the 1934 Johnson Act, prohibiting private credits to governments that had not repaid debts to the United States. The Soviet Union, as successor regime to the tsarist government, still owes the United States $837 million including accrued interest from World War I. In addition, lend-lease aid to the USSR totaling almost $11 billion during the Second World War has been bargained down to $674 million. A spokesman in Moscow nonetheless stated during the mid-1970s that this debt would not be paid unless the Soviet Union were granted most-favored-nation treatment.[31]

As early as 1958 Khrushchev had sent a letter to President Eisenhower with a shopping list that included as desiderata complete factories for production of petrochemicals, chemical fertilizers, textiles, artificial fibers, food processing, and plastics—all traditionally neglected sectors of the Soviet economy. In the past, a single piece of U.S. equipment would be purchased by the USSR for duplication purposes. This happened in the hydroelectric, steel, automotive, petroleum-refining, and precision tool industries.[32] Once successfully produced from the American prototype, no further machines were imported.

In a speech before the Supreme Soviet, the late Prime Minister Kosygin called for more trade as well as its facilitation. What he meant by the latter was lifting the U.S. ban on export of strategic goods, long-term American credits, and most-favored-nation treatment for the USSR. Kosygin boasted in late 1971 that within four years the Soviet Union would surpass in economic power "the sick man of the capitalist world," that is, the United States.[33] Khrushchev himself twelve years earlier had predicted that the communist-ruled world would produce half the global output of industrial goods by 1965 and that the USSR would outperform as well as attain a higher living standard than the United States by 1970.

TABLE 12.3
SOVIET–United STATES TRADE, 1968–1986
(IN MILLIONS OF DOLLARS)

Year	Turnover	Soviet Imports	Soviet Exports	Balance
1968	116.2	57.7	58.5	+ 0.8
1969	157.0	105.5	51.5	− 54.0
1970	191.0	118.7	72.3	− 46.4
1971	219.2	162.0	57.2	− 104.8
1972	637.7	542.2	95.5	− 446.7
1973	1,404.0	1,190.0	214.0	− 976.0
1974	987.0	612.0	350.0	− 262.0
1975	2,089.0	1,835.0	254.0	−1,581.0
1976	2,547.0	2,308.0	239.0	−2,581.0
1977	2,528.0	2,240.0	220.0	−2,088.0
1978	2,780.0	2,240.0	540.0	−1,700.0
1979	4,500.0	3,600.0	900.0	−2,700.0
1980	1,960.0	1,500.0	460.0	−1,040.0
1981*	2,410.7	2,171.1	239.6	−1,931.6
1982*	2,931.4	2,728.2	202.2	−2,526.0
1983*	2,482.6	2,050.9	431.7	−1,619.2
1984	3,884.0	3,283.9	600.1	−2,683.8
1985	2,865.4	2,422.8	442.6	−1,980.2
1986		*est.* 2,300.0		

*Figures for 1981–1983 are converted from rubles at the exchange rate of 0.7655 dollars to one (as of 7 September 1983).

SOURCES: *Statistical Abstract of the United States, 1974* (Washington, D.C.: GPO, 1974), p. 794; *New York Times*, 10 April 1975, citing *Ekonomicheskaia gazeta; Statistical Abstract, 1975*, p. 844; U.S. Bureau of the Census, *Highlights of the U.S. Import-Export Trade*, September 1976; International Monetary Fund, *Direction of Trade: Annual, 1970–1976* (Washington, D.C.: IMF, 1977), p. 291; *New York Times*, 21 October 1977; *Wall Street Journal*, 2 March 1981, p. 20; *Vneshniaia torgovlia*, no. 3 (March 1983), insert; ibid. (March 1984); U.S. Department of Commerce, *Statistical Abstract of East-West Trade and Finance* (Washington, D.C.: GPO, March 1986), p. 28; *Izvestiia*, 22 March 1986, p. 1, quoting U.S. Secretary of Commerce, Malcolm Baldrige.

Although commercial exchange with the United States increased more than sevenfold from 1972 through 1979 (see Table 12.3), the USSR refused to accept the Trade Reform Act, to which the U.S. Congress had attached certain restrictions. This proposed legislation would have granted most-favored-nation treatment over a period of eighteen months, rather than three years as the Soviets had wanted. Credits through the Export-Import Bank also were limited to $300 million rather than remaining open-ended. Finally, both Senator Henry M. Jackson and Congressman Charles O. Vanik had insisted[34] that large numbers of Jewish citizens be permitted to leave the USSR as a condition for passage of the bill.

Despite this setback at the government-to-government level, American private enterprise came forward with proposals to help Moscow obtain credits. The Bank of America offered to establish a syndicate that would raise half a billion dollars for financing Soviet imports from the United States. It had an earlier precedent from September 1973, when ten U.S. banks raised $180 million to build a fertilizer complex in the USSR. During all of 1985, the Soviets obtained approximately $4.5 billion in new credits from the West. An equal or perhaps larger sum may be required for the 1986 calendar year.[35]

Much of this hard currency, it was thought, would be used for the purchase of American grain under a five-year agreement. The USSR fulfilled its obligation during 1983–1984 and bought 9 million tons. The next two years, however, it only took the full quota of corn (4 million tons) and 2.8 million tons of wheat. Only 4 percent of the wheat quota was purchased during 1985–1986, even though the U.S. government offered to subsidize a price of $11 to $13 below domestic cost. Instead, the Soviets bought 5 million tons of wheat from Australia, Austria, the West European Common Market, France, and Yugoslavia. At the same time, they signed an agreement with Canada to purchase a minimum of 25 million tons of wheat and seed grain over a five-year period.[36]

Despite the official ban on sales of American products with military potential to communist-ruled states and the January 1980 embargo on high-technology equipment, many useful items have slipped through the system and ended up in Moscow. Part of the problem involves access from other Western countries to technology that the Soviets cannot obtain directly from the United States. Militarily valuable technology acquired by the USSR has included the following:

1. American companies sold more than $1.5 billion worth of equipment and technical information to build a truck factory on the Kama River near Kazan. The new vehicles were supposed to be for the civilian economy, but they were taken instead by the Soviet army for its invasion of Afghanistan. It continues to utilize them there. (See also Chapter 7.)

2. The USSR purchased navigation and electronic orientation devices from Litton Industries. The technology that came with

the equipment is now being applied to help Soviet aircraft and ships track U.S. submarines.

3. American and Japanese electronics, acquired purportedly for civilian air-navigation systems, have been diverted to missile guidance and fill an important gap in USSR technology.

4. The famous Gorky auto works, reportedly operated with U.S. computers and Japanese business machines, makes not only civilian automobiles and trucks but also amphibious assault vehicles and military trucks.

5. Precision ball bearings purchased from Bryant Grinder Corporation of Vermont are said by Pentagon experts to have aided the Soviets in developing their multiple independently targeted re-entry vehicles (MIRV) for strategic missiles[37] (see Table 12.4).

At the ninth annual meeting of the U.S.-USSR Trade and Economic Council, held in Moscow, about 400 American businessmen heard Mikhail Gorbachev call for improving commercial ties with the United States, which had continued to suffer since the December 1979 Soviet invasion of Afghanistan. He explained the three main obstacles as follows:

1. most-favored-nation treatment is denied the Soviet Union;

2. no serious trade can exist without credits; and

3. export controls have been created under the pretext that certain items can help USSR military production.[38]

THE U.S. ASSESSMENT

In his first press conference as the newly inaugurated president, Ronald Reagan replied to one of the questions as follows: "They [the Soviets] reserve unto themselves the right to commit any crime; to lie; to cheat, in order to obtain that [which will further their cause] ... I think when you do business with them—even at a detente—you keep that in mind."[39] After less than one year of dealing with Moscow, these four aspects of the USSR challenge were recognized in mid-1983 by the U.S. secretary of state:

First is the continuing Soviet quest for military superiority even in the face of mounting domestic economic difficulties ...
The second disturbing development is the unconstructive Soviet

involvement, direct and indirect, in unstable areas of the Third World . . .

Third is the unrelenting effort to impose an alien Soviet "model" on nominally independent Soviet clients and allies . . .

Fourth is Moscow's continuing practice of stretching a series of treaties and agreements to the brink of violation and beyond.[40]

All of the foregoing obviously break not only the spirit but also the letter of the May 1972 agreement on "Basic Principles of Relations Between the USSR and the United States," mentioned earlier in this chapter.

The question remains whether the Soviet Union ever has intended to abide by the treaties it has signed with the United States. A classified report on USSR violations of arms control agreements was presented on 31 January 1984 to a closed session of the U.S. Senate by the national security advisor to President Reagan and by CIA briefers. The following day, a comprehensive list of other treaties broken by the USSR also appeared in the *Congressional Record*.[41] Definite or suspected violations of only five are discussed in the "President's Report to the Congress on Soviet Noncompliance with Arms Control Agreements:"

1. Bacteriological and Toxin Weapons Convention (1972)—yellow rain;
2. Helsinki Final Act (1975)—notification of military exercises;
3. Anti-Ballistic Missile (ABM) Treaty (1972)—the Krasnoiarsk radar;
4. SALT II (1979)—
   a. encryption of missile test telemetry (radio signals) impedes verification,
   b. testing a second new type of ICBM (the SS-X-25) is prohibited by treaty,
   c. deployment of the SS-16 type of ICBM is banned by the treaty; and
5. Threshold Test Ban Treaty (1974)—likely violation of 150 kiloton underground test limit.[42]

In this same report, other examples from the SALT I (1972) and the unratified SALT II (1979) treaties were listed but not immediately revealed to the public.

The nonpartisan General Advisory Committee (GAC) on Arms Control and Disarmament later submitted a more detailed secret study

TABLE 12.4

SELECTED WORLDWIDE SOVIET ACQUISITIONS OF MILITARILY USEFUL
DOCUMENTS, HARDWARE, AND DUAL-USE PRODUCTS

Western Technology Acquired	Soviet Application/Improvement
Strategic Missiles	
Documents on Cruise Missiles Using Radar Terrain Maps	Cruise Missile Guidance
Documents on Heat Shielding Material for Reentry Vehicles	Ballistic Missile Warheads
Documents on Ballistic Missile Defense Concepts	Future Ballistic Missile Defense
Air Defense	
F-14, F-15, F-18 Documents on Fire-Control Radars	Four Soviet Fighter Aircraft
US Phoenix Missile Documents	Semiactive Air-to-Air Missile
Infrared Radiometer	Reduced Infrared Signature Aircraft
Fiber-Optics Systems	Aircraft and Missile Onboard Communication Systems
Air-to-Air Missile Documents	New Air-to-Air Missile
General Purpose Naval and Antisubmarine Warfare	
Aircraft Carrier Steam Catapult Design Documents	Aircraft Launching System for New Aircraft Carrier
US MK 48 Torpedo Documents	Antisubmarine Torpedo
Gamma Radiation Radiometer	Nuclear Submarine Wake-Detection Trailing System
Acoustic Spectrum Analyzer	Submarine Quieting
Powerful Acoustical Vibrator	Submarine and Ship Sonars
Space and Antisatellite Weapons	
Documents on Systems and Heat Shielding of the US Space Shuttle	Reusable Space System
Transit Naval Navigation Hardware	First-Generation Space-Based Naval Radionavigation System
US NAVSTAR Navigation System Documents	Digital Signal Processing for Counterpart Satellite System
High-Energy Chemical Laser Documents	Space-Based Laser Weapon
System 101 Processing Equipment	Digital Processing and Video for Space-Based Reconnaissance; Missile, Bomb, and Remotely Piloted Vehicle Command Guidance
Tactical Forces	
International Radar Conference Documents	Synthetic Aperture Radar for Aircraft Detection

Ground Support Equipment for US TOW Anti-tank Guided Missile	Countermeasure System
US Copperhead Laser-Guided Artillery Documents	New Laser-Guided Artillery Shell
Laser-Guided Missile Documents	Portable Antiaircraft System
Infrared Imaging Subsystem Designs	Fire-Control System of Future Tank
Millimeter Radar Documents	Antitank Missile
Pressure Measuring Instruments and Documents	Advanced Modeling for New Artillery Projectiles

Manufacturing and Technology

Kevlar 49 Fiber Documents for Missiles	Improved Missile Development
Complete Set of Manufacturing Equipment for Printed Circuit Boards	Copied for 11 Production Assembly Lines for Strategic Missile, Armor and Electro-Optics, and Radar Industries
DTS-70 Printed Circuit Board Testing System	Military Microelectronic Production System
Fiberglass Manufacturing Technology	High-Pressure Airtanks for Submarines
Computer Disk Memory Systems	Military Ryad Series Disk Drives
Bubble Memory Technology	Tactical Missile Onboard Memories
Technical Documents on Tests of Cold-Rolled Steel	Improved Structural Protection of Warships
High-Accuracy Three-Dimension Coordinate Measuring Machine	Copied for Several Industries

SOURCE: CIA, *Soviet Acquisition of Militarily Significant Western Technology: An Update* (Washington, D.C.: GPO, September 1985), pp 9–10.

to the White House that traces a pattern of USSR violations extending over the past quarter-century. The fifteen-page unclassified summary concludes that "aspects of Soviet conduct related to about half their documentary arms control commitments were found to constitute material breaches of contracted duties." In addition to the five mentioned above, the GAC report specified seventeen other violations and covered the test moratorium (1958), the agreement on Cuba (1962), the Limited Test Ban Treaty (1963), and the Outer Space Treaty (1967). One month earlier, Department of Defense testimony before the Foreign Affairs Committee in the House of Representatives revealed that the USSR has been jamming U.S. surveillance satellites used to monitor compliance with nuclear arms agreements.[43]

Despite the foregoing—and contrary to the impression often conveyed by Moscow—dialogue continues between the United States and the USSR in at least nine different forums. These include bilateral talks on improving the hot line and other channels of communication, strategic arms, intermediate-range nuclear forces, space weapons, nuclear testing, and non-proliferation of chemical weapons. Attempts to prevent the spread of nuclear weapons also are being discussed bilaterally, the treaty again reviewed in 1985. Multilateral negotiations include the 21-country Mutual and Balanced Force Reductions (MBFR) at Vienna, the 40-member Committee on Disarmament (CD) meeting under United Nations auspices in Geneva, and the 60-delegation biological weapons talks, also at Geneva.[44]

It should be noted that the USSR is making a concerted effort to prevent the United States from developing an anti-ballistic missile capability, which would replace the mutual assured destruction (MAD) strategy with one of assured survival. The MAD doctrine, supposedly holding both populations undefended and thus hostage, had never been accepted by Soviet decision makers. They only pretended and dissembled, while building the most powerful military machine in all history. This self-perpetuating elite in the Kremlin looks upon the United States as the main enemy (*glavnyi vrag*), the last remaining obstacle to the fulfillment of USSR foreign policy objectives.[45]

A good example of this attitude could be observed at the Reykjavik summit in mid-October 1986. Gorbachev unexpectedly presented a paper outlining Soviet proposals that resulted in tentative agreements on reductions of ballistic missiles and intermediate-range nuclear forces as well as an ultimate test ban. All of this depended upon U.S. agreement to confine its Strategic Defense Initiative (SDI) within the laboratory for a ten-year period. President Reagan refused to compromise basic security interests, and the meeting ended.[46]

In actual fact, an estimated 10,000 scientists have been testing a Soviet version of SDI over many years. Lasers for anti-missile weapons were fired in 1982 at a manned USSR spacecraft. Work on particle beams and kinetic energy weapons has continued far beyond the laboratory. Recent activities include expansion of the world's only ABM defense around Moscow, building a huge ballistic missile detection and tracking radar at Krasnoiarsk, maintenance of the world's only anti-satellite system, modernization of strategic air defense, and improvement of passive defenses.[47]

In conclusion, what can one say about the "new pragmatism" in USSR foreign policy vis-à-vis the United States? Despite a stagnation of the economy over the past decade, Western specialists predict an increase in Soviet military spending of 2 to 3 percent each year through the end of the 1980s. This may involve exploitation of other imperial assets: the sale of raw materials and weapons, extracting more from Eastern Europe through CMEA, perhaps a reduction in subsidies to Third World friends, and possibly some concessions regarding human rights of USSR citizens. As one expert suggests: the Soviet Union might be weaker and could have mellowed ten or fifteen years from now. However, "it would be a serious mistake to count on this."[48]

NOTES

1. *Pravda,* 4 July 1968, p. 2.
2. Known as the Baruch Plan after the U.S. representative to the U.N. Atomic Energy Commission, Bernard Baruch (U.S. Arms Control and Disarmament Agency [ACDA], *Arms Control and Disarmament Agreements,* 5th ed. [Washington, D.C.: GPO, 1982], pp. 5–6).

   Franklin Lindsay, who had accompanied Baruch to a private meeting with Arkadyi A. Sobolev, recalls that the latter listened patiently to a preview of the U.S. proposal and then replied: "The Soviet Union doesn't want equality. The Soviet Union wants complete freedom to pursue its own aims as it sees fit" (quoted by Flora Lewis in *New York Times,* 4 April 1983).
3. For the official USSR view of this period, see G. Trofimenko, "On a Pivotal Course," *Mirovaia ekonomika i mezhdunarodnye otnosheniia,* no. 2 (1975): 3–11.
4. It had been signed on 1 July 1968 but not ratified by the USSR and the United States until 5 March 1970. Text in ACDA, *Arms Control Agreements,* pp. 91–95.
5. For background information, texts, and signatories to these treaties, see ibid., pp. 34–47, 82–98, 99–108, 120–31.
6. U.S. Congress, House, Permanent Select Committee on Intelligence, Subcommittee on Oversight, *Hearing on the Sverdlovsk Incident: Soviet Compliance with the Biological Weapons Convention?* 96th Cong., 2nd sess., 1980, p. 12. See also David T. Twining, "Sverdlovsk Anthrax Accident," *Air Force Magazine* 64, no. 3 (March 1981): 125.
7. *New York Times,* 24 August 1983. The USSR also refused to send experts for observation of an underground nuclear test in Nevada (ibid., 23 March 1986).
8. Broadcast over Vienna radio, 17 July 1970.
9. Texts in ACDA, *Arms Control Agreements,* pp. 124–27.
10. Ibid., pp. 139–57, provides complete texts.
11. *Pravda,* 30 May 1972, published the declaration. See the *Department of State Bulletin* 66, no. 1722 (26 June 1972), pp. 898–99, for the English version.
12. ACDA, *Arms Control Agreements,* pp. 162–63, for the protocol; *New York Times,* 3 December 1974, for the communiqué.

13. See *New York Times*, 1 April 1977, on the press conference.

14. The treaty, protocol, memorandum, and the joint statement on subsequent negotiations are in ACDA, *Arms Control Agreements*, pp. 246–77.

15. *New York Times*, 11 March 1981.

16. U.S. Department of State, *Realism, Strength, Negotiations: Key Foreign Policy Statements of the Reagan Administration* (Washington, D.C.: GPO, May 1984), pp. 27–30, gives the speech.

17. *Pravda*, 22 December 1982.

18. Quoted in Richard F. Staar, ed., *Arms Control: Myth Versus Reality* (Stanford: Hoover Institution Press, 1984), p. 79.

19. Soviet and U.S. statements appeared in *New York Times*, 9 December 1983; Chernenko interview in *Pravda*, 9 April 1984. He told the same newspaper on 2 September 1984 that "Washington had broken off the negotiations," in obvious disregard of the truth.

20. U.S. Department of State, *Realism, Strength, Negotiations*, pp. 23–27, gives the text of President Reagan's address before the National Press Club in Washington, D.C.

21. *Washington Post*, 21 November 1983.

22. A report from NATO in Brussels, six weeks earlier, had already revealed that the USSR was deploying SS-21s in Eastern Europe (*Baltimore Sun*, 15 September 1983).

23. *Pravda*, 5 November 1983, p. 5.

24. *Washington Post*, 24 November 1983. See also Paul H. Nitze, "The Word and the Woods," *Wall Street Journal*, 23 March 1984, for the "walk in the woods" proposal and Soviet duplicity.

25. See "Introduction" by Richard F. Staar, *The Summit and the Peace Process* (Stanford: Hoover Institution Press, 1986), pp. vii–x.

26. U.S. Department of State, Office of the Legal Adviser, *Treaties in Force* (Washington, D.C.: GPO, 1980), pp. 214–17; U.S. Department of State, Bureau of Public Affairs, "U.S.-USSR Exchanges," *Gist*, August 1984, p. 1.

27. Herbert Kupferberg, *The Raised Curtain* (New York: Twentieth Century Fund, 1977), pp. 86–87.

28. From 516 USSR and 950 U.S. citizens in 1958, the numbers grew to nearly 16,600 Soviets and 91,800 Americans in 1977, including tourists during that last year (*Vneshniaia torgovlia*, no. 9 [September 1978]: 36).

29. Rozanne Ridgway testimony on "The Foreign Missions Act and Espionage Activities in the United States," 5 December 1985, pp. 9–10; *New York Times*, 23 October 1986, p. 4, for a chronology of these retaliatory measures.

30. *New York Times*, 11 November 1983; ibid., 4 March 1986.

31. Judy Shelton in the *Wall Street Journal* (European edition), 16 September 1986.

32. Anthony C. Sutton, *Western Technology and Soviet Economic Development, 1945 to 1965* (Stanford: Hoover Institution Press, 1974), 3:327.

33. See his speech to the Supreme Soviet, "On the Five Year Plan," *Pravda*, 25 November 1971, pp. 1–4.

34. *Congressional Quarterly: Weekly Report* 31, no. 20 (19 May 1973): 1218. The Jackson-Vanik amendment was attached to HR 10710 and appears in ibid., 32, no. 49 (7 December 1974): 3266.

   From 51,320 in 1979, emigration of Jews dropped to 1,140 during calendar year 1985 (*New York Times*, 8 April 1986).

35. "Financing the Soviet Empire," *National Security Record*, no. 90, (April 1986): 1–3.

36. Oswald Johnson, "Soviets Break Commitment," *Los Angeles Times*, 1 October 1986, and Montreal radio, 2 October 1986; *FBIS*, 3 October 1986, p. H-1.

37. See CIA, *Soviet Acquisition of Militarily Significant Western Technology: An Update* (Washington, D.C.: GPO, September 1985).

38. *Pravda*, 11 December 1985, p. 2, published the speech; for the tenth meeting, see ibid., 12 December 1986, p. 5.

39. Transcript in *New York Times*, 30 January 1981.

40. Statement of 15 June 1983 by Secretary of State George P. Shultz before the Foreign Relations Committee of the U.S. Senate, entitled "U.S.-Soviet Relations in the Context of U.S. Foreign Policy," *Current Policy* (Washington, D.C.: U.S. Department of State, 15 June 1983), no. 492, p. 2. See also his address in Los Angeles, ibid. (18 October 1984), no. 624, especially p. 4.

41. "Soviet Political Treaties and Violations: Chronology," *Congressional Record–Senate* 130, no. 8 (1 February 1984): S623-S633, 98th Cong., 2nd sess.; "Soviet Violations of Arms Control Agreements," ibid., pp. S652–54; "The President's Unclassified Report to the Congress on Soviet Noncompliance with Arms Control Agreements," White House Press Release, 1 February 1985.

42. *Congressional Record*, op. cit., pp. S648–49. See also U.S. Congress, Senate, Committee on Armed Services, *Soviet Treaty Violations*, 99th Congr., 1st sess. (Washington, D.C.: GPO, 1985).

43. General Advisory Committee on Arms Control and Disarmament, *A Quarter Century of Soviet Compliance Practices Under Arms Control Commitments, 1958–1983, Summary* (Washington, D.C.: 10 October 1984), p. 1; *New York Times*, 12 and 14 September 1984; ACDA, *Soviet Noncompliance* (Washington, D.C.: 1 February 1986); U.S. Department of State, "Interim Restraint: U.S. and Soviet Force Projections" (5 August 1986), *Special Report* No. 157, president's letter and unclassified report to the U.S. Congress.

44. Listed in the *New York Times*, 31 August 1986, and the *Wall Street Journal*, 23 September 1986, p. 25.

45. William T. Lee and Richard F. Staar, *Soviet Military Policy Since World War II* (Stanford: Hoover Institution Press, 1986).

46. Compare the television speeches, reporting on the above, by President Reagan in the *New York Times*, 14 October 1986, p. 4; by General Secretary Gorbachev in *Pravda*, 15 October 1986, pp. 1–2. See also text of U.S. offers in the *New York Times*, 18 October 1986, p. 5.

47. U.S. Department of Defense, *Soviet Military Power, 1986* (Washington, D.C.: The Pentagon, March 1986), pp. 41–57; William Kucewicz, "Moscow's Bigger Star Wars Drive," *Wall Street Journal*, 16 December 1986, editorial page.

48. Henry S. Rowen, "Living with a Sick Bear," *The National Interest*, no. 2 (Winter 1986), pp. 14–26; quotation from p. 26.

BIBLIOGRAPHY

Albano, Antonio. *Report of State Prosecutor's Office.* Rome: Appeals Court, 28 March 1984. Translation from the Italian.

Aliev, E. M. et al. *Mezhdunarodnye problemy Azii 80-kh godov.* Moscow: Mezhdunarodnye otnosheniia, 1983.

Albright, David E. *The USSR and Sub-Saharan Africa in the 1980s.* New York: Praeger, 1983.

Aleksandrov, A. M. et al., eds. *Radi mira na zemle: Sovetskaia programma mira dlia 80-kh godov v deistvii.* Moscow: Politizdat, 1983.

Alexiev, Alexander R. *The Soviet Campaign Against INF: Strategy, Tactics, Means.* N-2280-AF. Santa Monica, Calif.: Rand Corporation, February 1985.

Allen, Richard V., ed. *Yearbook on International Communist Affairs, 1968.* Stanford: Hoover Institution Press, 1969.

Amnesty International. *Report, 1986.* London: Amnesty International Publications, 1986.

————. *Torture in the Eighties.* London: Amnesty International Publications, 1984.

Anders, Karl. *Mord auf Befehl.* Tübingen/Neckar: Schlichtenmayer, 1963.

Anders, Wladyslaw. *Zbrodnia Katyńska w świetle dokumentów.* London: Gryf, 1982.

Andreev, Iu. V., and Shenaev, V. N., eds. *SSSR–Zapadnaia Evropa: Problemy torgovoekonomicheskikh otnoshenii.* Moscow: Mezhdunarodnye otnosheniia, 1986.

Andropov, Iu. V. *Izbrannye rechi i stat'i*. 2nd ed. Moscow: Politizdat, 1983.

Anikin, A. A. et al., eds. *Soedinennye Shtaty Ameriki*. Moscow: Mysl', 1982.

Anisimov, V. M. et al., eds. *Spravochnik propagandista*. Moscow: 1985.

Arbatov, G. A., and Oltmans, Willem. *The Soviet Viewpoint*. New York: Dodd, Mead & Co., 1983.

Arnold, Anthony. *Afghanistan's Two-Party Communism*. Stanford: Hoover Institution Press, 1983.

Ashby, Timothy. *The Bear in the Back Yard*. Lexington, Mass.: Lexington Books, 1987.

Avseneev, M. M., chief ed. *Krizis kapitalizma*. Moscow: Mysl', 1980.

Barghoorn, Frederick C. *Soviet Foreign Propaganda*. Princeton, N.J.: Princeton University Press, 1964.

Barron, John. *KGB: The Secret Work of Soviet Secret Agents*. New York: Bantam Books, 1974.

———. *KGB Today: The Hidden Hand*. New York: Reader's Digest Press, 1983.

Barecki, Józef, ed. *Rocznik polityczny i gospodarczy, 1981–1983*. Warsaw: PWE, 1983.

Beglov, S. I. *Vneshnepoliticheskaia propaganda: Ocherk teorii i praktiki*. Moscow: Vysshaia shkola, 1984.

Beichman, Arnold, and Bernstam, Mikhail S. *Andropov: New Challenge to the West*. New York: Stein & Day, 1983.

Bekarevich, A. D. et al. *Kuba: Stroitel'stvo sotsializma*. Moscow: Nauka, 1983.

Bergson, Abram, and Levine, Herbert S., eds. *The Soviet Economy: Toward the Year 2000*. London: Allen & Unwin, 1983.

Bertsch, Gary K. *East-West Strategic Trade: CoCom and the Atlantic Alliance*. Paris: Atlantic Institute for International Affairs, 1983.

Bittman, Ladislav. *The KGB and Soviet Disinformation: An Insider's View*. Washington, D.C.: Pergamon-Brassey's International Defense Publisher, 1985.

Blaustein, A. P., and Flanz, G. H., eds. *Constitutions of the Countries of the World*. Dobbs Ferry, N.Y.: Oceana, December 1985.

Board for International Broadcasting. *1986 Annual Report*. Washington: U.S. Government Printing Office, 1986.

Bobin, A. E. et al., eds. *Razvivaiushchiesia strany v sovremennom mire: Puti revoliutsionnogo protsessa*. Moscow: Nauka, 1986.

Bogdanov, R. G. *SShA: Voennaia mashina i politika*. Moscow: Nauka, 1983.

Bogomolov, O. T., ed. *Mirovoe sotsialisticheskoe khoziaistvo*. Moscow: Ekonomika, 1982.

Bogomolov, O. T. *Strany sotsializma v mezhdunarodnom razdelenii truda*. Moscow: Nauka, 1986.

Boiko, V. V., and Markin, L. V. *Ustnaia propaganda: Kriterii, pokazateli, usloviia effektivnosti.* Leningrad: Lenizdat, 1983.

Borisov, O. B., and Koloskov, B. T. *Sovetsko-kitaiskie otnosheniia, 1945–1980.* 3rd rev. ed. Moscow: Mysl', 1980.

Brezhnev, L. I. *Our Course: Peace and Socialism.* Moscow: Novosti, 1979.

——— et al. *Kommunisticheskoe dvizhenie.* 2nd rev. ed. Prague: Mir i sotsializm, 1980.

Brown, Archie, and Kaser, Michael, eds. *Soviet Policy for the 1980s.* London: Macmillan, 1982.

Brodskii, R. M., and Krasivskii, O. Ia. *Istinnoe litso sionizma.* L'vov: Kameniar, 1983.

Brutents, K. N. et al. *Sotsialisticheskaia orientatsiia osvobodivshikhsia stran: Nekotorye voprosy teorii i praktiki.* Moscow: Mysl', 1982.

Brysin, P. M. *Uchebno-material'naia baza nachal'noi voennoi podgotovki v shkole.* Moscow: Prosveshchenie, 1984.

Brzezinski, Zbigniew. *Game Plan: A Geostrategic Framework for the Conduct of the U.S.-Soviet Contest.* Boston: Atlantic Monthly Press, 1986.

Brzezinski, Zbigniew. *Power and Principle.* New York: Farrar, Straus & Giroux, 1983.

Butenko, A. P. *Sotsializm kak mirovaia sistema.* Moscow: Politizdat, 1984.

Bykov, O. N. *Mery doveriia: Real'nyi faktor uprocheniia mira.* Moscow: Nauka, 1983.

Byliniak, S. A. et al., eds. *Razvivaiushchiesia strany: Sovremennye tendentsii mirovykh khoziaistvennikh otnoshenii.* Moscow: Nauka, 1983.

Byrnes, Robert F., ed. *After Brezhnev: Sources of Conduct in the 1980s.* Bloomington: Indiana University Press, 1983.

Carrere d'Encausse, Helene. *Confiscated Power: How Soviet Russia Really Works.* New York: Harper & Row, 1982.

Cartwright, John, and Critchley, Julian. *Cruise, Pershing and SS-20. The Search for Consensus: Nuclear Weapons in Europe.* North Atlantic Assembly Report. London: Brassey's Defence Publishers, 1985.

Cate, Curtis, ed. *The Challenge of Soviet Shipping.* New York: National Strategy Information Center, 1984.

Chang, Pao-min. *The Sino-Vietnamese Territorial Dispute.* New York: Praeger, 1986.

Chernenko, K. U. *Izbrannye rechi i stat'i.* 2nd rev. ed. Moscow: Politizdat, 1984.

Cline, Ray S., and Alexander, Yonah. *Terrorism: The Soviet Connection.* New York: Crane, Russak, 1984.

Cohen, Sam. *The Truth About the Neutron Bomb.* New York: William Morrow, 1983.

Collins, John M. *U.S.-Soviet Military Balance, 1980–1985*. Washington, D.C.: Pergamon-Brassey, 1985.

Collins, Joseph J. *The Soviet Invasion of Afghanistan. A Study in the Use of Force in Soviet Foreign Policy*. Lexington, Mass.: D.C. Heath and Company, 1986.

Conte, François, and Martres, Jean-Louis, eds. *L'Union Sovietique dans les relations internationales*. Paris: Economica, 1982.

Conquest, Robert. *The Great Terror: Stalin's Purge of the Thirties*. rev. ed. New York: Collier Books, 1973.

————, ed. *The Last Empire: Nationality and the Soviet Future*. Stanford: Hoover Institution Press, 1986.

Crane, Keith. *The Soviet Economic Dilemma of Eastern Europe*. R-3368-AF. Santa Monica, Calif.: Rand Corporation, May 1986.

Currie, Kenneth M. and Varhall, Gregory, eds. *The Soviet Union: What Lies Ahead? Military-Political Affairs in the 1980s*. Washington, D.C.: U.S. Government Printing Office, 1985.

Dailey, Brian D., and Parker, Patrick J., eds., *Soviet Strategic Deception*. Lexington, Mass.: Lexington Books, 1987.

Damis, John. *Conflict in Northwest Africa: The Western Sahara Dispute*. Stanford: Hoover Institution Press, 1983.

Dash, Barbara L. *A Defector Reports: The Institute of the USA and Canada*. Philadelphia, Pa.: Delphic Associates, May 1982.

DeLauer, Richard D. *The FY 1985 Department of Defense Program for Research, Development, and Acquisition*. Statement to the 98th Cong., 2nd sess. Washington, D.C.: The Pentagon, 1984.

Dixon, Michael J. "The Soviet Union and the Middle East." In *The Soviet Union in the Third World, 1980–1982: An Imperial Burden or Political Asset?* Report no. 83–229 S. Washington, D.C.: Library of Congress, Congressional Research Service, 12 December 1983.

Dolgopolov, E. I. *Sotsial'no-politicheskaia rol' armii osvobodivshikhsia stran*. Moscow: Voennoe izdatel'stvo, 1986.

Donaldson, Robert H., ed. *The Soviet Union in the Third World: Successes and Failures*. Boulder, Colo.: Westview Press, 1981.

Doroshenko, I. A. et al., eds. *Feliks Edmundovich Dzerzhinskii: Biografiia*. 2nd ed. Moscow: Politizdat, 1983.

Douglass, Joseph D., Jr., and Hoeber, Amoretta H. *Conventional War and Escalation: The Soviet View*. New York: National Strategy Information Center, 1981.

————. *Soviet Strategy for Nuclear War*. Stanford: Hoover Institution Press, 1979.

Duignan, Peter, and Rabushka, Alvin, eds. *The United States in the 1980s*. Stanford: Hoover Institution Press, 1980.

Duncan, W. Raymond, ed. *Soviet Policy in Developing Countries*. 2nd ed. Huntington, N.Y.: Robert E. Krieger, 1981.

Dyadkin, Yosif G. *Unnatural Deaths in the USSR, 1928–1954*. Translated by Tania Deruguine. New Brunswick, N.J.: Transaction Books, 1983.

Dziak, J. J. *Soviet Perceptions of Military Power: The Interaction of Theory and Practice*. New York: Crane, Russak, 1981.

Ermolaev, V. I. *Iz istorii rabochego i kommunisticheskogo dvizhenii v Latinskoi Amerike*. Moscow: Mysl', 1982.

Fedoseyev, P. N. et al. *The USSR and Africa*. Moscow: USSR Academy of Sciences, 1983.

———. *Nauchnyi kommunizm: Uchebnik*. 6th ed. Moscow: Politizdat, 1984.

Feldbrugge, F. J. M., and Simons, W. W., eds. *Perspectives on Soviet Law for the 1980s*. The Hague: Nijhoff, 1982.

Filatova, A. I., ed. *Belaia kniga* Moscow: Iuridicheskaia literatura, 1985.

Filippov, V. I. *Mirovoe khoziaistvo: Tipy i zakonomernosti razvitiia*. Kiev: Vishcha shkola, 1983.

Finder, Joseph. *Red Carpet*. New York: Holt, Rinehart & Winston, 1983.

Firsov, F. I. *Lenin, Komintern i stanovlenie kommunisticheskikh partii*. Moscow: Politizdat, 1985.

Fomin, V. V. *SEV i drugie mezhdunarodnye organizatsii*. Moscow: Nauka, 1983.

Francis, Samuel T. *The Soviet Strategy of Terror*. Washington, D.C.: Heritage Foundation, 1981.

Gafurov, Z. Sh. *Natsional'no-demokraticheskaia revoliutsiia i armiia*. Moscow: Nauka, 1983.

Gankovskii, Iu. V. et al., eds. *Strany srednego vostoka*. Moscow: Nauka, 1980.

Gardner, H. Stephen. *Soviet Foreign Trade: The Decision Process*. Boston: Kluwer-Nijhoff, 1983.

Gavrilov, N. I., ed. *10 let efiopiskoi revoliutsii*. Moscow: Nauka, 1986.

Gelman, Harry. *The Brezhnev Politburo and the Decline of Detente*. Ithaca, N.Y.: Cornell University Press, 1984.

Germany, Federal Republic of. *Zahlenspiegel: Ein Vergleich*. Bonn: Bundesministerium für innerdeutsche Beziehungen, September 1985.

Gertsena, fond imeni. *Politicheskii dnevnik*. 2 vols. Amsterdam: Alexander Herzen Foundation, 1972, 1975.

Ghana. Ministry of Information. *Nkrumah's Subversion in Africa: Documentary Evidence*. Accra-Tema: State Publishing Corporation, n.d.

Glagolev, Igor S. *Post-Andropov Kremlin Strategy*. Washington, D.C.: Association for Cooperation of Democratic Countries, 1984.

Godson, Roy. *Labor in Soviet Global Strategy*. New York: Crane, Russak, 1984.

Golan, Galia. *The Soviet Union and the Palestine Liberation Organization*. New York: Praeger, 1980.

Goldman, Marshall I. *USSR in Crisis: The Failure of an Economic System.* New York: W. W. Norton, 1983.

Goncharov, L. V. et al., eds. *Agrarnye preobrazovaniia v stranakh Afriki na sovremennom etape.* Moscow: Nauka, 1982.

Gorbachev, Mikhail S. *A Time for Peace.* New York: Richardson & Steirman, 1985.

Goren, Roberta. *The Soviet Union and Terrorism.* London: George Allen & Unwin, 1984.

Gornung, M. B. et al., eds. *Razvivaiushchiesia strany-osnovnye problemy ekonomicheskoi i sotsial'noi geografii.* Moscow: Mysl', 1983.

Gorshkov, S. G. *Morskaia moshch' gosudarstva.* 2nd rev. ed. Moscow: Voenizdat, 1979.

Gosztony, Peter. *Die Rote Armee: Machtfaktor der Weltpolitik.* Munich: Wilhelm Goldmann Verlag, 1980.

Graham, Daniel O. *The Non-Nuclear Defense of Cities: The High Frontier Space-Based Defense Against ICBM Attack.* Cambridge, Mass.: Abt Books, 1983.

Grechko, A. A. *Vooruzhennye sily sovetskogo gosudarstva.* Moscow: Voenizdat, 1974.

Gress, David. *Peace and Survival: West Germany, the Peace Movement, and European Security.* Stanford: Hoover Institution Press, 1985.

Grimmett, Richard F. "Trends in Conventional Arms Transfers to the Third World, 1978–1985." *Congressional Research Service Report,* no. 86–99 F. Washington, D.C., May 1986.

Gromyko, Anatolii, A. *Aktual'nye problemy otnoshenii SSSR so stranami Afriki (80-e gody).*

——— et al., eds. *Krizis na iuge Afriki.* Moscow: Nauka, 1984.

Gromyko, Andrei, A. et al., eds. *Diplomaticheskii slovar'.* 3 vols. Moscow: Nauka, 1984–1986. Moscow: Mezhdunarodnye otnosheniia, 1985.

———, ed. *Istoriia diplomatii.* Vol. 5, Part 2. Moscow: Politizdat, 1979.

———, chief ed. *Za mir i bezopasnost' narodov, 1968.* 2 vols. Moscow: Politizdat, 1985.

Gromyko, Andrei A., and Ponomarev, B. N., eds. *Istoriia vneshnei politiki SSSR, 1917–1980.* 2 vols. Moscow: Nauka, 1980.

Gustafson, Thane. *The Soviet Gas Campaign: Politics and Policy in Soviet Decisionmaking.* R-3036-AF. Santa Monica, Calif.: Rand Corporation, June 1983.

Hacker, Jens. *Der Ostblock: Entstehung, Entwicklung, und Struktur.* Baden-Baden: Nomos Verlag, 1983.

Haig, Alexander M., Jr. *Caveat: Realism, Reagan, and Foreign Policy.* New York: Macmillan, 1984.

Hammond, Thomas T. *Red Flag over Afghanistan: The Communist Coup, the Soviet Invasion, and the Consequences.* Boulder, Colo.: Westview Press, 1984.

Hamon, Alain, and Marchard, Jean-Charles. *Action directe: Du terrorisme français à l'euroterrorisme*. Paris: Éditions du Seuil, 1986.

Hazan, Baruch. *Olympic Sports and Propaganda Games: Moscow 1980*. New Brunswick, N.J.: Transaction Books, 1982.

Heikal, Mohamed H. *The Cairo Documents*. New York: Doubleday, 1973.

———. *The Road to Ramadan*. New York: Quadrangle, 1975.

Henriksen, Thomas H., ed. *Communist Powers and Sub-Saharan Africa*. Stanford: Hoover Institution Press, 1981.

Henze, Paul B. *The Plot to Kill the Pope*. New York: Scribner's, 1983.

Hinton, Harold C., ed. *The People's Republic of China, 1949–1979: A Documentary Survey*. 5 vols. Wilmington, Del.: Scholarly Resources, 1980.

Hood, William. *Mole*. New York: W. W. Norton, 1982.

Hosmer, Stephen T., and Wolfe, Thomas W. *Soviet Policy and Practice Toward Third World Conflicts*. Lexington, Mass.: D. C. Heath, 1983.

Iakovlev, A. N. *Ot Trumena do Reigana: Doktriny i real'nosti iadernogo veka*. Moscow: Molodaia gvardiia, 1984.

Inozemtsev, N. N. et al., eds. *Mirovoi revoliutsionnyi protsess i sovremennost'*. Moscow: Nauka, 1980.

Institute for Foreign Policy Analysis. *East-West Trade and Technology Transfer: New Challenges for the United States*. Cambridge, Mass.: Institute for Foreign Policy Analysis, 1986.

International Institute for Strategic Studies. *Strategic Survey 1985–86*. London, 1985.

———. *The Military Balance, 1986–1987*. London: 1986.

International Research and Exchanges Board. *A Scholars' Guide to Humanities and Social Sciences in the Soviet Union*. New York: M. E. Sharpe, 1985.

Irkhin, Iu. V. *Revoliutsionnyi protsess v stranakh sotsialisticheskoi orientatsii*. Moscow: Izdatel'stvo Universiteta Druzhby Narodov, 1985.

Israelian, V. L. *Diplomatiia v gody voiny (1941–1945)*. Moscow: Mezhdunarodnye otnosheniia, 1985.

Iudin, Iu. A. et al., eds. *Partii v politicheskoi sisteme*. Moscow: Nauka, 1983.

Ivanov, A. A. *Sotsialisticheskii vybor v Afrike i ideologicheskaia bor'ba*. Moscow: Mezhdunarodnye otnosheniia, 1984.

Izmailov, A. V., ed. *Marksisty-Lenintsy Latinskoi Ameriki v bor'be za mir i progress*. Moscow: Progress, 1980.

Jackson, Richard L. *The Non-Aligned, the U.N., and the Superpowers*. New York: Praeger, 1983.

Jane's Fighting Ships, 1986–1987. London: Jane's Publishing Company, 1986.

Jasingh, Hari. *India and the Non-Aligned World*. Delhi: Vikas Publishing House, 1983.

Jensen, Robert G.; Shabad, Theodore; and Wright, Arthur W.; eds. *Soviet Natural Resources in the World Economy*. Chicago: University of Chicago Press, 1983.

Johnson, A. Ross; Dean, Robert W.; and Alexiev, Alexander. *East European Military Establishments: The Warsaw Pact Northern Tier*. New York: Crane, Russak, 1982.

Jones, Ellen. *The Red Army and Society*. Boston: Allen & Unwin, 1985.

Joseph, Philip, ed. *Adaptability to New Technologies of the USSR and East European Countries*. Brussels: NATO Economics Directorate, 1985.

Kanet, Roger E., ed. *Soviet Foreign Policy and East-West Relations*. New York: Pergamon Press, 1982.

Kaplan, Martin M., ed. *Proceedings of the Thirty-second Pugwash Conference on Science and World Affairs*. Geneva: Pugwash Council, 1984.

Kaplan, Stephen S. *Diplomacy of Power: Soviet Armed Forces as a Political Instrument*. Washington, D.C.: Brookings Institution, 1981.

Kashlev, Iu. B. *Ideologicheskaia bor'ba ili psikhologicheskaia voina?* Moscow: Politizdat, 1986.

Katz, Mark N. *Russia and Arabia: Soviet Foreign Policy Toward the Arabian Peninsula*. Baltimore, Md.: Johns Hopkins University Press, 1986.

Kegley, Charles W., Jr., and McGowan, Pat, eds. *Foreign Policy, USA/USSR*. Beverly Hills, Calif.: Sage Publications, 1982.

Kelman, Jacob M. *Anti-Semitism in the Soviet Union*. 3 vols. Jerusalem: Hebrew University, 1980.

Khachaturov, K. A. *Latinskaia Amerika: Ideologiia i vneshniaia politika*. Moscow: Mezhdunarodnye otnosheniia, 1983.

Kim, G. F., and Simoniia, N. A., eds. *Strukturnye sdvigi v ekonomike i evoliutsiia politicheskikh sistem v stranakh Azii i Afriki v 70-e gody: Sbornik stat'ei*. Moscow: Nauka, 1982.

Kirk, Grayson, and Wessell, Nils H., eds. *The Soviet Threat*. New York: Praeger, 1978.

Kirkpatrick, Lyman B., Jr., and Sargeant, Howland H. *Soviet Political Warfare Techniques*. New York: National Strategy Information Center, 1972.

Kissinger, Henry. *White House Years*. Boston: Little, Brown & Co., 1979.

Kiva, A. V. *Strany sotsialisticheskoi orientatsii: Osnovnye tendentsii razvitiia*. Moscow: Nauka, 1978.

Kommunisticheskaia Partiia Sovetskogo Soiuza. *XX s"ezd, 14–15 fevralia 1956 goda: Stenograficheskii otchet*. 2 vols. Moscow: Politizdat, 1956.

———. *KPSS v rezoliutsiiakh i resheniiakh s'ezdov, konferentsii i plenumov TSK*. vol. 11. Moscow: Politizdat, 1986.

Korgun, V. G. *Intelligentsiia v politicheskoi zhizni Afghanistana*. Moscow: Nauka, 1983.

Kovalev, A. N. *Azbuka diplomatii.* 4th rev. ed. Moscow: Mezhdunarodnye otnosheniia, 1984.

Koval'zon, M. Ia. *Teoriia revoliutsii: Istoriia i sovremennost', sbornik.* Moscow: Izdatel'stvo Moskovskogo universiteta, 1984.

Kremer, I. S. *FRG: Etapy "vostochnoi politiki."* Moscow: Mezhdunarodnye otnosheniia, 1986.

Kühne, Winrich. *Die Politik der Sowjetunion in Afrika.* Baden-Baden: Nomos Verlag, 1983.

Kulikov, V. G. *Kollektivnaia zashchita sotsializma.* Moscow: Voenizdat, 1982.

Kupferberg, Herbert. *The Raised Curtain.* New York: Twentieth Century Fund, 1977.

Kuznetsova, N. A. et al., eds. *Iran: Istoriia i sovremennost'.* Moscow: Nauka, 1983.

Laird, Roy D. *The Politburo: Demographic Trends, Gorbachev, and the Future.* Boulder, Colo.: Westview Press, 1986.

Lamphere, Robert J., and Shachtman, Tom. *The FBI-KGB War: A Special Agent's Story.* New York: Random House, 1986.

Lebedev, N. I. *SSSR v mirovoi politike. 1917–1980.* Moscow: Mezhdunarodnye otnosheniia, 1980.

——— et al., eds. *Nauchnye osnovy sovetskoi vneshnei politiki.* Moscow: Mezhdunarodnye otnosheniia, 1982.

Lee, William T. and Staar, Richard F. *Soviet Military Policy Since World War II.* Stanford: Hoover Institution Press, 1986.

Levitskaia, N. V.; Luganskaia, L. N.; and Lavrova, K. I. *Russkii iazyk: Uchebnoe posobie dlia soldat, ne vladeiushchikh ili slabo vladeiushchikh russkim iazykom.* Moscow: Voenizdat, 1982.

Lewis, William J. *The Warsaw Pact: Arms, Doctrine, and Strategy.* Cambridge, Mass.: Institute for Foreign Policy Analysis, 1982.

Lewytzkyj, Boris, and Stroynowski, Juliusz, eds. *Who's Who in the Socialist Countries.* New York: K. G. Saur, 1978.

Lindsey, Robert. *The Falcon and the Snowman.* New York: Simon & Schuster, 1979.

Lockwood, Samuel Jonathan. *The Soviet View of U.S. Strategic Doctrine: Implications for Decision Making.* New Brunswick, N.J.: Transaction Books, 1983.

Lokshin, G. M. et al., eds. *Bor'ba SSSR za mir i razoruzhenie.* Moscow: Mezhdunarodnye otnosheniia, 1982.

Löwenthal, Richard, and Meissner, Boris. *Der Sowjetblock zwischen Vormachtkontrolle und Autonomie.* Cologne: Markus Verlag, 1984.

Lowenhardt, John. *The Soviet Politburo.* Translated by Dymphna Clark. New York: St. Martin's Press, 1982.

Mako, William P. *U.S. Ground Forces and the Defense of Central Europe.* Washington, D.C.: Brookings Institution, 1983.

Marer, Paul. *Dollar GNPs of the U.S.S.R. and Eastern Europe.* Baltimore, Md.: Johns Hopkins University Press, 1985.

Markov, Georgi. *The Truth That Killed.* London: Weidenfeld & Nicolson, 1983.

Martin, L. J., and Chaudhary, A. G., eds. *Comparative Mass Media Systems.* New York: Longman, 1983.

Mastny, Vojtech. *Helsinki, Human Rights, and European Security: Analysis and Documentation.* Durham, N.C.: Duke University Press, 1986.

Mazurov, V. M. *SShA-Kitai-Iaponiia.* Moscow: Nauka, 1980.

McCauley, Martin, ed. *The Soviet Union After Brezhnev.* New York: Holmes & Meier, 1983.

McMichael, R. Daniel, and Paulus, John D., eds. *Western Hemisphere Stability: The Latin American Connection.* Pittsburgh, Pa.: World Affairs Council of Pittsburgh, 1983.

Medvedev, Roy. *All Stalin's Men.* Translated by Harold Shukman. New York: Doubleday, 1984.

Medvedev, Zhores. *Gorbachev.* Oxford: Basil Blackwell, 1986.

Meissner, Boris. *Sowjetische Kurskorrekturen: Breshnew und seine Erben.* Zurich: Edition Interfrom, 1984.

Menon, Rajan. *Soviet Power and the Third World.* New Haven, Conn.: Yale University Press, 1986.

Menzhinskii, V. I. et al., eds. *Mezhdunarodnye organizatsii sotsialisticheskikh gosudarstv.* Moscow: Mezhdunarodnye otnosheniia, 1980.

Michta, Andrew A. *An Emigre Reports: Fridrikh Neznansky on Mikhail Gorbachev, 1950–1958.* Falls Church, Va.: Delphic Associates, 1985.

Miliukova, V. I. *Otnosheniia SSSR-FRG i problemy evropeiskoi bezopasnosti, 1969–1982 gg.* Moscow: Nauka, 1983.

Miller, James A. *Strategic Minerals and the West.* Washington, D.C.: American-African Affairs Association, 1980.

——— et al., eds. *The Resource War in 3-D: Dependency, Diplomacy, Defense.* Pittsburgh, Pa.: World Affairs Council of Pittsburgh, 1982.

Mitchell, R. Judson. *Ideology of a Superpower: Contemporary Soviet Doctrine on International Relations.* Stanford: Hoover Institution Press, 1982.

Mlynar, Zdenek. *Nightfrost in Prague: The End of Humane Socialism.* New York: Karz, 1980.

Monkiewicz, Jan, and Maciejewicz, Jan. *Technology Export from the Socialist Countries.* Boulder, Colo.: Westview Press, 1986.

Moreton, Edwina, and Segal, Gerald, eds. *Soviet Strategy Toward Western Europe.* Boston: Allen & Unwin, 1984.

Morozov, V. G. et al., eds. *Ekonomicheskoe i tekhnicheskoe sotrudnichestvo s zarubezhnymi stranami.* Moscow: Mezhdunarodnye otnosheniia, 1983.

Mott, William C. *Strategic Minerals: A Resource Crisis.* Washington, D.C.: Council on Economics and National Security, 1981.

Mottola, Kari; Bykov, O. N.; and Korolev, I. S.; eds. *Finnish-Soviet Economic Relations.* London: Macmillan, 1983.

Myagkov, Aleksei. *Inside the KGB: An Exposé of an Officer of the Third Directorate.* Richmond, England: Foreign Affairs Publishing Co., 1976.

Nelson, Daniel N. *Alliance Behavior in the Warsaw Pact.* Boulder, Colo.: Westview Press, 1986.

Nerlich, Uwe, ed. *Soviet Power and Western Negotiating Policies.* 2 vols. Cambridge, Mass.: Harper & Row, 1983.

North Atlantic Treaty Organization. *NATO and the Warsaw Pact: Force Comparisons.* Brussels: NATO Information Service, 1984.

Ogarkov, N. V., chief ed., *Voennyi entsiklopedicheskiy slovar'.* Moscow: Voenizdat, 1983.

———. *Vsegda v gotovnosti k zashchite otechestva.* Moscow: Voenizdat, 1982.

———. *Istoria uchit bditel'nosti.* Moscow: Voenizdat, 1985.

Onikov, L. A., and Shishlin, N. V., comps. *Kratkii politicheskii slovar'.* Moscow: Politizdat, 1978.

Ornatskii, J. A. *Ekonomicheskaia diplomatiia.* Moscow: Mezhdunarodnye otnosheniia, 1980.

Ottaway, Marina. *Soviet and American Influence in the Horn of Africa.* New York: Praeger, 1982.

Oudenaren, John van. *The Soviet Union and Eastern Europe: Options for the 1980s and Beyond.* R-3136-AF. Santa Monica, Calif.: Rand Corporation, March 1984.

Ovsianyi, I. D. et al., eds. *Vneshniaia politika SSSR.* 3rd rev. ed. Moscow: Politizdat, 1978.

Page, Stephen. *The Soviet Union and the Yemens: Influence in Asymmetrical Relationships.* New York: Praeger, 1985.

Penkovskiy, Oleg. *The Penkovskiy Papers.* Garden City, N.Y.: Doubleday, 1965.

Peregudov, S. P. et al., eds. *Sovremennyi kapitalizm: Politicheskie otnosheniia i instituty vlasti.* Moscow: Nauka, 1984.

Pfaltzgraff, Robert L., Jr., and Ra'anan, Uri, eds. *East-West Trade and Technology Transfer.* Cambridge, Mass.: Institute for Foreign Policy Analysis, 1986.

Ploss, Sidney I. *Moscow and the Polish Crisis: An Interpretation of Soviet Policies and Intentions.* Boulder, Colo.: Westview Press, 1986.

Podlesnyi, P. T. *SSSR i SShA: Piat'desiat let diplomaticheskikh otnoshenii.* Moscow: Mezhdunarodnye otnosheniia, 1983.

Polmar, Norman. *Strategic Weapons: An Introduction.* Rev. ed. New York: Crane, Russak, 1982.

Pol'shikov, P. I. et al., eds. *Razvivaiushchiesia strany v mirovom khoziaistve.* Moscow: Mezhdunarodnye otnosheniia, 1983.

Popov, I. V. *Realizatsiia kompleksnoi programmy sotsialisticheskoi ekonomicheskoi integratsii stran-chlenov SEV.* Moscow: Nauka, 1983.

Prados, John. *The Soviet Estimate: U.S. Intelligence Analysis and Russian Military Strength.* New York: Dial Press, 1982.

Prange, Gordon W. *Target Tokyo: The Story of the Sorge Spy Ring.* New York: McGraw-Hill, 1984.

Proektor, D. M. *Osnovy mira v Evrope: Politicheskii i voennyi aspekty.* Moscow: Nauka, 1983.

Pugwash Council. *The Pugwash Conferences on Science and World Affairs.* Geneva, 1984.

Rahr, Alexander G. *A Biographic Directory of 100 Leading Soviet Officials.* 3rd ed. Munich: Central Research, Radio Liberty, RFE/RL, March 1986.

Raina, Peter. *Independent Social Movements in Poland.* London: Orbis Books, 1981.

Rakowska-Harmstone, Teresa et al. *Warsaw Pact: The Questions of Cohesion.* 3 vols. Ottawa: Canada, Department of National Defense, 1984–86.

Ratliff, William E. *Castroism and Communism in Latin America, 1959–1976.* Washington, D.C.: AEI-Hoover, 1976.

Rauft, Bryan, and Till, Geoffrey. *The Sea in Soviet Strategy.* London: Macmillan, 1983.

Rhoer, Edward Van Der. *The Shadow Network.* New York: Scribner's, 1983.

Richelson, Jeffrey. *Sword and Shield: The Soviet Intelligence and Security Apparatus.* Cambridge, Mass.: Ballinger, 1986.

Rokotov, S. M. *Sionizm: Orudie agressivnykh imperialisticheskikh krugov.* Moscow: Mezhdunarodnye otnosheniia, 1983.

Romerstein, Herbert. *Soviet Support for International Terrorism.* Washington, D.C.: Foundation for Democratic Education, 1981.

Rostow, W. W. *Open Skies: Eisenhower's Proposal of July 21, 1955.* Austin: University of Texas Press, 1982.

Rositzke, Harry. *KGB: The Eyes of Russia.* New York: Doubleday, 1981.

Roth, Paul. *Cuius regio—eius informatio: Moskaus Modell für die Weltinformationsordnung.* Graz: Verlag Styria, 1984.

———. *Sow-inform: Nachrichtenwesen und Informationspolitik der Sowjetunion.* Dusseldorf: Droste Verlag, 1980.

Rubinstein, Alvin Z. *Soviet Foreign Policy Since World War II.* Cambridge, Mass.: Winthrop, 1981.

Rumiantseva, A. M., ed. *Nauchnyi kommunizm: Slovar'.* 4th rev. ed. Moscow: Politizdat, 1983.

Sabel'nikov, L. B. *Voina bez peremiriia: Formy i metody ekonomicheskoi agressii.* Moscow: Mysl', 1983.

Sadykiewicz, Michael. *Die sowjetishe Militärdoktrin und Strategie.* Koblenz: Bernard & Graefe Verlag, 1985.

Saiadov, S. A. *Po zakonam internatsionalizma.* Moscow: Mysl', 1983.

Saivetz, Carol R., and Woodby, Sylvia. *Soviet–Third World Relations*. Boulder, Colo.: Westview Press, 1985.

Sakharov, Vladimir, and Tosi, Umberto. *High Treason*. New York: G. P. Putnam's Sons, 1980.

Sanakoev, Sh. P. *Voprosy sovetskoi vneshnepoliticheskoi propagandy*. Moscow: Mezhdunarodnye otnosheniia, 1980.

Savastiuk, A. I. *Osnovnoe protivorechie nashei epokhi i mirovoi revoliutsionnyi protsess*. Minsk: Nauka i tekhnika, 1980.

Sayilgar, Aclan. *Education of Foreign Revolutionaries in the USSR: Comintern Schools to Lumumba University*. Ankara: Baylan Press, 1973.

Scherer, John L., ed. *USSR Facts and Figures Annual*. Vol. 10. Gulf Breeze, Fla.: Academic International Press, 1986.

Schlessinger, James R. *Annual Defense Department Report, FY 1976 and FY 1977*. Washington, D.C.: The Pentagon, 1975.

Schmid, Alex P. *Soviet Military Interventions Since 1945*. New Brunswick, N.J.: Transaction, 1985.

Schmidt, Peter. *Wirkungen der "militärischen Entspannung" auf die Verteidigungspolitik der Natostaaten: Der Fall MBFR*. Munich: Tuduv-Verlagsgesellschaft, 1983.

Schönfeld, Roland, ed. *Reform und Wandel in Südosteuropa*. Munich: Oldenbourg Verlag, 1985.

Scott, William F., and Scott, Harriet Fast. *The Armed Forces of the USSR*. 3rd rev. ed. Boulder, Colo.: Westview Press, 1984.

―――. *The Soviet Art of War: Doctrine, Strategy, and Tactics*. Boulder, Colo.: Westview Press, 1982.

―――. *The Soviet Control Structure: Capabilities for Wartime Survival*. New York: Crane, Russak, 1983.

Scowcroft, Brent. *Report of the President's Commission on Strategic Forces*. Washington, D.C.: April 1983.

Seiffert, Wolfgang. *Kann der Ost-Block überleben? Der Comecon und die Krise des sozialistischen Wirtschaftssystems*. Bergisch Gladbach: Gustav Lübbe Verlag, 1983.

Sejna, Jan. *We Will Bury You*. London: Sidgwick & Jackson, 1982.

Shabaev, B. A. *Afrika: Iz proshlogo v budushchee*. Moscow: Nauka, 1984.

Shabalin, A. Ia. et al., eds. *Germanskaia Demokraticheskaia Respublika*. Moscow: Nauka, 1983.

Shakhnazarov, G. Kh. *Sotsializm i budushchee*. Moscow: Nauka, 1983.

Shastitko, V. M., ed. *Vneshniaia torgovlia SSSR so stranami SEV*. Moscow: Nauka, 1986.

Shenaev, V. N., and Andreev, Iu. V., eds., *SSSR–Zapadnaia Evropa*. Moscow: Mezhdunarodnye otnosheniia, 1986.

Shepeliuk, G. A. *Promyshlennaia integratsiia stran-chlenov SEV.* Kiev: Naukova dumka, 1982.

Shevchenko, Arkady N. *Breaking with Moscow.* New York: Knopf, 1985.

Shishlin, N. V., and Onikov, L. A., eds. *Kratkii politicheskii slovar'.* Moscow: Politizdat, 1978.

Shmelev, N. P. et al., eds. *Ekonomicheskie otnosheniia stran SEV s Zapadom.* Moscow: Nauka, 1983.

Shul'govskii, A. F. et al., eds. *Sovremennye ideologicheskie techeniia v Latinskoi Amerike.* Moscow: Nauka, 1983.

Shultz, Richard H., and Godson, Roy. *Dezinformatsia: Active Measures in Soviet Strategy.* New York: Pergamon-Brassey's International Defense Publishers, 1984.

Shvets, I. A., comp. *Kommunist: Kalendar'-spravochnik, 1983.* Moscow: Politizdat, 1982.

Shymakov, A. V., comp. *Knizhka partiinogo aktivista.* Moscow: Politizdat, 1983.

Sibilev, N. G. *Sotsialisticheskii internatsional.* Moscow: Mezhdunarodnye otnosheniia, 1980.

Sinclair, James E., and Parker, Robert. *The Strategic Metals War.* New York: Arlington House, 1983.

Smirnov, A. G.; Pobokova, O. P.; and Tkach, G. F. *Natsional'nye kadry osvobodivshikhsia stran.* Moscow: Nauka, 1980.

Socialist International. *Common Security: A Programme for Disarmament.* London: Pan Books, 1982.

Sodaro, Michael J., and Wolchik, Sharon L., eds. *Foreign and Domestic Policy in Eastern Europe in the 1980s: Trends and Prospects.* New York: St. Martin's Press, 1983.

Sokolovskii, V. D. *Voennaia strategiia.* 3rd rev. ed. Moscow: Voenizdat, 1968.

Soll, Richard S. et al. *The Role of Social Science Research Institutes in Formulation and Execution of Soviet Foreign Policy.* Arlington, Va.: SRI Strategic Center, n.d.

Solodovnikov, V. G. *Non-Capitalist Development: An Historical Outline.* Moscow: Progress, 1975.

——— et al. *Politicheskie partii Afriki.* Moscow: Nauka, 1970.

Solomon, Richard H., and Kosaka, Masataka. *The Soviet Far East Military Buildup: Nuclear Dilemmas and Asian Security.* Dover, Mass.: Auburn House Publishing Company, 1986.

Sorrels, Charles A. *Soviet Propaganda Campaign Against NATO.* Washington, D.C.: U.S. Arms Control and Disarmament Agency, October 1983.

Sosna, S. A. et al., eds. *Partii v politicheskoi sisteme.* Moscow: Nauka, 1983.

Sredina, G. V., ed. *Voenno-patrioticheskoe vospitanie sovetskoi molodezhi.* Moscow: Voenizdat, 1983.

Staar, Richard F., ed. *Arms Control: Myth Versus Reality*. Stanford: Hoover Institution Press, 1984.

————, ed. *Aspects of Modern Communism*. Columbia: University of South Carolina Press, 1968.

————. *Communist Regimes in Eastern Europe*. 4th rev. ed. Stanford: Hoover Institution Press, 1982.

————. *Poland, 1944–1962: The Sovietization of a Captive People*. Westport, Conn.: Greenwood Press, 1975.

————, ed. *Public Diplomacy: USA Versus USSR*. Stanford: Hoover Institution Press, 1986.

————. comp. *The Summit and the Peace Process: Addresses by President Ronald W. Reagan, 1985*. Stanford: Hoover Institution Press, 1986.

————, ed. *Yearbook on International Communist Affairs*. Stanford: Hoover Institution Press, 1969–1987.

Staniszkis, Jadwiga. *Poland's Self-Limiting Revolution*. Edited by Jan T. Gross. Princeton, N.J.: Princeton University Press, 1984.

Stent, Angela. *From Embargo to Ostpolitik: The Political Economy of West German–Soviet Relations, 1955–1980*. New York: Cambridge University Press, 1981.

Sterling, Claire. *The Terror Network*. New York: Holt, Rinehart & Winston, 1981.

————. *The Time of the Assassins*. New York: Holt, Rinehart & Winston, 1983.

Stookey, Robert W., ed. *The Arabian Peninsula: Zone of Ferment*. Stanford: Hoover Institution Press, 1984.

Stuart, Douglas T., and Tow, William T., eds. *China, the Soviet Union, and the West: Strategic and Political Dimensions in the 1980s*. Boulder, Colo.: Westview Press, 1982.

Sullivan, David S. *The Bitter Fruit of SALT: A Record of Soviet Duplicity*. Houston: Texas Policy Institute, 1982.

Suslov, M. A. *Marksizm-leninizm i sovremennaia epokha*. 2nd rev. ed. Moscow: Politizdat, 1980.

Sutherland, Douglas. *The Fourth Man*. London: Secker & Warburg, 1980.

Sutton, Anthony C. *Western Technology and Soviet Economic Development, 1945 to 1965*. Stanford: Hoover Institution Press, 1974.

Suvorov, Viktor. *The "Liberators:" My Life in the Soviet Army*. New York: W. W. Norton, 1981.

————. *Inside the Soviet Army*. London: Hamish Hamilton, 1982.

————. *Inside the Aquarium: The Making of a Top Soviet Spy*. New York: Macmillan, 1986.

————. *Inside Soviet Military Intelligence*. New York: Macmillan, 1984.

Swearingen, Rodger. *The Soviet Union and Postwar Japan: Escalating Challenge and Response*. Stanford: Hoover Institution Press, 1978.

Szymanski, Al. *Human Rights in the Soviet Union.* London: Zed Books, 1984.

Thomas, John R. *Natural Resources in Soviet Foreign Policy.* New York: National Strategy Information Center, 1985.

Tikhvinskii, S. L. et al., eds. *Diplomaticheskii vestnik, god 1982.* Moscow: Mezhdunarodnye otnosheniia, 1983.

Tolstoy, Nikolai. *Stalin's Secret War.* New York: Holt, Rinehart & Winston, 1982.

Tyson, James. *Target America.* Chicago: Regnery Gateway, 1983.

Ulam, Adam. *Dangerous Relations: The Soviet Union in World Politics, 1970–1982.* New York: Oxford University Press, 1983.

United Kingdom. Foreign and Commonwealth Office. Economic Service (International Division). *Soviet, East European, and Western Development Aid, 1976–1982.* Foreign Policy Report, no. 85. London, May 1983.

U.S. Congress. Commission on Security and Cooperation in Europe. *Report on Implementation of the Final Act to the Conference on Security and Cooperation in Europe: Findings and Recommendations Seven Years after Helsinki.* 97th Cong., 2nd sess. Washington, D.C., 1982. Committee Print.

———. Joint Economic Committee. *East European Economies: Slow Growth in the 1980s.* Vol. 3. 99th Cong., 2nd sess. Washington, D.C., March 1986, Committee Print.

———. *Allocation of Resources in the Soviet Union and China—1985.* Part 11. 99th Cong., 2nd sess., March 1986.

———. Office of Technology Assessment. *Strategic Materials: Technologies to Reduce U.S. Import Vulnerability.* OTA-ITE-248. Washington, D.C., May 1985.

———. House. Committee on Foreign Affairs and Commission on Security and Cooperation in Europe. Subcommittee on Human Rights and International Organizations. *Hearing on Abuse of Psychiatry in the Soviet Union.* 98th Cong., 1st sess. Washington, D.C., 1984.

———. Subcommittee on Europe and the Middle East. *United States–Soviet Scientific Exchanges.* 99th Cong., 2nd sess. Washington, D.C., 1986.

———. Permanent Select Committee on Intelligence. Subcommittee on Oversight. *Hearings on Soviet Covert Action: The Forgery Offensive.* 96th Cong., 2nd sess. Washington, D.C., 1980.

———. *Hearings on Soviet Active Measures.* 97th Cong., 2nd sess. Washington, D.C., 1982.

———. *Hearing on the Sverdlovsk Incident: Soviet Compliance with the Biological Weapons Convention?* 96th Cong., 2nd sess. Washington, D.C., 1980.

———. Committee on Foreign Affairs. *Special Study on Soviet Diplomacy and Negotiating Behavior: Emerging New Context for U.S. Diplomacy.* Vol. 1. H. Doc. 96–238. Prepared by Senior Specialists Division, Congressional Research Service, Library of Congress. 96th Cong., 1st sess. Washington, D.C., 1980.

————. Subcommittees on Europe and the Middle East and on Asia and Pacific Affairs. *Hearings on the Soviet Role in Asia.* 98th Cong., 1st sess. Washington, D.C., 1983.

————. *Report on Soviet Policy and United States Response in the Third World.* 97th Cong., 1st sess. Washington, D.C., 1981. Committee Print.

————. Subcommittee on International Security and Scientific Affairs. *East-West Troop Reductions in Europe: Is Agreement Possible?* 98th Cong., 1st sess. Washington, D.C. 1983.

————. Office of Technology Assessment. *Salyut: Soviet Steps Toward Permanent Human Presence in Space.* OTA-TM-STI-14. Washington, D.C., December 1983.

————. Senate. Committee on Armed Services. *Soviet Treaty Violations. Hearings Before the Committee on Armed Services.* 99th Cong., 1st sess. Washington, D.C., 1985.

————. Senate. Committee on Foreign Relations. Subcommittee on Arms Control, Oceans, International Operations and Environment. *Hearings on United States and Soviet Civil Defense Programs.* 97th Cong., 2nd sess. Washington, D.C., 1982.

————. Committee on Government Operations. Subcommittee on National Policy Machinery. *Report on National Policy Machinery in the Soviet Union.* 86th Cong., 2nd sess. Washington, D.C., 1960. Committee Print.

————. Subcommittee on National Security Staffing and Operations. *Study on Staffing Procedures and Problems in the Soviet Union.* 88th Cong., 1st sess. Washington, D.C., 1963. Committee Print.

————. Subcommittee on National Security and International Operations. Adam B. Ulam. "Communist Doctrine and Soviet Diplomacy: Some Observations." In *Memorandum on International Negotiation,* 91st Cong., 2nd sess. Washington, D.C., 1970.

————. *Hearing on International Negotiation.* Part 1, with Robert Conquest (15 December 1969). 91st Cong., 1st sess. Washington, D.C., 1970.

————. Part 2, with Leonard Schapiro (16 April 1970). 91st Cong., 2nd sess. Washington, D.C., 1970. pp. 29–66.

————. Part 3, with Dirk U. Stikker (26 February 1971). 92nd Cong., 1st sess. Washington, D.C., 1971. pp. 67–90.

————. Part 4, with Bernard Lewis (17 March 1971). 92nd Cong., 1st sess. Washington, D.C., 1971. pp. 91–123.

————. Part 5, with Robert F. Byrnes (2 April 1971). 92nd Cong., 1st sess. Washington, D.C., 1971. pp. 124–59.

————. Part 6, with Robert Conquest (30 April 1971). 92nd Cong., 1st sess. Washington, D.C., 1971. pp. 160–97.

————. Part 7, with William R. Van Cleave (25 July 1972). 92nd Cong., 2nd sess. Washington, D.C., 1973. pp. 198–246.

————. *The Soviet Approach to Negotiation: Selected Writings.* 91st Cong., 1st sess. Washington, D.C., 1969. Committee Print.

————. Select Committee on Intelligence. *Meeting the Espionage Challenge: A Review of United States Counterintelligence and Security Programs.* Report 99-522. 99th Cong., 2nd sess., 1986.

U.S. Government. Arms Control and Disarmament Agency. *Arms Control and Disarmament Agreements.* 5th ed. Washington, D.C., 1982.

————. *Soviet Noncompliance.* Washington, D.C., February 1986.

————. *The Soviet Propaganda Campaign Against the US Strategic Defense Initiative.* ACDA Publication 122. Washington, D.C., August 1986.

————. *World Military Expenditures and Arms Transfers, 1985.* ACDA Pub. 123. Washington, D.C., August 1985.

————. Central Intelligence Agency. *Biographic Report: USSR Institute of the United States and Canada.* CR 76–10864. Washington, D.C.: Directorate of Intelligence, 1976.

————. *CPSU Central Committee and Central Auditing Commission: 27th Party Congress.* LDA 86–10123. Washington, D.C., June 1986.

————. *CPSU Central Committee Executive and Administrative Apparatus.* LDA 86–10434. Washington, D.C., July 1986. Chart.

————. *CPSU Politburo and Secretariat: Positions and Responsibilities.* LDA 86–10436. Washington, D.C.: July 1986. Chart.

————. *The Cuban Economy: A Statistical Review.* ALA 84–10052. Washington, D.C., June 1984.

————. *Directory of Soviet Officials: National Organizations.* CR 86–11691. Washington, D.C., June 1986.

————. *Directory of USSR Foreign Trade Organizations and Officials.* CR 86–11692. Washington, D.C., May 1986.

————. *Directory of USSR Ministry of Defense and Armed Forces Officials.* LDA 86–11907. Washington, D.C., October 1986.

————. *Directory of USSR Ministry of Foreign Affairs Officials.* CR 85–14535. Washington, D.C., September 1986.

————. *A Guide to Political Acronyms.* PA 79–10474. Washington, D.C., October 1979.

————. *Handbook of Economic Statistics 1986.* CPAS 86–10002. Washington, D.C., September 1986.

————. *Soviet Acquisition of Western Technology: An Update.* Washington, D.C., September 1985.

————. *Soviet Civil Defense.* NI 78–10003. Washington, D.C., July 1978.

————. *The Soviet Weapons Industry: An Overview.* DI 86–10016. Washington, D.C.: GPO, September 1986.

————. *The World Factbook, 1986.* CR WF 86–001. Washington, D.C., June 1986.

————. Central Intelligence Agency and the Defense Intelligence Agency. "The Soviet Economy Under a New Leader." Report to the Joint Economic Committee. Washington, D.C.: March 1986.

————. Department of Commerce. *Statistical Abstract of East-West Trade and Finance.* Project DIE-47-86. Washington, D.C.: GPO, March 1986.

————. *1985 U.S. Foreign Trade Highlights.* Washington, D.C.: GPO, March 1986.

————. Department of Defense. *Annual Report to the Congress, FY 1987.* Washington, D.C., February 1986.

————. *Soviet Acquisition of Militarily Significant Western Technology: An Update.* Washington, D.C., September 1985.

————. *Soviet Military Power.* 5th ed. Washington, D.C.: The Pentagon, March 1986.

————. *United States Military Posture FY 1987.* Washington, D.C.: Joint Chiefs of Staff, 1986.

————. Department of State. *Chemical Warfare in Southeast Asia and Afghanistan: An Update.* Washington, D.C., November 1982.

————. *Country Reports on Human Rights Practices for 1985.* Washington, D.C., February 1986.

————. *Implementation of Helsinki Final Act, October 1, 1985–April 1, 1986.* Special Report no. 146. Washington, D.C., 1986.

————. *Lessons of Grenada.* Publication no. 9457. Washington, D.C.: GPO, February 1986.

————. *Patterns of International Terrorism, 1982.* Washington, D.C.: Office of Combatting Terrorism, September 1983.

————. *Realism, Strength, Negotiations: Key Foreign Policy Statements of the Reagan Administration.* Washington, D.C., May 1984.

————. *Report to Congress on Voting Practices in the United Nations.* Washington, D.C., 1984.

————. *Soviet Active Measures.* Special Report no. 110. Washington, D.C., September 1983.

————. "Soviet Influence on Afghan Youth," Special Report no. 139. Washington, D.C.: GPO, February 1986.

————. *Treaties in Force.* Washington, D.C.: Office of the Legal Adviser, 1980.

————. *Warsaw Pact Economic Aid to Non-Communist LDCs, 1984.* Washington, D.C., May 1986.

————. Departments of State and Defense. *Background Paper: Central America.* Washington, D.C., 27 May 1983.

————. *The Challenge to Democracy in Central America.* Washington, D.C., June 1986.

————. *Grenada: A Preliminary Report.* Washington, D.C., 16 December 1983.

————. *Grenada Documents: An Overview and Selection.* Introduction by Michael Ledeen and Herbert Romerstein. Washington, D.C., September 1984.

————. *Soviet Strategic Defense Programs.* Washington, D.C., October 1985.

————. General Accounting Office. *United Nations: Analysis of Selected Media Products Shows Half Oppose Key U.S. Interests.* GAO/NSIAD-86-98. Washington, D.C., April 1986.

————. General Advisory Committee on Arms Control and Disarmament. *A Quarter Century of Soviet Compliance Practices Under Arms Control Commitments, 1958–1983.* Washington, D.C., October 1984.

————. United States Information Agency. *Documents Pertaining to Relations Between Grenada, the USSR, and Cuba.* 3 vols. Washington, D.C., 1984.

U.S.S.R. Ministerstvo Vneshnei Torgovli. *Vneshniaia torgovlia SSSR v 1985 g.: Statisticheskii sbornik.* Moscow: Finansy i statistika, 1986.

————. *Narodnoe khoziaistvo SSR v 1985 g.* Moscow: Finansy i statistika, 1986.

Ustinov, D. F. *Sluzhim rodine, delu kommunizma.* Moscow: Voenizdat, 1982.

Valkenier, Elizabeth Kridl. *The Soviet Union and the Third World: An Economic Bind.* New York: Praeger, 1983.

Van Cleave, William R., and Thompson, W. Scott, eds. *Strategic Options for the Early Eighties.* White Plains, Md.: Automated Graphic Systems, 1979.

Vigor, P. H. *Soviet Blitzkrieg Theory.* London: Macmillan, 1983.

Vishniakova, A. S., ed. *Voprosy razvitiia mirovoi sotsialisticheskoi sistemy.* Moscow: Politizdat, 1983.

Volgyes, Ivan. *The Political Reliability of the Warsaw Pact Armies: The Southern Tier.* Durham, N.C.: Duke University Press, 1982.

Volkogonov, D. A., ed. *Marksistsko-leninskoe uchenie o voine i armii.* Moscow: Voenizdat, 1984.

Vol'skii, V. V. et al., eds. *Kapitalizm v Latinskoi Amerike.* Moscow: Nauka, 1983.

Voslensky, Michael S. *Nomenklatura: The Soviet Ruling Class.* New York: Doubleday, 1984.

Watson, Bruce W., and Watson, Susan M., eds., *The Soviet Navy.* Boulder, Colo.: Westview Press, 1986.

Weihmiller, Gordon R. *U.S.-Soviet Summits: An Account of East-West Diplomacy at the Top, 1955–1985.* Lanham, MD.: University Press of America, 1986.

Wesson, Robert G., ed. *Communism in Central America and the Caribbean.* Stanford: Hoover Institution Press, 1982.

Wettig, Gerhard. *Konflikt und Kooperation zwischen Ost und West.* Bonn: Osang, 1981.

Whelan, Joseph G. "Commitment in Perspective." *The Soviet Union in the Third World, 1980–82: An Imperial Burden or Political Asset?* Report No. 83–210 S. Washington, D.C.: Congressional Research Service, Library of Congress, 30 November 1983.

Whetten, Lawrence L., ed. *The Present State of Communist Internationalism.* Lexington, Mass.: D. C. Heath & Co., 1983.

White, Gordon; Murray, Robin; and White, Christine; eds. *Revolutionary Socialist Development in the Third World.* Lexington: University of Kentucky Press, 1983.

Whiting, Kenneth R. *Soviet Air Power.* Boulder, Colo.: Westview Press, 1986.

Wiles, Peter, ed. *The New Communist Third World.* New York: St. Martin's Press, 1982.

Willoughby, Charles Andrew. *Shanghai Conspiracy: The Sorge Spy Ring.* New York: Dutton, 1952.

Willrich, Mason, and Rhinelander, John G., eds. *SALT: The Moscow Agreements and Beyond.* New York: The Free Press, 1974.

Wolf, Jr., Charles et al. *The Costs and Benefits of the Soviet Empire, 1981–1983.* Santa Monica, Calif.: Rand Corporation, August 1986.

Wolton, Thierry. *Le KGB en France.* Paris: Grasset et Fasquelle, 1986.

Yao, Ming-le. *The Conspiracy and Death of Lin Biao.* New York: Alfred A. Knopf, 1983.

Yegorov, P. T.; Shlyakhov, I. A.; and Alabin, N. I. *Civil Defense: A Soviet View.* 2nd ed. Moscow: Vysshaia shkola, 1970. Translated and published in 1976 under the auspices of the U.S. Air Force by the U.S. Government Printing Office, Washington, D.C.

Yodfat, Aryeh Y. *The Soviet Union and Revolutionary Iran.* New York: St. Martin's Press, 1984.

Young, Brigitta. *Prospects for Soviet Grain Production.* Boulder, Colo.: Westview Press, 1983.

Zagladin, V. V. et al., eds. *Istoricheskaia missiia sotsialisticheskogo obshchestva.* 2nd rev. ed. Moscow: Politizdat, 1984.

———. *Mezhdunarodnoe rabochee dvizhenie.* Moscow: Politizdat, 1984.

Zagladin, V. V., ed. *Mirovoe kommunisticheskoe dvizhenie.* Moscow: Izdatel'stvo politicheskoi literatury, 1984.

Zagladin, V. V. et al., eds. *Revoliutsionnyi protsess: Natsional'noe i internatsional'noe.* Moscow: Mysl', 1985.

Zaleski, Eugene, and Wienert, Helgard. *Technology Transfer Between East and West.* Paris: Organization for Economic Cooperation and Development, 1980.

Zarodov, K. I., ed. *One Thousand Days of Revolution: Communist Party of Chile Leaders on Lessons of the Events in Chile.* Prague: Peace and Socialism, 1978.

Zemtsov, Ilya. *Policy Dilemmas and the Struggle for Power in the Kremlin—The Andropov Period.* Fairfax, Va.: Hero Books, 1985.

Zorin, V. A. *Osnovy diplomaticheskoi sluzhby.* 2nd ed. Moscow: Mezhdunarodnye otnosheniia, 1977.

Zwass, Adam. *The Economies of Eastern Europe: In a Time of Change.* Armonk, N.Y.: M. E. Sharpe, 1984.

INDEX OF NAMES AND ORGANIZATIONS